Western Times and Water Wars

A CENTENNIAL BOOK

One hundred books
published between 1990 and 1995
bear this special imprint of
the University of California Press.
We have chosen each Centennial Book
as an example of the Press's finest
publishing and bookmaking traditions
as we celebrate the beginning of
our second century.

UNIVERSITY OF CALIFORNIA PRESS

Founded in 1893

Western Times and Water Wars

State, Culture, and Rebellion in California

John Walton

UNIVERSITY OF CALIFORNIA PRESS
Berkeley · *Los Angeles* · *Oxford*

University of California Press
Berkeley and Los Angeles, California

University of California Press, Ltd.
Oxford, England

©1992 by
The Regents of the University of California

Library of Congress Cataloging-in-Publication Data

Walton, John, 1937–
    Western times and water wars : state, culture, and rebellion in
California / John Walton.
        p.   cm.
    Includes bibliographical references and index.
    ISBN 0-520-07245-6 (alk. paper)
    1. Owens River Valley (Calif.)—Social conditions.   2. Social
movements—California—Owens River Valley—History.   3. Water
rights—California—Owens River Valley—History.   4. Water rights—
California—Los Angeles—History.   5. Frontier and pioneer life—
California—Owens River Valley.   6. Paiute Indians—California—
Owens River Valley—History.   I. Title.
HN79.C22O949   1992
303.48'4'0979494—dc20   91-12889
                                                                     CIP

Printed in the United States of America
9   8   7   6   5   4   3   2   1

For Pris,
with love and gratitude

To the States or any one of them, or any city of the States,
    Resist much, obey little,
Once unquestioning obedience, once fully enslaved,
Once fully enslaved, no nation, state, city, of this earth, ever
    afterward resumes its liberty.

Walt Whitman, "Inscriptions,"
from Leaves of Grass, *1855*

Contents

Illustrations

MAPS

Tables

Preface

This is a book about social protest in the American West from the resistance to conquest of Native Americans to the present environmental movement. It is a work of historiography and sociological interpretation, an effort to recover the history of a community and to make sense of that experience as a source of general principles of social organization and action.

In the process of investigating this subject, I came across evidence that seemed to have gone unnoticed or little emphasized in previous interpretations of western development: the vital role of Native Americans in the labor force of frontier society, ethnic and gender conflict at the root of frontier culture, a pattern of dependent development in the American West analogous to modern Third World societies, the ironic compliance of pioneers and rebellion of bourgeois progressives, the perseverence of local protest traditions from populist class action to environmental movement, and the changing role of the state in local society. Taken together, these discoveries recommended a reinterpretation of portions of U.S. history and a comparison with related experiences of national development. Whatever the value of the empirical revelations, I hope to show that the American West in the period of national incorporation is as fertile a field for theoretically oriented social history as is Europe during its period of state formation. Indeed, in the end I hope to develop certain explanatory principles of collective action that apply across these settings and more.

The study, nevertheless, does not begin with an effort to generalize.

Quite the reverse. It is first a longitudinal analysis of a small community in eastern California from its preconquest Indian origins to its current incorporation within the physical infrastructure of Los Angeles. The story of the Owens Valley, as we shall see, is legendary—the inspiration for a number of histories, countless journalistic treatments, and a fair selection of novels and films. In California and adjoining regions, the "rape of the Owens Valley" is common parlance for the acquisition of its water by the city of Los Angeles at the turn of the century, and the danger of "another Owens Valley," the desiccation of an agricultural region for the sake of urban development, has been a clarion call for protest and governmental protection from the 1930s until today.

Nearly a decade ago, I began what was intended as a small inquiry into local rebellion in the Owens Valley during the 1920s. My purpose was to examine, by means of a case study, some of the theoretical ideas about rebellion that I had advanced in an earlier book. As the story of the Owens Valley–Los Angeles water war took shape, I realized that its larger meaning lay in the interplay of state incorporation and popular resistance, begun much earlier and continuing to the present. The small study became a large one. As I tried to integrate various kinds of evidence, it also became an experiment in research method and historical understanding. I have tried to find ways to tell a big story through the lens of a small case, to compare local societies across time, and to join the purposes of meaningful interpretation with those of causal explanation. Readers will judge, tolerantly I hope, how well this succeeds.

A word is required about my personal and analytical orientation to this study. Since the late 1920s, much has been written about the Owens Valley and its water wars with Los Angeles. Most of that writing dwells, explicitly or implicitly, on the propriety, justification, and public morality of the city's acquisition of land and water rights in the valley. Was it a question, as the title of one solidly researched monograph puts it, of "vision or villainy?" Did the city acquire its domain through deception and political machination, or by fair exchange and necessary small sacrifices for greater public benefits? Was Teddy Roosevelt's favorite aphorism, the greatest good for the greatest number, appropriately applied in this case? The single question, Was it right?, has obsessed historical research, owing perhaps to the contagious passion that has also generated popular treatments of the subject in film and fiction.

I do not join that debate for two reasons: because there is little new to be said about it and because the answer seems obvious in light of previous work. Los Angeles acquired a water supply from the Owens Valley because metropolitan growth would have been arrested without it and because city functionaries and their allies had the money, electoral support, and political muscle to realize their ambitions. Deception and coercion were among the many methods the city used at various times, but the fateful decisions were made in Washington. Owens Valley citizens who resisted the appropriation of their land and livelihood were victims of brute power in a broader reorganization of the state and urban society. And the whole conflict was unnecessary; Los Angeles could have compromised with valley farmers and merchants by leaving some of the water and private holdings behind (as, indeed, the courts later required it to do) without jeopardizing urban growth in the slightest. But Los Angeles was relentless in its effort to acquire every water right it could in the valley. Imperious in its own interest, it was arrogant in reponse to valley proposals for compromise. The city abused its power and, for that, has never stopped paying for its mistakes, while continuing to defend them.

In short, I stand with the critics of the city's policies, in part because these facts seem clear and in part because my subject is local society and its development largely in opposition to the city. Any objective analysis of protest or domination must begin with candor about one's analytical point of view. The perspectives that investigations invariably adopt need not entail error or distortion; but if they are suppressed they may masquerade as consensual wisdom. Researchers must examine themselves as well as their subject; the two are seldom related simply through the medium of neutral observation.

Others will differ with my appraisal, and of course there is no stopping the moral debate, now nearing its ninetieth year and still sprightly. The argument that follows, however, takes a very different direction. My objective is to explain the social protest undertaken by historical actors, not to evaluate whether they were justified in doing so by some external standard. Obviously, they felt that they were justified, and the questions become, Why did they feel themselves unjustly treated? and How did they construct ideas about justice and act on them in protest? In that sense, the moral debate that has occupied others, whether writers or participants, becomes evidence for this inquiry. How was the debate about justice formulated, how did it shift over time, and how did it influence the struggle? These questions lead to new revelations both about the Owens Valley and about theories of collective action.

I am grateful to a number of institutions and people for their help in this work. The investigation was supported financially by a series of Faculty Research Grants from the University of California, Davis. For access to their collections and staff assistance, I want to thank the

Bancroft Library and Water Resources Library both of the University of California (Berkeley), the California State Library (Sacramento), the California State Historical Society Library (San Francisco), the Henry E. Huntington Library (San Marino), the Inyo County Free Library, the Laws Railroad Museum, the Los Angeles County Library, the Los Angeles Department of Water and Power Library, the National Archives (Washington, D.C.), and the University of California at Los Angeles Library.

I owe a special debt to the Eastern California Museum at Independence, its staff including Kathy Barnes, and its director Bill Michael, who good-naturedly culled their files for documentary and photographic evidence, collected new data bearing directly on my interests, and brought me up to date on local events after my absences from the field. Inyo County can be proud of the services provided by the museum on a very modest budget. If better times are in store for the county, I hope that the Eastern California Museum receives a share proportionate to its effort at serving the public.

Residents and friends of the Owens Valley who provided me with expert information based on their own participation or research include Bob Bettinger, Gus Cashbaugh, Martha Davis, Mary DeDecker, Frank Fowles, Mary Gorman, William Kahrl, Enid Larson, David Lent, Richard Lingenfelter, Bill and Barbara Manning, Lillian Nelson, and John K. Smith. I am grateful to scores of other local citizens whom I interviewed anonymously about general issues.

I received useful comments on early drafts and selected chapters from Arnold Bauer, Craig Calhoun, Jack Forbes, William Friedland, William Hagen, Craig Jenkins, William Kahrl, Ira Katznelson, Ted Margadant, John Roemer, Norbert Wiley, and Aram Yengoyan. I am especially grateful to Buchanan Sharp, who made detailed corrections on the penultimate draft of the complete manuscript and shared with me certain parallels drawn from his own research and writing on English history. Howard Becker, once again, advised me to do the right thing when I was wavering. Beverly Lozano, also once again, did the illustrations, accepting only Paiute trinkets in return. In this project, as in previous connections, it has been a pleasure to work with Naomi Schneider and the University of California Press. My brother Craig and his wife Vera made fieldwork a treat with visits to their home on the desert and long conversations about western politics, ethics, environment, and literature. I hope that all who share those interests find something useful in this book.

ONE

Introduction

It is a paradox of modern democratic societies that the state is considered both the cause and the cure of injustice. The state is believed to foster social ills directly by conferring privilege on certain powerful constituents and indirectly by failing to serve the less coherent public interest. To ensure justice, citizens must then confront authority as outsiders, either by mobilizing in protest or by withdrawing their approval from the state. Nowhere is this presumed opposition of state and society so strongly maintained as in the United States. Thoreau's dissenting words seem axiomatic: "I cannot for an instant recognize that political organization as *my* government which is the *slave's* government also. . . . [T]he mass of men serve the state thus, not as men mainly, but as machines. . . . [T]here is no free exercise whatever of the judgement or the moral sense." Yet when less reclusive citizens than Thoreau urged that slavery and other injustice be corrected, it seemed equally obvious that they should engage the state and set it on the path of reform, not by revolution or abolition of the state but through renovation from within. Justice, in this view, depends on popular action ever vigilant against state tyranny, yet the state is routinely responsible for delivering justice.

This ambivalence toward the state and the divide separating it from trusted popular action are so ingrained in our political thinking that they affect even circumspect social and historical analyses. Social movements and the state are seldom treated together as interacting dimensions of the same political process. Rather, collective action generally is

understood as a problem of when and why people act in concert, presumably an uncommon event given its difficulties and costs, with explanations ranging from individual self-interest to coercion, or some
combination of interest and opportunity. In unrelated ways, the state is
typically understood as implacable structure, hegemonic control, socially autonomous direction, and the leaden hand of bureaucratic organization. The two concepts, collective action and the state, are lodged
in the different theoretical discourses of voluntarism and structuralism.
Given such mental habits, juxtaposition of the state and collective action implies antipathy, conflict, between a state that channels and in-
demnifies independent action and a popular insurgency that confronts
state rule as outsider and underdog.

When one begins to examine the relationship between collective
action and the state at close range, however, these oppositions collapse.
The modern state, as Max Weber observed long ago, is a human
community that successfully claims a monopoly of the legitimate use of
force in society; its claim to rightful domination depends upon law and
tradition for its social acceptance. Legitimacy is basic to the state's
capacity to rule, yet it is not confined to the state exclusively. The
modern state, on one hand, requires popular participation, and it
extends entitlements to its citizens that include the principles and
means to challenge legitimacy. Collective action, on the other hand,
whatever its grievance or ambition, draws on the same legal and
cultural foundations in constructing its own ideological proposals for
change. In short, the state provides certain means of collective action,
and protest appropriates principles of legitimacy to contest state rule.
This does not mean that the modern state is especially weak or that
popular insurgency possesses some previously unrevealed formula for
successful action. Rather, it suggests a complex relationship between
collective action and the state that is mediated by culturally constructed
legitimacy.

Such, as least, is the thesis of this study, although the story begins on
far more modest terrain. To the extent that the inquiry supports a
plausible alternative to prevailing explanations of collective action, it
does so by analyzing and interpreting a particular case in detail and by
exploring causal analogies in related cases. The case in point, that of a
valley and network of small towns in eastern California, provides an
example of state formation and incorporation, sustained protest, and
the creation of a distinct local culture.

THE SETTING

California's Owens Valley (map 1) has never known much in the way of worldly success—little wealth to speak of, few people among which to divide it, no cities or industry, sparse resources long since depleted by fortune hunters who came and went. But is has two things in abundance, both rare for California below the thirty-seventh parallel: water and history. The valley's archaeological and oral history predates its settlement by homesteaders in the midnineteenth century, and its recorded history was extensive before water became the essential connection with the surrounding world. That history is my subject because the relationship between this unprepossessing frontier community and the national state contains an explanation of the continuing struggle over how and for whom the western United States was developed.

Local enthusiasts would add the natural environment to any list of distinctions. *Bold* is the word that best describes the landscape. On its western side, the pine-covered Sierra Nevada rises from the valley floor at 4,000 feet to the granite peaks of Mount Whitney at 14,495. On the east, the barren White Mountains appear soft by contrast, despite their 11,000-foot stature. Wedged between ranges, and opening out to the Mojave Desert at its southern end, the valley is compact yet ineffably spacious—a clearly delineated space of human scale ringed nearly around by an awesome geography. Perhaps it is that very contrast that makes the valley at once cozy and forbidding. The mood shifts with the sun. In the early morning, the shadows of the Whites quickly recede eastward bringing typically bright days. In this "land of little rain,"[1] midday illuminates expansive pastures, larger stretches of sagebrush, the Owens River winding a leisurely course southward, businesslike towns, and, between today's settlements, the tumbledown markers of a once dense network of hamlets and farmsites. Afternoon steadily brings the return of long shadows from the sierra and with them a reminder of enclosed space. At midday the mountains seem to shrink, only to loom again at evening like a wall rising to seal the valley off from a cosmopolitan world to the west. Denizens of the region cannot escape the sense of living in a distinctly bounded place and, indeed, few of them want to. As a local writer, Mary Austin said long ago, there is a spell over the land.[2]

Lying along the eastern slope of the Sierra Nevada and running more than 100 miles from its well-watered north to the desert south, the

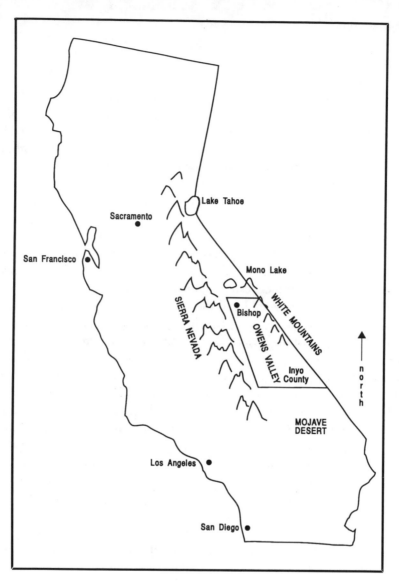

Map 1. California and Inyo County.

narrow basin looks forlorn today because its settlers have been replaced by urban owners. When John C. Fremont's expeditionary forces named the Owens Valley in 1845, it belonged to Indians. Paiutes irrigated fields from north to south and hunted and gathered their subsistence from the sierra to the White Mountains, an average distance of just ten miles. Today the valley belongs to the City of Los Angeles, which transports valley water 240 miles southward to supply a metropolitan area of 15 million people, leaving little behind for local subsistence. Between these periods the valley supported a frontier community that wrested the land from its indigenous claimants, only to see its own claim usurped by urban society and the state. Yet even today, people remain—descendants of the original Indians and pioneers, along with a host of new arrivals who have maintained their communities through 130 years of struggle among themselves and with their expropriators. If the valley appears as listless today as it did to Fremont's scouts, that is not because it remained untouched in the interim, but because it was touched so often. Invading forces transformed it from a natural habitat to a settler society and, in the twentieth century, to an appendage of the modern city. In addition to the precolonial landscape that greeted the first chroniclers, today we also see the archaeological remains of nineteenth-century settlement.

Generations of scholars have searched for a single key to western U.S. history, attaching diagnostic priority to the frontier as symbol and myth, the conquering spirit of manifest destiny, or the physical infrastructure that domesticated the wilderness. It is tempting to suppose, as some do,[3] that waterworks determined history in the arid American West; but the reverse is closer to the truth. History, the record of human agency and institutional development, explains what is significant about water—its varied uses, its appropriation, and the struggle over its benefits. In the American West, history has been a succession of struggles over dominion, of claims and counterclaims on the legitimate possession and use of resources bound up with the land, subsoil, water, air, the natural environment generally, and, in particular, with the social groups that won and lost in the struggle.

THE PATTERN

This book is both a social history of western development and an explanation of the changing patterns of collective action that made the history. Generally, its subject is the transformation of the American

West from Native American homeland to metropolitan hinterland. Concretely, it is a story of struggle as it evolved in one local society. In the Owens Valley, that history developed in a series of critical epochs and passages. Military conquest destroyed Paiute civilization but incorporated its technology and labor power as essential features of the frontier economy. Pioneer society was erected on the crude footings of state support, but was left to create its own civil society in the shadow of corporate capital, which dominated the principal sources of wealth. Frontier society was rent with conflict, from ethnic, gender, and class divisions within to aggrandizing monopolies without. Despite such constraints, settlers persevered in a cash-poor subsistence economy, awaiting the day when, as they gamely believed, progress would finally arrive. As admirers of Teddy Roosevelt and ardent supporters of federal reclamation in 1902, local citizens became convinced that progressivism meant their salvation. They saw that hope dashed four years later, when the federal government ceded development of the valley's water to Los Angeles. For the next eighty years the Owens Valley fought the city with methods that shifted from rebellion and violence to political protest and appeals to law. Battles lost during the 1920s in the name of community were pursued and finally won in the 1970s under the auspices of environmentalism. History provided strategic connections between these epochs as traditions from an earlier period were drawn upon and refashioned for new challenges. Local society was made and remade in the long struggle. As Raymond Williams notes about the English countryside, "community only became a reality when economic and political rights were fought for and partially gained. . . . [T]here is more community in the modern village, as a result of this process of new legal and democratic rights, than at any point in the recorded or imagined past."[4] In order simply to tell that story, however, much of the real and imagined past must be reclaimed.

Books about the American West generally fall into one of two categories: they either contribute to or criticize the myth of the frontier. Explanations for this obsession are plentiful. Few historical subjects enjoy such notoriety as the Wild West, and its prominence in popular culture attracts both embellishments and exposés. In deeper reflections, the influence of the frontier on American character and institutions has been a provocative thesis from the nineteenth-century studies of Alexis de Tocqueville and Frederick Jackson Turner to the critical modern writings of Edward Abbey and Donald Worster. Yet this fascination with the mythical West has given little encouragement to social history and historical sociology; research and theory devoted to the process of national incorporation are not on a par with, for example, studies of revolutionary transformation in France or of industrial class struggle in England. Herbert Gutman's general observation about the United States applies all the more forcefully to the West; most of its social history remains to be written.[5] Classical theses about the role of the frontier in U.S. development require critical assessment; and they receive it in this study. But preoccupation with the nature of the real West must be balanced with empirical study of how legend is socially constructed and selectively used in collective action. In this way, it is possible to join interpretive and explanatory approaches to social history.

This study simultaneously pursues interpretive issues and analytical questions of historical sociology.[6] Interpretively, the analysis focuses on culture as the system of meanings that people construct in social life and use to guide their action. In the following chapters, changing forms of social order and the state are examined in terms of the meanings they acquire in local society and consciousness. Action is understood to proceed from meanings lodged in culture or reformulated in ideology. If there is a method for analyzing these questions, it lies in recovering the voice and language of actors in their historical circumstances. Whether social history or historical sociology, the interpretation searches for people's purposes in the words they use to express them. Paiutes speak about their work, pioneers about farm life, small town editors about commerce, rebels about justice, and community leaders about legal and environmental protection. These voices quickly disabuse one of what Williams calls the "myth of the happier past"; but neither do they suggest steady progress. "Between the simple backward look and the simple progressive thrust there is room for long argument but none for enlightment. We must begin differently: not in the idealisation of one order or another, but in the history to which they are only partial and misleading responses."[7]

Analytically, the inquiry pursues a comparison and an explanation. This is a comparative longitudinal study focused on one case through distinct epochs and regimes. The periods are not imposed on local history according to some preconceived design; they emerged in both their nature and their duration from the historical evidence. Local society was orchestrated in many ways by the state, and the Owens Valley has experienced three state regimes. The expansionary state sponsored the Indian conquest, homestead settlement, and consolidation of frontier society from 1860 to 1900. The progressive state incorporated western regions into national society through reclamation, conservation, and land management from 1900 to 1930. Following the Depression and the expropriation of the Owens Valley, from the 1930s to the present the welfare state took responsibility for economic recovery, resource management, and environmental protection. Longitudinal comparison of these three periods makes it possible to trace the changing influence of the state on local society, to evaluate its scope and limits, and to focus more precisely on the local response and resistance to shifting forms of domination.

Each state form was associated with a distinctive pattern of collective action at the local level. Under the expansionary state, Paiute society resisted white control, particularly in response to coerced labor; farmers and merchants quarreled with one another over production and consumption practices; local groups periodically joined forces to oppose the trade monopoly of corporation-owned mines and to appeal to the railroad and the federal government for local services. Collective action was fragmented by class and status-group interests; political coalitions were rare and short-lived. Under the progressive state, efforts to incorporate the Owens Valley into regional and federal development plans provided the basis for community action, and during the 1920s, when state promises were betrayed, the community rose in rebellion. Although the progressive rebels attempted to bring their grievances before the California and federal authorities, their efforts to mount a successful social movement were turned back until welfare-state programs provided a legitimate legal challenge, particularly during the 1970s with new environmental legislation. Once this pattern is fully documented, we shall develop an explanation for the association and transformation of state forms and collective action: from the expansionary state and fragmented class action, to the progressive state and community rebellion, and then to the welfare state and the social movement.

THE PROBLEM

If this is a longitudinal case comparison, then the question arises, What is the Owens Valley a case of? First, although the American West is an immense and varied region, certain historical processes were central to its overall development, and the Owens Valley is remarkable as a microcosm in which those forces intersected. Each of the following factors affected both the American West generally and the Owens Valley in particular. Native Americans were dispossessed by military conquest and incorporated into the settler society as traders, laborers, and sometimes political allies in a fragile peace. Public land grants in various forms (such as preemption or homestead) subsidized and greatly facilitated settlement. Mining provided an important incentive for immigration and economic development, although its greatest benefits were monopolized by urban and national capital. The railroad opened the country but, like mining, introduced monopolistic practices and generated inequalities that gave rise to popular protest. Hardship was the permanent lot of most settlers, owing to inadequate transportation, weak markets, noncompetitive costs of production, trade monopolies, and local economies that hovered at the level of subsistence, barter, and self-provision. A pattern of uneven development stemming from these conditions was expressed in social divisions between men and women, whites and Indians, Anglos and Hispanics, all overlaid with class conflicts (for example, between farmers and merchants, or owners and workers). Alongside these schisms, western communities developed distinctive practices of cooperation and self-government—a civil society within sharp limits, which were misunderstood from afar as indicating lawlessness or an absence of society. The economic role of the state evolved from passive subsidization to active intervention, initially around irrigation and then in all aspects of western life, including reclamation, conservation, land management, Indian affairs, and most recently, environmentalism. The West, more than any other section of the United States, became the domain of state management and dissent over its legitimate claims.[8] In a general sense, therefore, this is a case of western development.

Second, these parallels argue for the wider relevance of this longitudinal case study, but not for generalizations about the multiform process of western development. I do not claim that the Owens Valley faithfully represents the larger history of the American West. Reasoning along that line would suggest a purpose to advance a theory that holds for and is tested against the general case. Instead, my purpose is to formulate a theoretical interpretation through close analysis of the case over time. Although I shall return to this logic in the final chapter, the research method pursues Arthur Stinchcombe's observation that "one does not apply theory to history; rather one uses history to develop theory."[9]

Beyond a general interpretation of western incorporation, the theory that develops from this study deals specifically with collective action and its changing forms. As a starting point, this study assumes that human agency is the central feature of historical change, although by no means the only one. Under conditions that are given, people organize in social groups and institutions and make their own history; and history made at one time becomes one of the conditions of action at another. From the standpoint of local society, the state looms large among the structures or conditions that affect collective action. The state's claim to legitimate domination is susceptible to challenge and change through collective action. Challenges to legitimacy, in turn, derive in important part from culture, which is embedded in tradition and ideology.

In the Owens Valley, each of these concepts has clear historical referents. The state assumed an increasing role in local society as it moved from patrimonial land agent to owner and author of economic development. As a web of meaning, local culture took root in a paternalistic order preoccupied with the Indian question, and it evolved around the symbols of community and progress. Collective action followed parallel transformations, from class and status-group protest over uneven development, to community rebellion, to social movement. The theoretical interpretation developed out of these elements explains collective action and its changing form through the interplay of state and culture.

TWO

Conquest and Incorporation

The American West, like so many frontiers of European expansion, was conquered by military force and incorporated into the geopolitical design of an alien nation. The formation of the United States during its most expansive period, the nineteenth century, followed a distinctive pattern, no less pernicious than other colonial adventures because its agents were as often settlers, miners, and traders as they were soldiers. Incorporation of the West was a policy, indeed a mission, conceived and implemented by the state, a colonial mode of domination even though other words were used to describe and celebrate it. The fabled pioneer agents of conquest, as well as their Native American adversaries, improvised roles in a struggle impelled by the military coercion and public-land incentives of an expansionary state.

In this respect, the American West bears a seldom recognized historical resemblance to other colonial societies. It is true, of course, that the United States expanded into contiguous lands rather than foreign acquisitions, and settled territories were regularly assimilated to the national union, with full rights of citizenship eventually granted to the new states and their individual members. Nevertheless, western expansion as a general socioeconomic process shared many of the characteristics normally associated with colonialism—and normally minimized in U.S. historiography. Indigenous societies in the new country were subdued by force, their land and labor seized for exploitation by the invader. The occupied territory was developed, not for the benefit of the local population, but in the interests of alien political and economic power. The result was a pattern of uneven development in which metropolitan monopolies exploited regional resources, exported their profits, and stifled the growth of local enterprise. The region was steadily incorporated as a dependent supplier of commodities to national and international markets, whose fluctuations now determined the rhythms of local prosperity. In combination, conquest and its ideological defense, a settler population with its own social order, and a fragile frontier economy all contributed to a blustery culture of paternalism—economically precarious pioneers obsessed with their superiority over the natives. And at the core of these contradictory forces, local society was rent by conflict and resistance.

My purpose in this chapter is not to argue that the American West was a literal colony—a term westerners used in a critical and pointedly ironic manner. Rather, I hope to demonstrate the complex ways in which Native American and white settler societies confronted one another, as well as some of the serendipitous generalizations that cover the incorporation of the West and other colonial experiences. Drawing on a variety of primary sources, detailed examination of a particular case will show: how conquest was accomplished principally as a result of the state's military and public land policies; the essential contribution of state subsidies and Indian labor to pioneer survival; similarities between the methods of labor control and the proletarianization of indigenous producers in the American West and other colonies; and the way frontier society was suffused by the ethic and practice of racial domination. This chapter, in short, analyzes the material and cultural foundations of frontier society.

Conquest came late to the Owens Valley. Remote from eighteenth-century Spanish mission society along the coast and *Californio* settlement in the Central Valley during the 1840s, the eastern sierra was crossed hastily and perilously by early migrants. Only in the late 1850s did whites settle the Owens Valley as miners or in commercial and agricultural activities that supplied the mines. For settlers, there never was a precapitalist interlude between their arrival and the mining boom—no traditional society based on land and custom in common. Although many were disappointed in their hopes for commercial gain, and during later economic recessions the region was reduced to a subsistence economy, from the beginning of its pioneer settlement the Owens Valley was conceived as a market economy. The establishment of commerce in food and minerals required state intervention by force and incentive. The indigenous population had to be brought under military control and the settlers subsidized with cheap public lands, both according to a well-established pattern of western development. Yet the Owens Valley also witnessed the fulfillment of another, less noted pattern. Conquest was achieved by the incorporation of Indians into settler society, not as a marginal dispossessed class but as essential wage labor. Social relations were shaped by this fact, coloring not only the Indian experience of exploitation but the culture of settler society.

THE BEGINNINGS

The first white sojourners to record their impressions of the Owens Valley in the 1850s described a tranquil and industrious Paiute Indian society. A. W. Von Schmidt, who led a United States survey party in 1855, observed, "This valley contains about 1000 Indians of the Mono tribe, and they are a fine looking set of men. They live principally on pine nuts, fish, and hares, which are very plenty."[1]

During the summer of 1859, U.S. Army Captain J. W. Davidson led a punitive expedition from Fort Tejon two hundred miles northeast to the Owens Valley in search of Indians presumed responsible for a rash of horse stealing in white settlements of the San Joaquin and San Fernando Valleys. Contact with the Paiutes soon changed Davidson's mind. "We are beginning to be convinced from close observation that these Indians are not only not horse thieves, but that their true character is that of an interesting, peaceful, industrious people, deserving the protection and watchful care of the Government."[2] A correspondent with the Los Angeles Star who accompanied the Davidson party noted that the Paiute headmen responded deliberately to the captain's praise for their peaceful intentions and to his offer of army protection. "Their reply was that such had always been their conduct and should ever be; that they had depended on their own unaided resources; that they had at all times treated the whites in a friendly manner, and intended to do so in the future."[3]

Despite the paternalism implicit in Davidson's offer of government protection, his observations gave more credit to indigenous agricultural invention than did subsequent chronicles.

> They have already some idea of tilling the ground, as the ascequias [irrigation ditches] which they have made with the labor of their rude hands for miles in extent, and the care they bestow upon their fields of grass-nuts, abundantly show. Wherever the water touches this soil of disintegrated granite, it acts like the wand of an Enchanter, and it may with truth be said that

these Indians have made some portions of their Country, which otherwise were Desert, to bloom and blossom as the rose.[4]

Von Schmidt and Davidson saw with pristine eyes the results of an indigenous civilization that had existed for thousands of years prior to white contact in the 1820s. The Old Spanish Trail from Tucson to Los Angeles initiated by Franciscans in 1775 cut well to the south of the valley, but Paiutes probably had contact with travelers, judging from their rudimentary knowledge of Spanish. Jedediah Smith and Joseph Walker separately pioneered trails through the valley in the 1820s and 1830s. By the 1840s traffic was brisk as California-bound wagon trains and John C. Fremont's expeditionary forces moved up and down the valley, the name of which Fremont bestowed in 1845 to honor his lieutenant, Richard Owens. Above the valley on the east, Paiutes had also established alpine villages in the White Mountains. "When in 1834 the trapping party of Joseph Reddeford Walker trekked east across the Sierra Nevada and entered Owens Valley to become the first white men ever to set eyes on the White Mountains, the range was already well-used—tracked with paths, dotted with camps, and littered with the debris of ten thousand years of human occupancy."[5] After twenty-five years of peaceful contact, the Indians who met Captain Davidson had good reason to suggest to him that they would do fine on their own unaided resources.

The Owens Valley Paiute comprise the southernmost subdivision of the Northern Paiute tribes, which occupy Northern Nevada and the eastern slope of California's sierra. Recent estimates suggest that just prior to white settlement, two thousand Paiutes were living in thirty permanent villages throughout the valley.[6] The villages were politically united in a smaller number of land-owning districts. Julian Steward's first ethnographies of the Paiute, based on investigations begun in the 1920s, list six districts in the northern sections of the valley, "each with communistic hunting and seed rights, political unity, and a number of villages,"[7] and seventeen settlements in the southern areas, where "most of the villages were independent, that is, constituted land-owning, political units. Some, however, especially those which lay in close proximity to one another, were apparently sufficiently allied to constitute larger bands like those [in the northern sections] at Big Pine and Bishop."[8] The bands were led by headmen, rather than chiefs, who governed in decentralized and limited ways subject to popular approval and ratification by a council.

The Paiute observed rules of land use based on ownership and common rights that varied by subsistence activity. Seeds and tubers, the most important foods, were cultivated and gathered in band-owned territories—elongated rectangles that extended across the valley between the summits of the two enclosing mountain ranges. Pine nuts were gathered in the mountains, but within distinct territories owned by bands and subdivided into plots assigned to families. Hunting and fishing, with some exceptions, came under common-use rights and were conducted on both an individual and a collective basis. Deer drives and mountain sheep hunts were communal undertakings. At the close of the pine nut harvest every fall, a six-day interdistrict festival was held featuring conferences, dances, gambling (with shell money), and a communal rabbit drive that produced pelts for blankets and clothing.

Outstanding among the achievements of Paiute society was the practice of settled agriculture based on irrigation systems constructed by the Paiutes. Although the practice was recorded by Captain Davidson and mapped by Von Schmidt, subsequent white settlers denigrated the Indians' accomplishments, claiming that they merely diverted streams to water wild plants rather than employing deliberate agriculture. This conventional wisdom was reflected, and in some ways established, by W. A. Chalfant's history of Inyo County, which appeared first in 1922 and was revised in 1933. Correcting the "bias" of an Indian agent stemming from "much sympathy with the Indians in their pathetic resistance to the inevitable white domination," Chalfant explained that "the products were the native plants, irrigated to a limited extent and not cultivated at all."[9] Julian Steward, relying on Chalfant's 1922 edition and on information obtained from the author, concluded similarly that the Paiutes practiced "irrigation without agriculture,"[10] and that they were "on the verge of horticulture but did not quite achieve it, for planting, tilling, and cultivation were unknown."[11]

Early observers were more discerning. In addition to the several-acre plots irrigated near Bishop Creek and Big Pine that Steward sketched, evidence from a variety of early maps and surveys shows at least ten separate irrigation works tapping creeks that ran eastward out of the sierra and covering, in series, a distance of 57 miles from north to south. The whole "irrigation system involved large plots totaling multiples of square miles."[12] The ditches lateral to each creek were clearly human constructions—spaced at regular intervals, each averaging 40 inches in width, the whole network regulated by dams that were annually erected and cleared. Indigenous agriculture had its own technology and social organization. The head irrigator enjoyed high status, having been elected or appointed to the post on the basis of skill. Digging sticks were used to cultivate plants; harvesting was done by women, who reseeded the ground as they filled baskets with their yield. Modern reappraisal of Steward's conclusions strongly suggests that "the Owens Valley Paiute were engaged in the practice of agriculture. They had developed a complex farming system on an agronomic scale that required substantial communal labor. This farming system involved a tremendous amount of work both in the initial phases of construction and laying out of the vast system of ditches and canals and in the annual dam-building, irrigation, and harvest."[13] Hunting and the gathering of pine nuts generated essential foods, but agriculture was tightly integrated with the broader patterns of social organization.

The puzzle, therefore, is less how the Paiute managed to build a self-sufficient agrarian society than why the white settlers and their experts chose to belittle this achievement. Mild irony attaches to Chalfant's own observation that in 1858 a delegation of Owens Valley Paiute traveled some distance to Fort Tejon and "asked assistance to put in crops next season, also someone to instruct them in agriculture, etc."[14] People groping on "the verge of horticulture" yet unable to achieve it would not likely be aware of their own needs for technical assistance or of where to look for answers. Rather, it was fundamental to white justification of the impending conquest that "the Piute is essentially a child of nature,"[15] an inferior race languishing without the benefits of civilization and therefore incapable of inventing civilized agriculture. "For all explanations of the essential weaknesses of savage society had as a basic tenet the assumption that Indians were not farmers, and all plans for civilizing Indians assumed they needed to be farmers."[16]

SETTLEMENT AND SUBORDINATION

White settlement of the Owens Valley is explained by a combination of the pursuit of natural resources and state expansion. The promise of mineral riches attracted individual Anglo prospectors from the increasingly monopolized gold fields of the California foothills and the silver lode of Virginia City, who joined Mexican miners exploring silver deposits in the Inyo Range. The state guarantee of military protection and cheap public land ensured the follow-up immigration of cattle-raising and farming purveyors to the mines. Of these influences, the role of the state was perhaps greatest, because it both made settlement possible and shaped its character.

Although legendary lost mines along the Old Spanish Trail lured prospectors to the Mojave Desert in the late 1840s, the first strikes affecting the Owens Valley came in 1859 at locations as far apart as Monoville (near Mono lake), the Inyo foothills (east of Independence), and Coso (in the desert southeast). Monoville alone grew to a camp of 2,000 by 1860 when new and more enduring discoveries were found in Aurora (Nevada) and the Russ District (east of Independence). Countless small claims filed at the same time reflected a deluge of prospectors spread over two mountain ranges from the high country of Mono County to the Mojave Desert. (See map 2, p. 68, for general locations.) An Indian agent writing in 1862 cautioned: "The discovery of gold and silver mines in the ranges of the mountains on the borders of the Great Basin make what was three years ago an unknown region at this time a great thoroughfare; and the importance of averting at this time such a calamity as an Indian war is more pressing, as it would prevent travel and deprive the country of valuable resources made known by the energy of our hardy pioneers."[17]

In August 1861 permanent white settlement commenced with Charles Putnam's adobe and stone house at the present site of Independence and Samuel A. Bishop's camp just west of the town that now bears his name. Bishop had driven five to six hundred head of cattle and fifty horses from Fort Tejon into the valley with plans to graze them on its luxuriant grasses and sell beef at the mining camps. A dozen more drives followed from the southern San Joaquin Valley to Aurora that summer and fall, with herds as large as fifteen hundred head. Although white-Indian conflict was unknown within the Owens Valley at this time, prospectors and travelers having passed undisturbed, the situation shifted as the grand thoroughfare became a cattle range. Grasses and grains were consumed or trampled by livestock. The Paiutes' fragile ecology and source of winter stores were seriously threatened. Mattie Bulpitt, a Paiute woman of 85 when she told her life story to an ethnographer in the 1930s, recalled the early years of settlement:

> Then the white men begin to come, one at first, then more and more, and from then on the valley was thickly settled with white people. The cattle begin to arrive with the settlers, little at first, then they begin to multiply. Through all this the Indians were very friendly, never complaining of the cattle and horses which roamed over their taboose [tubers] and sunflowers and other seeds producing food for the Indians. They used to irrigate these

fields. Eventually the white man begin to tell the Indian what to do. They told him not to pick the seed because if we pick seed from the plant, more plants will not grow. And when they go out to irrigate their seed beds, the white man says not to take any of the water. If you do my horses and cattle will not have anything to eat. Always the same story. Until the white man become abusive and was using force to keep the Indians from harvesting the seeds when they ripen. They begin to have a hard time because they were driven away from these places where they gathered different seeds for food. The conditions got worse when the Indians begin to get hungry.[18]

The Indian war that raged intermittently from 1862 to 1865 centered immediately on the killing of livestock and ultimately on the irreconcilability of Paiute subsistence and white settlement. With the exception of a few sympathetic Indian agents, whites failed to understand the devastating impact of their herds on the indigenous economy. Never a warlike people, the Paiute feared the armed invader but knew no effective means of resistance. Depredations began in the exceptionally harsh winter of 1861–62, when cattle and horses were taken by Indians to supplement winter stores already reduced by extensive grazing. The Paiute freely admitted some of these acts, but also noted that Shoshone bands from outside the valley were as often the predators, a fact lost on settlers indifferent to native ways and group differences. The first casualties occurred in late 1861, when a Paiute was shot in the act of taking a steer and within days a cowboy was killed in revenge. A truce was hastily arranged at Bishop's camp in January 1862. Its terms, although calling for blissful coexistence, addressed none of the real problems; and the political authority of its Indian assenters as "captains" or chiefs existed only in the minds of the whites. In fact, Indian groups were seriously divided, with many Paiutes tending to acquiescence and others aligning with more aggressive Mono and Shoshone bands led by the redoubtable Joaquin Jim.

Major accounts of the Indian war rely principally on white sources, reflecting at once a factual chronology more detailed than Paiute oral history and an overriding military perspective.[19] Juxtaposition of conventional descriptions with ethnographic reports from Paiute survivors given many years later balances this history by introducing the Indian voice and social conditions underlying the conflict. The war began in earnest in the late winter of 1862 as settlers mounted attacks to avenge and discourage livestock stealing. Emboldened by the ease of their initial massacres, white civilians pursued the enemy to the northern end of the valley, where they were abruptly repulsed by the massed, if poorly armed, forces of Joaquin Jim. The U.S. Army was summoned, two companies arriving from different directions as dozens of chastened civilians fled south and, as a measure of their intrusiveness, "took some 4,000 steers and 2,500 sheep with them."[20] For several months that spring the Indians reclaimed the valley, until army reinforcements established Fort Independence on July 4, 1862 (hence its name) and introduced their most effective weapon, starvation. Indian winter stores were destroyed, camps burned, and the survivors of these attacks chased into the mountains. The army commander's expressed aim was to "keep the Indians out of the valley and in the hills, so that they can have no opportunity of gathering and preserving their necessary winter supplies, and that they will be compelled to sue for peace before spring and grass come again."[21] Peace, from this standpoint, meant that white settlement and mining would proceed unhampered as the Indians passively accommodated themselves to civilization or, indeed, contributed their labor and resources to its forward march.

Many were not offered the choice. Edith Dewey explained that "there were times when we scarcely had anything to eat, when especially the white man never knew or stopped to realize that it was our land they settled themselves on and when we went to gather food that we thought was ours, which produced our only means of living and would chase us away. The men folk would always get us out to the mountains. . . . [W]e went up higher into the mountain till everything was alright again."[22] Ben Tibbitts said he was about ten or twelve years of age when the white man came. "Group by group they [the Indians] vanished into the mountains until they were all gone, [although] older folks would go down into the valley and hunt food. The soldiers continued to chase us through the mountains for about a year."[23] Mattie Bulpitt's experience with the destruction of food and shelter—"The soldiers came upon the camp and set fire to everything in sight"[24]—is confirmed by others.

Concerning their own use of violence, the Paiutes acknowledged emulating the acts of other tribes in seeking their proper revenge. In the early years, Hank Hunter recalled, "the feed was plentiful and the cattle were allowed to roam over the hills as they pleased. The Indians who lived nearby took advantage of this and began to kill the cattle on the sly, and many feasts were had." Settlers admonished a Paiute band through their leader whom they knew as Chief Chico, but "the warning meant very little to them and in a short time they were back to their cattle killing tactics." A massacre of guilty members of Chico's band ended the practice but left survivors, one of whom "continued to hate the white settlers because most of his relatives were killed" and exacted revenge until he was killed by his own people to pacify whites.[25] Mary Rooker noted that while many "Paiutes carried on, the Shoshones from the east commenced to rustle stock and slaughter them until the practice grew among the Indians of this valley."[26]

Indian resentment grew as a result of the betrayal of their initial goodwill toward whites and the injustices stemming from misunderstandings. Betrayal and error bred retaliation. George Robinson claimed that Paiutes helped the early settlers build shelters at Bend City: "[W]hile the Indians were doing this, the horses of the white man were fast disappearing. The white settlers unjustly accused the Indians who lived here when they saw all the time that the Indians who lived here used no horses." To prove their innocence the Paiutes tracked the horse thieves, who turned out to be two Shoshones, one of whom was shot by the whites as another escaped wounded. The wounded man and his band "came [back] over the mountains and made their way to a home occupied by a white man and his wife. It happened that the woman was alone so met her death at the hands of the Shoshone Indian who were out for revenge."[27] John Shepherd suggested that the Paiute themselves were capable of fearsome hit-and-run attacks when provoked. "The white people were not treating the Indians right and the Indians finally got tired of it." After asking for food at a settler cabin, "when the white woman closed the door on them the Indians got mad. They set a fire to the cabin and went away."[28] The woman and two children died in the fire.

The available accounts of the Indian war written by whites focus on a series of mismatched military engagements. The ethnographic evidence, although consistent on major events, emphasizes a more defensive posture among the Indians. Starvation and depredation jolted the Paiute from a cultural tradition in which aggression was generally limited to family, subsistence-plot, and ritual conflict. Retaliation was carried out by others besides the Paiute bands understood as the enemy by whites. And flight was a more typical response to settler incursions.

By fall 1862, without winter stores, many Paiutes began surrendering at Fort Independence, where another peace treaty was signed in October. Yet even here rival interpretations thrive. Although the army understood arrival at the fort as an act of submission, Paiute ethnographies repeatedly stress that the Indians were lured to the post by blandishments of peace and feasting. Indeed, many wary Indians chose to remain in the mountains owing to their suspicions about the purposes of the offer. Others "were glad and wished to make peace for they were starving."[29] Ben Tibbitts recalled a meeting at the fort: "[O]ur white father and friend said for us to forget the war and trouble. We are not going to kill one another any more. They have plans for all of us to come down to Fort Independence just as soon as we can and go to work for our white friends." After the meeting "all of the Indians and their families returned to their homes with food given to them by the white friends. This convinced them all the more that the white people were their friends, so they returned home to tell the families of the happiness and joy that would be theirs. In the next few days we went down to Fort Independence where we were captured and kept."[30]

An uneventful winter was followed in March 1863 by new Indian hostilities, signaled perhaps by the disaffection of several Paiute leaders from the fort. Whites expressed bewilderment at this development, in words that revealed the depth of their insensitivity to Indian grievances. "There has not been the slightest cause or provocation for this outbreak *except* that the Government has laid off a reserve and settlers are locating farms."[31] Paiutes who passed the winter in semicaptivity or in the mountains living on roots and worms no doubt saw spring as an opportunity to renew their resistance by returning to the land. In any case, the army reacted forcibly, calling in reinforcements that brought their numbers to 120 troopers and 35 civilians, shortly to be reinforced again, and initiating the most intense phase of the war with new attacks on Indian settlements and food supplies. More families surrendered to join those who had remained at the fort, bringing their numbers to one thousand by June.

In July the Paiute diaspora began. Nine hundred and eight Paiute, now clearly captive, were mustered at the fort for transportation to the Sebastian Indian Reserve near Fort Tejon under the armed guard of ninety-five troopers. The assembled families in wagons and on foot were told that anyone refusing to go would be shot. Indeed, many Indians assumed that their execution was imminent. "The only thing we could figure out was that we were going to be killed, and [we] were stubborn in obeying orders."[32] Fifty escaped the twelve-day trek, according to an army estimate; although that figure may be low. Susie Westerville recalled that nightly escapes along the trail were routine, and when the caravan crossed the marshes of Owens Lake "dozens and dozens of Indians hid among the tules [reeds]" until the main party had passed on. More drifted away after their arrival at Fort Tejon and returned to new settlements in the mountains above the Owens Valley.[33] In 1864–65, as the war wound down to sporadic outrages by both sides, Paiutes cautiously returned to the valley, living now in rude and rocky camps along the fringes of white settlement, where work was available. The army had prevailed and had won the liberty of unfettered settlement, but the cost was counted in the grudging acceptance and the small acts of everyday Indian resistance that would pervade the new pioneer society.

Edith Dewey's explanation of the war hits the essential point: "The white man did not want us to disturb his land."[34] A gloomy Indian agent added the obvious. "The mines, which are of unsurpassed riches, will cause thousands to permanently settle there during the coming year, and as heretofore throughout all of California, the rights of the Indian will be disregarded, and constant turmoil and war will be a natural result."[35] The three-year struggle cost the lives of at least two hundred Indians and thirty whites. In the end, whites achieved a tense domination of the valley now open to settlement under public-land laws. The imposed order, however, required army enforcement until 1877—fifteen years of nearly continuous military intervention on behalf of pioneer security. Gathered in camps and small plots at the edges of white farms, Paiute society was dispossessed of its land, independent subsistence, and the social order resting on those foundations. Arriving pioneers bemoaned the retrograde culture and living standards of these children of nature as they appropriated their irrigation canals. As a harbinger of things to come, Paiute men were soon working for meager wages as irrigators on the land that once formed their tribal commons and reflected their cosmos.

INCORPORATION

In addition to military intervention, the expansionary state assisted settlement of the Owens Valley through public-land laws that provided pioneers with cheap farmsteads. During the first decade of settlement, beginning in 1863, three methods of acquiring land were available: purchase of California state land, federal claims under the Preemption Acts of the 1830s, and claims under the recently passed Homestead Act of 1862. Under both federal laws, settlers could claim 160 acres for a $10 fee, $8 commission, and payment of $1.25 per acre after five years (or sooner by commutation) of proven use and improvement. "Settlers in the Owens Valley, until 1876, availed themselves of the Preemption and Homestead Laws in acquiring federal lands, or, to a lesser extent, purchased state school lands. Preemption and homestead filings were limited in size to quarter-section units, parcels sufficiently large in arid environments if the land was irrigable, but of little use on non-irrigable lands."[36] Of approximately 182 claims filed in the first decade, 92 percent were under federal law with the more established preemption method preferred (54 percent) to homesteading (38 percent). In contrast to much of the arid West, where federal acreage limitations proved unrealistic for profitable farming, the Owens Valley was readily irrigable, as the Paiute had shown.

The immediate deficiency confronting settlers, however, was labor. Ditches had to be maintained and new ones dug, land cleared, and roads built; and, most pressing, hands were required for the harvest. On the horizon of the settlers' quarter sections were the Indian camps—a dispossessed population of experienced cultivators with few means of subsistence, disenfranchised by the laws under which settlement was proceeding, subjugated by the army, yet desperate for some kind of livelihood. The obvious solution was to proletarianize the Paiute, recruit the men for manual labor and seasonal agricultural work and bring the women into household production and upkeep. This, indeed, was the course pursued by settlers, although its extent and importance are inadequately recognized in local histories and generally in the history and theory of western development.

Folklore and some scholarly interpretations comfortably assume that American Indians have little postcontact history worthy of attention beyond their doleful marginalization under the aegis of discriminatory policies. Anthropological research, preoccupied with important questions about aboriginal cultures, excels at reconstructing the precontact past, but displays only a limited interest in the varied ways in which white and Indian societies affected one another after conquest. Recent research has begun to fill this gap as the blunt notion of contact is replaced by nuanced processes of incorporation. Thomas Hall argues that Native Americans were incorporated in a world economic system, first by Spanish colonialism and later by the expanding United States, with varied effects depending upon the purposes of the incorporating state and the resources of the coveted nonstate societies. "Native Americans had two choices: become lower-class members of a capitalist state, or die resisting. Many took the second option. Only where Americans had no desire for the land were native groups given unwanted land for reservations. They were ignored and pushed outside the new economic order to become 'captive nations' and welfare recipients."[37]

Hall's interpretive study of southwestern societies (Pueblo, Comanche, and Apache) reveals one important pattern, but it is not generally true that indigenous groups were "ignored and pushed outside the new economic order." On the contrary, in regions like the Owens Valley, where incorporation took place for purposes of commercial market expansion, Indians were used adroitly as independent producers and wage laborers. Elsewhere, in perhaps the best-documented North American case, Rolf Knight writes about British Columbia:

> It is time that the generations of Indian loggers, longshoremen, teamsters, cowboys, miners, fishermen, and cannery workers, and others who labored in virtually every primary industry in BC were recognized. Wage work in the major industries of this province has been an intimate feature of Indian lives for five and more generations. Indian workers and producers have been important in some industries for well over a century—right from the start.
>
> Even this leaves out the previous history of Indian groups in BC as commercial trappers-traders and as occasional wage workers on ships and trading posts prior to 1858.[38]

Cardell Jacobson notes that "Oklahoma echoes the events that occurred in British Columbia. From the time of removal to the time of the Civil War, the cattle business was the backbone of the economies of the Five Tribes."[39]

Closer to the Owens Valley, John Sutter's New Helvetia colony, begun in 1841 at the future site of Sacramento in the Central Valley, made extensive use of coerced and contracted Indian labor. Albert Hurtado's study explains, "Force alone did not inspire people to work for Sutter; he could usually depend on some Indians to work a few weeks at a time in return for trade goods. . . . It was a complex combination of slavery, peonage, and free labor, defined by white and Indian perception and needs."[40] By the 1850s the early means of coercion were failing, and for a brief time Indians successfully demanded remuneration in cash and higher wages. But the system of wage labor was short-lived owing to a rapid decline of the Indian population, the ready availability of white labor, and early mechanization. At its peak, only about twenty Indians were employed.[41]

The Owens Valley Paiute played a more central and enduring role in the new settler economy. Pioneer society was built with the labor of whites and Indians working together in an exploitative yet closely interdependent social relationship. Indian labor was subordinated and was employed in a manner bearing greater resemblance to the colonial experience of Latin America and Africa than to conventional interpretations of North American settlement.

Paiutes began working for settlers as early as there was work to be done, despite continuing hostilities. Bend City was established in the summer of 1863 along the banks of the Owens River and throve for two years until it was overshadowed by nearby Independence, founded in 1865. George Robinson explained how settlers built adobe houses roofed with reeds "gathered for the white people by the Indians who lived in this part of the valley. The Indians went out every day to cut the common reed and tied them in bundles which then was carted away in wagons by the white man. The Indians worked the river all day trying to help the white man get settled."[42] Describing the Paiute as a "treacherous race" after fighting broke out again in the spring of 1863, settler Henry Hanks claimed that "the whites have treated them well, paid them faithfully for all services performed."[43] The wage-labor relationship combined with subsistence tenancy was firmly established by 1865–66, when settlers began producing field crops such as hay and wheat. "Property in the upper portion of the valley is perfectly secure, the settlers there are giving work to Indians, many of them cultivating their grass seed ground or having little patches of corn, or live securely on their fishing grounds without fear of white men." The "worst class" of Indians, who chose traditional subsistence practices, moved eastward; but "those who are in the valley prefer peace and to work, which they do for fifty cents a day and hogadie (food)."[44] By the standards of the time, the wage was low. Hurtado reports Indians in the Central Valley receiving 75¢ to $1 per day around 1850.[45]

By 1872, with the expansion of settler agriculture and a mining boom at nearby Cerro Gordo, labor shortages had developed, requiring regular harvest employment of Paiute men and women. Josiah Earl showed entrepreneurial talent by parlaying a productive homestead into a freight and supply business serving the mines. The newly inaugurated *Inyo Independent* newspaper noted approvingly, "In carrying on his extensive farming operations Mr. Earl has to depend almost exclusively upon Indians, and female Indians at that, for laborers. In fact, farmhands and miners both are very scarce in this country; not at all equal to the demand, so these Indians, even of the female persuasion, are mighty handy things to have around the house."[46] The labor shortage failed to generate much gratitude for these "things" around the house; whites grumbled that "the farmers are falling back on the slow and uncertain Piutes and Piutesses for help."[47]

The implication that Indian labor, especially female labor, was exclusively agricultural and provided merely a fallback necessity during the harvest season reflects more the pioneer penchant for self-congratulation

Indians Haying on Earl Ranch. Paiute Indians were incorporated extensively into the Owens Valley labor force. Seasonal agricultural labor was the most common form of wage work for Indian men. Hay stackers, working here with a derrick, were the most skilled and highest paid of the harvest laborers. (Guy C. Earl Collection, courtesy of the Eastern California Museum.)

than the weight of evidence. Dating his recollections from the end of the war, Ben Tibbitts noted that "several years later a saw mill was built on Big Pine Creek. There my folks received employment as laborers. It was there we learned to eat white men's food and learned to wash clothes. We looked forward to this every summer after that. When I became a young man I was employed at the saw mill. I earned 25 to 50 cents. Later the ranchers began to hire haying hands. An irrigator received 25 cents a day, and the haying crew would receive 75 cents a day. We worked from daylight to dark, and worked only to satisfy our master."[48] Mary Cornwell lost her husband when she was a young woman, and she assumed full responsibility for her daughter's upbringing. She took a job in the incipient service sector: "When Flora was about ten years we went to Bishop. I got a job washing dishes for Baulder, a restaurant man. I earned fifty cents a day and our food. We stayed there for about nine years."[49] Henry Levy's Independence Hotel and Livery employed Indian women to do the laundry.[50]

The majority of steady female wage employment was in domestic ser-

Gorman's Grain Field. Some Indian men and women lived on settler farms, took the white family's name, and worked beside their patrons in the field. Indian women specialized in winnowing the grain, a skill learned in native horticulture. (Connable Collection, courtesy of the Eastern California Museum.)

vice. On the Earl farm "an Indian woman did most of the heavier housework and was paid fifty cents per day."[51] Nellie Glen and Suzie Butcher were among the many Indian laundresses employed by families one day a week at the standard fifty-cents-and-food rate in the early years.[52] But Indian women were also preferred for threshing during the wheat harvest.

> Mr. Currie often hired squaws to thrash [sic] his wheat. He would spread a canvas on the ground and lay the cut wheat on this. The Indian women would take long sticks and beat it until the grain would fall out of the heads. They then placed some of this in their winnowing baskets, raising them high, and pouring the grain from one basket to another, letting the wind blow away the chaff. It was a most interesting sight to watch as the Indians were very skilled at winnowing.[53]

The most common employment for Indian men was ranch work, which peaked during the summer harvest but also required year-round attention. Haying was the main event of the agricultural year, when Indian labor usage and wages were greatest (even in the early years as

CONTENT.
2405.

Forbes

Paiute Laundress. Andrew Forbes ran a photographic studio in Bishop from 1903 to 1916 and documented Paiute culture as an avocation when he was not working as the town photographer or making scenic postcards for tourists. The most common form of wage work for Indian women was domestic service, particularly laundry at 50 cents a day. (Courtesy of the Seaver Center for Western History Research, Natural History Museum of Los Angeles County.)

high as $1 a day, depending on availability). Yet the larger ranches employed permanent crews of Indian cowboys, who tended herds, drove them to and from summer ranges in the mountains, broke horses, cleared new land, and irrigated. Speaking of her father's pioneering days, Helen Macknight Doyle recalled, "When he first came to the valley, and built a ranch house and corrals to winter the stock that roamed the mountain meadows during the summer, he employed Indians to dig post holes for fences and the ditches for irrigation. . . . [T]he bucks understood irrigating better than the white men and the mahalas [Paiute women] were faithful, good servants."[54]

At the Shuey place five miles south of Independence, Indians "formed a rancheria about three-fourths of a mile from our ranch and we employed them in many ways to help us. We paid the men and squaws each fifty cents per day and had them hoe, husk and shell corn."[55] The Cashbaugh homestead one mile east of Bishop was cleared by Indians in 1871 and became home to a Paiute family that had a camp one-half mile west of the main house. One man worked year-round cultivating, two women did regular gardening and hoeing, and a third washed. "We had Indians working for us all the time." One cowboy was with the family for 37 years. "Indians were good at all farm work—riding, irrigating, haying. They took pride in making a good stack of hay, better than the white man at haying." Yet the Indians also evinced resentment toward their white employers in carelessness, in the "slow and uncertain" pace mentioned previously, and in "playing tricks that made the whites work harder [such as when they] left the hay derrick in the wrong place" for those who followed.[56]

Farm work was not the only means by which Indian labor was incorporated into pioneer society, especially as time went on and the economy diversified. Road building to service the ore-hauling teams from nearby mines demanded durable laborers.

> John Shepherd has completed the toll road from the foot of the lake, via Darwin to the new survey, through the foot of Panamint Canyon, and it is now said to be a splendid road for any kind of teams. Shepherd did most of the work with his Indians under the command of Captain George, and we are told that the way the captain and his men slashed sage brush, and made rocks and dirt move, could not be surpassed by any equal number of white men that ever made road for wages.[57]

Indian miners reportedly took "considerable gold" from the Old Coso mine.[58] Gus Cashbaugh's father built a grist mill in 1865 with the construction labor of twenty-five to thirty Indians.[59]

By the turn of the century, the industrious Paiute Joe Lent moved from job to job as the pay and the white boss pleased him. When the Mono County saw mill where he was working at $4 per day shut down, he moved to haying at the Farington ranch for $2 per day, still a good wage at the time. That was seasonal work, allowing him soon to lay off and gather pine nuts before returning to the Mono mill as a crosscut-saw operator. Later he made a living as an Indian policeman for $20 per month (rising to $38 per month after three years), a railroad section hand, a highway construction worker, and a ranch hand again "mending broken ditches and building fences" because he liked the boss and his eyes could not take the dust of road work. Then he erected power lines, repaired the Lundy pipeline, and returned once more to ranching but refused to do irrigating or work under a particular fore-man, neither of which he liked, and got fired. That was all right, too, because he could eat by fishing or endure another stint of road work despite his bad eyes.[60]

Differentials between white and Indian wages were noticeable but not extreme, owing perhaps to frequent labor shortages. The general Indian wage of 50¢ a day rose for men to $1 for routine ranch work and as much as $2 for haying by the early 1900s. White cowboys earned a regular $1.25 per day or its equivalent, $40–45 a month.[61] Charles Mulholland, a newspaper publisher and Independence justice of the peace, kept a ledger itemizing expenses for his business and the 320-acre homestead he owned with his brother, Irv. Entries between 1900 and 1905 indicate that the Mulhollands employed individual Indians full-time at $40 per month during much of the year. Squaws and "1/2 squaws" were paid amounts ranging, respectively, from $4 to $7.50 and from $2 to $2.75 for unspecified numbers of days, but in multiples that suggest a base of 50¢ per day. In addition to one regular hand, Paiutes such as "Little Sam" or simply "Indian," were hired for brief periods at 75¢ a day or for lump sums of $5–15, suggesting casual labor at $1 daily. Entries of $40–60 for "hay hands" fail to specify number and duration, but the going rate of $2 per day is suggested by other items of unspecified harvest-season work that read "2 Indians @ 2.00, [total] 4."[62]

The U.S. Census of 1880 is the first serious attempt to enumerate Inyo County's Indian population. Although remote camps, divided families, and regular sojourning probably led to an undercount, the census taker found 637 Paiutes in the area, 194 of them children. Of the 443 adults, 377 (85 percent) were listed as having an occupation, and 66 were unemployed (table 1).

TABLE I.   OCCUPATIONS OF OWENS
VALLEY PAIUTES, 1880

	Men	Women	Total
Miner	1	0	1
Farmer	8	0	8
Housekeeper	0	17	17
Cook	0	2	2
Servant	0	4	4
Laborer	178	167	345
No occupation	29	37	66
Total	216	227	443

SOURCE: Compiled from the manuscript census schedule
(# 1) of the Tenth U.S. Census of Population.

The figures on Indian labor are striking in several respects. First, the proportion of adults in the labor force is quite high (83 percent) and equal for men and women. The census made no distinction between year-round and seasonal work in its occupational designation, and it was taken in June; both observations suggest that the figures were probably closer to the fall-harvest highpoint than to conditions prevailing all year.

Second, Indians were overwhelmingly classified as laborers; 92 percent of all those with an occupation and 74 percent of the entire adult population fell in this category. Regrettably, the census taker's categories were not refined enough to show much diversity in the types of Indian labor. Close examination of the manuscript census schedule shows that the enumerator began making elementary distinctions to the extent of identifying some as "farm laborer," but ceased the practice before listing many of the population.

Third, Indians played a vital and distinctive role in the labor force. In 1880 Indians comprised 22 percent of Inyo County's population, and 21 percent of the 1,794 persons in the total labor force were Indians. They were, in other words, equally represented and as fully employed as whites and Mexicans. Of the 818 persons identified as laborers, however, Indians comprised 43 percent. One would expect that the proportion of Indians among farm laborers would be higher yet, given what we know from descriptive evidence. Although the census taker did not use the category consistently, we can arrive at an estimate. White occupational classifications appear fairly discriminating; the census taker distinguished between farm laborer and other occupations such as teamster, packer, or woodchopper. If we assume that the white occupational count was accurate and that few Indians were non–farm laborers, then Indians would comprise approximately 65 percent of all farm labor at the seasonal peak. The estimate may be high, since qualitative information suggests that Indian labor was somewhat diversified in individual experiences if not in numbers. But other imponderables, such as Indian underenumeration, complicate our assumptions, such that the 65 percent estimate seems reasonable for these data.

Although the data are less than ideal, consistency among multiple sources supports several conclusions about wages and labor relations. First, in agricultural and household service work Indians comprised the majority of the labor force, worked for the lowest of common wage rates, and suffered sharp differences between male and female income. Despite these conditions, labor-force participation rates were high for Indians of both sexes. Second, among the minority of white males who did ranch work, often youths, wages were only slightly higher than those of Indians. Finally, however, proportionately fewer whites were engaged in wage labor; they tended to be farm and business proprietors. In the numerically and economically important mining jobs, Anglo and Mexican workers dominated, enjoying substantially higher wages—$4 per day in good times and $3 when wage reductions were enforced during slumps. Instances of good Indian wages were either in atypical jobs (such as in saw mills) or short-term seasonal work (such as haying). In general, wage inequality followed gender and sectoral (that is, agriculture versus mining) lines rather than intraoccupational divisions. Indians were assigned most of the menial and casual work for the least rewards.

A skeptical rejoinder to these conclusions would doubtless note that the defeated Paiutes were fortunate to have any kind of work and that the menial tasks they performed, although helpful, were not vital to the pioneer economy. In one sense, the settlers themselves refuted this argument with observations about the Indians' noteworthy skill in such essential work as threshing, irrigating, haying, and road building. Moreover, once threshing machines were available, farmers found the cheap labor of Indian women cost-effective and preferable because it resulted in less waste and cleaner grain for milling.[63] Large-scale mechanization in the valley was held off, in part, by the availability of cheap, skilled Indian labor. Most compelling, however, was the settlers' response to the threatened loss of their labor force. In spring 1873 the federal government hatched a plan for a Tule River Indian reservation in the southern San Joaquin Valley, where Native Americans from both sides of the southern sierra would be relocated and a definitive census taken. Editorial and public opinion in the Owens Valley dropped their preoccupation with the drunken and desultory habits of the Paiute and rushed to defend their own and, presumably, the Indians' best interests.

> To attempt to force them there [to the reservation] is simply to attempt an unmitigated swindle upon the government, an outrage upon the Indians and scarcely anything less upon the whites among whom they live. Their labor is of essential importance in public economy and supplies a want in that direction that no other can do as well. On this account their presence is a general benefit and the people here will universally protest against their removal, particularly as they are capable of much mischief if pushed to extremes. The Indians as a tribe are industrious and contented, peaceable and well disposed, and so they will remain if designing scoundrels will let them alone. The value of, and demand for their labor, both field and household, insures them good treatment at the hands of the whites, and a support free of cost to the government.[64]

> No catastrophe could befall our general farming interest that could equal the removal of our Indians to a reservation.[65]

> Large numbers of working Indians, now peaceably and profitably employed on farms, will be transmogrified into vagabonds, forced to steal or starve, if compelled to go to this worthless piece of ground. [White settlers] as a class protest against the withdrawal of their Indian laborers because they need them as such and that relation is mutually advantageous. [So dire is the problem that whites will make major concessions:] Large numbers of their Indians are anxious to and will become tax-paying citizens which of itself is an objectionable contingency, as the accession of that class of citizens is not desirable or desired by the whites, but nevertheless they will assist many of the red men to become citizens rather than see the reservation programme carried out.[66]

Settler protest succeeded, the reservation plan was dropped, and the status quo governing Indian labor and citizenship was preserved. Fifty years would pass before the Native American was given citizenship. In the meantime, disenfranchisement played a key role in maintaining the social relations of production by effectively discouraging Indian access to public lands. Strictly speaking, Indians were eligible to file homestead and preemption claims (if they renounced tribal affiliations and claims) but that "objectionable contingency" was blocked by settler practices motivated by the need for a labor force dependent on wages. One method to discourage claims was the law itself, which insisted that

Indians deny their culture in some respects. Another was bureaucratic obstruction.

> A few days since Mike Bishop, a Piute Indian, made application at this Land Office to pre-empt eighty acres of land adjoining Allison's place, Bishop Creek. Register McCallum refused the application on the general grounds that he did not think it legal, notwithstanding instructions from the Commissioners to Registers and Receivers which, to our view covers the whole case, admitting the Indian's right when he takes the oath supported by affidavits of two disinterested white persons, that henceforth he would live "all same as white man"—in other words, would wholly sever his tribal relations, renounce all claims or share to annuities, etc., all of which Mike did.[67]

> [As the Land Office explained, in something of a legal paradox:] "[T]he applicant to file is a Piute Indian and cannot voluntarily absolve his tribal relations. He is not a citizen of the United States within the meaning and intention of the law, therefore disqualified as a pre-emptor, and the application is refused." Other applications to file Indian claims have since been presented, but met the same fate.[68]

> [Time passed until another opportunity presented itself:] In March the Indian Homestead Act was approved. Mike made another application under that act. This time McCallum accepted it so far as to take $20 fees ($4 more than he had any right to) telling Mike to go back to Bishop Creek and forward necessary proofs (which, as in the previous instance, could have been obtained here). Mike did so, and thought it was all right till a few days since he came to inquire about his receipt. He was then made acquainted with the fact that our high-toned thief had pocketed the money, and that no filing had been made. This put Mike to the necessity of another 90 miles ride, to obtain the amount of fees, and to renew his application, making the third time.[69]

Yet another method to obstruct independent Indian proprietors who lacked Mike Bishop's perseverance and savvy was pressure to sell or abandon the plots they occupied under various forms of title. Mary Cornwell claimed that "there were some white people who wanted the land which is now the Crum Ranch. This was my husband's place by rights, but they finally got it. A man by the name of Sherwin who lived two miles north of here took me to Bridgeport [in Mono County] to see about my piece of land. We went to the land office. The 'big man' told me to continue living on my place. He said that it was my land. I stayed there for many years. Sherwin gave me food at the end of each month. He also gave me two dollars and a sack of flour. I finally sold it [to Sherwin] for $600.00. Now I had to leave."[70] Jennie Cashbaugh's family was defrauded by another Paiute acting as an agent "and in the end we found we were landless, some white people didn't want us on their land. We had to squat on some other land, but mostly wandered around."[71]

With the help of sympathetic whites who supported Indian filings with sworn statements about disavowal of tribal claims, a number of Paiutes successfully claimed and "proved up" public lands in plots ranging from 40 to 160 acres. A more encouraging report stated that "the Indians of the northern part of the valley are availing themselves of the privilege of entering lands under the Indian Homestead Law passed by Congress last March. Through their attorney, Mr. Sherwin, of Round Valley, some fifteen or sixteen of them filed Homesteads this week."[72] The report was overly optimistic. The 1880 census indicated only 8 Indian farmers (see table 1). By 1885, after more time for filing, and perhaps more settler pressure to sell or discourage proving up, county tax rolls show that of 640 land owners, only 9 were designated by the assessor as Indians.[73] Nine Indian farm proprietors represents 1.4 percent of the total at a time when the U.S. Census estimated that Indians numbered somewhere between 637 (1880) and 850 (1890) and comprised 22 percent of the county's population.

In summary, Paiute men and women entered the wage-labor force of pioneer society at an early date and worked in varied capacities, from the principal categories of domestic and farm labor to industry and services. In many of these undertakings the Indian was remarked as a worker superior in effort, skill, or knowledge to the white. Yet Indians invariably did manual labor subordinate to whites at the lowest wage rates—and expressed resentment about this relationship in foot dragging, pranks, and other forms of everyday resistance. Given the opportunity, some achieved independence from the wage labor system through farm ownership; but others were obstructed in the endeavor, or never tried. A cheap labor force was essential to pioneer prosperity, such as it was, and vigorous efforts were taken to maintain it.

In some important respects, the white settlers of the Owens Valley created a system of domination akin to colonialism in the white highlands of Kenya or Guatemala. Although European colonial practices varied widely, certain general features were typical. Indigenous groups were forcibly dispossessed of their land, resources, and infrastructure. From Africa to the Americas and Oceania, settler societies that engaged in commercial agriculture depended vitally on native laborers, who generally preferred to continue in their traditional economic pursuits. Participation in settler-controlled sharecropping or wage labor had to be coerced. The means by which this form of labor control was accomplished varied from commonplace land alienation to segregation on unproductive native reserves, outright bans on the cultivation of cash crops, the imposition of monetary taxes, and other forms of politically imposed wage dependency. Colin Leys's observation about the incorporation of Kenya's indigenous population applies as well to the Owens Valley: "Of all the ways in which capitalism wrought transformations in the pre-existing modes of production in Kenya the employment of wage labor stands out as the most far-reaching."[74] The explanation for these parallels lies not in some universal form of colonialism but in the structural conditions confronting modes of labor control that aspire to capitalistic market organization in the face of an available but recalcitrant labor force and political domination by a land-owning minority. The parallel between European colonies and the American West is not perfect, of course, but I believe it is on the track of a better explanation than the portrait of exceptional, marginalized Indians that pervades American studies.

RESISTANCE TO INCORPORATION

The Owens Valley Paiute resembled colonized peoples in yet another respect. By clinging to traditional subsistence practices where they could, and playing both systems depending upon opportunity, they were a semi-proletarianized labor force—a beleaguered society that nevertheless resisted economic and cultural domination. There had always been divisions within the indigenous culture. It is not surprising that by the 1870s some Paiutes aspired to such privileges of pioneer society as independent proprietorship, while others sought to maintain traditional ways of life. Most struggled with the tension between culture and survival.

Nowhere is the dilemma more explicitly demonstrated than in the conflict between wage work and subsistence practices wrapped in ceremony. Traditionally, families joined the fall pine-nut harvest, which was followed by a joint celebration of bands converging from all ends of the valley. Pine nuts and settler crops matured at the same time, posing the choice whether Indians would be farm workers or Indians. Sometimes opportunity costs urged the latter, or at least drove up wages.

> The Piutes *en mass* have skedaddled to the mountains to harvest the abundant crop of pine nuts with which the trees are loaded this year. After seeing in the Spring a fine prospect for pine nuts the usual four bits a day was no inducement for them to work; they wanted a dollar. But during the threshing the few natives who could be seen demanded "a dollar 'n hap one day, heap hogadie me likeum, whiskey too all same white man." And they got it

too—that is $1.50 per day. Pine nuts will be currency in the coming winter. A sack of pine nuts for a sack of flour has been the rule heretofore.[75]

The pine nut harvest being over, the mahalas, after three weeks absence, have returned to the washtubs, greatly to the relief of the white mahalas.[76]

As Joe Lent's occupational odyssey demonstrates, when it was possible Indians moved freely between the wage and traditional economies, abandoning, for example, the rigors of road work for fishing. The alternatives, however, were fast disappearing as settlement claimed more of the natural habitat, and the state (for example, game wardens) began to regulate its use. Ceremony persisted much longer than the subsistence activity it celebrated, particularly the harvest festival, which whites later attended and dubbed the Indian fandango.

If temporary withdrawal into the atrophying world of traditional culture was a passive form of resistance, more militant expressions were also common. The pranks, lassitude, and carelessness that grumbling settlers ascribed to Indian character are common forms of sullen resistance among slaves and indentured workers. Paiutes also developed methods tailored to their circumstances. Livestock continued to disappear long after the war, and crops were pillaged. Indians were "destroying by stealth the melon patches belonging to several settlers."[77] Unexplained fires seemed to ignite around Indian field crews and on farms adjoining their settlement at Camp Independence. Indigenous Luddism would appear the best explanation for a fired hay press.[78] Poaching on settler property and in streams was a common problem. One newspaper lament under the title "Should be Stopped" alleged that Big Pine streams were losing all their catfish to Indians who poisoned the waters with a concoction of mountain berries, gathered what fish they could use, and left the stream fouled with the rest.[79]

Indians took to wage work as their choices were steadily constrained, but never with unalloyed enthusiasm or indifference to their endangered way of life. Dispossessed of their land and forced to do the white man's work, they labored with pride and defiance. Indeed, in James Scott's multiform description of "everyday resistance,"[80] Indian pride of work was an expression of recusancy—an implied refutation of white superiority expressed in making a better haystack or displaying greater proficiency at irrigation and wheat winnowing. Resistance in the diverse forms of pride, sabotage, recalcitrance, and withdrawal suggests that tension pervaded the field of labor relations and that domination never succeeded in taking over the Indian's consciousness.

Ironically, the settlers displayed little awareness of the Indians' resentment, much less of their guile. Because pioneers regarded Indians as
children and savages, no one supposed them capable of critical reflection
on white ways. Yet no latter-day smugness will help to explain the
settlers' mentality. They misunderstood Indians because they had to deal
with them within the broader assumptions and aims of manifest destiny.
They brought to the Far West a repressive approach to the "Indian
problem" that, if anything, was less pernicious than the national policy
of wholesale Indian removal. Under a regime of sharp inequality, the
Owens Valley pioneers and Paiutes nevertheless lived together and fashioned a society as closely interdependent as its economy.

INDIANS AND WHITE SOCIETY

Social relations in the emerging society of whites and Indians were
determined by additional factors besides the important relations of production and wage labor. Just as Paiute culture animated resistance to
incorporation, white culture provided the framework within which economy, law, and social intercourse took a particular form, partly in response to the Indian. Where the Indian was concerned, the two cultures
intersected in the related principles of paternalism and violence. Paternalism defined the Indians' capacities and the civilizing responsibility of
whites; violence enforced, and sometimes abused, those norms. White
domination by these means introduced its own contradictions and vul-
nerabilities. The result was a thwarted society, never able to solve the
Indian problem and never doubting the methods it vainly pursued.

If the Indian was "essentially a child of nature,"[81] whites defined and
justified themselves as the parents. Their civilizing responsibility was to
protect and educate the Indian, to inculcate the habits of a more highly
evolved society, however harsh the necessary measures or reluctant the
beneficiaries. As Michael Rogin notes, paternalism meant that the
"parents did not simply replace Indians; they took upon themselves the
obligations of 'benefactors' and 'guardians.' For whites to indulge their
paternal wishes, Indians had to remain helpless children. Liberal paternal authority required its objects to have no independence or life of their
own."[82]

Paternalism in the Owens Valley fulfilled this description in ideology
and action. The first requirement was that an aimlessly natural society
be eradicated and, more important, replaced. Although this demanded
the regrettable use of force and disciplinary violence, such means were

justified by the salutary effects of a new paternal authority. For now it was possible to socialize the child into the civilized ways of work, property, and law. The task was formidable, slow, and always vexed by Indian backsliding—all of which emphasized the importance of the continuing military presence as a reminder of the costs of immaturity. Yet the settlers could also point to evidence of success in those "intelligent" Indians who learned English, worked dutifully, respected private property, and adopted white customs in matters ranging from dress to religion. Both theory and practice were sound. Settlers reasoned, in the words of their spokesman, W. A. Chalfant: "White domination, and its ability to make use of resources which to the Indian meant far less than the comparative comfort the conquerors have brought to them, were as inevitable here as they have been elsewhere as civilization advanced."[83]

Nowhere is paternalism expressed more literally than in the practice of naming Indians after white families. In effect, Indians were adopted as childlike servants and given a name like any new addition to the family. In Paiute society Mary Harry was Yowa-Khuya, and Ben Tibbitts was Tevegivih.[84] Jack Stewart was known in his own village as Hoavadunuki, which had no particular Paiute meaning, but Indians from other bands called him Tovowahazi because he was born in his mother's village of Tovowahamatu.[85] Disdaining Paiute culture, white settlers found these names unpronounceable and without significance. A first step toward civilizing the savages was to give them the Anglo or Spanish names of their employers. Typically, one or two Indian families became attached to a white family as permanent employees living on the homestead and acknowledged their adoption by taking the preferred family name. Because a proper white name was usually the result of stable employment, not all Paiutes had such names. Those identified in the U.S. Census of 1880 with names such as Old Sam and Whiskey Jim, or just "Indian," presumably worked for no single family.

Most Indians lived in traditional shelters of straw and branches, built on three types of site. First, rancherias or camps could be small plots located on the margins of settler farms where Indian employees were granted land use rights and maintained gardens. If the farm was sold, the tenants had no claim other than what might be negotiated with the next owner based on continued service. Second, the campodee or camp (the terminology is not applied consistently) was a recreated form of the village, embracing a number of families who squatted on unclaimed public land or were allowed to settle on government land. Such camps were quasi-reservations, although official reservations came much later

Winter House. The conical dwelling, called a *nobe,* was made of thatched tule reeds and designed for settled occupation, housing at least the man, woman, child, and dog pictured here. The wooden planks and dropcloth at the doorway are not indigenous building materials. In the right background are a dump or the remains of a campsite and a wooden building. (Courtesy of the Seaver Center for Western History Research, Natural History Museum of Los Angeles County.)

and did not have exactly the same boundaries. At Camp Independence, the largest of these settlements, Indians first resided under the wing of the army and later took full possession. Similar camps were located in each of the four principal towns, providing small plots and proximity to employment. Finally, the most autonomous settlements were scattered small camps on the valley's rocky fringes, inhabited by the poorest and least employable Indians. This tripartite division includes neither the small number of Paiutes who successfully purchased or homesteaded farms nor those who chose to remain in mountain or desert redoubts after the war.

The segregation characteristic of work and residence governed most social relationships. Rarely did settlers show any affinity for Paiute language and culture. Sam McMurry's parents homesteaded south of

Big Pine in 1873, so "Sam had grown up among the Indians and they trusted him. He could converse with them in their own tongue, as few learned to do well."[86] Typically, the Indians' use of English was ridiculed, and as a group they were referred to sarcastically as "the noble red man" or "aborigines." Later, when theatres came to the towns, Indians were assigned to a separate section in the balcony.

Anglo-Indian intermarriage was rare and earned adamant disapproval, unlike simple cohabitation. The novelist Mary Austin observed privately that "such families are not received by whites and the white man is cast off by his acquaintances—if he was *not* legally married it would be alright."[87] The same fate was reserved for Indian-white children, irrespective of the legal status of their parents' union. The large Mexican population provided a buffer between group prejudices. Mexican-Paiute intermarriage was common and the couple or their offspring evidently suffered no discrimination beyond that already experienced by Mexicans. Yet Anglo-Mexican intermarriage was also frequent and unremarkable, typically working to enhance the social status of the Mexican member of the partnership. The color line was fundamental, however; the marriage of a son of Big Pine's one black family to an Indian woman received the blessings of all.[88] Gender interacted with race in a decisive manner. In virtually all cases of intermarriage it was the woman who married "up." The idea, conversely, of a white woman marrying an Indian was beyond scandal.

Once the Indian was segregated and effectively supervised, paternalism urged the responsibility, indeed the self-interest, of white benefaction. The Paiute had to be trained in the ways of civilized society, and that education was the best safeguard against renewed hostilities between the races. Given the prerequisites, it is not surprising that the good works did not get under way until 1890 when the first Indian day school was established in Bishop. Martha Dixon, a teacher at the Inyo Academy, initiated the idea, sought approval from the Indian Commissioner in Washington, and raised funds locally to rent a building and pay teachers. Success in Bishop led to founding a second school in Big Pine, where the first teacher, a half-breed named Jose Turner, had to "name children" before class could begin with an official enrollment.[89] Methodist missionaries came at about the same time to offer Sunday school instruction. Among the malevolent forces threatening the Paiutes, however, these apostolics worried most about the "insidious ways" of Roman Catholicism "which has always been attractive to the Indians with its many symbols and ceremonies."[90] If church and school were the primary means of Indian socialization, organized extramural

Indian School. Although Forbes wrote "Piutes, Bishop" on the negative, this appears to be the class of the Indian School at Big Pine. Students of all ages are dressed for the occasion; a partially obscured white woman in the back row may be the teacher. Indian schools were maintained on reservations and through the civic efforts of settler families. (Courtesy of the Seaver Center for Western History Research, Natural History Museum of Los Angeles County).

activities paralleled the moral education of white youth. Paiutes were encouraged to field a baseball team and organize a brass band that marched in local parades.

Finally, paternalism was expressed with more immediate results in the practice of sponsorship. Indians deemed intelligent by virtue of their precocious acculturation were supported by white patrons in quasi-official, and paid, positions as imposed "captains" of their fellows; in the proof of homestead and other legal claims; and in subsidized vocational education outside the valley. Judging from the nature and numbers of these examples, only a small minority of Indians excelled sufficiently as apprentice whites to earn modest standing in pioneer society. Most lived apart, worked grudgingly, and contributed nothing to the validation of white society's civilizing mission. Indeed, relations between Paiutes and pioneers were characteristically tense—always fraught with violent conflict that seemed to threaten peace and prosperity. Whites worried continuously about the problem, but were undaunted in their paternalistic mission because the responsibilities of benefactor shaded easily into those of guardian.

Indians had to be protected from themselves and from renegade whites. Violence underpinned both the problem and the solution.

Fort Independence Indian Band. The Paiute reservation at Fort Independence had a brass band that played for valley-wide festivals and parades. Pictured here, standing from left, are Fred Glenn, Tony Harris, Alex Patton, "Happy Jack," Cleveland Buff, Harrison Diaz, Jim Reynolds, and kneeling from left, Johnnie Sims, Pete Thomas, Ben Hunter, an unidentified man, and Jim Earl. (Courtesy of the Seaver Center for Western History Research, Natural History Museum of Los Angeles County.)

The fact is well understood that most all the out-breaks of the semi-civilized tribes can be traced directly to the actions of a few unprincipled white men. There are white men—or men claiming to be white—in this valley, mean enough to sell whiskey to these same Indians for a few cents profit to be thereby gained, and to just such men may be ascribed the many bloody Indian wars. The best way to avoid Indian wars is to protect the Indians themselves. They are at the present time almost universally well treated, but it is in their power to do as much damage as at any time since the settlement of the valley. The presence of even a semblance of military force exerts a wholesome moral influence over the rough classes of both red and white.[91]

[As to the Indians alone:] Once made to feel the power of the whites, they are willing to be his useful servants when rightly protected as well as held in check by the military.[92]

[Concerning whites:] The cause of the whole trouble undoubtedly lays at the door of some white villain who sells them whiskey.[93] These felons will sooner or later create a serious disturbance unless something is done to bring them to justice.[94]

Conceived in two parts—protect the Indian and punish errant whites—the solution was doomed because neither part corresponded to realistic possibilities. The scourge of alcohol abuse was neither an exclusively Indian obsession nor an exhaustive explanation of Indian trou-

Bishop Harvest Festival Indian Baby Show. 1916   Forbes 2340

Indian Baby Show. Forbes caught the paternalistic flavor of interethnic relations in this shot of an Indian baby show held at the Bishop Harvest Festival of 1916. (Courtesy of the Seaver Center for Western History Research, Natural History Museum of Los Angeles County.)

bles. The Paiutes, moreover, had other reasons for defying paternalism, ranging from interferences with traditional practices to the rape and murder of their people. Finally, the law, which would theoretically enforce an evenhanded solution, was blatantly discriminatory in practice.

Many Indians took to alcohol with relish. The result was a visible dissolute element that hung around the towns gambling in traditional ways, loafing, and generally being vagrant. Another, overlapping element, was prone to violence. Indian violence was overwhelmingly an intragroup phenomenon, typically taking the forms of wife beating, lethal quarrels over whiskey or property, and murder stemming from long-festering disputes. Rare instances of violence by Indians against whites included harassing threats, aggressive pandering, and at least one beating of an unpopular farm boss. White drunkenness was perhaps equally common, and more troublesome in that it led to numerous white fatalities. Shooting affrays were weekly occurrences in the saloons and mining camps. Yet the problems were construed asymmetrically. Violence by Indians was attributed to the constantly reiterated and socially constructed problem of drunken Indians—who touched on whites' fears of savages run amok. Violence by whites was attributed to misguided individuals or the sometimes lamentable nature of rough-and-tumble life in the West. Local newspapers beat this tattoo for decades without variation, but never acknowledged the kind of story Joe Lent later told an ethnographer:

> I know of a little Indian child, a girl, about four or five years old who was taken over [when her mother died] by a white lady by the name of Mrs. Woods. The little girl's name was Elsie Lent. Her hair was white. She was a blonde; three quarters white blood. Mrs. Woods and Elsie came to Bishop one day to visit us. [Mrs. Woods] said to Elsie that she could stay with us for the night. It seems that when Mrs. Woods got back to town she did not go to the hotel, but stayed somewhere else and got drunk for the night. The next day towards evening, about six o'clock Mrs. Woods came out to our place with a horse and buggy still drunk. Mrs. Woods wanted to take Elsie back to town in the condition she was in and we told her we thought it was better for her not to take Elsie the way she was. When we said this to her she got mad and called us all kinds of names. She started to get up and walk to show us she was not drunk, but before she got very far she fell down on the floor. The Humane Society Officer [sic], Mrs. Mowel [intervened,] taking Mrs. Woods to town and put her in jail. I do not remember if they fined Mrs. Woods or sent her out of town. The next day Mrs. Mowel went out to our place and got Elsie and took her away to her own home. [Later] we were told that Elsie was sent to some white people's home, that she would be taken care of good. So what could we do being treated like dogs?[95]

Indian troubles also resulted from the clash of cultures. Paiutes had always practiced forms of retributive and ritual killing prompted by such ordinary events as incursions on family gathering territory or shamanistic bewitching. Particularly outrageous to whites was the custom of assassinating witch doctors who three times misdiagnosed patients. "A day or two ago information was received by Duncan Campbell, Justice of the Peace at this place, that the Indian Doctor, 'Little Joe' had been murdered by his tribe for malpractice in his profession."[96] Whites endeavored to quash the custom through symbolic arrests and scoldings, but with little success since no effective sanctions were available for regulating the internal affairs of Indians.

Paiute resentment over cultural intrusions paled against the fear of physical aggression by whites. Slayings of Indians persisted long after the war. "A few days since some Indians came in from Fish Lake and informed Major Egbert, Post Commander, Camp Independence, that white men were killing Indians out there. It is pretty evident that some lawless white men are doing their best to cause a serious disturbance."[97] In another instance, "a white semi-desperado and one or two of his friends at Bishop Creek rode up to an Indian farm and proceeded to help himself to what he found in a way no white man could brook for an instant. The Indian owner remonstrated, whereupon, the white brave pulled his revolver and begun to blaze away at the Indian and his mahala."[98] The implication that such atrocities were generally the work of white outcasts is tempered by Harriett Bulpitt's childhood recollections. "I remember there was a man here killed an Indian woman. I don't know why he did it. I think he was drunk. Well, of course, the Indians were up in arms. They were going to kill him. They hunted him everywhere, and I remember that the men, like my father and other men, that they all got armed with guns and and ammunition because they said they couldn't let that Indian really kill him. So they hunted for him, and they finally found him and got him safely away."[99] However unsavory, killings of Indians apparently did not warrant Indian justice or, for that matter, the attention of white tribunals.

Sexual abuse of Paiute women by white men was more common than homicide and was regarded as equally pardonable, despite newspaper histrionics condemning sordid individuals. "A Brutal Outrage" is the headline for one story, which continues:

[A] week ago last Sunday a brute called Roney Crane went to an Indian rancheria a few miles below Lone Pine and raped a twelve-year-old child of the local chief, Capt. Jim. He compelled her to terms under fear of her life, as he chased her some distance with a six-shooter, swearing that he would kill her, and others if they interferred. There were but a few old women and children in the camp at the time. The child was severely, if not dangerously injured. As soon as news of the outrage spread among the Indians, some thirty of them, well armed, went in pursuit of the beast; they did not find him. The dirty beast made good his escape.[100]

In another "Dirty Outrage," a gang of "five or six well known hoodlums rode up to the Indian camp west of town, and after knocking down and severely injuring Indian George with a stone for trying to rescue his squaw from their brutish clutches, they outraged her before his eyes."[101] Although in both cases the rapists were "well known" and the upright pioneers were genuinely offended, no arrests were made.

These crimes posed a special dilemma for white society. However gruesome, as crimes against savage nonpersons they belonged in their own mitigated class. The moral sting was nettlesome, but not traumatic. They were felt to be serious, however, as the contemporary rhetoric shows. The key is that the rape and murder of Indians were grave affronts, not to humanity, but to paternalism. White society was failing its civilizing mission and protective responsibility. Failing, that is, unless these were the isolated acts of hoodlums and desperadoes—exceptional outrages calling for exceptional rhetoric. If the facts proved otherwise, if the perpetrators were ordinary citizens, then the contradiction of paternalism was indeed serious. Under the dicey circumstance of hoodlum culprits who were nevertheless well known in the white community, failure to make arrests and a public spectacle conveniently veiled the contradiction.

Living among the settlers in the 1890s, the feminist and writer Mary Austin believed the atrocities stemmed from the social character, from "Christian pretence and democratic inadequacy," rather than from hoodlum deviance. White society offended the Indians generally, and it protected not the children of nature but their tormenters. Far from an aberrant outrage, she claims, "mahala chasing" was a local pastime.

Many of the younger Indian women were employed in the town as household help and it was no uncommon experience for them, on their way home unattended, to be waylaid by white men—in this instance two young girls, who had lingered behind to sweep the schoolhouse, and were afterward captured and detained for the greater part of the night by a gang of youths. The Indian girls closed their part of the episode by eating wild parsnip root—the convulsions induced by that bane being mercifully shorter than the sufferings already endured—and though the community did actually take measures to prevent the recurrence of such incidents, nothing was done to the offenders, who were sons, some of them, of the "best families." And not only at Bishop—I recall at Lone Pine a young wife kicked to death by a white man in a drunken fury at her resistance, and the Indian husband weeping in the broken measures of remediless dispair. "My wife all the same one dog."[102]

Similar accounts abound in the newspapers and oral histories of the period. Reflecting on the responsibility for interracial violence, one pioneer recalled: "[N]ever in all my association with Inyo's Piutes did I ever hear of a Piute man molesting a white woman."[103] Rape and murder, conversely, extended to the domestic front practices sanctioned during the conquest. Yet even the justifications of conquest contradicted the protective tenets of paternalism, and whites doubtless had an inkling that they were stuck with the contradiction. Should it begin to surface in the pursuit and prosecution of alleged desperadoes, the contradiction was comfortably suppressed by selective law enforcement. The proposition that the rapists and murderers were the settlers themselves could not be entertained.

The critical connection between paternalism and violence, finally, lay in the pioneer rule of law. In its own desultory fashion, law enforcement attempted to protect the Indians, but not at the expense of protecting, and defending, whites. As children and, of course, noncitizens, Paiutes had no standing in white courts. In fact, the Indian was subject to no legal system. It was assumed that residual tribal practices would maintain order, particularly with the help of white-designated captains. Yet at the same time the indigenous moral order was relentlessly undermined—indirectly through dispossession of the land, which eliminated the material bases of that order, and directly in suppression of the spiritual authority regulating matters such as medicine. Paternalism implied that all questions concerning the moral regulation of Indians were encompassed by familylike authority. The routines of daily life, however, continually brought the races into anomalous legal conflicts.

In practice, several implications flowed from the absence of any legal standing for the Indian. Crimes by Indians against one another were beyond the concern of white law. "On Wednesday last an Indian near Lone Pine was sent to the happy hunting ground by means of a butcher knife in the hands of another. The murderer was taken in charge by an officer, but as there was not legal grounds for holding him we believe he was handed over to his brethren to be dealt with according to their code."[104]

As a general rule, Indian testimony enjoyed no credence in court when the defendant was white, even though whites might condemn the deed. "The value of [Indian] testimony in certain cases was tested in the case of Jacob Dentz (for selling whiskey to the Indians) and found wanting; the jury refusing to give it credence sufficient to justify a verdict. The law gives Indian testimony all the legal value it safely can, and that value is sufficient to justify conviction in all notorious cases where the testimony is morally and substantially sustained by white men."[105] In this instance, however, the willing "victims" were Indian customers. When the liquor vending of one Aleijo Bardenebro in Lone Pine led to mayhem that "frightened into town for security" some of the farm families, he was "convicted on Indian testimony, and now enters upon a twenty-five days' term in the county jail."[106] The evident Hispanic ancestry of the perpetrator may have persuaded the court to accept Indian testimony in this case. In any event, the general rule exempted from legal action crimes involving Indian victims or testimony. By the mid-1870s local law enforcement had given up trying to convict anyone of selling liquor to Indians.[107] The rare crimes and affronts by Indians against whites, conversely, were subject to relatively unconstrained extralegal measures.

Settlers struggled to make the system work. The Indian problem, understood almost exclusively as a liquor problem, worsened in the public's judgment as time passed. Law enforcement took it up again, getting tough to the extent of imposing fines and occasional jail sentences. As evidence about how tough the policy really was, however, one summary of legal dispositions in whiskey-selling cases over an eighteen-month period in 1899–1900 showed eleven arrests and seven convictions. Sentences were neatly ordered by the perpetrators' ethnicity: Anglos were fined ($40) or given anywhere from ten to one hundred days in the county jail; Chinese, five months in the county jail; one Mexican, a year in the state penitentiary.[108] In 1885, for the first time intratribal homicide was prosecuted in white courts by mutual agreement.[109] But these were faint glimmerings of change against a gloomy background of continuing violence and mutual antipathy. Struggle as they might, the settlers found no way out of the impasse.

The legal system inspired by philosophical paternalism engendered practical difficulties. White violence, on one hand, made an embarrassing shambles of high-minded ideas about benefaction and guardianship; on the other hand, it created additional problems of unrest and attempted revenge among Indians. Legalistic paternalism exacerbated the problem. Pioneer society became ensnared in conflicts that eluded its ideology. Although there was no solution, the initiative for a tolerable modus vivendi came ironically from the Paiutes themselves.

FROM RESISTANCE TO NEGOTIATION

The resistance to settler domination, expressed so clearly in warfare and work, colored all social relations. Following the war, many of the valley's original inhabitants chose not to return to a life of white rule. The proportion was significant, judging from late nineteenth-century U.S. Census figures that put the Indian population (600–900) at half its prewar size (1,500–2,000) after the two hundred fatalities were counted. Among those who remained, "the Indian attitude was sullen and defiant for a long time."[110]

Whites believed Indians took their new names and identities with alacrity, rather than accepting them grudgingly or opportunistically. The evidence suggests that Paiutes made a distinction between the colonized self and the cultural self—between the role they assumed in instrumental relations with whites and their true identity—and guarded the latter from white appropriation. The census taker, for example, noted on the 1880 original schedules: "I did my best to attain the names of the Indians, but they would give only the names given to them by the whites and in no case their Indian names." In a cultural world hidden from whites, Indians enjoyed ridiculing their masters. Steward reports on a "widespread" dance featuring the "ceremonial buffoon," a satirical portrayal of white persons. "One wore a false beard, carried a cane, and walked stooping; a tall man stuffed his waist and carried a bundle on his back; another impersonated an officer, wearing a false face; a robust man impersonated a woman; a cowboy and a doctor were also impersonated."[111]

Important as these forms of everyday resistance were, they were not the only means by which the Paiutes struggled to preserve some semblance of cultural integrity. After losing the war, they continued to react to white attacks by hunting down the aggressors. By 1877 a new prudence born of mounting tension led the valley's district chiefs to convene "a conference among themselves, and also with the whites, relative to the situation as between the two races." The circumstances leading to the conference were not unusual. An Indian was accused by his fellows of traitorous mischief because he appealed for white intervention to avenge the killing of his brother-in-law by other Paiutes. The chiefs feared that this would bring down a wave of white retaliation in the climate of generalized antipathy, linked less to the incident than to the expansion of settlement and uneasiness over withdrawal of the military. Speaking for the chiefs, Captain Joe began by acknowledging "the utter folly of their entertaining thought of hostility to the whites" and offered instead a proposal: "He begged that it be agreed by the Indians and whites both, that if an Indian killed a white person, or attempted any outrage of any sort that he be given over to the whites at once for punishment according to law; that if a white man killed an Indian that the whites would deal with him as if it was a white man who had been the victim."[112]

The proposal conceded to the whites all legal jurisdiction over interracial conflicts, thus abandoning fading claims to a right of self-defense. The pragmatic reason for the concession was the desire to have white abuse of the Indian punished under the same law that applied to Indians' offenses against whites. The precedent, at least, was important. Although Indian fair-mindedness was roundly praised and the proposal informally accepted, no detectable change ensued. The settlers welcomed what they interpreted as a one-sided peace overture; they could not appreciate that a compromise was being offered by a culture they had never recognized. It was assumed that the Paiutes had simply come to their senses, and that consequently all would go smoothly in the future.

It did not, of course. Attacks on Indians by whites and other Indians continued unpunished. Intergroup relations were strained when the Indian victim was employed or esteemed by the pioneers. In the fall of 1885 an old Indian tenant farmer was murdered by the notoriously intemperate "Bronco Frank"—a Paiute known in his sober moments as Frank Broder, after John Broder his long-time employer. The incident mobilized concern, Paiutes swearing to avenge the old tenant with Bronco Frank's death, and whites wringing their hands again over the liquor traffic.

The upshot was a reconvened Indian congress that formalized the work of its predecessor. Once again, Paiutes assumed much of the blame and made concessions with self-imposed limitations. Indians would vacate the towns at night. Women consorting with or receiving liquor from white men would be "punished severely" (presumably by the tribe itself, although no details were given). More important, a new and more centralized interdistrict political system was adopted that involved limited self-government. A chief and sheriff were elected, one each for the northern and southern sections of the valley, who would take charge of policing Paiute communities. These four men went to the county courthouse at Independence to inform white officials of the new arrangement and to ask assistance in controlling the whiskey trade.[113]

These moves were conciliatory, even appeasing; the degree of self-government was small, and paternalism was expanded by the Indians' now taking some responsibility for the enforcement of white laws. No guarantees of legal equality were sought. The isolated Indian militants were not happy or cooperative; but neither did they have a plan or constituency. The new arrangement was clearly an evolution in the direction of white power. From a Paiute standpoint, the best that might be said is that it improved upon the available alternatives. The Indians had no choice over whether to accept or resist domination—they had been doing both for more than two decades with little to show for it—and self-government in the limited form of self-policing at least established a small principle of autonomy and kept the white sheriff out of some affairs. The peripatetic Joe Lent recalled his three years as an Indian "police" with satisfaction—$38 a month plus food, and a hat and a suit of clothes provided. He apprehended whites for selling liquor, "who got 30–90 days, but didn't bother the Indians."[114] A measure of autonomy in the field of law enforcement spread to other undertakings after 1885 as Paiutes began to establish their own schools. A slowly evolving peace came at the cost of abandoning ancestral claims, but these were largely nugatory, and the arrangement had its small compensations. And it achieved more than settler paternalism had done.

CONCLUSION

In 1934 Julian Steward observed that beyond the persistence of native art and shamanism, "Paiute culture has practically disappeared, [they] are more reticent and repressed than most Indians."[115] Begun 70 years earlier, that transformation resulted from the intersection of state expansion, a distinctive settler mode of production, and a paternalistic ideology that linked political and economic practice in the lifeways of pioneer society. No primary cause of the transformation can be singled out. The expansionary state was a political design and an ideological end; production depended upon state means and normative animation. It is convenient to specify these forces chronologically, but their transformative effect is found in their interaction, which produced a distinctive social formation.

The aims and methods of state expansion provide the essential context

of western American history. In the Owens Valley during the late nineteenth century, the expansionary state relied on two institutional means:
military force and public land grants. The two worked together in deliberate steps. The army dispossessed, routed, and ultimately subjugated
Native Americans. Among other effects on Indian culture and resistance,
this process resulted in the land being opened for white settlement. Once
in control, the state reallocated the land to settlers through preemption
and homestead policies that created inexpensive, small-scale proprietorship. Legend notwithstanding, the yeoman farmer was far from self-
sufficient. A labor force was required to clear the land, tend the crops
and livestock, build roads, and provide expertise about harvesting and
irrigation. Production became organized in a system of independent
white proprietors who depended on cheap Indian wage labor. Bereft of
alternatives—except flight, which many took—the indigenous Paiutes
provided that labor under conditions of coercive subordination. The
state played a key role in this respect, too. It held the Indians militarily
in check and restricted their access to citizenship and, for some time, to
public land. The Indian was anything but marginal to the formation of
a new social order. The conquest of the American West deserves a place
in the comparative history of colonialism and incorporation.

Settlers brought to the encounter with indigenous peoples a culture of
their own and customary methods for dealing with the Indian problem.
Paternalism provided a theory of Indian character and of the route to
civilization. Roy Harvey Pearce observes that "Americans after the
1770's worked out a theory of the savage which depended on an idea of
a new order in which the Indian could have no part. The Indian became
important, not for what he was in and of himself, but rather for what
he showed civilized men they were not and must not be."[116] Paternalism
urged that whites become the benefactors and guardians of Indians; the
latter responsibility entailed the use of violence that was seen as both
lamentable and a moral influence. But protection and violence foundered
on their mutual contradictions in daily life. Paternalism failed to achieve
its expected result, and although the pioneers could never quite appre-
hend that failure, it worried them in ways that colored their own moral
order. As Pearce concluded about the American experience generally,
"[t]he record is one of a failure in theory which made for a failure in
practice."[117]

Local conditions tailored the special fit of state expansion and ideological interpretation. The mines prompted agricultural settlement and
provided a cash market, however volatile, which in turn made possible

a wage-labor system. Paiute technology helped boost settler agriculture into irrigated cultivation for the market. Paiute culture produced an industrious and mild-mannered people. In paternalistic theory, all the elements of economic and civilizational advance seemed at hand. But paternalism met two staunch obstacles: internal contradictions that generated violence, and Paiute resistance to that violence. On the job, Indians alternately disassembled and pridefully outdid their overseers. They walked off the job when a return to traditional ways was possible. And they resisted the hegemony of white institutions by initiating alternatives that provided a modicum of autonomy.

Julian Steward was right, of course. By the early twentieth century Paiute culture had effectively disappeared. But the pioneer society that wrestled with it, and absorbed it, was itself a hybrid. The white institutions that confidently marched into the Owens Valley in 1860 wandered into the twentieth century in native adornment. The economy was as much a product of Indian as white labor, and the social relations governing its operation were colored by mutual accommodation. The legal system was two-tiered, and anemic when it came to controlling intergroup relations, particularly the baneful liquor trade. The races lived apart, the one patronizing and the other wary in their ritualized contact. Violence held paternalism in check, and tension suffused the social order. Civilization had arrived.

Pioneer Economy and Social Structure

In its original meaning, *pioneer* referred to one of a group of foot-soldiers who march in advance of an army with spades and pickaxes to dig trenches, repair roads, and prepare the way for the main body. That image of expendable labor captures better the actual experience of western settlers than does the conventional romance of self-sufficient individuals carrying civilization to the wilderness. Pioneers were experimental subjects, encouraged by state policy and popular ideology to explore the land, labor for its settlement, test its habitability and economic potential at their own risk, and report their results to waiting promoters. Investors, speculators, and large firms would follow to take charge in places where profit opportunities were good—and the pioneers could keep the rest. Just as Native American societies were forcibly fitted into an alien design of development, so the pioneer political economy was shaped decisively by its interaction with the expansionary ambitions of the state and of national capital.

The nineteenth-century state was weak by the standards of other colonial powers and what it would become at the close of the century. The state subsidized but did not regulate western expansion; it thus left in the hands of aggressive corporations the power to shape the development in fields such as mining and transportation. Western development struggled with dependency in much the same way as colonial and Third World societies are conditioned by and subject to the control of another economy. The relationship between two economies takes the form of dependency when the stronger economy can grow and become self-sustaining while the weaker can grow only with the help of the other. Dependent development means that the subject region or economy is developed not to fulfill its potential or to serve the needs of its local population, but mainly to further the interests of the dominant economy. Those interests typically, though not necessarily, run against the accumulation and equitable distribution of wealth in the dependent region. Dependent development, therefore, tends to be uneven. Certain local opportunities are fully exploited, while others are neglected or stifled. The model of dependent development does not imply that the path of socioeconomic change is rigidly determined or that actors in the subordinate region are incapable of autonomous action; rather, dependency is a structural fact of life around which struggle and accommodation revolve.[1]

This chapter documents the ways in which dependent development shaped the character of frontier society in the Owens Valley and laid the material foundation of a culture capable of great forbearance and also of occasional rebellion. It endeavors to formulate an empirical interpretation of frontier development in the United States, one that contrasts sharply with much historiographic tradition. My interpretation of uneven development is, however, similar in some respects to the concepts of internal colonialism advanced by critics of conventional historiography since the writings of Bernard De Voto and Thurman Arnold in the 1930s and expressed in a modern idiom by authors such as Richard Hogan, Patricia Nelson Limerick, and Donald Worster.[2] The characteristic features of this approach are best introduced through a contrast with historiographic tradition.

THE FRONTIER IN AMERICAN HISTORY

No theme is more central to the interpretation of American history than the influence of the frontier on national character and institutions. From the early seventeenth century, western expansion paced and in many ways defined the evolution of American society. The historian Frederick Jackson Turner was perhaps the most influential in a long line of commentators (from Alexis de Tocqueville to Daniel Boorstein) convinced that "to the frontier the American intellect owes its striking characteristics."[3] The philosopher Josiah Royce, a contemporary of Turner, went further; he argued that close scrutiny of a specific region would reveal fundamental truths about national development. "The American community in early California fairly represented, as we shall see, the average national culture and character."[4] The frontier acquired such importance because the advance of civilization in America coincided with westward movement. "The history of American civilization would thus be conceived as three-dimensional, progressing from past to present, from east to west, from lower to higher."[5]

What, then, did the frontier contribute to American character and institutions? The typical answer is youth, exuberance, pride, self-reliance, freedom from social restraint, boorishness, moxie, pragmatism—in a word, individualism. The frontier ethic of individualism inspired both admiration and misgiving. Walt Whitman is rhapsodic on the pioneers' heroism.

> For we cannot tarry here,
> We must march my darlings, we must bear the brunt of danger,
> We the youthful sinewy races, all the rest on us depend,
> Pioneers! O pioneers!
>
> O you youths, Western youths,
> So impatient, full of action, full of manly pride and friendship,
> Plain I see you Western youths, see you tramping with the foremost,
> Pioneers! O pioneers![6]

No less a poet, Tocqueville marveled at the robust equality of American society, but cautioned that its corollary "saps the virtues of public life. Individualism is of democratic origin, and it threatens to spread in the same ratio as the equality of condition. Individualism is a mature and calm feeling, which disposes each member of the community to sever himself from the mass of his fellows."[7] In the 1840s Tocqueville observed this paradox at work on the American frontier:

> In the western settlements we may behold democracy arrived at its utmost limits. In these states, founded offhand and as it were by chance, the inhabitants are but of yesterday. Scarcely known to one another, the nearest neighbors are ignorant of each other's history. In this part of the American continent, therefore, the population has escaped the influence not only of great names and great wealth, but even of the natural aristocracy of knowledge and virtue. None is there able to wield that respectable power which men willingly grant to the remembrance of a life spent in doing good before their eyes. The new states of the West are already inhabited, but society has no existence among them.[8]

Turner was more sanguine about the generative effects of the frontier on democracy, although he also appreciated Tocqueville's point. "American social development has been continually beginning over again on the frontier. This perennial rebirth, this fluidity of American life, this expansion westward with its new opportunities, its continuous touch with the simplicity of primitive society, furnish the forces dominating American character. American democracy is fundamentally the outcome of the experience of the American people in dealing with the West."[9] The frontier provides freedom and social mobility, yet it is "productive of individualism," "primitive" in its social organization based on the family, "anti-social," and infused with "antipathy to control," particularly in its distaste for strong government.[10]

The differences between Tocqueville's and Turner's views on individualism recede when these views are compared with those of Royce and more recent commentators who regard the development of community as the essential contribution of the frontier to the national experience. Royce believed that the "very horror" of lawlessness and popular violence in the early days so demoralized California pioneers that they began to form self-governing vigilance committees. With the evolution of "town governments of a more stable sort," Royce the philosophical idealist saw the triumph of "the State, the Social Order that is divine."[11] The great significance of the West, therefore, was not the absence of law and organized society during the initial period of settlement, but the deliberate process in which citizens took responsibility for arresting anarchy and building representative governing institutions.

Shorn of its metaphysical overtones, the Royce thesis is enjoying a revival. Daniel Boorstein's popular reinterpretation of the American experience claims that after the Civil War a new spirit of association blossomed and spread beyond parochial confines, and that communities were organized everywhere, from the producers on the open range and in the oil fields to the consumers in the cities. "Americans reached out to one another. A new civilization found new ways of holding men together—less and less by creed or belief, by tradition of place, more and more by common effort and common experience."[12] More exacting historical research has demonstrated that these bona fide communities displayed great variety, ranging from solidary religious (for example, Mormon) and ethnic settlements to physically separated "communities of hardship" on the prairie and "frustrated communities" in the mining areas, where individualism ultimately reigned.[13]

Cast in terms of individualism versus community, the debate about the nature of frontier society begins to lose its bite. On one hand, these alternatives are seldom exclusive. Even cursory examination suggests that the question is less whether community took root on the frontier than what kind of communities existed there. The major interpretations, moreover, are reconcilable in detail. Tocqueville's celebrated argument that the American penchant for voluntary associations in response to the problem of individualism merges neatly with Royce's stress on self-governing vigilance committees as the first step toward social order.

On the other hand, the similarities between the major interpretations are more profound, and provocative, than the differences. All of the interpretations assume that a unitary societal pattern exists and is created by the welling up of countless local experiences. The character of society is the sum of its localized parts, and the nature of those parts is unaffected by any prior influences of social organization or the state. Frontier society is created de novo in the struggle of ungoverned pioneer men and women—themselves a distinct breed of individual, as Whitman suggests—against the elements, the Indians, and one another. Repetition of the experience in varied settings produces a general frontier ethos that then becomes the defining feature of the society. Most curious about such accounts is that, except in the work of Royce and in very recent scholarship, they are based on little or no close analysis of local society. The lawless frontier where "society has no existence" is as much an imaginative construction as the individualistic American character it purportedly spawned; each is cited to validate the other. Henry Nash Smith aptly identified the true importance of "the American West as myth and symbol" in broad-brush interpretations of national culture: that the West was indulged not for what it was but for how it served the efforts of Americans to understand and justify themselves.[14]

Examined in its own right, however, frontier society may support a very different interpretation of national development. If settlers came in groups with shared motives and depended on one another for survival, one may conclude that their individualism was colored by the exigencies of their collectivism. If they confronted Indians less with "manly pride and friendship" than with the means of state violence, their society already embodied principles of political organization. If that society was egalitarian, the mechanisms for allocating public lands helped to make it so. If the Far West, at least, was colonized for its minerals and its agricultural potential, for the complex political ends of manifest destiny, then it was orchestrated in important part by a societal design. If, in short, we reverse the assumption that the nation was formed through the welling up of pristine local experience, then a more nuanced interpretation of frontier society becomes possible, in which the process of political and economic incorporation shapes local society as it interacts with conditions on the ground.

The epochal interpretations of Tocqueville, Royce, and Turner are not so much inaccurate as incomplete and causally misspecified insofar as they address local society. If the Owens Valley fairly represents the general organization of settler communities, there is something vaguely apposite about descriptions that refer to an absence of society or an antipathy toward control. But these are only glimpses. Frontier society, it is true, erected only a flimsy scaffold of institutions responsible for public welfare, in part because it lacked the financial resources to support responsible local government and in part because it relied heavily on the federal government. The absence of resources was itself the result of a pattern of uneven and dependent development in which little of the wealth generated locally remained there. Yet the deficiencies in formal, public institutions were compensated by the informal, civil society which throve and assumed broad responsibility in its own way. The problem, therefore, is to explain the nature of this civil society, the conditions that called it into existence, the culture that drove it, and the consequences of its efforts.

THE PEOPLE

Tocqueville could have been speaking of the Owens Valley in 1870 when he noted about the western states that "the inhabitants are but of yesterday." In that year, the first census counted 1,956 Inyo County residents living in an area that had no permanent white outposts until 1861 and very few settlers before the county was established at mid-decade. Rapid growth continued during the 1870s, reaching 3,000 by the end of the decade. The essential social fact about these recruits for pioneer society was an incongruity of origins and aspirations. They came from an amazing number of U.S. states, foreign countries, and alien cultures; yet they had impressively similar ambitions, supported by modest means.

Forty percent of the population was foreign born and 57 percent had at least one foreign-born parent. Great Britian (England, Ireland, Scotland, Wales) and British North America (Canada, Newfoundland, Nova Scotia) contributed the largest single bloc of foreigners: 15 percent of the total population. People from Mexico made up 12 percent of the total; many were of course not foreigners but indigenous Californios whose residence predated U.S. acquisition of the territory in 1846. Germany led the remaining nationality groups (6 percent), followed by smatterings from China, France, and sundry countries of Western Europe. Even in 1870, before the return of many exiled Paiutes, 18 percent of the population was nonwhite, including some Blacks and Asians along with the Indians. If the 1,956 residents are divided into Anglo-Americans on one side and nonwhite, Mexican, and non-Anglo Europeans on the other, these cultural minorities together account for roughly 40 percent of the population.

Given the recency of California's incorporation into the United States, it is not surprising that a relatively small number of Owens Valley settlers migrated from adjacent regions in the San Joaquin Valley and the mining towns of Northern California. Although California led other states as a place of migrant origin within the United States, it contributed only 13 percent of the Inyo County population; 15 percent if combined with Nevada as a regional catchment area. No other state ranked close to California; New York followed at a distance with 6 percent. Moreover, no U.S. region dominated. After New York, three states each contributed about 3 percent of the Inyo population: Pennsylvania, Ohio, and Missouri. The next bunch, with 1–2 percent each, included Maine, Indiana, Virginia, Iowa, Tennessee, and Kentucky. The Owens Valley pioneers represented the full spectrum of populated areas in the United States—the Northeast, South, and Midwest.

Why did they come? The question is best answered by the settlers themselves. Alexander Kilpatrick was born in Edinburgh, Scotland, but "heard the call of the West" and came to the mining town of Bodie, where he made metal castings. Frank Olivas fled Apaches in Mexico and "came first to Los Angeles, and shortly after to Inyo county, finally settling in Lone Pine where he was a packer and miner."[15] The promise of mining riches often faded once the settlers arrived in the Owens Valley, and they took up other pursuits. John Shuey relates how his father "had been in the Georgetown mines near Sacramento in 1849. Excitement had been started about mines on the eastern slopes of the Sierra Nevada mountains and in the Inyo Range on the east side of the Owens River Valley and Father Shuey caught the fever. However, by the time we got there the miners had not found much gold and interest was abating, [so he decided] to try raising stock and a little farming."[16] Alden Plumley's grandfather and great uncle "were attracted by the promise of gold and silver in Virginia City [but] the brothers soon gave up mining and moved to the Bishop area. There they took up land."

Others came to farm and raise livestock. "Having missed the Gold Rush of 1849," Thomas and Ezra Goodale of Connecticut settled first on a nursery in the San Joaquin Valley and later "brought seedlings of apple, peach, and prune trees to the Independence area, and in the late 1860s took up [between the two] a 360-acre homestead." Clem Meyers left his father's cattle ranch in Merced, California, to establish himself in the same business at George's Creek in the early 1870s. Samuel McMurry came directly from Illinois to Big Pine when his brother "wrote of the great possibilities for farmers in the Owens Valley."[17]

Although mining and farming were by far the dominant attractions, they were not the only reasons for migration. Some came with the army and decided to stay. James Haberlin was an Irish deserter from the British Navy who "jumped ship in New York, changed his name to Malone, and joined the U.S. Army. He escorted a wagon train across the plains and arrived at Camp Independence in Owens Valley in the summer of 1864 with a wife and baby."[18] When his enlistment expired, Malone yielded to his wife's preference for civilian life and "they bought an old pioneer ranch about two miles from the fort."[19] As the population expanded, an itinerant few came to offer their professional services. Dr. Woodin "had been originally a successful consulting physician in New York, but had contracted tuberculosis, from which he had recovered in the high electrified air of Inyo, where he had been drawn while it was in the flush of its mining era by the contagion of gambling in his blood."[20]

On the whole, Owens Valley immigrants shared Doc Woodin's gambling spirit. The California frontier offered four major footholds on the climb to a better life: mine, farm, army, and town services. But these were seen as mere steps on the way to promised prosperity and a reasonable chance at riches. California was both a destination and a dream.[21] In Bordeaux, France, Charles Meysan "heard of the California Gold Rush and decided to migrate." He went first to the western sierra foothills, and in 1869 "the family decided to make their home [and open a general merchandise store] in Lone Pine as the mining boom at Cerro Gordo looked very good."[22] In Petrolia, Pennsylvania, Helen MacKnight Doyle recalls, her father read "alluring tales that led to a country of gold," developing an obsession that eventually drove him to Bishop Creek. "The trouble with this country is that it's all finished. I can always make a bare living here, but everything is surveyed and what chance has a surveyor in a country that is already laid out and finished? Think of the opportunities in California, not only in my own line of work but, through the work, being able to get in on the

TABLE 2. OCCUPATIONAL STRUCTURE OF
INYO COUNTY, 1870 AND 1880

	1870 (N = 1,404)	1880 (N = 1,794)
Professional	1.5%	2.2%
Merchant, manager	5.0	1.5
Clerk, services	2.1	4.0
Farm, ranch	19.4	13.1
Mining	26.4	7.9
Trades	7.1	8.6
Labor	20.1	45.6
Housekeeping	14.0	17.2
Army	3.6	—
Total	99.2%	100.1%

SOURCE: Compiled from the manuscript census schedules (# 1) of
the Ninth and Tenth U.S. Censuses of Population.

ground floor of good mining properties! Why, they're making million-
aires out there overnight!"[23]

The Owens Valley pioneers came with a premeditated plan based on
what they thought they knew of California and what they hoped. They
would have to work in their own line, at least at first, but their work
would be handsomely rewarded. Windfalls could be expected, too.
American culture promised social mobility in proportion to industry
and probity. The frontier represented many things to these pioneers,
from savages and natural resources that required conquest, to arduous
work that was understood as the price of fortune. But most of all the
frontier was an idea, and it was the idea that drew them.

The 1870 census taker found these pioneers hard at work in a variety
of pursuits (table 2). The largest occupational category was that of
miners and ore processors (millers and smelters), who together comprised 26 percent of the 1,400 persons in the labor force. Categories can
be misleading, however; about one-third of the 20 percent of the work
force classified as laborers, especially teamsters and packers, worked
directly with the mines transporting ore and equipment. Similarly, although only 19 percent of the working population identified themselves
as farmers (or stockmen), the majority of laborers were engaged in
agriculture, and more than half of the women listed as housekeepers

were directly involved in farm and farm-household production. A reasonable estimate is that mining and agriculture provided the livelihood directly for 70 percent of the working population.

In 1870 women comprised 29 percent of the white population, but only 14 percent of adult whites. Men typically migrated west alone or with a male relative or friend. Once settled and gainfully employed, those who had families sent for them. When women arrived they brought with them, or soon bore, children, doubtless including as many boys as girls. But the adult settler population remained heavily male in the early decades.

As was true for the society at large, the occupational structure was greatly affected by social divisions based on gender, ethnicity, and national origin. Virtually all white women were classified as either housekeepers or, if they were not adults, as having no occupation. Only a dozen were described variously as servants, teachers, and (perhaps widowed) farmers. Two-thirds of the miners were either noncitizens or foreign born. Mexicans, with a few Chileans, constituted the largest single ethnic group among miners, representing one-third of the total. Roughly another third came from Ireland, England, France, and the German states. The remainder originated mainly in U.S. states such as Pennsylvania, Illinois, and Kentucky, where, like their European fellows, they had learned their trade in coal mines. Laborers on farms were predominantly Paiutes. In 1870 the number of Chinese was small but growing rapidly. Initially they worked as cooks and farm workers; by 1880 they had branched out to construction, laundry, and the proprietorship of a few stores and restaurants—which whites, with some justification, regarded as opium dens. Although prostitution was actively practiced by a small staff, particularly in the mining camps, the 1880 census taker counted only two Chinese women in the trade. At the other end of the spectrum, Jewish families from San Francisco founded several of the major commercial enterprises, including the Levy and the Marks and Cohen general merchandise stores. In 1870 the incipient class structure was equally a system of status-group stratification based on gender and ethnicity.

The pioneers brought their dreams and varied occupational skills to the Owens Valley, but little more. Few possessed any capital to speak of, only small sums of money and what belongings they could haul or ship west. In the early years men came alone with the bare requirements for their journey and took mining jobs, hoping to save enough to bring their families. "Cristobel Carrasco was born in San Jose, California on

July 30, 1868. In 1870 his father, who had been working at Cerro Gordo for a year, went to San Jose and brought his family to Lone Pine by team. Some families were living at Cerro Gordo at that time, but most men left their families at Lone Pine and came home whenever they could, which was not very often."[24] Thomas E. Jones was born in Wales, where he entered the coal mines at the age of twelve. After saving for a decade to make passage "to the Golden West, he arrived in San Francisco in early 1860 and immediately started for the nearby gold camps. In 1864 T. E. and his brother John E. Jones, Mr. Evans, and Mr. Miles started by way of Aurora for Round Valley, where they expected to make their home." Thomas took up 160 acres and began raising wheat, while John went to the railroad terminus at Carson City, Nevada, to retrieve his family "with a four-horse team and big wagon loaded with food, farming implements and other supplies—a big item in those days as everything, except beef, was very high."[25] Andrew Neel Bell was an exception who prospered in the western sierra mining camps and invested his capital in a flour mill there, "but sold out to join his brother, Tom, in Owens Valley. At first they had a saw mill on Big Pine Creek and purchased 180 acres of land."[26]

Public records show the modest fruit of their labor and initial investments. The 1870 census provides the value of real estate and personal property held by 1,246 adult white and Indian men (no women were classified as independent property holders). Fifty-four percent of these men held no personal property worthy of census enumeration, and 63 percent had no land. The 467 men who controlled land through purchase or 160-acre public claim possessed property with an average value of $1,153, based primarily on the land itself. The 577 farmers and other persons engaged in transport and storekeeping owned personal property valued at an average of $942.

What did they bring to the frontier or acquire as the means of their livelihood? Inyo County tax assessment rolls provide detailed information on real estate and personal property, although the earliest surviving ledger is for 1882 and probably overstates the affluence of pioneers in the previous decade. For assessment purposes, land and personal property were rated well below the estimated market value in the census. Andrew Clark was the Baptist minister of Bishop Creek's first church and a prosperous farmer of 110 acres, which he worked with his wife Rachel and seven children. The Clarks were a socially prominent family. Their assessed valuation of $2,750 included, in addition to the land and improvements (house, barns, outbuildings, corrals), the following

items and values: two watches ($25), furniture ($50), firearms ($15), a
sewing machine ($20), a library ($25), fixtures ($25), machinery
($150), two wagons ($75), harness ($40), six American horses ($240),
four halfbreed horses ($40), three mixed-breed cows ($60), three calves
($15), eighteen stock cattle ($180), a dozen poultry ($5), two mules
($50), and thirteen beehives ($65). Jim Sherwin, one of the rare Indian
homesteaders, lived in nearby Round Valley on 160 acres with a cabin
and no personal property; the land was valued at $300. Tom Bell, a Big
Pine Indian assessed at $250, possessed only 160 acres and a shack.
Hiram Huckaby, an average homesteader worth $515, had fewer ma-
terial possessions cluttering his 160 acres than the Reverend Clark, but
he owned the same kinds of things: furniture ($20), farm utensils ($20),
wagon ($50), harness ($10), three halfbreed horses ($60), two mixed-
breed cows ($40), two calves ($10), and a dozen poultry ($5).

The slim distinction between relatively humble and prosperous farmers merits emphasis. The William Baker family of Big Pine had an
assessed worth of $3,710, nearly three times greater than the $1,360 of
the Benigno Aguirre family of Milton, although both homesteaded 160
acres. Baker's land and improvements totaled $2,800, Aguirre's $820.
But their possessions and other means of production were quite similar:

	Baker	Aguirre
Furniture	$100	$ 25
Firearms	30	10
Sewing machine	20	20
Farming utensils	25	10
Wagons (2 each)	100	50
Harness	20	—
Saddles	—	10
Halfbreed horses (5 each)	200	50
American horses (3)	—	75
Colts (4)	40	—
Mixed-breed cows (5, 2)	100	40
Calves (8, 5)	40	25
Stock cattle (10, 13)	100	130
Poultry (3 dozen, 2 dozen)	10	10

	Baker	Aguirre
Hogs (2, 3)	10	15
Mules (2)	—	50
Beehives (2, 4)	10	20
Corn (3 tons)	105	—

White farmers enjoyed a relatively homogeneous class situation irrespective of differences in net worth, which were due chiefly to the value, not the amount, of their land. Most lived modestly. In the early years there were a few exceptions; for example, Frank Shaw by the 1880s had acquired a 960-acre land and cattle company valued at $17,450, but even his family's wealth was principally in livestock (1,000 stock cattle valued at $10,000), and their personal possessions included nothing more frivolous than the standard watch, furniture, and sewing machine. More significant differences in class situation separated homesteaders from the Indians and Chinese, of course; and from town residents, who typically owned a lot, house, and furnishings, and perhaps a business inventory, but on average had much less net worth owing to the key difference, land ownership. Conversely, the farmers who arrived with negligible capital acquired what fortunes they had through the state and the public land laws. If wealth were measured in cash, personal possessions, or style of life, they were overwhelmingly a humble lot.

The first social structural effects of these class and status characteristics could be seen in the towns, whose locations are indicated in map 2. Lone Pine, near the southern end of the valley and adjacent to the Cerro Gordo Mine, was peopled in equal measure by the families of Mexican miners and Anglo ranchers. As the transportation hub between the mines and Los Angeles, it hummed with the interplay of cultures and commerce. Mexican Independence Day was the great celebration of the year, and fiestas were held "always on the Sixteenth of September, and on the two yearly visits of Father Shannon."[27] Although Lone Pine's high concentration of miners, Mexicans, and saloons lent it a wicked reputation, Mary Austin noted of its people, "there is not much villainy among them. What incentive to thieving and killing can there be when there is little wealth and that is to be had for the borrowing! If they love too hotly, as we say, 'take their meat before grace,' so do their betters. Eh, what! shall a man be a saint before he is dead?"[28]

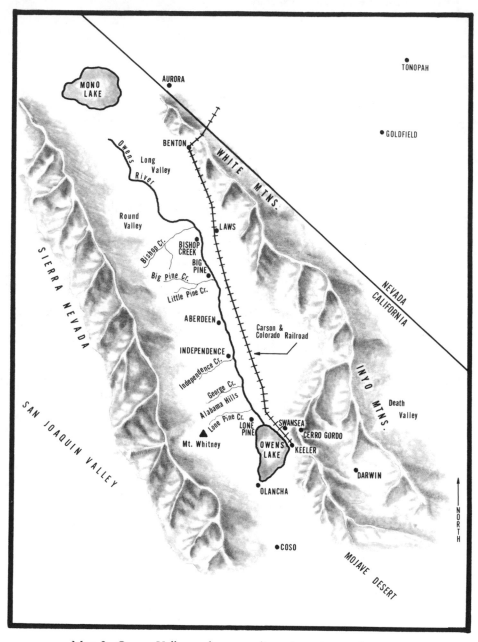

Map 2. Owens Valley and surroundings, late nineteenth century.
(Map by Lozano.)

Main Street, Bishop (formerly Bishop Creek). Although taken in the early twentieth century, this view of Main Street captures Bishop's frontier town appearance. Two hotels and a grill on the left side of the street and a drugstore and bargain store on the right typify small proprietor and merchant enterprises. Homes and cottonwood trees appear in the background. (Courtesy of the Eastern California Museum.)

Bishop Creek (incorporated in 1903 as Bishop) lay 60 miles to the north, in richer farm country at the upper end of the valley. Although its population was diverse, the local culture was predominantly Anglo, and the economy was predominantly one of small farmers. Bishop Creek and its surrounding hamlets (Round Valley, Milton, Sunland, Owensville, Poleta) with 624 residents was the largest population center in 1870 (the other towns had 400–475), which meant that it also concentrated the greatest number of women and families. If Lone Pine was loose, Bishop Creek was temperate, frugal. When the Methodists joined the Baptists with a second church and the spring runoff turned its pastures to marshes, smug residents of Independence called it "gospel swamp." Big Pine, 15 miles south of Bishop Creek, was closely allied with its neighbor in economy and mood. Another 30 miles separated Big Pine from the county seat of Independence to the south, itself just 15 miles north of Lone Pine. This made for something of a north-south split. As the valley ran southward, elevation, water, soil, and piety diminished. Independence hosted the army until 1873 (and a small garrison until 1877) and was closely linked to mines in the Sierra Nevada and Inyo Mountains. Agriculture tended more to stock raising and orchards than in the north, although wheat and hay were grown everywhere. Agriculture and mining intersected in Independence as nowhere else. Slightly smaller than the other towns in 1870, it was nevertheless the leading town in civic affairs, a meeting point though clearly southern, and a center of opinion—host of the valley's only important newspaper until 1885.

The settlers were a culturally diversified lot who shared one idea, prosperity through labor. Their only resources were undercapitalized ambition, rough skill, and determination. Men came first and laid the craggy foundation of a stratified society in which the women who followed had little choice but to assume their place alongside other minorities. Yet if women, Mexicans, Indians, and Chinese were lowly (in that order), no one else was very high. The towns amalgamated traits of the population and economy in distinctive ways, becoming emollient communities and a distraction from the daily rigors of pioneer life.

ECONOMIC DEVELOPMENT

Economic development in the Owens Valley was a product of mining, agriculture, and their interaction. Other features of the local economy, its occupational structure, markets, and commercial life, were fundamentally derivatives of a pattern set by the peculiar integration of the two major enterprises. In time, the economy shifted from one of relatively independent smallholders to one characterized by a growing concentration of land and by external dependency. The shift was effected in large part by the local penetration of national capital and state policy.

Initial settlement took place around Independence and relied primarily on Preemption Act and Homestead Act claims of 160 acres. In some instances settlers availed themselves of their legal right to claim up to 320 acres by using the two laws in succession. Although the first filings of 1863 were canceled when people fled Indian resistance, permanent entries were proved up in the late 1860s as agricultural communities began to flourish. Because farming on quarter-section parcels required irrigation, the 1870s saw a greater rate of settlement in the northern valley around Bishop Creek, where streams descending from the eastern sierra were more numerous. By 1880, the largest farming population was located in the neighborhood of Bishop Creek and Round Valley. Adopting Paiute methods and expertise, the farms were established on the western side of the valley, where streams could be readily diverted, rather than along the Owens River, which would require major canal excavations beginning in the 1870s. Judging by canceled entries, the farm failure rate was high in the initial years but soon reversed itself. "Successful homesteading began slowly in the Owens Valley, for during the 1860s the number of entries that were ultimately canceled exceeded those that were carried to patent [due to] the extreme hardships initially encountered by pioneer settlers in this isolated frontier. Eventually (throughout the 1870s), the number of patented homestead entries outpaced canceled entries by more than two to one." During the early years the valley was populated by bona fide pioneer smallholders "for in 1880 seventy percent of the valley's farms were 160 acres or less in size and ninety-two percent of all farms were no larger than 320 acres."[29]

The austere beginnings of settlement are illustrated by the serious obstacles and slim opportunities facing agricultural production. Robert Shuey, with his wife Nancy and their three children, turned from mining to agriculture in 1866 on a homestead south of Independence.

> He hired a man with a plow and three yokes of oxen to break up the wire grass sod for corn. It was impossible to break this sod with a harrow and the first year we went along with an axe and striking one blow in the sod made a hole into which we dropped four grains of corn. Closing the hole with one blow of the pole of the axe. The land was damp and rich, the corn came up quickly and grew rapidly. Then father got Indians to cultivate right around each hill and pull out the sunflowers that grew faster than the corn. With this rude cultivation we grew a fine crop of corn that year. We paid the men and squaws each fifty cents per day and had them hoe, husk, and shell corn. We sold all the corn we could produce to the Eclipse [mine] mill for mule feed, getting from 10 to 15 cents per pound delivered.[30]

Guy Earl recalls that the farm of his parents, Josiah and Adilade, was more prosperous, although the census taker evaluated it equal to the Shuey place at $2,500.

> We had a ready market for all the truck garden stuff and other produce of the farm, because the miners at the camp were glad to get it. As soon as the vegetable season began, about the first of June, my brother and I drove our spring wagon loaded with garden truck to Independence and peddled it from

house to house. It was a cash business and we always brought home from twenty-five to forty dollars each [thrice weekly] trip, all practically clear gain less Indian wages.[31]

Neighbors Jacob and Henrietta Vagt employed one white laborer on a modest farm valued at $1,500 that owed much to the agricultural expertise they brought from Germany. After visiting "Vagt's fine farm just beyond Camp Independence," local editors Pleasant Chalfant and James Parker reported: "[W]e saw good crops of corn growing on ground from which a crop of hay had been previously cut the present season. Mr. Vagt has a number of varieties of grapes, peaches, and other fruits all producing remarkably well."[32]

Market production in the northern end of the valley got off to a slower start, but it progressed as it reached for more distant markets. While still single, the elder Augustus Cashbaugh homesteaded 160 acres and claimed another 80 at Bishop Creek. He cleared the land with Indian labor and oxen by dragging a heavy timber over the ground to uproot sage brush. The farm produced vegetables and milk for sale at the Benton mines, beef, hay, and all of the requirements for subsistence. Blocks of ice cut from ponds frozen in the winter helped preserve farm produce in root cellars for year-round sale and use. Cashbaugh married into the Dehy family in 1873, finding as others did that the frontier farm depended on women's labor and, often, on the mutual support of related families. Men frequently migrated with a brother or uncle and soon established families on adjacent parcels. The Reverend Andrew Clark and his brother Thomas, their wives Rachel and Barbara, eleven children between the two families, and two more brothers, William and Milton, all came to control 480 acres at the center of Bishop Creek. Thomas and John Jones began raising wheat in Round Valley before the latter's family, including Mary and four children, joined them in 1865. Thomas married Harriet Williams, a Welsh immigrant, eleven years later, and together they raised a large family. The Jones families raised grain, fruit, and vegetables on 320 acres, getting a good start when a government contractor from Fort Independence paid them $100 per ton for 20 tons of barley. "The soil is productive for wheat, oats, barley and corn and vegetables in general. We raise good fruit, apples, peaches, plums, apricots, etc., but not very profitable for grapes. The early and late frosts are detrimental to fruit every year, but when we do have fruit it is good. The average per acre of [grain] is 1200 to 1700 pounds."[33] Behind success stories of this kind one usually finds extended-family enterprises sharing land, capital, and labor.

Shepherds. French and Basque shepherds trailed large flocks through the Owens Valley en route from the Bakersfield and Lancaster areas to summer ranges in the eastern sierra. Although the traveling herds brought cash trade to local merchants, the sheep damaged valley grazing and unfenced crops, leading to conflicts between homesteaders and town business owners. (Courtesy of the Eastern California Museum.)

In the early years stock raising was more common in the southern valley, but nowhere the dominant agrarian mode, owing to the small size of the parcels. Most farmers had a few beef cattle, but only a handful such as Frank Shaw held extensive range lands and made their living principally in ranching. There was, however, something of a middle ground because small farmers customarily grazed cattle on unclaimed public land—"a clear gain" in the studied calculations of Josiah Earl. For a long time valley citizens were firm advocates of the no-fence law common in California counties, a political position encouraged by free access to government lands as well as the high cost of fencing quarter sections. Yet local farmers were plagued by the huge herds of sheep and cattle driven through the valley from the San Joaquin for summer pasture in the sierra and for sale at the mining camps. Drives reportedly as large as 50,000 sheep tramped through the valley in early spring and fall, threatening unfenced field crops and the supply of grass for local live-stock. The retinues of Basque, French, and Italian shepherds and shearers provided a stimulus to local business, but the herds imposed environ-mental costs sufficient to cause the enactment of a head tax on sojourning sheep, which was divided among the affected counties.

Perhaps the most significant characteristic of the agrarian economy from the standpoint of social life was the mix of market and subsistence production. If Guy Earl's vegetable wagon did a brisk cash business, it was exceptional. Mary Alice Robinson of Big Pine comes closer to the typical recollection. "The people raised their own meat and vegetables and, for the necessary things they needed from the store, they traded their produce. There was no great amount of money here, but people got by without needing all the luxuries."[34] In lieu of costly imports available only for cash, such as coffee and sugar, farm families used such substitutes as roasted barley grain and honey from their own beehives. John Jones wrote that he made shoes and clogs for his wife and children and himself. "Then I built a house. Just think of my wife making candles, sugar, molasses, starch, and even I and the children cutting and burning green cottonwood to have ashes for her to make soap, and I got deer skins to make coats and pants!"[35] Augustus Cashbaugh "raised everything on the ranch," made candles from beeswax, stuffed mattresses with corn stalks, and preserved fruit with vinegar made from apple juice; but he stopped short when it came to Buckingham boots and Arbuckle coffee purchased locally and certain mail-order furniture from Weinstock and Lubin in Sacramento.[36] Just to the north in Mono County "every farmer traded much of his produce to merchants in Bodie and Lundy for merchandise, so he did not have much money. [The stores had] percales and calicoes which the women of Mono bought to make their own clothes and those of their children by hand. Underwear was often made from flour sacks."[37] During recurrent national and local depressions when money was scarce, "much of the business was done by trading. For instance, comb and canned honey was becoming popular and was practically legal tender."[38]

A surviving ledger from a Bishop Creek general merchandise store reveals more detailed evidence, as well as price data. The store (unnamed in the ledger, though possibly Leece and Watterson) served town and farm customers, and the accounts run from 1899 to 1901. Although the prices are higher and the extent of market transactions is greater than in the early pioneer period, these figures are suggestive. The most common cash purchases included such items as coffee (priced at 25–50¢ for unspecified amounts), tobacco (25¢), overalls (75¢), shoes ($1.35–2.75), boots ($3.00), canned sardines or salmon (35¢), oysters ($1), pepper (15¢), cloves (20¢), chocolate (15¢), soap (25¢), baking powder ($1.15), oatmeal ($1.10), calico (45¢), elastic (25¢), ladies' hose (50¢), thread (10¢), buckets (30¢), matches (5¢), castor oil (50¢), machine oil (20¢), crackers (10¢), macaroni ($1.00), candy (10¢), envelopes (10¢), and fish hooks (10¢). The average monthly bill was $10 to $20 for regular customers with charge accounts. Some traded labor services for credit. Lou Girard, for example, earned $30.70 in merchandise for digging 410 post holes. Many bartered farm produce for credit: Mrs. Evans regularly delivered rolls of butter in lots of six to twelve at 35¢ each; Mrs. Croscup received $3.36 for 96 pounds of potatoes and 99¢ for 33 pounds of apples; E. Brown contributed lumber and eggs at 10¢ a dozen; Andy Welsh earned $51.81 for 4,230 pounds of oats and $49.95 for 5,308 pounds of barley. The resourceful Gus Cashbaugh exchanged a large load of melons valued at $15, practically covering one month's charges for overalls, pepper, coffee, butter, ladies' hose, a lamp chimney, two buckets, vanilla, muslin, thread, and baking powder.[39]

Trading assumed a central place in the local economy because farmers found themselves in a perennial squeeze between monetary requirements and a limited cash market for valley agriculture. Isolated in the early years, the local market was constrained by geography or transportation costs, and by a population that increased slowly—mostly by the addition of more farmers. Supply and demand, moreover, encompassed a limited range of products. As the towns grew or the mines boomed, farmers earned cash income mainly from fruit, vegetables, hay, grain, meat, and dairy products. Labor, imports such as farm equipment, and final proof on homestead land ($200 plus fees) all required cash payments. Much of the small farmer's income revolved in this circuit, leaving the greater part of the subsistence economy to self-provision and barter. In the early years, the army post provided a rare and valued cash market. That probably explains the settlers' strenuous objections to its troop reductions and subsequent closure in the 1870s, although the troublesome Indian was their public argument. With land and labor costs as low as they were going to go and little advantage to mechanization, the farmers' future depended on larger markets; and markets, for the most part, meant the mines.

The mines, of course, had drawn the first settlers, their military protectors, the working population of miners and teamsters, and the farmers themselves. But the camps and boom towns acted less magnetically as markets for local producers. The paradox is explained by the monopoly of control over production and transportation created by the bullion kings, particularly at the Cerro Gordo, Inyo's fabulous silver lode, which paced the local economy during the first two decades and transformed Los Angeles into a major city.

Cerro Gordo was discovered in 1856 by Pablo Flores, but was worked only irregularly until the late 1860s. News of the strike began attracting small operators equipped with rustic Mexican technology for smelting silver in adobe ovens. The Spanish name Cerro Gordo, which translates as fat hill, was soon shortened as miners and prospectors from scattered parts of California and the Great Basin converged on "the hill," filing nearly one thousand claims by 1870.[40] Among the adventurers were two San Francisco entrepreneurs who came with more sophisticated visions of the wealth that could be commanded by strategic investment and organizational control. Mortimer Belshaw, a mining engineer with experience in Mexico, arrived in April 1868 with two essential resources: a promise of financial backing from San Francisco investors, and knowledge of new smelting technology that employed the largely ignored galena deposits on the hill. Victor Beaudry was a merchant who had established a general store at Independence in 1865 and another a year later at the camp, where he lent money generously and soon acquired shares of various claims for unpaid debts. Although Belshaw "began producing silver-lead 'base' bullion at a faster rate than the United States had ever known" in August 1868, Beaudry was in the race, with a less efficient slag furnace already in operation and a smaller smelter working by 1870. Wily beneath their competitive instincts, the rising tycoons became partners and major shareholders in the Union Mining Company, which soon controlled most of Cerro Gordo's ore processing and a number of lead and silver mines.[41]

The Union monopoly extended far beyond the production process in ways that shaped the regional economy. With his investors' capital, Belshaw had constructed a toll road rising 5,000 feet from the shores of Owens Lake to the camp at an elevation of 9,000 feet. Pack mules were replaced by ore and supply wagons on the controlled Yellow Grade Road, which provided the only access for transporting large loads to and from the mines. Charcoal and water for operating the smelters as well as all supplies for the burgeoning town arrived on Belshaw's road at a cost of $1 for wagons and 25¢ for a horse and rider. Equally important, Belshaw created a labor monopsony—many workers selling their services to effectively a single buyer—by paying top wages for experienced miners, always in demand at the four-dollar-a-day camp. By 1869, some eight hundred to one thousand men were employed in all mining and smelting operations, with the Union mine and its affiliates retaining the largest share. Although the effects of this organization were felt only indirectly through the valley communities, more decisive consequences stemmed from the developing transportation monopoly. The Union smelters were capable of producing silver ingots faster than they could be moved to Los Angeles and, ultimately, by ship to San Francisco for refining and sale to the U.S. Mint. In 1869, Belshaw and Beaudry helped finance the Cerro Gordo Freighting Company and contracted with the Los Angeles teamster Remi Nadeau to transport silver bullion by twenty-

Cerro Gordo Mine. The "Comstock lode of eastern California," Cerro Gordo Mine produced over $10 million in silver bullion during the late 1860s and the 1870s. Discovered originally by Mexican miners, "fat hill" soon became a monopoly of San Francisco corporate capital, which exported virtually all profit. (Courtesy of the Eastern California Museum.)

mule teams down the precarious grade and 200 miles across the Mojave Desert to Los Angeles. On the return trip Nadeau's wagons came loaded with provisions from wholesale distributors in Los Angeles.

> Los Angeles was now a bustling mining center. At the Commercial Street platform [Nadeau's wagons] unloaded their cargoes, repairing then to Los Angeles Street's wholesale houses to be loaded with return merchandise. Bales of hay, casks of wine, potatoes—everything from a frying pan to a crate of live chickens—headed for Owens Valley. The simultaneous arrival of the land boom and Inyo trade brought a sudden prosperity to Los Angeles. The farmers swarming into Southern California found a ready-made market for their surplus produce in the high-sided wagons bound for the silver mines of Inyo. Nadeau and the other teamsters were buying Los Angeles County's entire surplus feed crop. Los Angeles continued to enjoy the Owens River commerce, which by 1874 had grown to a total monthly traffic of 700 tons and piled up an annual freight bill of more than $700,000. About half of this income the Cerro Gordo Freighting Company was spend-

Bullion Awaiting Shipment from Cerro Gordo. Advances in smelting technology made it possible to produce silver ingots faster than they could be hauled out by independent wagon teams. Mine owners contracted with Los Angeles freighters who supplied the camp with provisions, transported the silver, and left little mine trade for local merchants, farmers, and teamsters. (McGrath Collection, courtesy of the Eastern California Museum.)

ing over Los Angeles counters at the rate of almost a thousand dollars a day. Some 2500 tons of barley and 3000 tons of hay, constituting respectively 27 per cent and 40 per cent of Los Angeles County's yield, were consumed annually by Cerro Gordo teams. "The value, direct and indirect, of the Owens River trade . . . as furnishing a market for surplus products" stated the Los Angeles *Star*, "is almost beyond computation."[42]

Despite the colonial dependency in which Owens Valley producers were cast by the mining monopoly, local political sentiments were divided and ineffectual when it came to challenging the cartel. In 1869, eastern investors established a smelter called the Owens Valley Silver-Lead Company at Swansea on the shore of the lake. Endeavoring to drive out competition, Belshaw used toll charges on his road to obstruct ore shipments destined for the new smelter. The Swansea company circumvented this move and, when Belshaw sued for toll violations, was exonorated in an Independence jury trial. In the valley, a petition drive successfully pressed the county board of supervisors into reducing toll rates, but the supervisors resisted further suggestions from citizens and the *Inyo Independent* that the county appropriate the road. At that point, Belshaw got himself elected to the board as the representative for the Cerro Gordo District, perhaps to deflect any further political interference. An alternative road construction project funded by public subscription was equally unsuccessful at breaking Union control. It failed to find a navigable path that did not coincide in key places with the Yellow Grade.

The most serious challenge came through the courts, when a coalition of smaller mine owners known as the San Felipe faction attempted to establish a prior claim to Belshaw's galena vein. With the support of local law enforcement, Belshaw at first attempted an underhanded foreclosure on the rival claim, which led to a protracted law suit. Despite a brilliant defense by Union attorney and local favorite Pat Reddy, an Inyo jury in the "big suit" ruled against Belshaw for the second time. Now, however, the county's political mood split between support for antimonopolism and appreciation for trickle-down benefits from the Union mine. According to one Los Angeles historian, "The people of Inyo, their sympathies with the bullion kings who had built Cerro Gordo, thought the decision an appalling injustice. Chalfant [the editor] of the [*Inyo*] *Independent*, siding now with Belshaw, declared his pioneering endeavors had 'done more to benefit this county than all other primary enterprises combined.'"[43] Although the evidence thus far is only suggestive, the split may have been along class lines—the juries, recruited valley-wide and representing farmers and working people, being opposed to a monopoly that excluded local producers, while the newspaper reflected town entrepreneurial interests still hopeful of sharing in the trickle-down benefits of corporate capital.

While the decisive lawsuit was being appealed in the summer of 1873, "Belshaw and Beaudry were stepping up production to drain the mountain's wealth before they could be forced to give up the Union mine."[44] Mining efforts at the Union were redoubled for the next two years: a new hoisting works built at the main shaft, an expanded water system installed, the Stevens sawmill in the sierra west of Lone Pine financed for additional supplies of lumber and charcoal, and wages boosted to $5 a day. Of the total $17 million in silver extracted from the hill, "it is estimated that Cerro Gordo produced, and Remi Nadeau delivered, 5,290 tons of bullion worth $2,000,000 to Los Angeles in

1874 alone."[45] The power of the Union Mining Company carried another day as the popular opposition (the petitioners against toll charges,
the juries and their constituents, and the small mine owners) saw their
legal victories turned to economic defeats. In 1876 the San Felipe faction merged with Belshaw and Beaudry as lesser partners in the Union
Consolidated Mining Company.

By then, however, the boom was over. Cerro Gordo's silver veins
were exhausted, and production slumped from 1875 until 1879, when
the Union Con was abandoned. New discoveries at Coso and Darwin
absorbed some of the labor force and refocused the chastened hopes of
valley loyalists. Indeed, local reaction to the cycle of monopoly boom,
external profit, and returning hardship was muted. By the close of
1872, *Inyo Independent* editors Chalfant and Parker fully understood
the economic consequences of dependency on crumbs from the silver
table, but Belshaw and Beaudry were criticized only mildly in the newspaper—for a myopic sense of the general welfare rather than for rapa-
ciousness. The editors were more disposed to blame local farmers and
businesspeople for deficiencies in entrepreneurial spirit. Behind this
ambivalent assessment lurked a hopeful, if prodding message—a good-
natured Protestant asceticism. The Owens Valley could, indeed would,
prosper despite the shortsighted Belshaws of this world when citizens
applied push and pluck to the revealed general interest.

> Hitherto, as is well known, the farmers of this county have derived but an
> infinitesimal portion of the benefits pertaining to the immense freighting
> interests of their own section. It has fallen almost entirely into the hands of
> those neighboring counties and in amount has been sufficient to very mate-
> rially aid in building up a large and prosperous city of 10,000 inhabitants
> [i.e. Los Angeles]. And what have we here, right at the fountainhead of this
> wealth, to show in proof of its existence? Two or three little villages, which
> have not derived benefits enough from the business of their own county to
> make their combined growth one-tenth of that of this distant city! Various
> circumstances have tended to produce this disadvantageous result, but if our
> people had taken time by the forelock and shown a true enterprising spirit,
> the whole condition of affairs would have been changed for the better a
> thousand fold. It is useless for the farmers and business men generally of this
> valley to lay back on their reserved rights and growl at certain individuals
> because the latter do not go out of their way to pitch money ready coined
> into their pockets. It is true these men—the bullion producers—might have
> more clearly identified themselves with the general welfare of the county. We
> have given form to complaints of this lack of true public spirit, [but] the fault
> lies at the doors of the business men (so called) and farmers generally of this
> valley. The mere profits of hauling which if divided up, as it might have been,

Hauling machinery to Casa Diablo Mine Bishop Cal 263 A.A.Forbes

Teamsters. Local teamsters operated at the fringe of the freight trade. Here machinery is hauled to the small Casa Diablo mine near Bishop Creek. The corporate-freighter monopoly led local teamsters and merchants to unite in opposition to the mines and to make efforts to open new trade opportunities. (Courtesy of the Seaver Center for Western History Research, Natural History Museum of Los Angeles County.)

among our own people would have made this one of the most prosperous little counties in the state. The men of enterprise, not the opportunities, were lacking.[46]

The editorial opinion is noteworthy as a statement of frontier ideology rather than as a fair diagnosis of economic woes. Citizens had in fact displayed acumen and enterprise within the limits of uneven development. Twice they attempted to curb the monopoly, or at least channel some of its wealth in their own direction. In the summer of 1872, the grassroots petition drive urging county supervisors to appropriate the toll road in the public interest had tried to open the freight business to local competitors. Later that fall, farmers worked to create an association that would, by threatening boycotts, pressure merchants to handle local produce rather than imports. Teamsters allied themselves with this effort and petitioned Belshaw directly to eliminate freight contracts in favor of competitive bidding open to Owens Valley haulers.[47] And the free enterprise that they recommended to the Union they put into practice by supplying other small camps outside Cerro Gordo's ambit.

The valley residents were deficient in class unity and political organization, not enterprise. An important part of their failure to crack the

monopoly was the division between, on one hand, farmers and teamsters, who favored aggressive efforts to insinuate themselves into the
monopoly, and on the other hand, county politicians and commercial
interests, who saw the mine owners as benefactors tainted only by an
understandable selfishness. But local analyses and ambitions had no
influence on the far-flung mining industry. Belshaw and Beaudry had
other worries: competition from big capital in the Swansea smelting
works, the profit expectations of their San Francisco financiers, and
practical problems ranging from water and fuel supplies to a perpetual
backlog of silver ingots waiting to be transported.

As provisioners to the big mines, Owens Valley farmers and merchants had three handicaps that were beyond remedy. First, the supply
line to Cerro Gordo did not run from north to south through potential
feeder communities in the valley but barely touched its southern extremity at Lone Pine. Local analysts understood the problem and talked
confidently about a more direct road running north from the mines and
on to San Francisco; but no such road existed, and formidable economic interests were committed to improving the Los Angeles route.
Second, had such a road existed it is doubtful that valley farmers could
have supplied all of the Union's needs in the late 1860s, although they
certainly would have benefited from a share of the action. Finally, given
these limitations on transportation and available markets, local farm
prices were not competitive. For example, Nadeau's wagons delivered a
hundredweight of flour for $6.50, while local mills asked $7 to $7.50.[48]
Farmers in Los Angeles County enjoyed access to the voracious Cerro
Gordo market through wholesalers served by rail feeders and Nadeau's
freight monopoly. The Owens Valley, in short, was becoming an eddy
in western America's broad stream of uneven capitalist development.

If entrepreneurial enthusiasts understood the problem, they did not
speak of it in those terms. Rather, they continued to talk approvingly of
local prospects and to hope for incorporation within the expanding
system. By 1880, with the collapse of Cerro Gordo an accepted fact,
those hopes were kindled by the long-awaited railroad and its promise
of access to distant markets. Hard times encouraged tempered optimism.
From 1876 onward very little money circulated in the valley.[49] A certain
sobriety appeared, combining antimonopolism as the lesson of the recent
past with gratitude for having survived hard times. "Events did not
unhinge society half so much as was feared. And it is the realization of
this fact that has induced a feeling of confidence in the future of the
country, through the influence of which a degree of 'settledness' has been

produced which of itself is the harbinger of prosperity for its people."[50] Rumors had circulated before, and it was agreed that "a railroad is about our only hope for a boom of solid proportions."[51]

Early in 1882 optimism resurged as surveyors from the Carson and Colorado Railroad in Nevada began evaluating sites for the line. Local reaction was concerted and generous. When the key issue became a choice between a line running along the unpopulated eastern side of the valley near the mines or a route 5 to 10 miles westward through the towns, citizens convened public meetings to encourage town service and even offered free lots for depots. A committee of "leading citizens" presumed to provide C&C management with "the facts" about where the line should locate. Citing the progressive slogan that would later haunt them, they urged a plan "to secure the construction of a road where it will accomplish the greatest good for the greatest number."[52] Disappointment soon followed.

Backed by the San Francisco financier D. O. Mills, the railroad was intended to stimulate new mines and profit from ore shipments, not to encourage agricultural production. The Carson and Colorado entered the valley on the northeast and ran straight for 70 miles along its eastern side to the old mining terminus at Keeler on Owens Lake. That route was chosen because of its lower construction costs and its convenience to the only potential clients of interest to the financiers. Mills, "the money power behind this road," was dubious about its investment wisdom from the beginning. Yielding to promoters from the Bank of California, he "resisted all inducements" to serve the towns, and even after the line was completed in April 1883 he noted skeptically, "[W]e either built it 300 miles too long or 300 years too soon."[53] Although local boosters were glad to have a railroad and looked to the day when it might prove an export stimulant, they were also disappointed with its results. Town access to the line depended on stage-connected terminals along the eastern side of the valley—one for each settlement, making a total of ten from Laws to Keeler. Worse yet, the railroad managers refused to make shipping contracts with Bishop Creek farmers, whose prices were higher before delivery than the market prices in Sacramento.[54]

The railroad was both a sign of and an inducement to changes taking place in the 1880s. It signaled a shift away from the smallholder economy and toward export production capable of yielding a profit above the freight rates—mainly production of cattle. By itself the railroad would not have had nearly the effect that it had in combination with another national intervention, this one in the form of state policy. The

Desert Land Act of 1877 was designed precisely for arid regions like the Owens Valley, providing 640 acres at $1.25 per acre to claimants, who were required to reclaim land with irrigation but not necessarily to settle on it. Although John Broder and Jonathan McMurry each filed in the first year of the new law, additional entries "remained insignificant" until 1886, when "there began a genuine rush for Owens Valley's unclaimed public land." By the mid-1890s virtually all of the valley's public land had been claimed, and the Desert Land Act had become the single most frequently used means of acquisition: 36.9 percent of the acreage was entered in this manner, by contrast to homesteading in second place with 31.5 percent.[55]

The boom in large-parcel entries had three explanations. First, entrymen paid the small fee and earnest money of 25¢ per acre merely to use the land for grazing cattle. Typically, they had no serious intention of building costly irrigation works and proving up by paying the remaining $1 per acre after three years. It was a legally abusive way of renting the range until cancellation or any subsequent claim occurred. The scheme guaranteed three years' use of the public pasture for 25¢ an acre, and that use right was customarily extended until a new claimant came along. Second, however, a number of valid claims were patented as cooperative irrigation works or ditch companies were started by groups of neighbors. From the late 1870s until the early 1890s, a score of such ditch companies were organized. Contiguous farmers subscribed anywhere from $20 to $100 plus their own labor to dig canals regulated by head gates that served each member-property. The ditches were dug as tributaries to the larger creeks and especially the Owens River, which crossed a much larger territory than had previously been irrigated with stream laterals. Third, in addition to stockraisers and a new breed of large-scale farmers, others simply filed claims on the land for speculation. "These canals triggered a rush of land hunters from outside the region. The majority of desert land entrymen were speculating on the increased values that would result from the extension of the canals across these lands."[56]

A San Francisco firm, deceptively named the International Immigrant Union, recruited settlers through newspaper advertisements and charged a fee for assistance in selecting parcels, a service that was free at the U.S. Land Office. Rhapsodic in its support for settlement, the *Inyo Independent* was slow to criticize any kind of speculation.[57] For a few years in the early 1880s, with the surge in land claims, promised settlement, and new canals, hopes for a boom were unleashed again—and, before long, disappointed once more.

The last decade of the nineteenth century saw the end of pioneer society. The era of smallholders and a relatively egalitarian social order was supplanted by uneven development, which began with the mines and spread to the farms. When the promise of balanced economic development stemming from the railroad and desert land reclamation proved chimerical, hard times returned. Depression in the 1890s had more transformative effects than the slump of the late 1870s. Dependent development brought contradictions: smallholder penury in the midst of overall growth, more farms and more concentrated land holding, failed homesteaders and confident ranchers—polarization, in short. The Owens Valley felt the effects of national depression on its farm prices in the years following 1873 and 1893, as well as the effects of the steady decline in the value of silver throughout the period. But the synchronization of the local and national economies was imperfect; specific conditions brought the most acute hard times to the valley in the 1880s and early 1890s.

The economic depression impressed everyone as the worst the valley had yet experienced, and its explanation seemed equally obvious to everyone. Reacting in an editorial to the charge that they were "often too optimistic about the economic prospects of the valley," the *Inyo Independent* left no doubt about their plight. "Never since white people came to the country was business so dull and money so scarce."[58] The railroad, "our only hope for a boom," had not altered the bedrock problem of production costs. A survey conducted by the newspaper showed that the Los Angeles prices for oats, barley, corn, wheat, butter, eggs, poultry, and vegetables were all below those of Inyo County, where only hay was priced competitively—and that advantage was eliminated by freight charges. "Farm produce of any kind cannot be exported beyond one or two of the nearest mining camps in Nevada." But the problem of costs was constrained from the other end by the price of necessary imports for more efficient farming. "The freight on general merchandise and farm implements and machinery is about $60 per ton from San Francisco and with such crushing odds against them the farmers cannot make their business pay."[59]

Small farmers were cornered, forced to give up or go into debt by mortgaging patented homesteads. The mortgage rate jumped 50 percent in the late 1880s, and the uncommon circumstance of farm tenancy

FOUR

Frontier Civil Society

The American West was a distinctive kind of society—an experienced world of social relations and cultural meanings that ran deeper than the exigencies of state control or dependent development. Patterns of land tenure, labor control, subsistence production, weak markets, and unequal exchange all determined the possibilities of frontier society; but its significance as a way of life was culturally created within the wide borders of material necessity. Civil society gave the frontier its special character as well as its shallow reputation for rugged individualism, recusancy, and rough justice. In this chapter, I shall argue that those traits are overdrawn, that the vital practices of voluntary association from which so many western stereotypes derive are themselves explained by the practical requirements of governing newly formed communities.

Frontier communities were confronted immediately by awesome responsibilities that ranged from building a rudimentary infrastructure of roads and canals to establishing an effective order of government and law. They met the task, moreover, with few financial or institutional resources. The federal government encouraged their creation but assumed none of the cost beyond initially securing and distributing the land. Civil society responded to this problem by constructing a workable community and investing the result with cultural meaning. Once we understand the frontier as a cultural accomplishment, we also understand the significance of its elements and the historical process that fitted them together.

PUBLIC AUSTERITY AND CIVIC INITIATIVE

Civil society comprises the network of institutions beyond the family
that are not, strictly speaking, part of government or the formal economy. It includes social institutions closely linked to those sectors but
governed primarily by the moral order rather than the state or the
market: churches, lodges, voluntary associations, public service organizations such as the volunteer fire department, political clubs, artistic
societies, reform groups, private schools, economic cooperatives, irrigation societies, vigilance committees, festivals, and social movement
organizations. As the examples hint, civil society was well developed in
the Owens Valley, contrary to ill-considered judgments about the frontier as a place where, in Tocqueville's phrase, "society has no existence." Frontier society is best explained not by asking whether organized communities throve, since informed observers agree they did, but
by inquiring into the distinctive nature of civil society. That question, in
turn, requires appreciation of the wide compass of social responsibility
left to civil society by a laissez-faire economy, the state, and the narrow
competence of local government.

Inyo County was established by the California legislature in 1866
with Independence as its provisional seat; a similar effort two years
earlier had been dropped because of Indian troubles. The new county
was staffed by a salaried, if meagerly paid, judge, district attorney,
sheriff, clerk, and treasurer, and, on a part-time basis, an assessor, a
superintendent of schools, a surveyor, a coroner, and five supervisors
elected from districts.[1] Formally, county government was charged with
responsibility for creating and maintaining schools, roads, bridges (an
important matter because the Owens River bisected the valley), and
hospitals and care for the indigent sick; assessing and taxing property;
printing public information; and providing law enforcement. In practice, however, these functions were shared in varying degrees by voluntary efforts in the pioneer period. The first schools were constructed
by groups of neighbors who supplied small cash donations, materials,
labor, and sometimes land. The county paid teachers, typically women,
a small salary; but the arrangement was precarious. In Mono County,
which had the same system, "the county paid thirty dollars per month,
and Joe Scanavino boarded the teacher. Mr. Scanavino wanted [her] to
dig potatoes along with teaching, so she quit."[2] Costly roads were built
through public subscription that paid the private contractor's costs for
Indian labor, and road maintenance was supported by toll charges set

by the board of supervisors. The county supported hospital care for the indigent, but on a contract basis with local physicians and private homes equipped with sickbeds. Law enforcement was the most thoroughly public responsibility; but even here the county contracted with residents to house trusted prisoners, and the sheriff relied on vigilantes, not always by choice.

Conventional interpretations of the American West cite a vaunted individualism in circular explanations of both the origins and the consequences of frontier social organization. In fact, pioneers orchestrated by the state and national economy, and struggling to manage environmental and imposed hardships, were probably less individualistic than their eastern counterparts. On one hand, they developed versatile instruments of civil society. On the other, their rudimentary institutions of local government were constrained less by individualism or aversion to social restraint than by the sheer cost of public services in a cash-poor economy. Although Inyo County expressed its interest in public welfare with high tax rates (second among all California counties, they claimed, at $3.10 per $1,000 of assessed value), the net income generated from austere farms and mercurial mines was inadequate to meet local needs.[3] The county operated with a large public debt even as it provided limited services.

The newly formed government faced an imposing set of demands, ranging from the mechanics of raising revenue and keeping the peace to building the physical infrastructure. Road construction illustrates some of the basic problems. An intricate system of farm-access, intertown, and town-to-mine roads was required for commercial development; yet the distances involved and the required water crossings made any road a costly project. Private subscription for construction costs and tolls facilitated communication with mining districts, but the income generated was seldom sufficient for maintenance, and other routes were left to the initiative of individual farmers. The problem was made worse by inadequate drainage, the spring runoff, and seepage from irrigation ditches that left roads deeply rutted and often impassable. The county was blamed for not taking responsibility.[4] Fire protection was a crying need in this arid region where high winds fanned sparks from wood-burning stoves. Disastrous fires were a common occurrence; in 1886 virtually all of Independence was burned to the ground. Recognizing that municipal fire protection was far beyond the capacity of local government, town businesses led by the *Inyo Independent* began campaigning in 1870 for money, equipment, and volunteers for a fire department. "Our town is a fast increasing cluster of highly flamable houses, but awaiting an accident or the incendiaries' torch."[5] Although a volunteer fire company was created after public meetings the following year, it was poorly equipped and ineffective—bucket brigades from the creek running through town delivered water faster than the prized fire engine. In the conflagration sixteen years later, "no fire fighting apparatus was available, and the flames ran unchecked until thirty-eight buildings in the central part of the county seat had been swept away."[6] When the monstrous earthquake of 1872 severed roads and destroyed homes and the county courthouse, no one even considered public assistance as an avenue of reconstruction.

Owens Valley citizens displayed no desire for freedom from social constraint when it came to needed public services. They volunteered for collective undertakings, supporting the norm that only people "laboring to build up permanent institutions" such as schools would ensure the future against the "selfish policy" of those, like the mine owners, who intended to make their fortune and leave.[7] Yet private efforts to meet collective responsibilities went only so far before the problem came back to county finance. The county sought state assistance and incurred bonded indebtedness to meet the major costs of law enforcement, the courts, and hospital care for the indigent sick, leaving it in the red by $90,000—just about the amount of the annual budget. Part of the problem stemmed from a high rate of tax delinquency, doubtless involving many farmers trapped in subsistence production.[8] Tax reforms were proposed, notably a heavier contribution from the mines, which were assessed only on their property (buildings, smelters) rather than on the value of their holdings or their ore deposits. But the proposal failed because it coincided with the decline of Cerro Gordo.[9] Indeed, Belshaw sued the county over its assessment of the Union smelter under existing standards, claiming that it was worth only $6,840, not the county's figure of $231,000, a difference which translated into $5,800 in overdue taxes.[10] The outcome of the suit is unclear, perhaps because the mine was nearing its collapse of 1879, after which methods of taxation were irrelevant.

The effects of weakly financed government were felt most acutely in law enforcement. The newspaper complained that law in Inyo County was a shambles because clever lawyers able to get convictions would not work for the lowly wages paid the district attorney, preferring the more profitable defense of criminals. In one typical year, eighteen homicides led to only six trials, with half of those resulting in acquittals. The redoubtable Pat Reddy typified the problem, defending celebrated male-factors and declining invitations to work for the district attorney's office.[11] Dissatisfaction with the management of "criminal matters," the newspaper claimed, "was without doubt the prime cause of the late vigilante manifestations."[12] The interpretation is valid within limits. Spontaneously mustered vigilance committees were at the sheriff's dis-posal to pursue Mexican social bandits, including the legendary Tiburcio Vasquez, who preyed on stagecoach routes in the southern valley. Vig-ilantes took matters into their own hands when the culprits were whites selling whiskey to Indians or a Portuguese gunman responsible for Sheriff Thomas Passmore's death in a shooting affray in Lone Pine.[13] To be sure, there were instances of mob rule, such as the lynching of a Chinese man sentenced to life in prison for killing a white woman—despite misgivings of several jurors about the evidence of his guilt.[14] More often, however, vigilantes were anything but lawless executors of frontier justice. They provided a supplementary police force of volunteers doing a job that the county could not afford to compensate, and they enjoyed moral support from the community for their efforts. It was a question of "popular justice" under regrettable circumstances:

> The courts have fallen into disrepute. [Vigilantism] is mistaken from abroad for the wild lawlessness inseparable from a rude state of society. No one observing from a distance would suppose that the men who participate in these affairs are in most cases upholding rather than overturning society, and that they occupy the foreground only because of the inefficiency of the judicial machinery. They will not disappear until we have some short, im-partial and certain method of punishing crime.[15]

Although the charitable interpretation of vigilance committees should be tempered in light of their vigor for pursuing interracial crimes, within the limits of pioneer society they represented in one field the general necessity for civic action. Civil society substituted for gov-ernment in a variety of crucial roles. The local press reported the news with a fervor for making opinion and mobilizing action, albeit from a staunchly centrist position. It led campaigns, for example, to regulate the Cerro Gordo toll road, to attract the west-side railroad line, to expose land fraud, to provide fire protection, to increase public salaries, and to control the whiskey trade. In addition to popular justice and the press, two institutions at the core of civil society were the Protestant associations and the ditch companies.

The term *Protestant associations* suggests that churches and quasi-religious groups worked in tandem under the general inspiration of a secular ethos. Coeval with pioneer society, the Baptist church (founded in 1869) and the Methodist church (1873) attracted hundreds of members and sponsored civic activities such as schools and missionary work among the Indians. Emphasizing social mobility, the Methodists drew a distinctly higher-status parishioner (judging from their membership rolls) and took the initiative for establishing the county's first private high school in 1889, the prized Inyo Academy. Yet secular Protestantism extended further, to women largely responsible for an active temperance movement, for example. The reformers lobbied against the whiskey traffic and for a "local option law" prohibiting liquor sales in the county (which succeeded much later), sponsored lectures, and even converted a saloon into an ice-cream parlor, demonstrating the convivial possibilities of sobriety.[16]

Among men Freemasonry was by far the most influential group with a Protestant provenance. Chartered in 1872 as the first lodge of any kind in the county, the Ancient and Accepted Order of Freemasons (or F&AM, for Free and Accepted Masons) spread from Independence to Bishop Creek and Big Pine, recruiting many of the local elite in commerce and agriculture. In December 1873, for example, the Masons of Independence elected their officers for the next two years: Henry Isaacs, a clerk and merchandise store owner; Andrew Bell, a prosperous farmer and miller; Harry Egbert, a lawyer; Isaac Harris, co-owner of the largest merchandise store; Charles B. White, a physician and county hospital contractor; John and James Shepherd, large farmers and road contractors; James Brady, a mine owner; John B. White, a clerk; and one anomalous S. B. Upton, a farm laborer. In 1875 and 1877 many of these men were reelected, with the addition of C. F. Stoutenborough, the owner of a general merchandise store and J. D. and Omie Mairs, farmers and owners of a livery stable and a store. Chalfant and Parker, the editors of the *Independent,* and their successor, Charles Mulholland, were members.[17] The Masonic Order provided local businessmen a trusted circle of respectable associates. As Max Weber observed about the Protestant sects generally, Freemasonry ensured creditworthiness in a risky commercial environment.[18] The stress on respectability also encouraged a civic spirit in the lodges, expressed in school fund raising and the funeral rites promised to each member. When Sheriff Passmore was killed in the line of duty, his fellow Masons turned out pallbearers and a cortege of forty carriages. Yet, as a secret society, the Masonic Order acted mainly behind the scenes, promoting solidarity among members of the com-

mercial, political, and social elite. Their unity would play a key role in
the struggles looming ahead in the twentieth century. In pioneer society,
Freemasonry was important as an expression of community and middle-
class culture. Observations drawn from a study of contemporaneous
Freemasonry in Oakland, California, apply as well to the Owens Valley.

> It brought together men, primarily native Protestants, who shared belief in
> American social, political, and religious ideals. It perfectly reflected that
> fusion of Protestantism and democracy which characterized American mid-
> dle-class culture. Committed to equality, it tempered rugged individualism
> with an insistence on brotherly love. Most importantly, it demanded adher-
> ence to the moral virtues that made for respectability—temperance, sobriety,
> and industry.[19]

The ditch companies provided an altogether different contribution to
civil society—communities of neighbors brought together by the requirements of production, the accidents of their location along common
waterways, and their mutual need for cooperation in constructing irrigation systems. Among the seventeen irrigation societies that existed by
the turn of the century, eleven were in the Bishop–Big Pine area. They
varied in size, from fifty to seventy members in the larger Owens River
Canal Company, Bishop Creek Ditch Company, and McNally Ditch
Company, to a dozen or so in the smaller Big Pine Canal Company and
Rawson Ditch Company. Their single purpose, to capture and equitably
deliver water for irrigation, involved multiple tasks. The companies
were formed through subscription of a certain number of shares, depending on the irrigable acreage and the amount of water required by
each farm, at a standard cost per share. The largest single task that
absorbed subscription fees, of course, was to dig the canals, some to a
depth of 8 feet and a length of several miles. Each company of shareholders elected a board of directors whose job was to submit to a
membership vote the proposed water allotments and assessments for
regular maintenance (repairing breaks, dredging silt and brush). Assessments could be paid, at least in part, with labor. The great significance
of the ditch companies was that from necessity, and with the Paiute
heritage, settlers entered into economic cooperatives governed by democratic methods in the production process. Of course, not all agriculturalists were members of irrigation societies. Dryland farmers, cattle
and sheep ranchers, holders of riparian rights along creeks, and many
settlers in the southern valley had no need or opportunity to participate.
For those who did, however, the ditch companies provided their most
important resource and an immediate acquaintance with civil society.

Community Christmas Tree and Celebration in Big Pine, 1923. Holidays were civic events and occasions for neighbors to gather together. Here well-dressed townspeople look on as children line up for presents from Santa Claus. (Mendenhall Collection, courtesy of the Eastern California Museum.)

The Owens Valley towns boasted a number of other voluntary associations. The two political parties had central committees, and both the People's and Temperance parties turned out respectable numbers. Other lodges were organized, such as the Odd Fellows, and most of them, like the Masons, had women's auxiliaries. A drama club put on plays and dances, which were materially supported by other groups. Later the Farm Bureaus came along, and women formed an Improvement Association. The list goes on, including even an Early Pioneers club which emphasized the social distinction between pre-1872-earthquake residents and latecomers.

Local festivals provided another dimension of associational life. They were frequent, because each of a number of organizations sponsored its own annual event and every town specialized in a seasonal fete. From the early years, the Paiutes' fall Fandango at Fort Independence became a valleywide, intergroup holiday and later coincided with Bishop Creek's Harvest Festival. Lone Pine was renowned for its September 16 Mexican Independence Day celebration. Bishop Creek held the traditional Fourth of July picnic at Keough's Hot Springs. The county fair and Farm Bureau or lodge picnics punctuated the holiday calendar. Although the festivals clearly served the purpose of entertainment, they also had a civic function. Elected officials addressed their

1810.   1884.

MEXICAN NATIONAL
HOLIDAY!

═══SEPTEMBER 16, 17, 18.═══

At Lone Pine, Inyo County, Cal.

───o───

PROGRAMME:

At 11:30 P. M. of the 15th the National Flag will be raised with appropriate remarks by

S. B. PADILLO,

followed by **SALUTES**, and with

Music by the Band.

───o───

Following this will be a song entitled *THE HIDALGO MARCH*, by local talent.

At Sunrise on the 16th a National Salute will be fired. The literary exercises will commence at 10 A. M. and will consist of the following:

Reading of the Declaration of Independence.

Oration, and remarks by Enrique Lopez and other persons.

The National Air will be rendered by local talent.

At sunset a National Salute will be fired.

On the evening of the 16th there will be a

-:-:-Grand Display of Fire Works!-:-:-

───o───

At 8 o'clock P. M. *Sharp*, there will be given

A DANCE

───AT───

RICHARDS & CASTRO'S HALL.

Admission Free.

Supper at the --- Lone Pine Hotel.

Tickets (Admitting Lady and Gent) $2.00.

On the 17th there will be various amusements, especially

═══Foot Racing.═══

All persons are cordially invited to be present on the above occasion, as a good time will be guaranteed and perfect order insured.

By order of the Committee,

FRANK MIRANDA,	President,
M. CASTRO,	Secretary,
BELLES CARRASCO,	Treasurer,
RUPERTO CARRASCO,	Collector.

☞ J. G. Dodge will carry passengers to and from the Lone Pine Depot at reduced rates.

Mexican National Holiday (Newspaper Ad). Each valley town hosted a major annual festival. With a large Mexican population originating from the early mining days, Lone Pine sponsored the September 16 Mexican Independence Day celebration. (*Inyo Independent.*)

assembled constituents, farm and business advisors shared the latest wisdom, valley ambitions were articulated in yearly reviews of their progress, and, particularly as time went on, local political initiatives from petition drives to new organizations were promoted in this forum.

The critical point in all this is not so much the sheer number of voluntary associations as the density of their social bond. In communities of several hundred people (many of them children, Indians, and miners, who lived in separate worlds) the likelihood was high that white adults would find themselves tightly affiliated in some subset of church, lodge, school, fire department, vigilance committee, ditch company, or political club. These linkages, moreover, frequently involved organizations with clear civic responsibilities—groups of citizens united to provide for themselves what local government and their own hard-won tax dollars could not provide.

COLLECTIVE ACTION

In addition to supplementing public service needs, civil society provided a base and facility for political action. Petitioning the authorities, ranging from the county and federal governments to the mine owners, was a strategy developed in the earliest days. In 1872 a petition to the California legislature to enact a trespass law was circulated throughout the county and signed by four hundred supporters, who wished to protect fields from wandering livestock while avoiding the high cost of fencing.[20] In 1870 and again in 1877, petitioners beseeched the "proper authorities" for extended mail service.[21] The controversy over the Cerro Gordo toll road produced three separate petitions demanding that the county buy the busy commerical artery and provide easier access for local teamsters and merchants.[22] After Independence was designated as a provisional site for the county seat, various local initiatives attempted, unsuccessfully, to move government operations to the commerical hub of Lone Pine or to redraw the northern border so as to make Bishop the seat of Mono County. Each of these proposals was put forward as a solution to the familiar problem of inadequate public services.[23] Anticipating the withdrawal of federal troops in 1872, political strategists agreed that a petition was "useless or worse" in dealings with the army. Petitions were selected as the means for urging the governor to send new military protection during Indian troubles of the late 1870s and the 1890s, but to no avail.[24] The poor condition of the roads and the low salaries of county officials were also addressed in petitions.[25] Although few of these petition drives succeeded, the frequency with which citizens carried assorted problems to a variety of authorities demonstrates a politically energized community alert to local needs and state legislative possibilities. In a state dominated by the political interests of large landowners and the railroads,[26] these undertakings indicate a healthy regard for government rather than any distaste for its restraints.

Collective action was not limited to petitioning. When local citizens mounted valley-wide protest alliances they showed better results. The first important collective action following the Indian wars was the 1872 struggle with the Cerro Gordo monopoly, which won little more than public regulation of the toll road. The repertoire of strategies, including petition drives, efforts to create a farmer's association, and the allied mobilization of teamsters, established a precedent for cooperative action that would be reactivated and refined over the next fifty years. The next major campaign began in 1878 following rumors that the U.S. Land Office at Independence was scheduled for removal to the mining town of Bodie in Mono County. The news

> produced a storm of indignation and depth of feeling never before equalled by anything of the kind emanating from the head of government. The underhanded manner in which the scheme had been brought about, lying premises on which the action was based, its obvious injustice, the unusual political weight brought to bear, all tend to intensify the general sense of an injustice received, and indignation toward the scheming rats, yet unknown, who instigated it.[27]

A mass meeting was held at the Independence courthouse "for purposes of entering a protest," and editor James Parker was selected to write resolutions for a petition sent to the secretary of the interior, both U.S. senators from California, and congressional and state representatives. The land office provided the most fundamental of all services as the place where public land claims were located, filed, and patented. In this instance the passionate and defensive protest succeeded. Yet a few years later mass meetings and citizen committees failed in proactive efforts to route the railroad through valley towns.

Two important collective actions in 1889 elaborated the pattern and helped solidify it as a tradition that would be called upon in the twentieth century. The Hillside Water Company had begun damming lakes in the foothills above west Bishop and running its own ditches from these new reservoirs to customers in the valley. With the headwaters of the Bishop Creek irrigation cooperative thereby threatened, "settlers went and closed the ditches made by the company and declare that they will not allow water to be taken from the stream until their own wants are supplied."[28] The first of many organized and militant water protests succeeded to the extent of forcing a fair apportionment decision on the courts.

Two months earlier, the citizens of Bishop had convened an "enthusiastic meeting" to come to grips with the trade question and the economic downturn. "The time has come for some radical action by the people of Inyo County to correct the depressed business interest [caused by railroad freight rates that] threaten to ruin local farmers and bankrupt the entire community. The time has come when it is imperatively necessary for the community to combine for mutual protection and cooperation." The idea, quickly endorsed by a public meeting in Lone Pine, was to open a southern trade route to Los Angeles, "find a way out of [the] valley via Mojave," and break the railroad's "chains of oppression." The alliance hoped to incorporate four groups with mutual interests: farmers, merchants, miners, and teamsters. "The general uprising is not a fight, not antagonistic to the railroad, but a forced struggle for self preservation."[29] As spring came, signs of progress were detected in a new mail route to Los Angeles and a locally awarded commercial contract. But signs were all that materialized; the alliance never really mounted a movement. However animated the enterprising spirit, valley ambition could not dissolve the obstacles of local production and transportation costs, limited markets, and an enveloping national recession. Locally, they were unable to supersede class interests and ideological ambivalence to take any action beyond supplication.

One movement proved an exception to this pattern of small defensive victories and big developmental flops. Begun in 1886, the populist-inspired Farmers' and Producers' Cooperative Union enlisted nearly one hundred farm families from throughout the valley. "We simply desire equality, equity, and fairness, protection for the weak, restraint upon the strong." Their organizational meeting at the Methodist Church novelly urged that farmers bring their wives, who "are equally interested with us; the organization will be stronger and counsel wiser with them."[30] The first meeting defined broadly the "classes of producers" who would be served by the Union and suggested a cooperative system as a likely vehicle. Rival meetings on the same day recommended that they reconvene on the following Monday at the Good Templars Hall in Bishop Creek, where, despite bad weather, recruits appeared "in goodly num-

bers." As specific proposals emerged, the influence of the national Farmers' Alliance was unmistakable. Owens Valley producers had to cooperate rather than compete through "indiscriminate individual shipments."
The sense of the meeting was that they needed "some organized combination for mutual protection; that if we systematize our industries and
ship our products through one channel—one agency honestly and efficiently managed—we would thus maintain a more respectful attitude
with buyers and consumers." When a few skeptics wondered whether
successful examples of the cooperative system existed, an article was
read from the *Kansas Patron* averring that once "toiling masses" were
now "doing a cash business."[31] Meetings that wrestled with practical
issues continued into the summer; "to fix the scope of such organization
was the real difficulty," because some wanted one large co-op and others
a separate cooperative store, marketing union, or technical assistance in
stock breeding. During the next year, plans moved to reality as the
co-operative became the largest incorporated entity in the valley, with
capital stock of $5,000 raised in $10 shares. The corporation established
a Producers' Union Store ("produce taken in exchange"), a Stockbreed-
ers' Association, and a Cooperative Creamery that operated successfully
for many years. Although the Producers' Union fell short of populist
visions for an all-embracing consumer and marketing co-operative capable of export, it achieved impressive tangible results by organizing
valley farmers in the local market and relieving some of the financial
strain that ruined so many in these hard times. Among the many resourceful institutions of civil society aimed at providing essential services
in lieu of effective government, the Producers' Union uniquely innovated
a workable, if limited, solution to the plight of dependent development.
    It would be a mistake, however, to equate civil society with populist
collective action. The ideological egalitarianism so evident in the Producers' Union and the antimonopoly struggles with the railroad and
mines vanished when some of the same citizens acting through the same
institutional framework turned to social issues, especially where those
concerned Indians. The liquor trade befuddled, indeed outlasted, pioneer
society despite a staunch temperance movement and strenuous denunciations of the white miscreants and the lax law enforcement that perpetuated the outrage. Drunken Indians, and ultimately their white suppliers, were responsible in the public mind for a large share of immorality
manifested in lassitude, pandering, gambling, fights, murders, insolence,
and general indifference to work discipline. Yet next to such histrionic
analyses of the moral order, saloons throve in all the towns, mainly on

settler trade; and liquor vendors were well known and easily tolerated. Indeed, the breweries created by early pioneers of German origin flourished as a model of locally controlled enterprise. The liquor industry was one of the very few industries combining local capabilities with a brisk market, and high-minded temperance beliefs did little to discourage this display of enterprise. Collective action foundered on the contradiction—at least as long as the problem was framed in ways that quickly revealed the connection between Indian consumption and business profit.

In the summer of 1901, however, circumstances conspired to recast the issue. Wages of agricultural labor were on the rise, reportedly by 50 percent during the previous haying season, and another advance of equal magnitude seemed likely. Concerned farmers issued a meeting call: "United action wanted to settle the Indian wages question." In one creative stroke whiskey, wages, and farmers' rights were joined. "Shall the farmers of this valley submit to the dictation of illicit whiskey vendors and the Indians in the matter of farm wages?" No, said "something over a score of solid citizens," who pledged themselves not to pay over $1.25 a day to Indians harvesting hay and not more than $1.00 for general farm work. Paternalism made wage restraint a civic virtue, since the "wage increase is not to the advantage of the Indian, but his detriment" leading directly to "more whiskey consumption and less usefulness." The pledge was widely circulated, acquiring so many signatures that the signers became identified as the Committee of 145.[32] But evidence on labor shortages and daily wage rates during the harvest—by 1900 averaging $1.50 to $2.00 (even $3.00 when an abundant pine-nut harvest lured Indians)—suggest that the committee failed. The requirements of agricultural production and business profit overshadowed the debatable virtues of wage restraint. By itself, that is of no special significance; collective actions failed frequently, for varied reasons. Twenty-six years earlier the temperance lobby had lost a closely contested local campaign to ban liquor sales in the northern valley, because commercial interests retained Pat Reddy to challenge the legality of special voting districts.[33] Taken together, however, frustrated actions like those of the Committee of 145 demonstrated a more fundamental failure. Civil society reached its limits where normative consensus faltered.

THE LIMITS OF CIVIL SOCIETY

The normative limits were strict because civil society required a relatively encompassing consensus on what to do and how to do it, and a willingness to do it together. Where individual interests and class situations coincided, as was sometimes the case, much could be accomplished, notably in the area of providing public services. Equally often, however, interests conflicted, and collective action diminished proportionately. The divergent interests of town merchants (saloon keepers, brewers, and their colleagues in a variety of service businesses) and farmers on the question of Indian wages was but one fissure in a society striated by lines of potential group conflict. Town-farm divisions appeared in other forms, such as resentment of the subsistence economy and blame for cash shortages. Merchants cited inefficient farming, while producers lamented weak marketing and consumer preference for imports. While farmers protested the ravages of migrating sheep herds, merchants welcomed their trade. Yet local commerical and agricultural interests were united in sharp disputes with the mining economy and its beneficiaries (including some local laborers, suppliers, and service contractors). The towns themselves, particularly Bishop and Independence, competed for valley leadership and the meager patronage of the county seat. County printing contracts were behind a rivalry between Bishop's *Inyo Register* and Independence's *Inyo Independent*. North and south were separate economies and, in some ways, distinct societies. Within agriculture, conflicting interests separated homesteading farmers and stock raisers, a division that overlapped with geography. In short, local society was underpinned by cross-cutting economic ties and by potential and active class divisions.

Many of these schisms were superseded in collective action; but when they were not, violent conflict provided the discolored litmus of civil society's absence. Violence, of course, appeared in many forms, few of them consistent with picaresque depictions of western lynch mobs and gunfights. Shootings were common enough, but usually motivated by gambling or personal disputes played out in saloons and mining camps. Indians killed one another with some frequency for ritualistic reasons (inept medicine or bewitching) and took murderous revenge for the misdeeds of liquor vendors, especially Chinese. Yet when we look further for a pattern of *social* violence rooted in group situations and aimed at persons or property, two surprising revelations appear.

First, by far the most common circumstances of violence were routine quarrels over property rights and economic justice. The destruction of pastures and gardens by wandering livestock led to bitter quarrels and sometimes to the theft, maiming, or slaughter of animals.[34] Disputes over property lines, and therefore over acreage or access, were common as a result of crude original surveys and were the source of long-running feuds and even homicides.[35] Perhaps most endemic were conflicting claims to water rights, a problem that, unlike the others, led to both a welter of lawsuits and to summary violence, including murder.[36] Quarrels involving economic justice generally centered on wages, employment, or commerical transactions.

Second, when people took the law into their own hands, it was not typically with the gun, but with the incendiary's torch. Arson was the preferred instrument of retributive justice in a repertoire that included shooting, theft, vandalism, maiming livestock, breaking ditches, and (when they came into use) cutting fences and opening gates. Although these methods were sometimes combined, the popularity of incendiarism lay in its relative safety from punishment, semianonymity, versatile application, and forceful message. Symbolically, arson acquired status as a grave sanction from its use against food supplies and settlements in the Indian wars and from the legacy of social protest in European immigrant cultures.[37] Pragmatically, it fitted a variety of situations calling for blunt expressions of moral grievance that clearly distinguished themselves from any predatory intent.

The reported frequency of confirmed arson and suspicious fires is impressive. Moreover, the number is probably underestimated in weekly newspapers serving limited areas of the valley and depending on word-of-mouth sources. Support for that conjecture comes from comparing independent sources. Although the local press is the principal surviving source for reports of arson incidents, several deliberately set fires are mentioned in the store ledgers and business correspondence of the Lone Pine merchant Charles Meysan. None of the Lone Pine incidents described by Meysan was reported in the newspapers published at Independence and Bishop although those papers tried for valley-wide coverage and sometimes did report other cases of arson outside their immediate precincts. Therefore we may assume that the frequency of arson was even greater than the surviving reports indicate, although its general pattern may be fairly represented, judging from the similarity of Meysan's and the newspapers' accounts. Table 4 lists fifty-two incidents of proven or probable arson reported in the local press. The reports vary in the amount of detail they provide; they often give little evidence or surmise about motive. The unevenness of the accounts requires that the incidents be grouped according to some notion of type and then that the cases of the various types be read across, for a more comprehensive analysis. Indeed, approached in that fashion the very sketchiness of some reports becomes meaningful as an indication of the resigned

TABLE 4. ARSON: PROVEN AND PROBABLE INCIDENTS, 1870–1909

Date	Time	Target	Victim	Explanation	Legal or Other Action
Aug. 12, 1871	—	Lumber pile	—	Arson, insane act	None
July 13, 1872	—	Haystack	R. Van Dyke farm	Arson, Indian malice	None
Sept. 21, 1872	—	Building	—	Arson, Indian malice	None
July 19, 1873	—	Stable	Hightower and Co.	Unknown arsonist	None
Oct. 2, 1875	3 A.M.	New residence	Mr. Gerrish	Vagabond arsonist	None
Nov. 13, 1875	Night	Stable, haystacks	H. G. Plumley farm	Suspected arson	Arrest and dismissal
Mar. 18, 1876	Midnight	Hay yard, law office, and store	Bennett, Rowley	Suspected arson, second victimization	None
July 1, 1876	Midnight	Store	McMurry and Moore	Arson	None
July 8, 1876	Morning	Haystack	Stage company	Suspected arson	None
July 22, 1876	Midnight	Brewery	C. A. Walter	Arson, threats by known person	None
Sept. 23, 1876	1 A.M.	Haystacks, farm building, fine house	W. G. Watson farm	Following quarrel with neighbor	None
Nov. 11, 1876	10–11 P.M.	Polling place	—	Voting prank	None
Nov. 25, 1876	—	Mexican shanty	—	Suspected arson, Indian arsonist	Indian fatally shot
July 21, 1877	—	Coal pile at mine	Cerro Gordo Company	Suspected arson during labor troubles	None
Aug. 4, 1877	Night	Haystacks	C. M. Joslyn farm	Suspected arson	None
Aug. 18, 1877	—	Mine works	Union Consolidated	Arson	Later arrest for another arson
May 12, 1878	—	Mexican hall	—	Arson	Warrant issued for known suspects

Date	Time	Structure	Owner	Description	Outcome
June 15, 1878	9 P.M.	Barn	Mr. Bond	Tramps suspected of carelessness or malice	None
July 20, 1878	—	Stable	Paul Bennett	Indian carelessness, second victimization	None
Aug. 17, 1878	10–11 P.M.	Mine building and works	Beaudry Co.	Arson during labor troubles	None
Aug. 17, 1878	11:30 P.M.	General store	J. H. Stoutenborough	Arson by known perpetrator	None
Apr. 5, 1878	7 P.M.	Bridge	Inyo County	Arson	Miner arrested
May 3, 1879	2 A.M.	Hotel and mining town buildings	—	Suspected arson during labor troubles	None
July 19, 1879	2 P.M.	Hay press and stacks	Shepherd farm	Indian carelessness	None
Mar. 25, 1882	—	Fine house	Wm. Harrell	Possible arson	None
Aug. 26, 1882	4 A.M.	Store, house, and brewery	J. H. Stoutenborough	Arson, threats by Indians, second victimization	None
Apr. 28, 1883	—	Haystack	James Shaw ranch	Possible arson	None
May 19, 1883	—	House	Mrs. Williams farm	Suspected arson	None
Dec. 5, 1883	Night	Fields	Mrs. Lewis farm	Possible arson	None
Dec. 5, 1883	—	Haystack	Al Briggs farm	Possible arson, previous owner had fire	None
Mar. 7, 1885	—	Fields	E. Robinson ranch	Indian mischief	None
Jan. 27, 1887	—	Haystack	J. M. Horton farm	Arson	None
July 20, 1889	—	Barn	John Dodge farm	Possible arson	None
Apr. 4, 1890	9 A.M.	Livery stable	J. G. Dodge	Possible arson, second victimization	None
July 23, 1890	3 A.M.	Commercial block	Ben and Michael Lasky	Possible arson, multiple instances	None
June 27, 1892	7 A.M.	Yard of general store	Ben Lasky	Arson	None

(continued)

TABLE 4 (continued)

Date	Time	Target	Victim	Explanation	Legal or Other Action
June 2, 1893	2 A.M.	Commercial building	Thomas Boland's building, housing Lasky General Store	Possible arson, repetition	None
Sept. 8, 1893	3 A.M.	Home, office	Dr. Woodin	Possible arson	None
Mar. 2, 1894	10 P.M.	Home	S. A. Densmore	Arson	Chinese arrested, dismissed
July 20, 1894	Night	Shack	T. J. Goodale	Arson and homicide	Neighbors James and Wm. Hines tried, found not guilty
Sept. 21, 1894	4 A.M.	Hospital contracted to county	Mrs. Lewis	Possible arson, second victimization	None
Dec. 20, 1895	9:30 P.M.	General store	Rhine	Arson	None
Dec. 27, 1895	Night	Livery stable, haystack	Julians	Arson	None
May 19, 1899	2 P.M.	Haystack and buildings	Mairs ranch	Possible arson, vandalism at family business	None
Jan. 5, 1900	10 P.M.	Haystack	Chas. Walter farm	Suspected arson, second victimization, neighbor quarrels	None
July 26, 1901	10 A.M.	Haystack	R. P. Hessions farm	Possible arson	None
June 6, 1902	Early A.M.	General store, doctor's office	Rhine, Woodin	Possible arson, second victimization	None
July 24, 1903	Midnight	Store, corral	A. W. Eibeshutz	Suspected arson	None
Jan. 4, 1907	—	Town building	Gollober	Malice leading to arson	None
Jan. 4, 1907	Early A.M.	Saloon	Clarence Johnson	Suspected arson	None
Feb. 13, 1909	Night	Aqueduct construction camp		Arson	None
Feb. 14, 1909	Night	Aqueduct construction camp		Arson	None

SOURCES: *Inyo Independent*, 1870—1910; *Inyo Register*, 1885–1910; Eastern California Museum, Charles Meysan store ledger and business correspondence.

tolerance accorded to arson in a society where popular justice was recognized as the only possible form of justice in matters beyond the capacity of the feeble law-enforcement agencies.

As a method of social protest, arson spanned the possibilities of class relationships. Indians fired the haystacks and buildings of their farm employers, miners burned ore-processing works, businesses were victimized by disgruntled customers, and farmers took revenge on one another over property disputes. The violence took place within and between classes. Based on the circumstances of socioeconomic setting, suspected perpetrators, victims, and targets, three types of arson are discernible: labor (both farm and mine), market, and property.

Arson associated with farm labor usually involved Indians. Their grievances were seldom mentioned by newspaper accounts, which preferred to dwell on charges of irresponsibility, sloth, or childishness. Just as black slaves in the American South were perceived as careless rather than defiant, Paiute resistance was ignored or characterized as mischief. "On their ranch near Lone Pine, R. Van Dyke and partner lost about 40 tons of hay through the cussedness of a juvenile Piute. The hay had been spread out to dry, and the little fellow attempted to test its dryness with a match."[38] Inexplicably, Indians started a fire on the ranch of E. Robinson "that would have destroyed haystacks and buildings" had not help arrived in time; "the miserable lazy Indians are a worse nuisance than skunks or coyotes."[39] Some suggestion of motive is provided in the case of a fire on the ranch of James and John Shepherd, prosperous farmers at Georges Creek who also employed Indians in road construction.

> At about 2 o'clock P.M. Thursday last a fire started near some outhouses [and] bid fair to sweep all the stacked hay, granaries, stables, etc. At the same moment a Petaluma hay press was aflame, and cinders were flying in every direction; yet by the almost superhuman exertions of Mr. Jas. Shephard, members of the household and some Indians, the press and all the stacks were saved. The fire originated from some coals and ashes carelessly thrown out by an Indian employed about the place.[40]

Although the evidence is ambiguous, Paiute Luddism may have been responsible in this case. On one hand, Indians were known to have perpetrated certain fires, although it was usually assumed that they acted out of carelessness rather than with deliberate intent. On the other hand, carelessness is implausible in this instance involving experienced farm workers who knew the hazards of fire; the conspicuous hay press was a form of mechanization that threatened the best paid and most skilled harvesters, the hay stackers.

The generalized character of protest arson is demonstrated by its use in labor disputes far removed from Indians in the field. As the mines began to falter and wages were reduced, a series of fires broke out. "In Cerro Gordo last Saturday night an incendiary attempt was made to burn about 50 tons of coal close to the lower furnace of the Union Company."[41] One month later, a fire of unknown origin that destroyed the mine's hoisting works was attributed to an errant spark.[42] A year later, however, the causes of this and other protests were finally understood.

> About 10 or 11 o'clock on the night of the 7th instant quite a large frame building at Cerro Gordo, situated between the Beaudry furnace and house and nearly opposite Belshaw and Co.'s store, took fire and was destroyed. It was unquestionably the work of incendiaries. During the blaze an attempt was made to fire the company's new iron hoisting works, a quarter of a mile further up the hill. The whole matter is said to have grown out of the hatred entertained toward the company's management by some former employees or the Mexicans, more immediately provoked by a late, and the third reduction of wages.[43]

The Union mine was not the only target during the arson wave. In June 1878 the Stevens Sawmill, built in the sierra to supply Belshaw's works with lumber and coal, was damaged by a fire conveniently attributed to the "carelessness or malice" of two tramps noticed in the area.[44] When the mining camp at Darwin was destroyed by a fire originating in an unoccupied hotel, observers "supposed that the fire was caused by an incendiary."[45] Such suspicions were given support when the authorities arrested the arsonist who torched the 265-foot Lone Pine Bridge that crossed the Owens River connecting the Cerro Gordo and Darwin.

> John T. Dely was taken into custody, a native of Limerick, Ireland, about 30 years of age, and an engineer and machinist by trade. He has been in the county at times for five years, during which, as he stated, the county had combined into a conspiracy against him; he has not in that time averaged four meals a week, and life had become insupportable; if guilty of any crime he had been driven to it. He is the person supposed to have fired the Union Con hoisting works at Cerro Gordo immediately after being discharged from work in July last. Witnesses will testify as to his threats of burning the steamers on the lake and the bridge.[46]

In a second form, arson transcended the class situation of labor, affecting market relations in general. Although the motives for protest are elusive, commercial establishments and their proprietors were common targets. Charles Walter's Star Brewery near Camp Independence was discovered in flames under circumstances that left "scarce a doubt it was the work of an incendiary. Among these were threats from a certain irresponsible individual, made but a few days previously, that he 'would ruin him (Walter) before he was much older' or words to that effect." Evidently the threat was not sufficient to produce an arrest of the "certain individual," and nothing more is known about any grievance that may have prompted it. "There is not much likelihood that the deed can be brought home to any one, whatever the moral conviction in regard to his identity."[47]

In many of these cases the perpetrator was known or suspected. Sometimes the same store or proprietor was a repeated victim of fires. Years after the Star Brewery fire, a haystack on Charles Walter's farm near Camp Independence was burned, raising the possibility that Walter himself was the target, rather than some feature of his business or farm operation.[48] John Stoutenborough's general merchandise store in Bishop Creek suffered an arson attempt, or perhaps a warning, in August 1878, when coal oil boxes were stacked against an exterior wall and lighted. The flames were noticed from Hutching's saloon across the street and soon extinguished. Although the newspaper was confident that "in this case the perpetrator [was] known, and doubtless proof [would] be found to send him below for a few years," no arrest was reported.[49] Four years later the store, a brewery on the premises, and adjoining businesses were wrecked in a fire that caused a huge explosion of blasting powder in Stoutenborough's warehouse. "The current opinion as to the cause of the fire is that it was caused by drunken Indians— doubtless the correct one. A 'noble red' was heard to say last evening that he would burn Stoutenborough, Briggs and Brown, and offered to bet $4 on the proposition." No information is provided about the Indian's complaint, whether it concerned the store's liquor-selling practices, or whether it had any connection with the earlier fire. On the contrary, although an Indian was the presumed agent of the deed, moral responsibility was fixed on Chinese whiskey vendors and the local law-enforcement agents that tolerated them. "The Chinese quarters of town should be besieged and everyone compelled to evacuate. The Piute element should not be allowed to remain within the town limits after sunset."[50]

Yet liquor and ethnic conflicts hardly explain the frequency of arson, its recurrent targets, and the sometimes intricate planning devoted to the act. A neighbor of the McMurry and Moore store in Big Pine was the author of an attempt so elaborate as to suggest extensive premeditation.

The fire was the result of a deliberate attempt by a sneaking coward to destroy property, and take life, too. A lot of shavings, whittled with a knife, had been placed in a sugar box and thoroughly saturated with kerosene. In the same box, with their necks projecting through holes in the cover of the box, were two bottles filled with the same explosive liquid. In the midst of the shavings was a short piece of candle held in place by nails, and so arranged as to be easily lighted without disturbing the surroundings. By means of a ten foot measuring pole sharpened at one end the incendiary placed this very effective sort of a torpedo on the shed roof over the store part of the building. At this stage it seems he became fearful of the results to himself if he set fire directly to the contents of the box by means of the short piece of candle, and, to avoid this risk, he took a sack filled with hay and placing it along side the fire box, set fire to it and made off hurriedly as his footprints plainly prove. The hay blazing up so brightly caused the timely alarm [when its light was detected from a nearby house].[51]

In this case, once again, the question of responsibility appears as a peculiar dilemma. Although contemporaries noted that "very little doubt exists among those on the ground as to who the guilty party is," and everyone agreed that "the incendiary is the meanest of all criminals, and the most difficult to guard against,"[52] no legal action followed.

The ready explanation is that these commercial fires were arranged to collect on insurance claims. Indeed, the practice was well known in the adjacent Death Valley region as a method for promoters to escape the clutches of eastern investors in bogus mines, with an additional bonus from the insurance companies.[53] The suspicion is perhaps justified in cases like that of Bertrand Rhine's Inyo Mercantile Store, which was destroyed by an unexplained fire. The store was insured for $7,000; the proprietor's estimated loss was $8,000 to $9,000.[54] But very few stores were so well insured, and many merchants and farmers stated that they had no insurance at all—and they stayed to rebuild. The failure to pursue legally suspected arsonists is therefore not explained by a supposed conspiracy to defraud insurance companies.

The motives behind commerical arson are more veiled than for the other two types, perhaps because of what the public exposure of those motives would reveal about business practices and local grievances. When Indians and Chinese were plausible perpetrators, the problem was witheringly exposed. In the more typical instances, where the known culprits were white, a curtain descends on questions of agency and motive. Before looking behind that curtain at what is being concealed and why, several hypotheses deserve mention. From the diversity of suspected arsonists and business victims, one should assume that varied grievances prompted these attacks. Liquor sales led to quarrels over price, quality, or availability, and particularly to rowdy customers. During hard times, when barter and subsistence production were the only sources of farm income, many residents were heavily indebted to the general merchandise stores,[55] and some may have resorted to violence if their credit was stopped. The prices charged consumers or paid to farm suppliers were potential sources of conflict. Generally, merchants and producers were divided along multiple lines of economic interest, and these divisions could have inspired resentment. The available evidence does not allow evaluation of these alternatives; but it speaks clearly to the conflictual nature of market relations, and by its silence on certain particulars it suggests that something important is being concealed.

In the third type of property arson, that stemming mainly from quarrels among farmers, the evidence is more complete. It is clear, for example, that some grievances originated from long-standing disputes over property boundaries, livestock, and water. Arson and gunplay were combined in popular justice and, when the stakes were high or when conventionally enforced laws were involved, these cases were taken to the courts. A classical feud between William Watson and Thomas Volkert illustrates these points. Both farmers claimed rightful possession of a small strip of land that separated their homesteads south of Bishop Creek. Relations between them were already strained when Watson went looking for some of his livestock on the Volkert ranch. Discovering the animals in a barn, Watson went in. He received a crippling wound in the hand from Volkert's shotgun. After a lull of several years, Watson's entire farm (house, grain, haystacks, and stables) was destroyed by fire, "clearly the work of some diabolical incendiary. This last disaster, accidental or otherwise, leaves him without a vestige of hope. He is a most worthy man."[56] Neighbor Volkert then abandoned his disputed claim, which was briefly taken up by James Wright. But in the following year "the remains of James Wright were found lying in a spot of sand near Owens River. The man's neck was broken and marked as if it had been done by a rope."[57] No connection was established between Wright and Watson. Volkert returned to his original homestead a month later and, when he found Watson removing grape vines from the contested strip separating their farms, ordered him off at gun point. Now Watson complained to the sheriff, who jailed the less popular Volkert, the latter refusing to pay a fine of $250 for assault and spending 250 days with the county. That, however, did not end Watson's troubles. Despite a crippled hand, he was soon embroiled in a knife fight over wandering livestock with the new occupants of Volkert's farm.[58]

We do not know whether Volkert torched Watson's farm or whether Watson hung Wright. Individual exploits, probably lost to historical record, are less significant than recurring patterns, which allow plausible inferences about retributive justice. Two further case studies help establish such a pattern. Property rights, disputed in the previous case, merged easily with water conflicts in others. On January 19, 1894, the following announcement was published in the *Inyo Independent* and repeated for the next four weeks.

Public Notice

> I take this means of notifying S. A. Densmore that his irrigating ditch running through my land is damaging my property by making deep cuts and washes. And you are hereby notified to repair said ditch and put it in condition to prevent further damage.
>
> C. A. Walter[59]

The tempestuous Charles Walter had been involved in previous arson cases. We do not know whether his public notice achieved the desired result; but when the back pantry of Densmore's home in Independence was ignited with kerosene in early February, the action could have been understood as another warning. The same means could easily have been applied to the house itself. "The deed must have been perpetrated by some person familiar with the premises as no noise was made either on entering or leaving the place, and a spaniel always left in the house made no alarm and was outside in the morning."[60] If Walter had reason to deliver a second and stronger message to the offending Densmore, neither the local law-enforcement officers nor the avuncular press were about to expose the customary method for settling differences between settlers. Indeed, both seemed to cooperate in the charades that followed. A Chinese man whom Densmore had recently discharged from his employ was arrested for the pantry arson on the evidence of footprints near the back gates judged by investigators as "the imprints of a China shoe." The accused not only had motive, he also had a bad reputation, having reportedly served a term in the Nevada State Prison. All that was missing was an explanation of how the man came to make the acquaintance of Densmore's spaniel. The best indication that the Chinese man's arrest was a smokescreen is his release a week later because there was insufficient evidence for a trial, "although there is no doubt that he was the perpetrator of the deed."[61] Walter, whose public notice had surely attracted attention, was never mentioned in connection with the investigation.

Not all quarrels between farmers ended so conveniently or, when they involved water, so promptly. A final case shows how arson and homicide could combine in a long-running dispute that moved in and out of the courts. The brothers Ezra and Thomas Goodale were early pioneers who established a de facto claim to water drawn by ditch from Saw Mill Creek at Blackrock in the late 1860s. As neighboring homesteads were settled, controversies over rights to the creek and ditch erupted regularly over a period of twelve years, because Ezra never bothered to file a water right. In 1881, after filing a rival claim, "Robert Arnold cut the ditch of water claimed by Ezra Goodale and proceeded to appropriate it for his own use."[62] Goodale swore a complaint to the sheriff, resulting in Arnold's arrest. A two-year lawsuit followed. A jury awarded $200 in damages—one-fifth of what Goodale had asked.[63] But the question of water rights was not definitively addressed in the verdict, and disputes continued. When Ezra died in 1891, Thomas took over management of the ranch. A new quarrel was brewing with James Hines, the owner of the neighboring homestead, which shared access to Saw Mill Creek. Both Goodale and Hines made camps on the creek near their ditch heads to oversee any water diversion. In July 1894 the "brush house" at Goodale's camp caught fire, and he promptly requested the judge at Independence to have Hines arrested for arson. Returning to the site in advance of the sheriff, Goodale was shot from ambush and died a few days later.[64]

James and his brother William Hines were arrested for murder, but Pat Reddy's able defense won a not-guilty verdict.[65] Although Reddy enjoyed a huge statewide reputation by the 1890s, local jurors may have been swayed by something stronger than prestige in such a clearcut case. Thomas Goodale, too, was respected as an authentic pioneer and had been a candidate for U.S. senator in 1877, before family illness forced him to quit the race. More likely, the jury was party to the moral order that had evolved around settler quarrels. They may have declined to enter a dispute that belonged properly to the realm of popular justice—a tradition of social control,[66] revealed in the practice of arson, that regulated more comprehensively and effectively affairs beyond the ken of law-enforcement agencies and consensual collective action.

When these cases are seen against the background of the fifty-two instances listed in table 4, the evidence suggests that arson was often employed as a warning and was only resorted to for purposes of retribution when moral suasion failed. Milder warnings sometimes preceded reluctant escalation. Most fires attacked attention-getting, but limited, targets. Haystacks were commonly chosen; they had both tactical and symbolic advantages. They were easily fired without detection, by means of a bottle of coal oil and a burning wick, and if the winds were calm the damage was limited to the isolated stack (but often they were not). In one graphic case the incendiary divided a haystack before torching half of it. Equally important, the fired haystack symbolized the agrarian origins of the retributive act, whether expressed by Indian laborers or white neighbors. The victim would probably know which, since a lot more was known than was said, at least for the historical record. The deed was usually accomplished by stealth in the middle of the night, but for purposes of ambiguity rather than strict anonymity—which might have compromised the act's meaning. The incendiary's art was to convey a clear, if modulated, message, while leaving the authorities "helpless" to prosecute the crime. And it worked, as indicated by the number of perpetrators who were known but acknowledged to be safe from legal action. As table 4 indicates, only five arson or murder arrests were made, including the dubious Chinese shoe case, and only one person was convicted—the unfortunate Irish miner who included a costly county bridge among his targets.

It is difficult to evaluate the success of retributive justice at ending grievous practices or otherwise resolving disputes. A functionalist interpretation would claim that the persistence of arson over the years implies that it had results. There is probably some truth here—reforms by victims may explain why most did not experience repeated assaults. But that explanation has major limitations. Miners and Indians had very little power to alter their circumstances by intimidation. Among farmers, moreover, violence frequently provoked counterviolence. At best, the climate in which retributive justice was tacitly approved probably urged restraint on offenders singled out in front of their neighbors. At worst, it was an inefficient system that engendered at least as many conflicts as it resolved.

The grievances expressed in arson were fundamentally economic, centering on farm and mine wages, mechanization, commercial transactions, property, and water. Many were bona fide class conflicts, as in the cases of miners, Indian field hands, and consumers or debtors. Intraclass quarrels among farmers were also common and equally responsive to economic conditions. About half of the incidents in table 4 occurred during the months from July to September, when the harvest and commercial activity were at their peak. Similarly, slightly more than half took place during the hard times of 1875 to 1883, followed by

another upsurge in the recession of the early 1890s. This study, like
E. P. Thompson's study of England's forested rural areas, reveals "a
deeply divided community, subject to arson and violence, and the divisions not according to any regular socio-economic stratifications."[67]
In the Owens Valley the divisions occurred among laborers, consumers, and farmers on one side, and merchants, capitalists, and other
farmers on the other. Their quarrels were economic, in the main, whether among peers or between class antagonists. The interpretation stressing social control has to be grounded on this shifting subsoil of economic hardship.

The regulative failings of the economy, the state, and civil society left
settlers with the necessity of devising their own moral code for dealing
with obdurate conflict. Arson and violence provided forcible means for
handling disputes, but they also had their own etiquette. On one hand,
they were tacitly accepted—when it came to apprehending suspects,
identities were readily concealed and scapegoats were boisterously embraced, with imaginative attention to detail. The farther away responsibility was placed the better, which explains the popularity of scapegoats
such as vagabonds, Chinese, and paternalistically exculpated Indians.
The principle was versatile in application. When the elegant new house
("not excelled by any private residence in the county") of Mr. Gerrish
in Independence was torched before it could be occupied, suspicion
focused on "some passing communist with a view of creating a diversion
that would render it possible to effect a burglary elsewhere in town."[68]
On the other hand, acceptance of popular justice was contingent on its
respecting the operational arena of civil society. Murder—and the burning of public bridges—required the mobilization of official justice, even
if it proved forgiving. Popular justice worked best by not disrupting the
game of respectability and not challenging legal tolerance.

A rule-clarifying case arose when Pat Reddy was retained to defend
the suspect in a widely publicized murder trial. The rumor soon spread
that a score of vigilantes had come to Independence intent on burning
Reddy's stable and lynching the murder suspect. The public reacted
with unprecedented chastisement of their fellow citizens. "The community generally has been thrown into a state of excitement, wonder and
final indignation beyond anything of the kind ever experienced here
before [by] a gang of men, some of them hitherto recognized as good
men and citizens [but now involved in] committing midnight arson and
murder, deplorable outlawry." A "Warning" signed by "Many Citizens
of Bishop Creek" expressed a "burning shame and disgrace to the law

abiding citizens" and pledged "time and money in hunting out" the vigilantes by a new force of countervigilantes.[69] The matter was soon settled when the original insurgents explained, or improvised, that their objectives had been misunderstood. In a published "Card to the Public" four Bishop men said: "[O]ur meeting was for the capture of [another fugitive]. While we were in meeting, some indiscreet person, either in joke or earnest, proposed to fire Mr. Reddy's stable and the whole meeting, so far as we know, refused to do any such thing."[70]

The larger point was that vigilantes and arson had their socially accepted place and this was not it. Lynching a convicted Chinese murderer was seen as something of a public convenience, and arson aimed at concluding conflicts that the law could not or would not tackle was accepted as rough justice. The rule was that popular justice could operate with relative impunity in those areas conceded by law enforcement, but it could not intervene where the law was at work. The relationship, moreover, was asymmetrical. On its own initiative or at the request of citizens, law enforcement could intervene, handing over to the courts a dispute about land or water, for example, or the choice of punishment for a misdeed. Movement in the other direction was proscribed. As long as the rules were observed, law, civil society, and retributive justice could coexist, if not always in harmony then in creative tension.

In summary, civil society on the frontier grew vigorously in the wide space left unregulated by the institutions of an externally oriented formal economy and a weakly financed public sector. Collective citizen action augmented public services and rallied the population to occasional political organization and economic cooperation. Yet civil society met formidable limits of normative consensus where economic interests divided the population, and weak institutions, especially legal ones, left irreconcilable quarrels. Some problems, such as disputes over water and property rights requiring authoritative intervention, were simply beyond the ameliorative capacity of civil society. In the capacious gaps, settlers had to defend their own interests with violence, threats, and sundry means of retributive justice. Arson was the most extensively practiced and revealing of these. It showed how even in the organization of retributive justice, society existed. A distinctive moral order grew up around social violence, defining its appropriate circumstances, restraining its use, and enveiling its unseemly necessity. Both law and lawlessness were socially regulated spheres of action. Law enforcement deferred to and collaborated with both civil society and the morality of social violence. Each responded to changes in the other. As government slowly enhanced its fiscal capacity, it took over services such as roads and hospitals from civil society. Violence diminished with the advent of agrarian democracy in the ditch companies.

Yet, after more than thirty years of struggle to make frontier society work for the settlers, these three elements had established their special places in a seamless weave. Weak government, strong civil society, and morally organized violence were by now traditional—carefully balanced parts of the frontier way of getting things done. When new problems came along, such as expropriative intrusions from Los Angeles, and the law did not satisfy popular notions of justice, tried methods like arson were readily available. Society existed in hearty and nuanced forms that Tocqueville, Turner, and the like could not appreciate from afar. What seemed like lawlessness to outside observers was tacitly understood as social control within frontier civil society. The concept of individualism describes very little that was important. The meaning of the society lay in a culture steadily fashioned from exigency and hope.

FRONTIER CULTURE

The concept of culture effectively synthesizes the foregoing chapters on conquest, the pioneer economy, and frontier society. By culture I understand the meanings that people construct for their lives and environment. Culture is produced in material conditions; it shapes those conditions and endows them with significance, prompting varied responses to the social and physical world. Culture shapes both historical subjects and their analysts.[71] In Clifford Geertz's words, "[M]an is an animal suspended in webs of significance he himself has spun, [and] culture [is] those webs." The analysis of culture is an interpretive "search for meaning," the study of particular attempts by particular peoples to place things "in some sort of comprehensible, meaningful frame."[72] In the late nineteenth-century American West, culture was expressed in assumptions about the appropriateness of social practices and, especially, about where local society was headed. Propriety and prosperity were seen as the keys to an ever hopeful future. The meaning of any particular occurrence was ascertained by considering its role in the unfolding of this trajectory.

In that terse summary are compressed many layers of meaning, which require unpacking. Settlers built a new society in the Owens Valley during the short space of forty years at the end of the nineteenth century. Of course, they borrowed heavily from the national heritage, Paiute achievements, immigrant cultures, and state patrimony. Yet the consciousness of creating something new was pervasive; it was a way of describing and justifying the frontier, of investing it with meaning. When any question arose about, for example, the settlers' efforts, Indian oppression, or the sluggish economy, volumes were spoken in the words "We built this country, we made productive farms from barren desert." Newness took many forms. The diverse settler society was new in the sense that few if any had ever lived among such motley fellows, certainly not among Indians as co-workers and seldom with neighbors who spoke a different language. The land was new or at least unused by European standards. Perhaps the overriding fact of newness was that everyone had come to build a new life measured by better fortune than they had known.

From the beginning this was a male-centered society. Men came first, built a habitat adapted to their needs, and long dominated in sheer numbers. The women who followed assumed vital roles in the farm labor force, and some slowly achieved business and professional careers, mainly in teaching. But patriarchy governed their lives, weighed on their spirits, and occasionally inspired rebellion. Mary Austin's autobiographical reflections on the time describe the great gulf created between men and women by the pursuit of prosperity. Between the man's inadequate situation and future success,

> there was a hiatus always about to be bridged by his "getting into something." This was an attitude prevailing among men of Inyo; one on which they constantly reassured one another. *Something* was due to happen soon. There was the promise of the land; its rich and alluring possibility; there was the residue of the romantic mining experience; also something must be allowed to the allure of the desertness. Men . . . spent their lives going around and around in it, always keyed to the expected, the releasing discovery. With the women it was not so; they felt, as they hung there suspended between hopes that refused to eventuate, life slipping away from them.[73]

> There was a spell of the land over all the men. Men talking together would inevitably express the deeply felt conviction, "Well, this country is bound to go ahead sometime; just look at it." Women hearing it would look at one another with sharp—or weary—implications of exasperated resignation.[74]

Pioneer women lived in a society whose overriding ambitions were not of their choosing. And they lived, day to day, on isolated farms

seeing very little of other women their own age. Loneliness was the
mood they used most often to describe their condition. Public life was
organized predominantly around the exclusive affairs of men—lodges,
ditch companies, politics, and saloons. To the lesser extent that women
participated in organizational life, it was in the secondary groups open
to them: lodge auxiliaries, temperance associations, and family-oriented
institutions such as church and school. Loneliness, therefore, also expressed the absence of a legitimate place in society for women as
women. It encompassed a more general ennui that only the rare feminist
like Mary Austin would express openly. Evidence on the strains of
patriarchal family life appears in biography, oral history, and ironic
public announcements.

Mary Austin lived apart from her husband, practiced her writing
craft, earned a small salary for herself and their retarded daughter
teaching at the Inyo Academy, and eventually divorced—all in the face
of bitter social criticism. Women like her were characterized derisively
as having "views." Divorce was rare and brought ostracism. Belle Mc-
Donald wanted to end her bad marriage to Angus, the stern Scotsman
and Big Pine blacksmith. "In those days divorce was utter disgrace, so
it was only after long deliberation on his part and appeal on hers that
he finally consented, but only with the understanding that he was to
keep the children and she was to leave."[75] Occasionally women simply
left their husbands and suffered public humiliation. The following type
of notice appeared often in the local press.

> Caution. My wife, Maud B. Day, having left my bed and board without any
> cause whatsoever and against my consent, I will not be responsible for any
> debts she may contract from and after this date.
>
> Charles E. Day[76]

Luna Hutchinson, a farm woman and writer, carried on a spirited
dialogue on "the woman question" with the editors of the *Inyo Independent,* urging "woman's equality with man in the marriage contract."
In articles signed only "L. H." she argued that although all women were
denied the vote, a married woman labored under additional burdens
because she could not control property independent of her husband,
enter contracts to buy or sell without his consent, or inherit the full
value of his estate. The editors coyly noted that "L. H. comes up man-
fully in support of her cause," but found it "absurd to charge their

[women's] meager showing to lack of opportunity." If the doctrines L. H. advocated were "unsound," the editors indulgently allowed, they were at least well written.[77] When Helen MacKnight returned to the valley with a medical degree, she had to fight against "the criticism and scorn of the other physicians in the town"; she earned a sparse income by treating Indian patients and emergencies in mining camps that no other doctor would handle.[78] In addition to the small number of rebels like Austin, Hutchinson, and MacKnight, there were many more who endured their condition or channeled their energies into womens' activities like the temperance movement or the Improvement Association. In this masculine culture, however, "there were women of [Austin's] generation who never outgrew the paralyzing impuissance of this singular obliviousness to their claim on consideration."[79]

Sexism was one component of a more general world view which gave cultural signficance to interrelated forms of discrimination—each with its special features. White-male paternalism suffused the society. Measured by the number of people affected and by its insidiousness, its most pervasive effect was the spiritual enervation of women. Measured by the degree of its coercion and degradation of people, however, its greatest effect was on Indians of both sexes. In its most virulent form, paternalism was expressed as racism or, in the idiom of the time, as nativism, aimed principally at the Chinese. Chinese migrant labor in California suffered the animosity reserved for low-wage competitors in the labor market, compounded by a politically expedient brand of racism that misused Asians in the battles between capital and labor.[80]

If Paiutes suffered derision as "aborigines" and "noble redmen," they also received a patronizing tolerance denied the "moon-eyed sons of joss" or "children of the celestial kingdom." Routinely, "celestials" residing in small Chinatowns in Bishop Creek, Independence, and Lone Pine were raided, summarily convicted of crimes, jailed, and killed by whites and Indians alike with no fear of retaliation. Defenseless Chinese thus provided a convenient focal point for free-floating anger. Close relations between whites and Chinese were less common than those between whites and Indians—going no further than the employment by some whites of a farm "cookie" or a house-and-garden servant—and this gave free rein to hatred fanned by other forces. Chinese were regularly blamed for crimes such as liquor sales to Indians; but the most energetic vituperation focused on their status as competitors in the labor market and, no doubt, in commerce, including the whisky trade.

Suffragettes. Although undated, this Forbes photo seems to have been taken in 1916 as the questions of Indian citizenship and voting rights were coming to the forefront. Here Forbes has staged in his studio the county clerk registering three Paiute women voters. The masking on the left side of the backdrop suggests that he worked on the image for some unrecorded purpose. We may infer that, of the parties involved (the county clerk, Forbes, and the Paiute women), some or all advocated Indian voting rights before the victory of women's suffrage in 1920. (Courtesy of the Seaver Center for Western History Research, Natural History Museum of Los Angeles County.)

"If American working men were to consent to live like Chinamen, they would soon be working for Chinese wages."[81]

Nativism reached its heights during the 1880s, when local hard times coincided with national and west-coast hysteria over the Chinese Exclusion Act. Banishment was urged in demonstrations throughout the western cities and towns where Chinese had been brought for mine labor and railroad construction. The Owens Valley enthusiastically joined the campaign. Taking up "the Chinese Question," the *Inyo Register* expressed avuncular concern and judged that a boycott of Chinese labor was the only effective solution. Anti-Chinese smokers could do their part, too, when local stores began to supply "white labor cigars."[82] Employers united in the cause and announced their patriotic intentions.

White People Wanted

At the request of Hotel Keepers, Mine Managers, and other business men, and many housekeepers, notice is hereby given that at least fifty white cooks can find employment here in Inyo County. These people earnestly desire to get rid of Chinese, and will do so as rapidly as other help can be found to take their place. Fair wages will be paid to sober, civil and reliable white help. Negroes will be employed at once in preference to Chinese; the people want to get rid of these pests.[83]

If the campaign succeeded, it was only to the extent of shoring up chauvinistic group solidarity. The number of Chinese in the labor force remained constant. White cooks combining sobriety, civility, and reliability must have been rare, and blacks were probably leery of the job. Getting there and living unmolested were problems, judging from the experience of a black man tarred and feathered in Mojave or the house servant "Nigger Sam" Meredith whitewashed in Big Pine.[84]

Sexism and racism, of course, were national problems fostered in special ways by settler society. The white-male chauvinism of frontier culture was fueled by economic austerity, yet it was also mellowed in some ways by an unalterable population diversity and dependence on the skills and services of ethnic minorities. Mexicans occupied an interstitial position that demonstrated a softer face of prejudice. Mexicans were tolerated and sometimes embraced, at least on ceremonial occasions and in the case of long-time residents who chose to become integrated with white society. Mexican settlements at Cerro Gordo and Lone Pine were coeval with pioneer homesteads, and Mexican miners were acknowledged experts in their essential trade. They enjoyed an aloof respect that did not preempt personal abuse but militated against the perniciously patterned discrimination experienced by women, Indians, and Chinese. Other non-Anglo groups such as the Germans, French, and Basques suffered no prejudice.

Necessity and diversity lent a certain cosmopolitan flavor to frontier culture. Chauvinists were not necessarily hicks. They paid close attention to national affairs, California politics, and legislative changes affecting their interest. They identified with trend-setting San Francisco, and the more affluent families traveled there (not so much to Los Angeles) for shopping, vacations, and college education. Many never read books and probably could not afford them, but those who did exhibited contemporary middlebrow tastes. Perry Wilkes, a book salesman from Kern County, did well with the *Illustrated Bible, Scenes of a Wild Life in the Far West,* and *McCabe's American History.*[85] I. N. Townsley started a local subscription agency whose best sellers included: the *Personal Reminiscences, Anecdotes and Letters of General Robert E. Lee;* the *Encyclopedia of Things Worth Knowing, or 25,000 Wants Supplied; The Science of New [married] Life;* and Mark Twain and C. D. Warner's *Gilded Age,* which was enjoying a successful run on Broadway at the time.[86]

A drama society was formed in Bishop that staged plays for recreation, profit, and charity and provided one of the few activities open to women. Churches and schools sponsored most of these refinements. The Methodist Inyo Academy in Bishop shone across the valley as a beacon of cultural achievement and civic pride. The churches distinguished themselves in secular reform, perhaps because they provided a channel for womens' citizenship. By the turn of the century Mary Austin's stories and essays, written at Independence and collected in *The Land of Little Rain,* were recognized locally, after critical acclaim in San Francisco and Los Angeles—Ambrose Bierce found "unexpected interest [in her] tang of archaism."[87] Local resentment of her views receded with invitations for readings and book-signing parties.[88] Valley-wide festivals included on an equal footing the Fourth of July Picnic, the Indian Fandango, and the Mexican Independence Day celebration. People shared a hybrid culture that connected unequally privileged groups. The harsh world of white paternalism was tempered by a progressive strain in the arts, leisure, and social reform.

Frontier culture thus embodied and enacted a paradox—the meanness of austerity, paternalism, and swaggering ambition interlaced with wit and sensitivity. This cultural amalgam was a product of many in-

fluences, including necessity, diversity, and cosmopolitanism. Moreover, populism and maturation each played an important role. Valley
farmers practiced economic co-operation and mounted perhaps the
most successful collective political action in the populist-inspired Farmers' and Producers' Cooperative Union. The Republican and Democrat
Parties vied evenly for local support, alternating victories by thin margins in the 1880s. The People's Party entered electoral politics in the
1890s, easily outrunning local prohibitionists and winning 11 percent
of the vote in the national elections of 1892, and 14 percent in 1894.
With the fusion of the Democrat and People's Parties, however, Inyo
County delivered an impressive 64 percent for Bryan in the presidential
race of 1896 and 61 percent in 1900.[89] The culture of populism drew
on rural prejudices and nativism, to be sure, but it also articulated an
ideology of antimonopolism and egalitarianism that Owens Valley citizens had evolved on their own in dealing with the agrarian economy
and external capital. Paternalism diminished in populist circles, which
invited women's participation and preached equality.

Maturation was a process of change in which newness shaded into
permanency. The rough-hewn methods of citizen action, popular justice, and violence conceded space to electoral politics and reform. Contemporaries felt it as a new settledness. By 1900 the literary and drama
circle drew better crowds than vigilante meetings. Describing the Sali-
nas Valley, directly west over two mountain ranges, John Steinbeck
observed the stages and substructure of this maturation.

> A new country seems to follow a pattern. First come the openers, strong and
> brave and rather childlike. They can take care of themselves in the wilder-
> ness, but they are naive and helpless against men, and perhaps that is why
> they went out in the first place. When the rough edges are worn off the new
> land, businessmen and lawyers come in to help with the development—to
> solve problems of ownership, usually by removing the temptations to them-
> selves. And finally comes culture, which is entertainment, relaxation, trans-
> port out of the pain of living. And culture can be on any level, and is. The
> church and the whorehouse arrived in the Far West simultaneously. And
> each would have been horrified to think it was a different facet of the same
> thing.[90]

The Owens Valley had its churches, its seldom mentioned whore-
houses, and the social infrastructure in between, from lodges to political
clubs. The business interests Steinbeck notes acquired greater importance as homesteaders faded into the background. The influential Ma-

sons typified this shift in a characteristic blend of Protestant respectability, commercial enterprise, and restrained populism. As maturation
proceeded, culture fermented the mixture of paternalism, nativism, cosmopolitanism, populism, and Protestant ethic. Each provided an interpretive lens through which meaning was apprehended. Paternalism, in
Herman Melville's apposite phrase, supplied the "metaphysics of In-
dian-hating."[91] Nativism provided the pioneers with an explanation for
failures in civility, liquor sales, and violence in the resonant notion of
alien sabotage. Populism usefully indicted externally controlled markets
and monopolies. Local blame was placed, uncontroversially, on the
feebleness of the enterprising spirit.

Although these interpretive themes combined in diverse ways under
specific sets of circumstances, the characteristic amalgam was hopeful
expectation. It was the "coming boom" vaunted in the press or, in Mary
Austin's words, the conviction that "something was due to happen
soon." Even though the something was only vaguely conceived, its
expected result was so clear it could be visualized, tasted, and spoken in
one word: prosperity. The meaning of diverse events, from new railroad
rumors to a bumper crop of potatoes, was usually found in the progress
they signaled. Prosperity had three great interpretive advantages: it was
easy to understand, pleasant, and a ready symbol to paper over divisions between whites and Indians, town and country, merchant and
farmer. It made sense of their history and their impasse. Had it not been
for . . . (naming, according to one's disposition, bullion kings, railroad
capitalists, a weak spirit of enterprise, production costs, market access,
or freight monopolies), prosperity would have been realized. Conversely, when "something" cleared the obstacle, the natural state of
prosperity would then be established despite the bothersome delay. This
was the dense matrix of meaning. It explained everything from the
necessarily harsh means the settlers took to civilize the Indians in the
1860s to the perilous developmental path they confidently followed into
the twentieth century.

CONCLUSION

Tocqueville notwithstanding, society enjoyed a healthy existence in the
American West. But it was a predominantly civil society in which the
major responsibility for social order and collective goods fell to volun-

tary associations. Weakly financed local government did what it could, mainly in the fields of law enforcement (with the help of vigilantes and Indian police) and public works (with help from subscriptions and corporate improvements). Cooperative societies provided the rest of what was available, ranging from agricultural infrastructure to education. Even when local government and civil society worked in harmony, their limitations were such that much was left undone or left to the informal mechanisms of popular justice. The special character of frontier society lay in the pragmatic balance and normative interplay of state, economy, and civil society—although much of that went unnoticed in contemporary interpretations formulated at a distance in a highly ideological context. Frontier culture explained all this to its members and endowed the pioneers' labor with moral significance. Paternalism and popular justice were complementary aspects of one meaningful system. Indians, other minorities, and women had reason to resist its onerous implications, and some of them did so in ways that tempered their oppression. What is more impressive, perhaps, is the unanimity of their belief, the firm faith in coming prosperity, that persisted even in the worst of times.

Recent scholarship, of course, has come a long way since Tocqueville and Turner, both in revisionist interpretation and in solid empirical work. As we have seen in connection with conquest and incorporation, a number of writers now take a critical position on the role of the state, ethnic conflict, and dependent development.[92] In an early paper focused on the social psychology of the frontier, Allan Bogue identified the problem of inadequate revenues underlying formal institutional weaknesses, but did not carry that into an analysis of the compensatory strengths of civil society.[93] Conversely, rich portraits of frontier communities seldom relate customary practices to political economy.[94] Richard Hogan's study of development and politics in six Colorado towns, however, is a valuable synthesis of the "consensus" and "conflict" analytical approaches, and the towns' development provides a fertile contrast with that of the Owens Valley.[95] From its separate regional vantage point, the present study supports Hogan's conclusion that the frontier "was granted autonomy as part of a strategy for controlling the perimeter of the governed territory. The state facilitated entrepreneurial economic and political development and coopted frontier elites who succeeded in establishing effective social control. This process fostered economic and political expansion through the penetration of capital and the annexation of new territory."[96] In both regions conflict arose between settlers encouraged by the state's expansionary policies and the corporate monopolies in mining and transportation. Political life in the Colorado towns centered on class struggle:

> When labor was economically independent and politically organized, as were the Colorado gold miners and the farmers of northern Colorado, boosters [merchants and speculators] courted the interests of labor, defending the rights of persons in public Carnival government. When nonlaboring classes [corporate owners and large-scale ranchers] controlled frontier industry, as in the transportation and southern Colorado farming and ranching settlements, local government was a private, corporate [caucus] affair in which nonlaboring industrial and commercial classes united in the defense of property and public order.[97]

Hogan's class and political alignments were not duplicated in the Owens Valley, for several reasons. The rural California class structure was not as differentiated, as we have seen. On one hand, for much of the nineteenth century agricultural producers shared a common, modest class situation; and on the other hand, powerful corporate interests were involved in the local economy for only a limited time and, with the exception of Belshaw's short tenure on the board of supervisors, did not attempt to control local government. Similarly, Owens Valley merchants and boosters shifted their sentiments back and forth between farmers and mine owners, and most of the time they pursued their own interests separately. In general, political alliances were conveniently short-lived, and action was mounted on the basis of fragmentary groups. The principal classes—merchants and farmers—of necessity sometimes joined their meager forces against outside capital (not, as in Hogan's study, because labor was well organized, but because capital had no use for Owens Valley local interests); yet more frequently they spurned collaboration. Among other differences from the Colorado towns, local government in the Owens Valley was not a prize to covet. Indeed, although class and ethnic fights were common enough, class struggle was not the moving force of local politics. Civil society was the centerpiece of local life, a tradition that ran deeper than formal government and regulated disputes as well as cooperation in culturally meaningful ways.

Why, then, dwell on Hogan's study? First, because the initial parallels are strong and corroborate an interpretation based on the role of the state and dependent development. Second, because the combined evidence suggests that political conflict was endemic in both regions and that although it took different concrete forms, it revolved around the intervention of national interests and failed to achieve any unified action during the frontier period. In Colorado, that led to "the ultimate defeat of local resistance to incorporation into the national political economy," a fate also observed by other writers.[98] In the Owens Valley, however, nineteenth-century culture and political struggle laid the bases for a new era of resistance to incorporation; the resistance that was beginning would not be defeated so handily as in Colorado. An explanation of the differences may reveal a dimension of western history obscured by current debates that focus on consensus versus conflict.

FIVE

Rebellion

At the turn of the century, the Owens Valley directly experienced the consequences of a national change from a weak yet expansionary state to a strong and consolidated Progressive state. Initially local society welcomed the change and, with some justification, saw it as the fulfill-ment of the promise of prosperity. But philosophical promise soon turned to politics and politics to betrayal, at least from the standpoint of local ambition. Animated by a culturally rooted sense of injustice, Owens Valley communities and classes for the first time united in pro-test. A new repertoire of collective action was elaborated, based on traditions of popular justice and thoroughly modern claims on the state.

From 1904 to 1928, an alliance of citizens rose in rebellion to save their communities. The local struggle engaged the insinuating ambitions of metropolitan expansion that reached 240 miles northward from Los Angeles in search of the rights to land and a water supply. California's Little Civil War pitted a pioneer community of farmers and burghers against an urban growth coalition of merchants, manufacturers, devel-opers, public officials, and technically expert aqueduct builders. Partic-ipants understood it as a confrontation between urban progress and the continued existence of local society—a confrontation in which the state would determine who won and who lost.

PROSPERITY

The boom awaited by Owens Valley boosters since the collapse of Cerro Gordo in the mid-1870s finally came at the turn of the century. Although modest and unenduring, renewed prosperity vindicated local society. Optimism had not been ill-founded. Dreams of flourishing communities (maps 3, 4, and 5) and individual mobility could become realities, meaning that the ideological premises of pioneer society were valid and durable. Disappointing experiences with the mining monopolies, avaricious railroads, and local incivility were, perhaps, aberrations. Evolution, after all, was a slow process and now the twentieth century seemed to have finally delivered on nineteenth-century hopes. The populist temper had rallied in 1900 to give Democrat William Jennings Bryan 61 percent of the Inyo County vote, though he lost nationally to William McKinley;[1] in 1904 the county gravitated to Republican Theodore Roosevelt, who won a 56 percent majority there.[2] Owens Valley populists and their former antagonists in town commerce were equally willing recruits in the Progressive Movement, a national trend seen as tailor-made to the aspirations of local development. The Progressive themes of good government, scientific efficiency, antimonopoly, and entrepreneurialism articulated the local faith.[3]

The source of renewed optimism lay once again in the mining economy. From 1900 to 1904, a series of gold strikes were made in southwestern Nevada in the Bullfrog-Rhyolite-Beatty district and at Goldfield and Tonopah.[4] For the communities lying one hundred miles west of the new discoveries, "far more important in effect was the creation of nearby cash markets which demanded the best efforts of the agricultural lands of the Owens Valley."[5] This boom, however, stimulated more than just agricultural production. In 1902 valley investors had created the Bishop Light and Power Company to supply local needs. The mines in southern Nevada lured the Colorado-based Nevada-California Power Company, which purchased the Bishop power company and the rights to reservoir sites for power generation in the eastern sierra held by the Hillside Water Company of Bishop. The Nevada-California soon became the Southern Sierras Power Company and proceeded to build a series of power plants in the valley and transmission lines to the new mining towns, among other destinations. The Owens Valley became a center for the export of electricity, and although the enterprise was controlled by Colorado capital, it proved a stimulus to local construction, jobs, and commercial activity.

Shortly after the Nevada gold strikes, efforts were made to revive Cerro Gordo with a new smelter at Owens Lake that promised to extract profitably silver from ores previously ignored. By contrast to the Belshaw-Nadeau monopoly, "early in 1906, the new company began

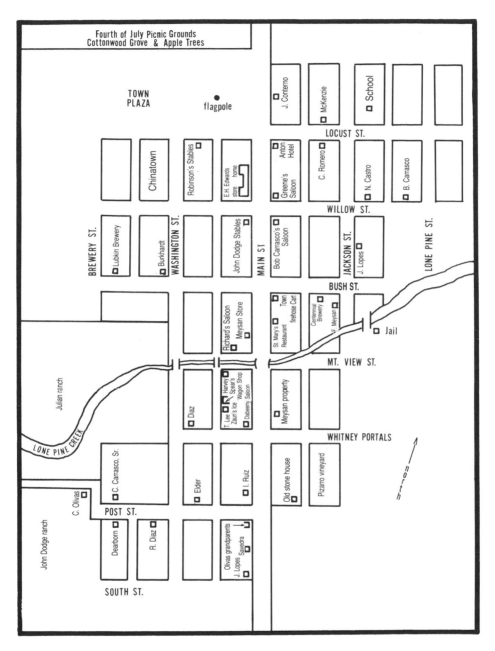

Map 3. Lone Pine, circa 1900. (Map by Lozano.)

contracting local teamsters to freight low grade silver ore from the mine dumps at Cerro Gordo to the smelter currently under construction at Keeler."[6] Although this scheme flopped, it led indirectly to a second boom at Cerro Gordo when employees of the silver-smelting company discovered that the old Union mine contained great quantities of zinc. From 1911 to 1919, Cerro Gordo and the railroad town of Keeler shared their good fortune with Owens Valley agricultural producers, merchants, and teamsters. Unfortunately for the local economy, the boom was short-lived (the big years were 1915 to 1918) and in the end generated only one-half the earnings carried away by the bullion kings of the 1870s.

If the mines and power company were the engines of economic growth, commerce was its pilot. Bishop advertised itself as "the chief business center of Eastern California," an unimpressive claim since it was the only incorporated town in the region; but the description added "there are two banks, two newspapers, and numerous business establishments of other kinds, some of which would do credit to a city four times as large."[7] In 1912, when Bishop's population stood at 1,200, the recently established Chamber of Commerce claimed "about 100 wide-awake" members,[8] and by 1916 the thirty-two-page county phone book listed 302 subscribers to the Bishop exchange.[9] As business grew so did the general wealth. From 1900 to 1920 the assessed value of property in Inyo County rose from $1.8 to $5.9 million.[10]

Wilfred and Mark Watterson, sons of a prominent sheep-ranching family, established the Inyo County Bank in 1902; its resources were estimated at $700,000 at the time of incorporation in 1911. As a measure of commercial activity, several general merchandise stores served Bishop, but "probably no other town of this size in California can show so striking an example of business growth as is seen in the progress of the well known firm" Leece and Watterson, Inc.

> Thirteen years ago [in 1899] it was a small concern in small quarters. Today its position of leadership in the commercial life of eastern California is scarcely disputed. Many of its extensive lines of stock are purchased in carload lots, and during at least one season one of the greatest factories in the country shipped more of its output to this house than to any other in the state, outside the distributing depots in San Francisco. This incidental fact is evidence of the volume of business done, as well as the spirit of improvement among the people of the valley.
>
> The lines carried include domestic and builders' hardware, stoves, ranges, oils, paints, farm machinery, vehicles, cream separators, and in fact every line of goods found in hardware stores. In addition, high class lines of

Corner of Main and West Line Streets, Bishop. The First National Bank was the Bishop branch of the Watterson Brothers' Inyo County Bank, and its building housed the U.S. Post Office at the rear. A meat market, real estate office, and army store separated the bank from the Masonic Lodge, with the star on top. (Curtis Phillips Collection, courtesy of the Eastern California Museum.)

silverware, cut glass and cutlery are carried. The sporting goods department is practically as complete as a city gun store would offer, including an extensive line of English fishing tackle. The greater part of a separate two-story building is required to house the extensive line of fine vehicles, California-made harness and plumbing goods.

The firm is the sole Inyo agency for the John Deere Plow Co., the Oliver Chilled Plow Co., the Studebaker line of vehicles, buggies and automobiles. They are also agents for the American Steel and Wire Co., and handle Ellwood, American and Union Lock fencing, all of which are received in carload shipments. Their agencies include that of the Dupont Powder Co., and in this connection a heavy stock of mining supplies is carried.[11]

The passage, drawn from a promotional tract published in 1912, is rhapsodic and doubtless a better indicator of the commercial mood than the volume of sales at Leece and Watterson. Yet it suggests important changes, which are corroborated by other evidence. It displays, first, a new spirit of optimism about local growth—plaudits rather than pleas for a spirit of enterprise. Second, the history of this firm indicates that commercial activity had expanded rapidly in a short time. Third, the Watterson family connection with ranching, banking, and merchandising indicates that certain families with agrarian roots were diversifying and becoming a business elite. Finally, judging from the sundry product lines that moved well at Leece and Watterson, the local economy was changing. Farmers were fencing their land, new construction was thriving, and the automobile had arrived, perhaps to begin overcoming the perennial problem of isolation.

Real estate speculation played an intriguing role in this development. By 1900, public land claims had fallen to a trickle as most of the good parcels had long since gone to patent.[12] Farmers and their agents could now sell these public land claims commercially, and some of them seized the opportunity. J. L. Gish advertised that he would "sell part of this fine ranch . . . one of the finest farms in Inyo County. When I purchased this land in 1903 I was told that I could not make a living on it. It was then all sagebrush, and I paid $950 for 160 acres which I now value at $300 per acre."[13] At least six real estate brokers operated from Bishop alone, but the more remarkable fact was that the "beautiful Owens Valley" was being advertised and sold by agents from Los Angeles to Fall River, Massachusetts. The Van Bokkelen Brothers in San Francisco offered "irrigated farms in small and large tracts" and urged, "[W]rite us today for illustrated booklet and full information."[14] The Homeseekers Bureau of Bishop and Fall River (eastern office) offered acreage and ranches ranging from $625 to $65,000: "What Inyo County has within its borders no pen can adequately describe, nor brush delineate, nor human tongue recount."[15] Notwithstanding, they offered a "Book of Facts." The booklet was a joint publication of the Inyo County Board of Supervisors, the Chamber of Commerce, and the horticultural commissioner. It appeared in various editions (with and without illustrations) under titles such as *Inyo County, California* and *A Few Facts about the Famous Owens River Valley.*[16] The promotional pitch started plainly enough: "Come to Beautiful Owens Valley to Live—Inyo County is the Switzerland of America," but in a section devoted to the "social conditions of Inyo from a law and order standpoint" it made the misleading claim that with "litigation so small, and injuries so few, Inyo's condition has been exceedingly good."[17] At this early date, tourism and sport fishing were emphasized among the county's attractions to visitors and sought-after permanent residents.

Although we shall never know how many were actually lured by these collaborative efforts of business and local government, the people came. As table 5 shows, the years 1900 to 1910 enjoyed a 60 percent

TABLE 5. SELECTED MEASURES OF INYO COUNTY
DEVELOPMENT, 1900–1930

	1900	1910	1920	1930
Population, Inyo County	4,377	6,974	7,031	6,600
Population, Bishop	540	1,190	1,304	850
Number of farms	424	438	521	218
Farmland (acres)	141,059	110,142	140,029	94,567
Mean farm size (acres)	333	252	269	434
State average farm size (acres)	397	317	250	224
Percentage of farms owner occupied	76	82	80	40
State average percentage of farms owner occupied	61	76	74	82
Annual value of crops (ten-year average) ($)	394,846	532,643	1,503,195	245,507
Annual value of livestock (ten-year average) ($)	574,229	1,153,767	2,596,985	412,205
Annual value of mineral production (ten-year average) ($)	218,014	273,603	1,186,764	450,151
Population, Los Angeles	102,479	319,198	576,673	1,238,048

SOURCES: *Twelfth, Thirteenth, Fourteenth,* and *Fifteenth U.S. Census of Population* and *U.S. Census of Agriculture;* "Thirty-fourth Report of the State Mineralogist, California State Division of Mines," *California Journal of Mines and Geology* 34 (October 1938): 374–75.

increase in the county's population from 4,377 to 6,974, while the population of Bishop more than doubled. Indeed, growth was focused on the towns, as the number of farms remained fairly constant from 1900 to 1910 and then moved upwards slowly until 1920. The amount of acreage in farms actually declined in the first decade of the century because land was withdrawn from settlement by the federal government. The irrigated acreage (not shown in the table) rose from 41,000 to 65,000 acres between 1900 and 1920. Average farm size, which had been going up as a result of filings under the Desert Lands Act, began to drop from 1900 to 1910, probably because more minifarms were established in and around the towns by people who made their living in nonagricultural pursuits. The percentage of owner-occupied farms also dropped slowly, suggesting an increase in the number of tenants. From the earliest period of data collection, the value of agricultural produc-

Bishop in the 1920s. This 1921 photograph of Main Street shows continuing hopes for local prosperity. While the Interstate Telegraph office on the left maintained communications with the outside world, the Store for Women offered in its logo value, courtesy, and service. On the right, the Bishop Theatre advertised "Yes We Show All This. Never Less Than Seven Reels," and the sign above proclaimed "Owens Valley the Home of the Pear." (Courtesy of the Eastern California Museum.)

tion rose steadily until the 1920s. During the 1880s, as we saw in chapter 3, stock raising superseded crop production; although that pattern persisted in the twentieth century, both forms of production rapidly increased, especially from 1910 to 1920. The agricultural boom and the coincident surge in mineral production owed much to the effects of World War I on rising prices, though local factors were also at work.[18]

Finally, table 5 illustrates two dramatic changes that are the focus of this chapter. First, as Inyo County moved toward modest prosperity, a rapidly expanding Los Angeles loomed to the south as the nation's largest city west of Chicago by 1930. Second, following Inyo's early burst of prosperity, local development ended and decline set in during the 1920s. The first fact explains the second, but not without a long story.

STATE ENCROACHMENT AND AGRARIAN PROTEST

In 1902, on opposite sides of the country, two innovations of statecraft set in motion events that would soon transform the Owens Valley from a rural haven to a contested terrain of bureaucratic expansion. In February the City of Los Angeles regained public control over its water system, laying the foundation for what would become the nation's largest municipally owned utility. In June, the U.S. Congress passed Senator Francis Newlands's Reclamation Act, which provided for unprecedented government participation in the development of western water projects. In each instance the state, both federal and local, responded to the experience of several decades, which testified that only public responsibility could meet the complex capital and jurisdictional requirements of infrastructural development in the western United States.

The circumstances leading to the Newlands Act are representative of the state's expanding role in society at the turn of the century. Although federal intervention in the management of western lands was but one in a series of progressive state empowerments, it was arguably one of the most critical. "The concept of the welfare state edged into the American consciousness and into American institutions more through the scientific bureaus of government than by any other way, and more through the problems raised by the public domain than through any other problems."[19] Beginning in 1878, when John Wesley Powell published his cautious yet imaginative plan for the development of western "hydrographic basins," the problem of how to organize and finance irrigation projects brought together three sets of antagonistic parties: federal government scientists, who urged public responsibility; western cattle ranchers and the political representatives of eastern farmers, who opposed it; and land speculators and western politicians, who moved from skepticism to favor once their particular interests were satisfied.[20] Pressure for a federal solution mounted in 1891 following a severe drought, the collapse of private investment in irrigation schemes, and the convocation of the first National Irrigation Congress.

The early plans of Major Powell and Senator Newlands proposing federal works financed through public land sales were judged too radical by Congress. Yet the same interventionist principle, with significant compromises requiring fewer acreage limitations and less withdrawal of private land from speculation, was embraced in 1902 when the House passed the Reclamation Act (and established the U.S. Reclamation Service) by a vote of 146 to 55 with 150 abstentions. The shift is explained by chance and changing political structure. Following McKinley's assassination in 1901, Theodore Roosevelt brought to the Republican White House new energy for political reform, executive aggrandizement, and a personal enthusiasm for western irrigation.[21] Yet Roosevelt also stepped

a rural haven to a contested terrain of bureaucratic expansion. In February the City of Los Angeles regained public control over its water system, laying the foundation for what would become the nation's largest municipally owned utility. In June, the U.S. Congress passed Senator Francis Newlands's Reclamation Act, which provided for unprecedented government participation in the development of western water projects. In each instance the state, both federal and local, responded to the experience of several decades, which testified that only public responsibility could meet the complex capital and jurisdictional requirements of infrastructural development in the western United States.

The circumstances leading to the Newlands Act are representative of the state's expanding role in society at the turn of the century. Although federal intervention in the management of western lands was but one in a series of progressive state empowerments, it was arguably one of the most critical. "The concept of the welfare state edged into the American consciousness and into American institutions more through the scientific bureaus of government than by any other way, and more through the problems raised by the public domain than through any other problems."[19] Beginning in 1878, when John Wesley Powell published his cautious yet imaginative plan for the development of western "hydrographic basins," the problem of how to organize and finance irrigation projects brought together three sets of antagonistic parties: federal government scientists, who urged public responsibility; western cattle ranchers and the political representatives of eastern farmers, who opposed it; and land speculators and western politicians, who moved from skepticism to favor once their particular interests were satisfied.[20] Pressure for a federal solution mounted in 1891 following a severe drought, the collapse of private investment in irrigation schemes, and the convocation of the first National Irrigation Congress.

The early plans of Major Powell and Senator Newlands proposing federal works financed through public land sales were judged too radical by Congress. Yet the same interventionist principle, with significant compromises requiring fewer acreage limitations and less withdrawal of private land from speculation, was embraced in 1902 when the House passed the Reclamation Act (and established the U.S. Reclamation Service) by a vote of 146 to 55 with 150 abstentions. The shift is explained by chance and changing political structure. Following McKinley's assassination in 1901, Theodore Roosevelt brought to the Republican White House new energy for political reform, executive aggrandizement, and a personal enthusiasm for western irrigation.[21] Yet Roosevelt also stepped

into a broader current of state transformation. Beginning with the Populist Movement, a "crisis of electoral control" had plagued the Republican and Democrat parties for two decades. Politicians responded with "programs and popular appeals that could win business confidence as well as national elections . . . [at the same time] permitting a gradual accumulation of administrative powers in presidential hands."[22] In 1900, both parties courted western interests by including irrigation proposals in their national platforms.[23] Behind the electoral crisis, however, was a deeper reorganization of the state, a "search for order"[24] in an urban-industrial society now unmanageable with the instruments of nineteenth-century statecraft. "After 1900, the doors of power opened to those who saw a national administrative apparatus as the centerpiece of a new governmental order. . . . By transforming ideological conflicts into matters of expertise and efficiency, bureaucrats promised to reconcile the polity with the economy and to stem the tide of social disintegration."[25]

The only issue that concerned Los Angeles at the turn of the century was when the next boom would begin. After a period of dramatic expansion in the 1880s, when the city's population increased by $3\frac{1}{2}$ times, the next decade was comparatively slow—the population merely doubled (see table 5). As land developers and publicists went to work informing the world that "God made Southern California—and made it on purpose,"[26] the second of many booms occurred; the population tripled from 1900 to 1910. Nineteen-twenty saw more than a half-million residents, and the million mark was passed before the end of that decade. Yet in 1902 this expansion was far from assured. Local planners knew that the future of Los Angeles depended above all on a greatly expanded and permanent water supply.

Growth was a self-conscious plan in Los Angeles, the expressed ambition of city officials and entrepreneurial interests organized in the Merchants and Manufacturers Association. Their aim was to supplant the west-coast economic leadership of San Francisco, which symbolized boss rule and union corruption, by building a western mecca on the bedrock of good government and the open shop. If the dream depended on water, the reality focused on organization. The city had to reclaim its lease-holding private water company and create a public agency capable of raising big capital through bond issues and of entering into arrangements with other governmental units, because any augmentation of the local water supply would have to come from outside city and county boundaries.

The movement for municipalization did not spring from some early impulse toward progressive reform . . . [and] did not represent in Los Angeles a

wholesale rejection of free enterprise. Instead, the essential support for the movement came from the business community itself. The movement for municipalization emerged in the context of a greater effort by Los Angeles' business leaders to assert their independence in the stewardship of the city's social, political, and economic future.[27]

The key figure in the municipalization campaign was Fred Eaton, the son of a prominent local family and a water expert by virtue of his service as chief engineer for the private utility and his election to the office of city engineer in 1886. Eaton became chairman of the Republican City Central Committee, and in 1898 he was elected mayor; during his incumbency he completed the negotiations that created the Los Angeles Department of Water and Power (DWP). It is reasonable to assume that Eaton pursued municipalization with a specific plan in mind, as he was the first to propose the idea of a gravity-fed aqueduct stretching 240 miles from the Owens River to Los Angeles. Indeed, such was Eaton's interest in the project that some time between 1904 and 1905 he began taking options for himself on Owens Valley land that the city, if it adopted his plan, would have to purchase later.[28] "Eaton had turned to municipalization as a way to gain access to the far greater amounts of capital that public financing can provide. But he never conceived of the project as anything other than a private scheme that would work to his personal profit."[29]

As the newly created city utility and the federal agencies moved into the Owens Valley, the outlines of conflict began to appear. By spring 1903 the Reclamation Service was carefully scouting locations for its maiden projects, the success of which would shape the agency's political future. Engineering reports on the Owens Valley were highly favorable, estimating that a dam and reservoir could increase by two to three times both the amount of irrigated acreage and the value of agricultural production.[30] Learning of the proposed project from inquiring engineers and from the withdrawals of public land for potential construction, local citizens were reported "very favorable to government aid and the sentiment now seems to be strongly in favor of having the Reclamation Service assume full charge of all existing canals."[31] Meanwhile, however, Eaton and other Los Angeles agents were reconnoitering the same landscape, filing options, and, according to later accounts, even posing as Reclamation Service employees in order to gain a foothold for the city's veiled plan. As scandal eventually revealed, the conflicting projects were confounded in the intrigues of one man, Joseph Lippincott, who was both the chief of the key southwestern region for the

Reclamation Service and a private consultant to the city. Individual ambition and duplicity throve along with high-minded social planning, and the two projects became intertwined in the moral response of the citizenry as the conflict took shape. Local suspicions of treachery were aroused as private individuals filed options to purchase land in places where the reclamation project would naturally locate. Further investigation revealed the hand of Lippincott, and valley residents blamed city agents for undermining the federal project. Yet the seed of rebellion grew from the larger confrontation of two entrepreneurial bureaucracies whose conflicting designs urged the application of state means to the attainment of different political and economic ends.

As their fears of city meddling were steadily confirmed, local citizens turned naturally to traditional methods of political protest. The mobilization that began in 1904 responded to outside intervention initially on the basis of narrow class interests. Citizens were quick to penetrate the city's scheme and the threat it posed to the reclamation plan backed by most farmers. A petition drive was mounted "on official statements that it would be advantageous to show the people's attitude toward the proposed [Reclamation Service] project."[32] Appealing to the secretary of the interior, 380 signatories who controlled 104,242 acres wrote:

> We, the undersigned—the Poeple [sic] of the "Owens River Valley", Inyo County, State of California, in consideration of the fact that in this Valley we have a large body of arid land, both public and private, and this land by partial development has proven that it is possessed of more than ordinary fertility, and that the climatic conditions offer every inducement to thorough and prosperous habitation, and recognizing the fact that our limited means will not permit of the development of our water supply to its maximum efficiency, and also recognizing the urgent Need of the consolidation and systematizing of the existing rights and conditions for this efficient development, and further wishing to impress upon you the great benefit that will accrue to the poeple of the Owens River Valley in particular and to the poeple of the West in general from this development—do hereby earnestly petition and urge that the investigations and surveys now well under way, in this the "Owens Valley Project" be continued and prosecuted with all possible dispatch consistent with econemy [sic] to a point which will prove the merits of this Project.
>
> In consideration of the work already done we sincerely thank you and we will heartily cooperate with you in your efforts and will agree to the proper and just adjustment of existing rights and make all reasonable concessions consistent with equity and fairness.[33]

The language, if florid, was carefully chosen. The authors made it clear that the Owens Valley offered just the sort of project the Reclamation Service was looking for; efficient development would follow

from a public investment beyond the limited means of private citizens. Moreover, great benefit would result for the people of the region and the West. But, without mentioning Los Angeles or the southwestern chief, they stressed the urgent need to consolidate existing rights under the ambit of the federal project before something else might happen. The secretary did not reply, perhaps because he had already been informed by Lippincott of the city's plan and the choice that loomed.

The impending conflict became public on June 29, 1905, when the *Los Angeles Daily Times,* under the headline "Titanic Project to Give City a River," announced "the most important movement for the development of Los Angeles in the city's history." The announcement was not authorized by the city and was premature for the federal government, which was still deliberating whether to proceed with the reclamation project. The news galvanized all parties. In the valley mobilization turned to protest. A meeting in Bishop "attended by a large and enthusiastic assemblage" named a citizens' committee to organize the opposition and plead their case to Washington.[34] The nine-member committee requested an investigation by the secretary of the interior into the propriety of actions by the Reclamation Service.

> We, the members of the Citizen's Committee, appointed by the people of the Owens River Valley in mass meetings assembled, respectfully and earnestly petition that a thorough investigation be made of the proceedings of the Reclamation Service officers in connection with The Owens Valley Project. We believe that the officers of the Reclamation Service are, and have been, using their services to acquire the water rights of this valley for the City of Los Angeles instead of for the reclamation of arid lands. If this is accomplished it will mean the eventual ruination of this beautiful valley and conversion of the same into a barren waste of desert.[35]

The Citizens' Committee was composed almost entirely of modest agriculturalists. George Clarke, a farmer and member of the recently elected Bishop City Council, chaired the group. Only one committee member held a significant amount of land: Harry Shaw (the son of the cattle baron Frank Shaw, who owned 15,000 acres) was a middling stock raiser with 2,400 acres valued at $22,508. The rest were farm proprietors on a modest scale with holdings ranging from 120 to 760 acres, valued at $500 to $4,800.

Elected committee members were not the only ones moved to political action. Stafford W. Austin, Mary's husband at the time, wrote to President Roosevelt with an official protest that named the perfidious Lippincott as the culprit in the undoing of the federal project.

I am Register of the United States Land Office at this place [Independence]. In behalf of the people of this district I wish to protest against the proposed abandonment of the Owens River Project. The whole outrageous scheme is now made plain. Mr. Lippincott while drawing a large salary from the Government was employed by the City of Los Angeles [and] betrayed the Government by turning this important project over to the city. Will you in justice to the Owens River Project, and to the people of this district, see that this matter is thoroughly investigated. In the interests of fairness and of the honor of the Reclamation Service, I appeal to you not to abandon the Owens River Project.[36]

William Dehy, the district attorney of Inyo County, also writing on official stationery, appealed to the populist values he believed Roosevelt represented, noting that local aims were in harmony with

the policy of the administration to do its utmost toward enabling the plain everyday American to provide a home for himself and his family, [the policy that] stands for the peopling of the valleys and the conversions of the deserts into well watered valleys rather than the overcrowding of large cities. If the Government's reclamation project for this valley is abandoned in order that the City of Los Angeles may add to its wealth and population, it will mean the depopulation and devastation of the whole Owens River Valley for the thousand people who now have vested water rights, and homes here can not, in the very nature of things, withstand the encroachments of a large and wealthy city.[37]

Mary Austin, who would soon leave the valley for a celebrated literary career, published an elegant essay in the *San Francisco Chronicle* defining the value question as "how far it is well to destroy the agricultural interests of the commonwealth to the advantage of the vast aggregations of cities."[38] But the people spoke more vividly to the president through a farm woman from the hamlet of Poleta a few miles east of Bishop. Lesta Parker best expresses the guileless faith that homesteaders invested in the progressive administration.

Pres. Theodore Roosevelt
Washington D.C.

Dear Friend:

Look on your map of California, along the Eastern boundry south of Lake Tahoe and you will find a county named "Inyo". Running onto this county from Nevada through a small corner of Mono Co. you will see the Carson and Colorado R.R. which after it enters Inyo follows along the Owens River until they both come to Owens Lake, an alkiline body of water. It is about this river I write to you.

This river after it leaves the narrow mountain canon, runs through a broad and fertile valley for 100 miles. The first 20 miles of which is all or nearly so, in cultivation, further south ranches become more scattern. It has four prosperous towns.

Indeed the people are very very proud of thier little valley and what thier hard labor has made it. The towns are all kept up by the sourrounding farms. Alalafa is the principle crop. They put up to from two to four ton per acre and it cost from $1.25 to $1.75 to put it up and sell for $4 to $7 per ton, so you see the county is very prosperous. As there is about 200,000 ton raised in the valley if not more every year. Cattle raising is a great industry.

There never has been any capitolist or rich people come here until lately and all the farms of the Owens Valley show the hard labor and toil of people who came here with out much more than their clothes. And many had few of them.

Now my real reason for writeing this is to tell you that some rich men got the government or "Uncle Sam" to hire a man named J. B. Lippancott to repersent to the people that was going to put in a large damm in what is known as Long Valley. But—Lo! and Behold! Imagine the shock the people felt when they learned when Uncle Sam was paying Mr. Lippancott he was a traitor to the people and was working for a millionare company. The real reason for so much work was because a man named Eaton and a few more equaly low, sneaking, rich men wanted to get controling interest of the water by buying out a few or all of those who owned *much* water and simply "Freeze Out" those who hadn't much and tell them to "Git".

Now as President of the U.S. do you think that is right? And is there no way by which our dear valley and our homes can be saved? Is there no way by which 800 or 900 homes can be saved? Is there no way to keep the capitolist from forcing the people to give up their water right and letting the now beautiful alalafa feilds dry up and return to a barren desert waist?

Is there no way to stop this thievering? As you have proven to be the president for the people and not the rich I, an old resident who was raised here, appeal to you for help and *Advice*.

My husband and I with in the last year have bought us a home and are paying for it in hard labor and economy. So I can tell you it will be hard to have those rich men say "stay there and *starve*" or "Go". Where if we keep the water in the valley it won't be only 3 years until the place will pay for it self.

So Help The People of Owens Valley!

I apeal to you in the name of the Flag, the Glorious Stars and Stripes,

> Yours Unto Eternity,
> Lesta V. Parker.[39]

As the themes of protest suggest, the movement in 1905 was inspired by agrarian interests. Petitioners stressed the bountiful agricultural

achievements of the valley and its even greater potential with an irrigation project. Reflecting one aspect of the national progressive agenda, they stressed that Owens Valley would fulfill the Reclamation Act's intended purpose of efficient growth. Reflecting the closely related populist values, they dwelt on the benefits that would come to the plain everyday American devoted to converting western lands into prosperous small farms—an ideal aroused by the reform administration of Teddy Roosevelt. The virtues of rural life were compared with the pathology of overcrowded cities. The moral tenor rose when they turned to the wrong that needed righting, and the restoration of fair play that must follow the alleged betrayal of the public trust. Corruption stemmed from the city, but they had faith in the federal government. Citizens welcomed federal intervention as a solution to both the capital requirements for development and the city's threatened invasion. "We will heartily cooperate" with a fair and equitable government, they say, warning in the same breath that their survival is at stake.

Proper understanding of a popular movement requires that we analyze both its social bases and its political objectives as they are expressed in "languages of class. It is not a question of replacing a social interpretation by a linguistic interpretation, but rather it is how the two relate."[40] In their letters and public statements, Owens Valley citizens employed language that affirmed their right to the rewards of labor, and their expectation not only that the state would ensure fairness but that it should favor the little people devoted to building the West against acquisitive cities and capital. Pioneer communities and the state, in their view, cherished equality and property. These values were rooted in the movement's social base.

The social composition of the 1905 protest is presented in table 6. The occupations of the signers of the 1905 petition and the members of the Citizens' Committee were ascertained by looking up their names in the Inyo County tax assessment roll and the Great Register of voters, sources that provide, respectively, the value of property owned by and the occupations of all individuals residing in the county.

The social bases indicated in table 6 complement the movement's political agenda. Of the valley's working population, 41 percent were engaged in agriculture (farming and ranching), with a further 39 percent engaged in skilled trades, mining, and manual labor.[41] The occupations of signatories to the 1905 petition show a dramatically different pattern.[42] A resounding 80 percent were farmers and ranchers, with very few from the working class (skilled trades, mining, or labor); busi-

TABLE 6. OCCUPATIONAL STRUCTURE OF THE OWENS
VALLEY AND PROTEST PARTICIPANTS, CIRCA 1905

	Valley, 1908 (N = 1,250)[a]	Petition Signers, 1904 (N = 333)	Citizens' Committee, 1905 (N = 11)
Professional	4%	4%	18%
Commercial and managerial	5	5	0
Clerical and service	11	6	18
Farm and ranch	41	80	55
Skilled trades and mining	25	4	0
Labor	14	1	0
Housewife	—	—	9
Total	100%	100%	100%

SOURCES: Eastern California Museum, Index to the Great Register, Inyo County, 1908; National Archives, petition "To the Right Honorable Secretary of the Interior of the United States," 1905.

[a]In 1908 women did not have the vote and their exclusion from this enumeration produces some bias in the occupational structure. Moreover, the numerical total of male occupations in 1908 underestimates the economically active by approximately 150 due to missing data.

ness and the professions were represented approximately in their population proportions. The Citizen's Committee had a similar profile.[43]

Table 7 provides some useful additional data. The protesters closely resembled the general population in the amount of land they held and its assessed value. Their leaders in the Citizens' Committee, however, were clearly the more affluent farmers with mean holdings and assessed values double the rank-and-file figures; but the leaders were nevertheless middle class next to the large cattle ranchers. The somewhat higher property values of the protesters in comparison to the population doubtless reflects the greater mobilization in the Bishop area and the northern end of the valley, where prosperous irrigated farms were concentrated and where sentiment favoring the reclamation project was strongest. Generally, the 1905 protest expressed a political strategy aimed at rescuing the federal irrigation project, drew its support principally from middling agriculturalists in the northern region of the valley, and followed the lead of the more affluent among them. Resurgent

TABLE 7.   SOCIOECONOMIC CHARACTERISTICS OF THE
OWENS VALLEY AND PROTEST PARTICIPANTS, CIRCA 1905

	Valley, 1900	Petition Signers, 1905	Citizens' Committee, 1905
Mean size of landholding (acres)	317	301	621
Mean value of property assessment ($)	1,589	2,447	5,065

SOURCE: Eastern California Museum, Inyo County tax assessment roll, 1900.

commercial interests in the towns took little part in the controversy, perhaps because they saw promise in more intimate ties to Los Angeles.

Although Lesta Parker was advised by the acting secretary of the interior that "the matter will be carefully considered by this Department," the final decision to terminate the reclamation project issued from the president and his inner circle; the citizens "lost without ever having had the opportunity to have their representative present."[44] Echoing the progressive dictum of the greatest good for the greatest number, Roosevelt explained: "It is a hundred or a thousandfold more important to state that this [water] is more valuable to the people as a whole if used by the city than if used by the people of the Owens Valley."[45] The flaw in this reasoning, however, was that the choice was not either-or. Sylvester Smith, the congressional representative for Inyo County, had offered a compromise in which a reclamation project would give local needs first priority, with surplus water passed on to the city, but only for domestic use. Other compromises are easily conceived, such as city priority with some guaranteed allotment for valley farmers. But Los Angeles wanted all it could get.

Two political circumstances explain the city's determination. First, although the planned aqueduct was fully the responsibility of the Department of Water and Power (DWP) and its chief engineer, William Mulholland, the project enjoyed energetic support from Los Angeles business leaders, represented by the influential Merchants and Manufacturers Association. It is reasonable to assume that these interests had Eaton's confidence while he was laying the groundwork for a new water supply and had Mulholland's cooperation during subsequent reconnaissance of Owens Valley properties. Indeed, in November 1904, immediately after the Reclamation Service decided to suspend temporarily its work in the Owens Valley, a syndicate of important Los Angeles inves-

tors purchased 16,000 acres of land in the San Fernando Valley, the city's northern suburb where the aqueduct would terminate in a storage reservoir. The investors, who later profited handsomely when the San Fernando Valley was brought under irrigation, included Henry Huntington of the Pacific Electric Railway, E. H. Harriman of Union Pacific, W. G. Kerchoff of the Pacific Light and Power Company, Joseph Sartori of the Security Trust and Savings Bank, L. C. Brand of the Title Guarantee and Trust Company, Moses Sherman of the Los Angeles and Pacific Railway, E. T. Earl of the *Los Angeles Express,* and Harrison Gray Otis of the *Los Angeles Times.*[46] When Mulholland went to Washington, D.C., to deal with the compromise proposed by Congressman Smith, he took along the president of the Chamber of Commerce. As William Kahrl's detailed study of these maneuvers observes, in the relationship between the DWP and Los Angeles investors "[n]o conspiracy was necessary; their objectives were the same."[47] And other city interests would be served by the project, including those expressed by the voting public on subsequent bond issues.

Second, Los Angeles interests enjoyed direct and influential access to Roosevelt through California's Senator Frank Flint and the president's close friend and adviser, Forest Service chief Gifford Pinchott. The showdown on the reclamation project came in June 1906, when Flint's bill giving Los Angeles title to public lands for the aqueduct right-of-way was about to be reported out of the House Public Lands Committee with Smith's compromise amendment included. After a meeting with Flint and Pinchott, the president persuaded the House committee to delete the amendment and bring the bill to a prompt vote.

Histories of the Los Angeles–Owens Valley controversy look no further than the successful application of political influence by city interests to explain Roosevelt's decision. This overlooks the president's own ambitions and political strategy and the special part that California played in them. The Roosevelt administration met a national political crisis with efforts to expand the efficiency and administrative capacity of the state as it also endeavored to incorporate supportive constituencies. Roosevelt courted western interests with the Reclamation Act and courted urban reformers, especially in eastern machine cities, with progressive measures such as publicly owned utilities. Booming Los Angeles with its municipal water department was a trophy that the hunter's eye did not miss. "An avid aggrandizer, the president understood and encouraged those aggrandizing executive officials who sought to construct small empires out of the growing demand for public management."[48]

Roosevelt traveled often to California and especially admired the vigorous progressive movement in the state, itself "solidly arrayed . . .
behind a philosophy of massive public works to make possible the
urbanization of California."[49] If Roosevelt ever received the letters and
petitions from Owens Valley residents, they would have appeared poi-
gnantly trivial against the weight of political considerations favoring Los
Angeles. The Owens Valley fell neatly into a groove made for it by the
transformation of the state in the progressive era.

Protest was calmed, if not eliminated, when the aqueduct construction began in 1908, and it remained so for several years after the
project's completion in 1913.[50] (The route of the aqueduct is shown in
map 6.) Negotiations continued between the city and local committees
such as the informally constituted Owens Valley Associated Ditches,
later the Water Protective Association, comprised of the heads of local
canal companies. Initially they petitioned the federal government to
restore lands withdrawn from settlement for the aqueduct right-of-way.
Later they focused on the extent to which the valley might share in the
city's largesse: would the city build a storage reservoir from which
water could be drawn in amounts consistent with local growth, would
the city guarantee continued irrigation of 60,000 acres or some lesser
but assured amount, would the city deal with popularly chosen local
association representatives rather than exclusively with individual property holders? Although intricate maneuvers surrounded each point, the
valley won no tangible concessions in the years leading up to 1920.
Under no obligation or any real pressure, the city refused to adopt any
fixed policy guaranteeing the local future.[51] Nevertheless, these were
peaceful years; the city took only the excess surface water, and agriculture throve on the rising prices during World War I.

Stability rested on the city's commanding political position and federal backing. Locally, moreover, the 1905 protest had succumbed to
opportunism. The question became how to hitch local progress to the
city's rising star. Business representatives looked hopefully at evidence
that the aqueduct would stimulate the economy. Aqueduct construction
provided an important source of employment; although the crews were
provisioned from Los Angeles, the city required local co-operation. The
federal government had graciously provided the aqueduct right-of-way
over most of the 240-mile distance. But the channel also had to pass
through privately held land within the valley. In 1908, a number of
farmers and ranchers willingly offered their land, or parts of it, for sale
to the city. Among the sellers of 192 parcels were Irv Mulholland,

achievements of the valley and its even greater potential with an irrigation project. Reflecting one aspect of the national progressive agenda, they stressed that Owens Valley would fulfill the Reclamation Act's intended purpose of efficient growth. Reflecting the closely related populist values, they dwelt on the benefits that would come to the plain everyday American devoted to converting western lands into prosperous small farms—an ideal aroused by the reform administration of Teddy Roosevelt. The virtues of rural life were compared with the pathology of overcrowded cities. The moral tenor rose when they turned to the wrong that needed righting, and the restoration of fair play that must follow the alleged betrayal of the public trust. Corruption stemmed from the city, but they had faith in the federal government. Citizens welcomed federal intervention as a solution to both the capital requirements for development and the city's threatened invasion. "We will heartily cooperate" with a fair and equitable government, they say, warning in the same breath that their survival is at stake.

Proper understanding of a popular movement requires that we analyze both its social bases and its political objectives as they are expressed in "languages of class. It is not a question of replacing a social interpretation by a linguistic interpretation, but rather it is how the two relate."[40] In their letters and public statements, Owens Valley citizens employed language that affirmed their right to the rewards of labor, and their expectation not only that the state would ensure fairness but that it should favor the little people devoted to building the West against acquisitive cities and capital. Pioneer communities and the state, in their view, cherished equality and property. These values were rooted in the movement's social base.

The social composition of the 1905 protest is presented in table 6. The occupations of the signers of the 1905 petition and the members of the Citizens' Committee were ascertained by looking up their names in the Inyo County tax assessment roll and the Great Register of voters, sources that provide, respectively, the value of property owned by and the occupations of all individuals residing in the county.

The social bases indicated in table 6 complement the movement's political agenda. Of the valley's working population, 41 percent were engaged in agriculture (farming and ranching), with a further 39 percent engaged in skilled trades, mining, and manual labor.[41] The occupations of signatories to the 1905 petition show a dramatically different pattern.[42] A resounding 80 percent were farmers and ranchers, with very few from the working class (skilled trades, mining, or labor); busi-

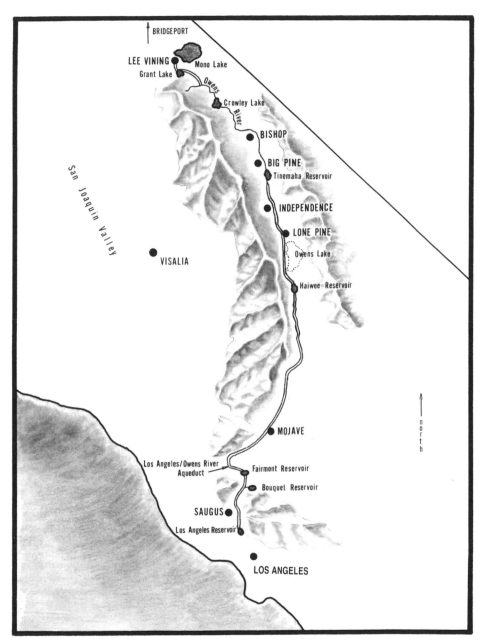

Map 6. Route of the Los Angeles Aqueduct. (Map by Lozano.)

former editor of the *Inyo Independent*, who sold 1,020 acres for $10,120; brewer John Lubkin, 240 acres for $5,300; realtor and County Assessor Ben Yandell, 440 acres for $4,080; farmer and merchant A. W. Eibeshutz, 160 acres for $900; and even banker Mark Watterson, who would later oppose city sales, but at this time received $8,700 for 440 acres.[52] The agrarian protest of 1905 foundered on the commercial hopes of a profitable partnership with Los Angeles.

REVOLT OF THE BURGHERS

Decisive troubles and a second stage of protest began in the summer of 1919. A serious drought prompted the city to begin tapping groundwater pumped from wells into the aqueduct, thereby dropping everyone's water table. The privately owned Southern Sierras Power Company followed suit by conserving its storage reserves for power generation and restricting the flow of irrigation water for local use. In a harbinger of renewed mobilization, "Citizens [took] Action to Save Their Crops."

> A delegation of probably fifty men went to Hillside Reservoir and raised the gates enough to permit the flow of 2500 inches into Bishop Creek. [After refusing to release the water themselves] Messrs. Katz and Rhudy of the Southern Sierras Power Co., a man at each elbow, [were] escorted out. Men at the gate then raised it, after which everybody sat in and had lunch. No damage was done to person or property.[53]

Although local newspapers failed to note the historical roots of this action, which repeated a scene from 1889, editorial opinion provided a pivotal interpretation of new purpose in the unrest: "The interests of every person, business or profession are those of the farmer. The sympathy of the community is solidly with the farmers. The backing of the community will be theirs."[54] Town interests, which failed to support the farmers in 1905 and even welcomed the aqueduct, now began to think through the full implications of city control over the water supply.

In the face of new uncertainties both sides adopted more aggressive strategies. Realizing its vulnerability to weather and local protest, the city began wholesale purchases of land, water rights, and ditch companies. City property acquisitions soared from a yearly half dozen or so to 104 in 1923 and 250 in 1924.[55] Residents alleged a "checkerboarding" pattern to the purchases, which focused on strategically located parcels and left other working farms cut off by city-owned abandoned plots and unmaintained canal sections. Although the city denied any such calculated plan behind the escalating purchases, the effect was the same. "A feeling of insecurity has long pervaded the area: ranch improvements were curtailed and finally ceased, real estate values declined until property, both town and rural, was unsaleable; business as well as farming stagnated."[56]

Renewed mobilization in the valley was energized by the threat not only that agriculture would suffer, but also that city purchases would depopulate the farms, stifle local banking and commerce, and ultimately destroy the towns. The new movement began to coalesce around two objectives: to restrain city purchases of individual farms and to ensure the conditions of continued agricultural production.

Desperately needing an organizational vehicle for their protest, in the spring of 1922 citizens set out to establish an irrigation district based on an innovative application of California state law. The Wright Irrigation Act of 1887 authorized formation of irrigation districts as special units of local government where a majority of landowners in an area obtained the approval of the county board of supervisors and two-thirds of the electorate within the affected boundaries. Under the Wright Act and in common practice, irrigation districts provided a collectively beneficial alternative to the riparian rights doctrine, which grants priority use to property owners along the banks of a waterway. Democratically sanctioned irrigation districts were given the authority to distribute water among all landowners in a river basin through the powers of eminent domain, taxation, and bond sales for the construction and maintenance of irrigation works. In the Owens Valley, of course, co-operative ditch companies had accomplished the latter well in advance of the legislation. In 1922 a new use for the irrigation district was conceived. The idea was to unite all property owners and canal companies in a single legal association that could bargain exclusively with the city over land sales and water rights. The novelty of the proposed Owens Valley Irrigation District was that it would include owners of town lots, and their water rights, in association with farmers and ranchers.

Petitions signed by four hundred registered voters qualified the measure for a vote. Local festivals played their traditional part in the new cause. At the Fourth of July picnic that year, for example, experts on the formation and operation of irrigation districts were brought in from the San Joaquin Valley, and their informative presentations were followed by a political rally on behalf of the ballot measure. The proclaimed virtues of an autonomous and freely elected property owners' associa-

Keough's Hot Springs. Panoramic view of the popular resort south of Bishop. Keough's Hot Springs was the site of Farm Bureau and Fourth of July picnics, events that were used to mobilize the community behind the Owens Valley Irrigation District in the early 1920s. Owner Karl Keough was also a rancher, merchant, and a leader of the resistance movement. (Mendenhall Collection, courtesy of the Eastern California Museum.)

tion with legal standing blended nicely with the Independence Day celebrations. A ballot in December 1922 approved the district by a margin of 599 to 27, and a further ballot in August 1923 authorized it to issue bonds by a vote of 702 to 80.[57] The new movement was launched with the support of 90 to 95 percent of the electorate, an outcome "better than the most sanguine had ventured."[58]

Now the water war began in earnest. In reprisal for the successful irrigation district elections, city crews began reclaiming water for the aqueduct by breaking dams and canal heads.[59] Early in 1924, Los Angeles unsuccessfully sought an injunction in the Inyo County Superior Court to prevent the sale of irrigation district bonds. The injunction was requested by two minor characters in the conflict evidently acting for a trio of city allies who opposed the Watterson brothers' unrivaled leadership of the local movement: the attorney L. C. Hall; the large-scale property owner William Symons; and George Watterson, the uncle and banking rival of Mark and Wilfred.[60] By far the most threatening offensive, however, was the city's accelerating campaign to buy up farms and water rights in enough locations to isolate irrigation district members who held out against selling their properties.

Keough's Hot Springs, Interior. (Mendenhall Collection, courtesy of the Eastern California Museum.)

As the resolve of both sides stiffened, the shoots of desperation appeared. Drought and falling agricultural prices brought general hard times. City purchases engendered bitterness toward those who sold out. Many were uncertain about which way to go—whether to accept or reject an attractive city offer for their farms. Litigation over water rights and pumping increased as both sides sought an ally in the courts. The Hillside Reservoir action led to a water allotment decision partly favoring the farmers; but the court refused to forbid groundwater pumping for export on city land.[61] Broader negotiations were stalled, with the city unwilling to recognize the irrigation district or announce a definite policy on any matter concerning the valley's future, such as a storage dam or a guarantee of irrigated acreage.

Protest mobilization spread in proportion to the growing threats. "The Inyo County Federation of Women's Clubs has been for several weeks working quietly but efficiently to bring the water situation before the club women of Los Angeles."[62] The Bishop Business Women's Club listed its "grievances against the city of Los Angeles in regard to the all absorbing topic, The Water Question":

First—The almost complete standstill of all trade in our community.
Second—The depreciation of property values.
Third—The threatening future which may bring failure to those of us who own a business, and
Fourth—The loss of employment by those who work for others.

We feel that these mental evils, which have been produced by the unfair acts and dealings of the city of Los Angeles, are having a demoralizing effect, not only on the men and women of the community, but on the minds of our boys and girls.[63]

A. B. Whieldon, who owned the Owens Valley Land Company, said "I have been unable to continue my work here, being compelled to look elsewhere for saleable lands." The Bishop Farm Loan Association claimed that the Federal Land Bank of Berkeley had told them "that owing to the uncertain conditions involving the Owens Valley Irrigation District from purchases by the city of Los Angeles, . . . loans would be suspended."[64] Economic and town life were suspended as doubt increased. Investment was withheld. Federal agencies refused valley war veterans the loan benefits to which they were entitled, citing economic uncertainty in the region. Local lending stopped, real estate stagnated save for the city's bidding, farm production dropped, and schools began to close.

Anger over the city's efforts to undermine the irrigation district literally exploded in May 1924, after Los Angeles filed a lawsuit against four canal companies (deliberately ignoring the irrigation district) and a long list of individual farmers that included virtually every water user in the northern valley. The suit claimed that all users above the aqueduct intake on the Owens River between Independence and Lone Pine were wrongfully diverting water to which the city was entitled by its purchases of all or parts of several canal companies during the previous year. Exasperation overwhelmed the resistance movement. In the resisters' view the action was "brought mainly for the purpose of demoralizing this county, frightening the people, and depressing land values." Springing from their deepest cultural reflex, one response summarized their outrage: "The defendants in this case, the water owners and users of this section, are the men who helped build the west."[65] Although the prose of the Big Pine Herald editor Harry Glasscock often ran to histrionics, this time it proved prophetic. On May 21 a huge explosion ripped a hole in the aqueduct.

This first dynamite assault on the Los Angeles aqueduct symbolized a shift from conventional protest to open revolt. During the following months a new mix of strategies evolved, with the aqueduct as its attention-getting centerpiece. Throughout the summer local activists rallied at mass meetings and gathered in late-night strategy sessions at the home of Wilfred Watterson. They wanted to press Los Angeles to accept the irrigation district as the valley's sole bargaining agent; later they met to plan a desperate appeal for state intervention in the controversy.

Under fire, the city's Public Service Commission shifted perceptibly. To prevent further protest the city would halt land purchases in an "exempt zone" surrounding Bishop, provided a full aqueduct was maintained. The city would allow no status to the irrigation district in acquisitions elsewhere. A large meeting at the high school auditorium with Wilfred Watterson presiding denounced the plan as simply a continuation of "the policy heretofore followed of acquiring water and water lands in Inyo County by dealing with us as individuals and not as a community." Alternatively, valley representatives attempted to move the dispute on to broader terrain by cultivating support from the Los Angeles Chamber of Commerce. Watterson's proposal to the chamber acknowledged that the city might justifiably buy out most of the valley and suggested that "the owners of the lands and water are willing to leave determination of values of this property to a 'Valuation Commission' composed of not less than five disinterested business men to be mutually agreed upon."[66]

It is not true, as some writers have claimed, that the resistance movement was mainly interested in pushing up the price of the land with the intention of selling for big profits at the right time. The pervasiveness of this judgement in recent and otherwise justifiably popular books requires special note. Kevin Starr, for example, despite citing sources that argue the contrary, observes that "most Owens Valley farmers, led by the banker brothers Wilfred and Mark Watterson, preferred a windfall over a lifetime of toil. Long since out-maneuvered by Los Angeles and the pro–Los Angeles policies of Washington, they understandably wanted out on favorable terms."[67] In 1924, frustrated by the city's failure to respond to any proposal, the movement did pose the dramatic choice that Los Angeles *either* restore the valley's agricultural potential *or* buy all the offered farms at prices determined by an independent commission. Nevertheless, as long as the movement was united, most of its actions were aimed at ensuring the first alternative. As in any community, some wanted out and were doubtless happy to sell, but most did not sell at this time,[68] despite the city's attractive prices. As the effort and numerical support behind the irrigation district suggest, their preference was clearly to live and prosper in the valley. If their fight could not secure that objective, then it would settle for no less than a fair and independently determined financial settlement. The Farm Bureau formulated the most complete version of the proposal and presented it to city officials through the Chamber of Commerce.

> It is deplorable that the farmers of any community should have to continually fight the encroachments of any large city. If the city must have the water, and it seems that such is the case, what wiser plan would there be than to make preparations to buy out the entire valley, not at your price, not at our price, but at a reasonable price fixed by a competent board of appraisers. In no other way can the city give justice to the people of the valley, unless it be to restore it to its development of two years ago, and to carry on a constructive program, believing that there is enough water to properly irrigate the Owens Valley and to supply the San Fernando Valley and the City of Los Angeles. . . . We recommend either the complete purchase of the valley at a fair valuation or the institution of a program which will bring the proper agricultural development of the Owens Valley.[69]

The Public Service Commission called the proposal greedy speculation and simply repeated its previous position with the specification that the exempt zone might include 30,000 acres. Locally this was seen as merely a "continuance of past unfair and destructive methods."[70] In mid-November a special committee of the commission met with Bishop representatives, but with no new ideas and to no avail—"the same old bunk" according to the *Independent*.[71] Six months of political maneuvering within legal limits had produced nothing. The pent-up movement was at an impasse.

At dawn on Sunday November 16, 1924, seventy men from Bishop, led by Wilfred Watterson, drove south in a caravan of Model T Fords and took possession of the Los Angeles Aqueduct at the Alabama Gates spillway. Among the insurgents was an engineer and former aqueduct employee recruited to open the hydraulically operated gates and remove the assorted handles and levers with which normal operation could be restored. Within hours a crowd of several hundred gathered to watch the city's water supply cascade down the open spillway onto the desert floor. This was a bold and risky effort to create an event of such notoriety that the governor, on receiving preplanned requests from the county sheriff and the district attorney, would be forced to send the state militia to oust the trespassers and restore order, thereby publicizing the extremity of local conditions. The valley story would finally be told in a forum beyond the city's control. Progressives in their own way, the insurgents believed that state intervention and public opinion would produce a just settlement. It was, in any case, the only move left to them.

At first, the publicity gambit seemed to work. Newspapers as far

Occupation of the Los Angeles Aqueduct. On the Sunday morning of November 16, 1924, a group of about seventy local citizens took control of the aqueduct at the Alabama Gates control house and diverted the city's water supply through the spillway into the dry bed of the Owens River. This wide-angle photo shows the insurgents along the canal (which is obscured behind them) and the control house at the top, their automobiles in the middleground, and the much-tracked sand and full spillway in the foreground. (Courtesy of the Eastern California Museum.)

away as Paris reported the occupation. The *Literary Digest* coined the phrase "California's Little Civil War" and suggested that national eyes were on Los Angeles and that its reputation for "decent dealing" now hung in the balance.[72] Even the *Los Angeles Daily Times* took a sympathetic view of the rebels.

> At the foot of the Alabama hills . . . are grouped 100 or more automobiles, dust ladened and bearing the scars of long arduous journeys over mountains and deserts. Others are continually joining in groups, coming from the Inyo hills to the eastward, from Independence, Big Pine and Bishop from the northward, from Lone Pine and the desert stretches southward.
>
> Who are these people who have hurled the boldest of defiance at the officials of Los Angeles? Grouped around at the dozen camp fires are several women, sturdy women with bronzed faces and hands calloused by household toil. They are the women of Bishop, wives of ranchers, Bishop's leading business and professional men who have taken upon themselves the big job of feeding scores of Owens Valley men who have opened the flood gate.
>
> The city can afford to be liberal in its settlement with these pioneers whose work of half a century it will undo.[73]

The insurgent's plot was enacted in most scenes save the finale. The mood at the spillway turned festive as several hundred supporters

Full Aqueduct, Looking South. On their arrival, the initial occupying force raised the American flag as a symbol of their struggle for the rights of a frontier community, and posed for the camera before opening the spillway. (Courtesy of the Eastern California Museum.)

Dry Aqueduct, Looking North. Within a day the deep channel was empty, and the "army of occupation" had grown to several hundred. (Courtesy of the Eastern California Museum.)

Peace Put Under Way in War Over City's Aqueduct

Ranchers of Owens Valley "Sitting Tight"

CAMP AT AQUEDUCT GATE IS CENTER OF FAMILY LIFE

Some Women Cook for Watchers While Others Care for Tots; Girls Form Orchestra

BY OTIS M. WILES
"Times" Staff Correspondent
[EXCLUSIVE DISPATCH]

ALABAMA CONTROL GATE, LOS ANGELES AQUE-DUCT, Nov. 19.—Through the Alabama control gate, the strategic position on the Los Angeles Aqueduct, between Independence and Lone Pine, a stream of flowing water is rushing down into the waste land of the Owens River bed today. Above the gate the turbulent mountain stream is dashing southward. But at this point it veers to the east and the huge concrete ditch is drained. Not a drop is following on its intended course.

At the foot of the Alabama hills, said by geologists to be the oldest mountain formation on the continent—even older than the Sierras—are grouped 100 or more automobiles, dun-laden and bearing scars of long arduous journeys over mountains and deserts. Others are continually joining in groups, coming from the Inyo hills to the eastward, from Independence, Big Pine and Bishop from the northward, from Lone Pine and the desert stretches to the southward.

Who are these people who have hurled the boldest of defiance at the officials of Los Angeles who guard the destinies of the city's water supplies and its source?

Grouped around at the dozen camp fires are several women, sturdy women with bronzed faces and hands calloused by household toil. They are the women of Bishop, wives of ranchers, Bishop's leading business and professional men who have taken upon themselves the big job of feeding the scores of Owens Valley men who have opened the flood gate. Among them is Mrs. Eva Glasscock, the kindly woman in khaki breeches and mountain boots, who is chief of the commissary.

Mrs. Glasscock is the wife of Harry A. Glasscock, publisher of the Owens Valley Herald and the Inyo Independent. Each morning at 7 o'clock she drives to the control gate from Bishop, fifty-seven miles to the northward, and drives back again at 9 p.m. Today, in addition to superintending the feeding of the men, Mrs. Glasscock also admitted running an issue of her husband's paper off the press. "And all of us have kiddies to take care of and feed and send to school," she said.

The barbecue has just ended. It has lasted all the afternoon. Mrs. Glasscock and her women helpers had charge of it. Bishop declared a holiday. Practically all of the town places of business were closed. The business men were at the head gate, and signs on their locked doors said so. They donated the food and they have been doing so since the gate was first "captured," and they intend to do so until an amiable settlement is reached.

The Bishop butchers supplied the meat, the Bishop bakers donated the bread and the Bishop grocers donated the other food, and fifty Bishop women each made a pie.

The barbecue ended, 350 residents of Owens Valley congregated in groups about the scene. Here was Sheriff "Charlie" Collins gnawing at a big chunk of barbecued meat. And these were the people who elected him.

Over there "Cop" John Fishman is sitting on a rock and talking to the boys. "Cop" Fishman was one of the earliest settlers in Owens Valley. He came here back in '68 with a twenty-mule team that con-

sumed eighteen days on the trip. He admits having trouble with naked Indians and tells a vivid tale of the quake of '72 in Owens Valley, when twenty-six persons were killed and when the Owens River was shaken a mile off its original course. "Cop" Fishman says his neighbors here at the head gate are right and he says he will stick with them to the finish—whatever the finish may be.

"The river used to be ours," he said, "the Aqueduct took it away, and now the ranchers are all dry."

Over here, by one of the improvised tents used as sleeping quarters for the men, stands "Doc" Boody, one of Bishop's physicians. He is looking after the physical condition of the men who remain night and day on the scene. Through the desert heat of the day and the chilly night.

"I came here nine years ago to live, after everybody said I was going to die," he said, "and this is the only place on earth I can live in and I'm going to remain living here until I die a natural death. They can't drive me out."

And weaving in and about among the groups of bronzed men, smiling women and laughing children is Rev. E. E. Schoffler, "the fighting parson" of Owens Valley. The "fighting parson" is pastor of the Bishop Baptist Church. Where his entire congregation is found, there he will be found also, he declares. He is carrying on, in visioning the day when peace, harmony and prosperity will once more visit Owens Valley, although it be a distant day.

The "fighting parson" has brought down an armload of song books. He has passed them among the 350 ranchers that cling to the Alabama hillside.

An orchestra with several khaki-clad girls dragging drums and musical instruments with them, climbing up the slope a chord or two is sounded and 350 lusty throats join in the singing of "Onward, Christian Soldiers," the song sweeping across the barren Owens Valley and re-echoing against the tinted Inyo hills of the east.

Mid-day passes, the sun dips behind the suncrest of the high Sierras. Long shadows creep across the valley as chilly winds, kissed by the snows, slip down from the mountain heights. Dusk settled and the determined ranchers remained at their posts. Bonfires began to grow on the hill sites, and a welcome aroma of hot coffee drifts across mesquite stretches and the overall ranchers remain on into the night.

Darkness descends and the women folks, wearied by their day's toil feeding their men—the guardian of their homes—join their husbands about the fires. Some are nestling their babies, others are "feeding" a phonograph with operatic selections.

And the men of the Alabama toll gate remain on. Talking quietly in groups and never asking—how long?

Los Angeles Daily Times, November 20, 1924. After four days, *Times* photographers had been to the occupation site and returned home with their film. Photographic layouts and stories described the picnic at Alabama Gates, portraying the encampment of "350 ranchers" as a center of family life, entertainment, and local solidarity. (Courtesy of the *Los Angeles Times.*)

joined the trespassers in the excitement and solidarity against anticipated retaliation. "Civil war feared" said one Los Angeles newspaper.
The county sheriff, a friend and sympathizer, appeared with the oblig-
atory order to desist and began recording names for summonses. But
the rebels declined his request, explaining that they would occupy the
gates "until we gain our point," and many, to affirm their participation,
told the sheriff, "Put my name down" on the list. When the county's
Superior Court Judge Dehy was pressed by Los Angeles officials to issue
arrest warrants, he disqualified himself in the case, citing a personal
interest. No arrests were made. Local law was with the rebels.

By the third day of the picnic at Alabama Gates, seven hundred
people had joined in. Most came from Bishop, fifty miles to the north,
where a professionally painted billboard posted at the principal intersection read: "If I am not on the job you can find me at the Aqueduct."
Recruits spelled each other in night-long vigils, training searchlights on
the highway approach from Los Angeles. Neighbors brought food. The
fourth day featured a grand barbecue provisioned by Bishop grocers
and a rancher who cabled Karl Keough "aboard the aqueduct" to say
that some "cattle are just north of you across the ditch. Tell Jim to
collect the fat ones for your barbecue. You are welcome as long as they
last."[74] Western movie star Tom Mix, who was filming in the near
Alabama Hills, brought his crew and a Mariachi band. The *Los Angeles
Daily Times,* underestimating the crowd at 350 participants, nevertheless observed: "Owens Valley Ranchers Picnic as Water is Wasted";
"Camp at Aqueduct is Center of Family Life—Some Women Cook for
Watchers While Others Care for Tots"; and "Girls Form Orchestra."[75]
Behind their festivities, however, local citizens demonstrated a resolute
purpose to defend their community and way of life.

Governor Friend Richardson upset the rebel plan by refusing to send
the state militia as requested by Inyo County Sheriff Collins, Superior
Court Judge Dehy, and District Attorney Hession—sympathizers all.
But the governor did agree to a special investigation by State Engineer
W. F. McClure. McClure's report, published in December, concluded:

The opening of the gates was a most popular move. Men, women, and
children were there, 500 to 800 or more in number. Business and professional men left homes and businesses and repaired to the place, some five
miles or so north of Lone Pine. The people of the valley were as a whole
drawn closer together in sentiment during those four days than they have
been in years. Is it consistent or reasonable to expect an American community of 3000 or more souls so united in sentiment to be content with the

seemingly determined program of a city situate [sic] 200 or more miles away being put into operation without protest?[76]

As a partisan and editor of the *Inyo Register*, W. A. Chalfant spoke for the insurgents, stressing the broad support enjoyed by the insurrection at Alabama Gates and its roots in an "American community . . . driven to the defense of its rights."

> Inyo's public buildings would not have been large enough to hold those who [would have] stepped forward to take the places of whoever might be taken from the scene. Nobody at the aqueduct was unwilling to share the penalties of his neighbors—and nobody there had the least idea of tamely standing punishment for defending his livelihood and home. There was not a firearm on the hill; but any attempt to force eviction by an authority except on the people's own terms would have meant bloody battle. Nor would that have been all; beyond question it would have meant a blow to the aqueduct that would have dwarfed all earlier happenings. For do you think that men who have been driven to the last ditch by schemers who have openly said they would get the property for half price would lay down? There were men on the hill at the spillway who practically face ruin because of the city's machinations; men who are seeing the work of a lifetime destroyed. These men and women are Americans of one of the most thoroughly American communities in California—add that to your other information about those whom mouthpieces of the city officials term "mob," "anarchist," and so on. They are people intelligent, well informed, resolute and determined. I have written "they," make it "we," for this community has no division in this matter.[77]

On the morning of the fifth day the occupation ended without the desired intervention of the militia or immediate concessions from the city. The rebels did at least receive the publicity they sought and official attention. The governor and an influential bankers' association in Los Angeles, moved by the city's embarrassment from favorable publicity for the threatened "pioneers," offered to mediate the dispute with the Los Angeles authorities. Yet in the end nothing was settled. With the pressure off, the city stepped up its purchases of farms and town lots from an average of 250 a year in 1924 and 1925 to 450 in 1926.[78] In response, the aqueduct—now guarded by private police in the city's employ—was bombed repeatedly during the next three years.

Twenty years of protest and disappointment had transformed the Owens Valley political agenda. Evolving from its agrarian origins of 1905, the resistance movement of the 1920s spoke in a more universalistic language based above all on the values of community. The early protest themes of populism and agricultural productivity were transformed into more inclusive sentiments that stressed the mutual interests of town and country, farm and business, community survival, and a way of life. Encouraging support for the irrigation district, the *Inyo Register* set the new mood: "Let us set aside all considerations of individual squabbles and relative rights and unite on the great issue of keeping for the Owens Valley, to be adjusted among ourselves, the water which by nature and justice belongs to it. Give the irrigation district your support. Any other attitude will be that of individualism rather than for the community; and in the end, what is best for the whole community is best for the individual interest."[79] The irrigation district attempted with some success to promote collective solidarity by discouraging individual property sales and electing a representative committee to act as the bargaining agent for town and country proprietors in dealings with the city.

The political program of the early 1920s was measured and pragmatic, in contrast to the sentiment and bombast of public statements in the 1905 protest. Town and farm groups that formed the alliance endeavored, first, to constitute themselves as a legitimate public entity under state law. The irrigation district was formally established by popular vote; its elected board of directors, headed by Wilfred Watterson, mapped the strategy for the resistance movement. The innovative political purpose was to appropriate the instrumentalities of the state itself, rather than to fight as a solitary interest group. With their vehicle empowered, local activists next put forth a program of moderation. They sought guarantees that they would be included on the rising tide of city development. Their principal demands included city construction of a storage reservoir; local preference for irrigation water before its export; a guaranteed allotment of irrigated acreage; recognition of the irrigation district's authority over land sales and broad policy issues; and, if all else failed, a promise that the city would buy all valley land and water rights in one purchase for a sum determined by independent appraisal. The last proposal led detractors in Los Angeles to charge the resistance movement with cynical speculative motives hidden behind their public appeals for justice. Although the charge reveals something about the city's obsession with speculative development, a bloc sale at this time was not a live option, and valley strategists invested the great majority of their effort and hope in attaining some workable compromise. Speculative ends would have suggested a set of political means very different from those the defenders of community actually adopted. And even though city prices were reasonably good, people did not sell en masse as long as the resistance movement continued. Although the salience of the various demands shifted over time, the principle was always the same. Los Angeles would have to deal fairly with the valley's legitimate representatives united in the irrigation district.

Yet, beyond this forceful assertion of principle, local ambitions were moderate and disposed to compromise. The requirements of urban expansion were never questioned, and after 1905 the city's right to surplus Owens Valley water was not an issue. The only proviso was that urban growth not be accomplished at the cost of local ruin. The Bishop Chamber of Commerce spoke for everyone when it said:

> We recognize and admit the importance of an ample water supply for a great and growing city, and the further fact that Los Angeles has been compelled, to a considerable extent, to look to Owens Valley for that supply.
>
> We do not admit the justice, however, of such domestic and municipal use being made the excuse for despoiling fertile farm acreage of one section in order that the territory nearer the city could be built up whether for the benefit of speculators or for other reasons, and particularly when this could have been avoided.[80]

Reasonable or not, Los Angeles and the DWP under William Mulholland would concede none of these points. The city's strategy was to humor the resistance movement with protracted negotiations over its demands, particularly the question of a dam and storage reservoir, while simultaneously undermining its solidarity with individual property purchases. City intransigence is best explained by the absence of any constraint to compromise. The federal government had long since granted the right to exploit the valley, and the State of California had declined to get seriously involved in what was conveniently defined as an interjurisdictional dispute. Also, the city was looking far into the future, to a time when it would need all of the water. As the plan of piecemeal land acquisition went forward in the Owens Valley, city officials were commuting to Washington, D.C., for negotiations on the Boulder Canyon project and another aqueduct from southern Nevada to Los Angeles. And there were human facets to the conflict. Former friends William Mulholland and Fred Eaton were at odds over the latter's scheme to profit from the sale of land he had acquired at the proposed site of the storage reservoir. Mulholland, the single greatest influence in water policy, preferred the valley's demise to Eaton's enrichment at city expense.[81]

Try as they might, members of the irrigation district could make no headway against these obstacles to compromise. Intrepid acts designed to publicize the injustice of it all became their only recourse. Each instance of property violence was preceded by a collapse of hopeful initiatives for local self-determination. The May 1924 aqueduct bombing followed immediately on a city lawsuit that thwarted water diversions by the canal companies, now constituents of the irrigation district. The occupation of Alabama Gates was precipitated by a completely unsatisfactory counterproposal to local insistence on irrigated acreage guarantees and the storage reservoir.[82] The reluctant rebels acknowledged their problem. In December 1924, Mark Watterson wrote to Mary Austin, requesting help:

> We are having a desperate struggle against the City and the only weapon we have is publicity, and that is about the only thing the City of Los Angeles seems to fear.
>
> If you could have an interview with the representatives of the Associated Press and give them a strong statement of your views . . . under the heading of something like this:
>
> > MARY AUSTIN TAKES UP THE CAUSE OF THE OWENS VALLEY RESIDENTS AGAINST THE GREAT CITY OF LOS ANGELES
>
> I believe it would do us an immense amount of good.[83]

Years later, *Inyo Register* editor W. A. Chalfant confided to Mary Austin, "that incident at the spillway became almost 'a shot heard 'round the world.' I have always held it to be a justifiable advertising move, though I did not support the subsequent dynamitings that occurred."[84] The rebels wanted to force the city to negotiate, and their only means became appeal to public opinion which, they hoped, would somehow enforce their rights. It was the only avenue left.

VIOLENCE AND POLITICS

The early years were remarkably free of violence. As the resistance movement grew and broadened its social base, the protest repertoire was adapted from local tradition and was flexibly combined with innovations.[85] The occupation at Alabama Gates reenacted the collective methods for enforcing popular justice developed by vigilance committees and co-operative ditch companies. The customary petition drives and town meetings, sometimes convened at fairs and holiday picnics, provided the means for creating a new kind of irrigation district. The district and the courts were then used to redefine the city-county struggle as a dispute between equals before the law.

Violence in the service of popular justice was a well-developed local tradition (as the history of arson shows) but it was banished from the protest repertoire during the first twenty years of the water war. When the Hillside Reservoir gate was opened in June 1919 by fifty members of the Bishop Creek Water Association, for example, workers at the scene were "escorted out . . . after which everyone sat in and had lunch."[86] Los Angeles first introduced property violence in response to organizing victories by the irrigation district. "In the summer of 1923 representatives of the city of Los Angeles dynamited the dam at Convict Lake, above all the ditches, in order to break the ditches on the Eaton Ranch in Long Valley, forcibly doing this in order to get more water for their impoverished aqueduct."[87] In at least one instance of ditch breaking, residents mobilized to defend their property after city crews cut a canal and diverted its flow into the aqueduct.

Rifles Protect Big Pine Canal

On Monday night a competent force of guards put an injunction on [the diversion] by locating at the scene, fully armed and determined that it should not be made.[88]

In the early hours of Wednesday, May 21, 1924, the resistance movement took the violent offensive by dynamiting the aqueduct just below the Alabama Gates. Although the city estimated the damage at $25,000, most of that in water lost during a two-day shutdown for repairs, the blast was less effective than planned. The force of several hundred pounds of exploding dynamite lifted a huge boulder alongside the channel, but most of the debris fell back into the hole. Private detectives hired by the city and the metropolitan "wobbly squad" dispatched to the scene reported evidence of an elaborate attack. The area was covered with footprints and tire tracks suggesting to the sleuths that fifty participants had been involved. The dynamite was supposed to have come from a warehouse in Laws owned by the Wattersons. Investigators claimed that witnesses reported a caravan of eleven automobiles originating in Bishop on the previous evening and passing through Big Pine to gather supporters along the way. Within a day of their arrival detectives were telling reporters that forty to sixty people were involved, of whom seventeen were already identified.

Despite these confident claims, detective Jack Dymond working for the Los Angeles district attorney complained that local sentiment was obstructing the investigation.[89] Dymond predicted that the culprits would never be brought to trial because no local grand jury would indict, and no court convict them. Los Angeles offered a $10,000 reward and gamely speculated that the federal government would soon enter the case because the saboteurs had short-circuited interstate telephone lines to make good their escape.

Theories about the responsible parties proliferated in the early aftermath, many the invention of urban reporters. The *Los Angeles Examiner* had it narrowed down to maniacs, anarchists, or Wobblies. The latter possibility was endorsed by the *Los Angeles Times* on the strength of rumors about a "known Red leader" who had been fired from his job on the aqueduct. The water department suspected "spite workers" based on the dynamiters' intimate knowledge of the aqueduct and where a charge would do the most harm. More intriguingly, Los Angeles District Attorney Asa Keyes theorized a plot enacted by valley dissidents in the service of city private interests opposed to municipal ownership. Efforts by valley representatives to cultivate support from business groups in Los Angeles fed this surmise.[90] But much of this speculation faded as the city's well-publicized investigation revealed local actions and motives.

> According to the evidence now in the hands of the authorities most of the men implicated in the dynamiting plot came from points north of Big Pine, while a few are thought to have been recruited in Big Pine and a few from the rim of the desert. All of them planned and plotted the wrecking of the big ditch some weeks before the explosion. [T]he scheme is looked upon by the persons believed to have been involved as a matter of self-protection. The small ranchers and land owners of the upper portion of the Owens Valley declare that unfair methods have been used by Los Angeles in obtaining water rights for the Aqueduct to the disadvantage of the local ranchers. The direct reason for the attempt to wreck the Aqueduct is believed to be traceable to the number of suits started by the city of Los Angeles against ranchers and landowners in Owens Valley to settle once and for all various water rights. The landowners, according to their statements, will be forced to appear in court at their own expense and defend the suits or else lose all of their water rights.[91]

Despite the revealing investigation, no effort was made to charge the suspects. City officials claimed that seeking convictions through county law enforcement agencies was fruitless, a charge vigorously denied by Inyo District Attorney Jess Hession. More likely, the city had insufficient evidence for indictments against the bombers. The exploded dynamite could not be traced, and no witnesses to the actual deed came forward. In Jack Dymond's informed opinion, "every resident of the Owens Valley knows who did the dynamiting, but no one will tell. Some of the most prominent and wealthy farmers and ranchers in the Owens Valley are involved."[92]

Valley solidarity was impressive but not complete. The small opposition group led by L. C. Hall, William Symons, and George Watterson
posed a serious threat to the irrigation district. In 1923 they had persuaded fellow members of the McNalley Ditch Company to sell, giving
the city a foothold for its lawsuit against "wrongful diversions" from
the aqueduct intake, and in the following year they continued to encourage individual sales within the district's boundaries. In the eyes of
movement supporters, these men were traitors and deserving targets of
intimidation. In August 1924 seven men barged into a Bishop restaurant, abducted attorney Hall, and dropped him in the countryside with
a warning to leave the valley.[93] Local lore maintains that Hall escaped
tar and feathers only by rendering a secret Masonic gesture, which
prompted mercy from the lodge brothers among his tormentors.[94] Symons and Watterson also received threats, suggesting that movement
support was in danger of flagging without forceful reminders intended
for potential rank-and-file defectors.

During the summer of 1924, movement strategy embraced a flexible
combination of popular justice, protest demonstration, and political
negotiation. Coincident with the May 21 bomb, Wilfred Watterson and
a local delegation met with the Los Angeles Chamber of Commerce,
asking that they investigate water department purchases that were freez-
ing out unwilling sellers and potential buyers other than the city. A
similar two-pronged approach accompanied the Alabama Gates action,
when Mark Watterson joined the occupation while his brother met with
the bankers' Los Angeles Clearing House. In both cases the plan was,
first, to call attention to their plight in dramatic fashion, and second, to
gain influential allies in a realigned political contest. When the May
bombing failed to shock the city into a conciliatory mood, and indeed
brought a swarm of "spies" into the valley, strategy shifted to the publicity advantages of nonviolent resistance in the aqueduct takeover.

This time the results were more encouraging. Although the governor
refused to send the state militia as Inyo officials requested, the picnic at
Alabama Gates was a public relations coup. Newspapers around the
country sympathized in stories about hearty pioneers defending their
farms and the bankers' clearing house endorsed a resolution promising
to help bring about an equitable solution. State legislators, worried about
the Los Angeles precedent of urban appropriation as it might affect their
own rural districts, took the McClure Report under serious consideration. Acting on its recommendation, the lawmakers approved the Reparations Act of May 1925, which authorized compensation for damages

suffered by persons or municipal corporations as a result of any other person, firm, or public corporation entering their watershed for purposes of export. Although the act failed to specify procedures (other than "arbitration and compromise") for determining damages, it allowed submission of financial claims for "injury, damage, destruction or decrease in value of any such property, business, trade, profession, or occupation resulting from or caused by the taking of any such land or waters."[95]

Immediately after the act was passed, the Owens Valley Reparations Association, in Bishop, and the Big Pine Reparations Association were formed and began assembling extravagant lists of financial losses. Together, 431 Bishop and 117 Big Pine claimants demanded nearly $3 million, or about half the assessed value of all the 1,470 taxable properties held in 1920—many long since sold to the city. Losses were calculated in six categories, allowing multiple claims by individuals: business, occupational, professional, real property, personal property, and trades. Fred Bulpitt wanted $4,869.82 for business losses to his grocery store and $30,600 for his real property. The Bishop Ice Company claimed $16,811.26, and Dell Yandell's insurance agency $310.58. For lost earnings, Dr. C. E. Turner asked $4,516.50; twelve carpenters and barbers in Bishop claimed $1,200 each; and thirty-five Big Pine Indian farm laborers wanted $720 apiece. The Seventh Day Adventist Church of Bishop estimated its lost property value at $2,800.[96] Los Angeles refused to recognize any of these claims until the act was tested in the courts.

Ironically, the Reparations Act narrowed the field of resistance by shifting the struggle away from irrigation district autonomy toward the monetary value of implicitly conceded property and livelihoods. The hope of preserving the valley began to fade, at least as an organizational principle. Vagaries in the law, moreover, allowed Los Angeles to proceed with individual buyouts pending court evaluation and enforcement. Under the circumstances, the city sought to avoid the reparations question by further purchases of land and water rights within the canal companies at generous prices, thereby embracing all claims in a single, conventional real estate transaction. Indeed, these attractive sales were made contingent on the seller's signed agreement to renounce any further claims against the city. As many of the ditch companies were broken up, the irrigation district lost its base and rationale. Of necessity, the resistance movement shifted its organizational base to the less principled reparations associations and the newly created, more defensive, Owens Valley Property Owners' Protective Association. The Protective Association provided a weaker vehicle, lacking status as a public organization and steadily appealing to a smaller circle in the stalwart Owens River Canal Company (or "Keough pool" after Karl Keough and his Bishop neighbors). Effective resistance was losing many of its former alternatives.

The last offensive in the water war began in April 1926, when a city well under construction on the former Watterson ranch near Bishop was dynamited. After a two-year lull, this second blast renewed the violence that would continue in waves through the summer of 1927. Between 1924 and 1931, eleven separate attacks on the city's water system were reported in the *Inyo Independent:*

Date Reported	Site	Description
May 21, 1924	Alabama Gates	Concrete wall of aqueduct rent by large explosion
April 4, 1926	Bishop ranch	City well feeding aqueduct destroyed by dynamite
May 12, 1926	Alabama Gates	Ten-foot hole blasted in concrete aqueduct wall at site of May 1924 explosion
May 26, 1927	No Name Siphon	Large-diameter iron pipe carrying aqueduct water destroyed near Little Lake in most costly blast
May 27, 1927	Big Pine	Intake to city power plant destroyed
June 5, 1927	Cottonwood Creek	Concrete aqueduct wall damaged 12 miles below Lone Pine
June 19, 1927	Tuttle Creek	Sixteen-foot hole dynamited in aqueduct wall 2 miles below Lone Pine
June 25, 1927	Alabama Hills	Bomb exploded on hillside in attempt to block aqueduct with landslide
July 16, 1927	Alabama Hills	Fourteen feet of aqueduct wall damaged at site of June 25, 1927, attack

assembly accused Big Pine rancher George Warren of "working with the city and interfering in the plans to obtain reparations." Notified of the group's order that he leave the valley within forty-eight hours, Warren responded: "Tell 'em I'll stay, tell 'em to go to hell." Subsequent investigations identified the Shelley Hill meeting as a turning point in the "general conspiracy" now being mobilized for a final defense.[105]

On May 6, 1927, the Los Angeles City Council unanimously denied all of the $2.8 million in reparation claims submitted by the Bishop and Big Pine associations. In support of its decision the council noted that since Los Angeles had entered the valley in 1907, the assessed value of Inyo land and property had risen from $43,000 to $200,000. Far from causing damage and property loss, the aqueduct had enhanced the valley's economy.[106] President Ben Leete and Secretary Frank Spaulding of the Owens Valley Property Owners' Protective Association cabled their response to Mayor Cryer: "Four times have we asked that the troubles between property owners here and [in] Los Angeles be left to arbitration. Four times has this offer been rejected. . . . This policy, which is unheard of in the United States, can have but one result namely to inflame real American citizens to violence."[107]

True to their word, the rebels altered the course of tactical bombing and negotiation in a new wave of assaults, designed to damage the water system. The fourth and most spectacular explosion in the series destroyed a 450-foot length of the nine-foot diameter pipe at No Name Syphon, which carried the valley's water through steep hills and canyons near Little Lake to the desert beyond. No sooner had the damage been estimated—at $50,000 to $75,000—than the next blast eliminated the intake to the Big Pine power house, shutting down all electrical power. The choice of these two targets suggests careful planning and intimate knowledge of the water system. The group of twelve men who invaded the city's installation at No Name Canyon in the early morning hours led two Indian guards away to avoid injury. In both instances telephone lines were short-circuited to cover the dynamiters' escape.

Los Angeles responded to the escalation in kind. Six armed guards were sent to No Name Canyon with orders to shoot to kill. The city offered a $10,000 reward for information leading to conviction, and it now echoed the valley's 1924 appeal for intervention by the state militia. The Los Angeles Times reported that six hundred special police were awaiting orders, "concentrated and ready to do battle."[108] A new force of hired private detectives and city investigators was dispatched to apprehend the culprits. Five days after an ineffectual blast south of Lone Pine on June 5, the city sent one hundred armed guards to patrol the length of the aqueduct. City agents roaming the valley were nothing new. Leete and Spaulding complained in their earlier telegram of "spies [and] professional detectives whose residence is Los Angeles, but who are now deputy sheriffs of Inyo County. . . . [P]roperty owners are constantly shadowed by these imported gum-shoe men. Evesdroppers around homes are common."[109] Now, however, an armed occupation was in force; the initial contingent of one hundred was soon doubled. Patrols moved up and down valley roads at all hours. Searchlights were trained on the hills west of the aqueduct in "a state of virtual warfare."[110]

If anything, the occupation challenged the bombers' ingenuity. In a game of hide-and-seek with the guards, four more blasts hit the aqueduct, one aiming to cover it in a landslide. As patrols concentrated in one place, diverse forms of sabotage mushroomed elsewhere. More charges, which had failed to explode, were discovered. City wells were incapacitated, searchlights shot out, and phone lines cut. With intrepid action multiplying, however, the detectives were closing in.

Major C. Percy Watson was arrested in Big Pine on June 30, 1927. The warrant, issued in Contra Costa County near Oakland, alleged that Watson had come there to purchase and transport illegally 400 pounds of blasting gelatine and 300 pounds of TNT (subsequently Alameda County, which includes Oakland, arrested him on the transportation charge). In the complaint filed by the Los Angeles Board of Water and Power Commissioners, Watson and A. J. Betker, a Bakersfield oil worker, were accused of violating state laws controlling explosives. They were not charged with dynamiting the aqueduct, a crime within the jurisdiction of Inyo County. Detection had been simple. Empty explosives boxes were found at No Name Syphon clearly marked with lot numbers of the Hercules Powder Company in Pinole, California. Investigators found company officials co-operative. They remembered Watson well and noted that their initial suspicions about such a large order had been allayed by the major's knowledge of explosives and his seemingly professional purpose. Watson had concealed any connection with the publicized Owens Valley by giving Betker's address in Bakersfield as his own. The Pinole office had called the company headquarters in Wilimington, Delaware, and obtained permission for the sale. Faced with ample evidence of the transaction, Watson freely admitted purchasing the explosives, but denied any involvement in the aqueduct bombings. As an explosives expert and former army officer, Watson explained, he was engaged in experiments testing "shell-proof armor" on his Big Pine ranch.

Watson had come to Big Pine in 1924 and purchased a 58-acre ranch for $12,000; the city now wanted to buy it for $25,000. As a stalwart of the Protective Association, Watson refused to sell, endorsing organizational demands for higher prices (perhaps $60,000 for his place) and reparations should a bloc sale prove the only recourse. Declaring in one breath that he would prove his innocence of the bombings, in another he charged that "the entire population of the little valley is aroused against the city of Los Angeles. They are tired of being spied upon, but there is nothing they can do. Wells have been placed adjoining my property by the city and all of the water drained off from my property. This is a common practice to install wells and drain off water underground thus drying out the farmers."[111]

Watson's connection with the resistance movement became clear when he was arrested and spirited off for arraignment in Contra Costa County. "Mass meetings were held in valley towns, and feeling against summary methods used in effecting [his] arrest ran high. All classes of people throughout the valley contributed to the $5,000 bail fund."[112] Wilfred Watterson recalled, "My brother got in touch with one of Watson's friends and gave him a note filled out for five thousand dollars and asked him to go out and get three or four names on it and the money would be advanced. In a few hours the note came back looking like a petition to the Governor of the state as it had about one hundred and fifty names on it."[113]

The city's dilemma in the Watson case stemmed from suspicions that Inyo officials would not prosecute one of their own. District Attorney Jess Hession was charged with a conflict of interest as he was the former counsel of the reparations association and was due a fee should the claims succeed. Although unstated, the city's valid interpretation was that the dynamiters came from local organizational ranks. True in some respects, the charge misjudged Hession's professional scruples. When the city requested that the U.S. Attorney General appoint a special prosecutor, Hession angrily called the grand jury into session, saying he would subpoena "every water board member, city official, and city detective who knows anything" about charges that law enforcement was compromised because of rumors that prominent local citizens were involved in the bombings. "This is Inyo County's reply to the Los Angeles Water Board's statements that we have never done anything to bring the dynamiters to justice."[114]

Behind the seemingly separate battles over criminal prosecution and reparations, the fundamental city-county struggle orchestrated all other moves. The Protective Association wanted state intervention and arbitration of reparations claims in the atmosphere of urgency created by the bombings and the resulting statewide sympathy. By contrast, going to the courts, as the governor urged, would not only prolong the issue beyond the staying power of the insurgency, but also insulate the decision from the public opinion the association had done so much to rally. The dynamiters had little fear of local indictments, both because they could count on exoneration by a local jury and because Hession's subpoena showed that the city had no case without witnesses from the still-solid ranks of the resistance. The city labored precisely at blocking any conflation of the two issues. Let the Reparations Act be tested in court, said the city and, now, Watterson's erstwhile colleagues in the Los Angeles Clearing House.[115] If keeping the criminal matter out of Inyo's jurisdiction meant a weaker case against Watson, that was preferred to a high-risk trial that would use the reparations question as a defense. Indeed, no new indictment was sought when the Contra Costa charges against Watson were dropped due to technicalities involving the admissibility of his partner's testimony.

At this point disaster came upon the resistance movement from an unexpected direction. When the Inyo County Bank failed and the Watterson brothers were charged with embezzlement, all other activities sank in the same boat. The bank failure is best analyzed separately; it is treated in the "Decline" section of this chapter. Its bearing on the violent phase of the movement is twofold. First, most forms of protest and any hope of preserving the valley's economy collapsed with the bank. Second, District Attorney Hession's prosecution of the Wattersons convinced the city that the suspected dynamiters, too, could be tried in Inyo County.

In February 1928 the city handed over to Hession the results of its investigation into the aqueduct bombings, much of it the work of the Pyles National Detective Agency, headquartered in Los Angeles. Claiming that at least fifteen ringleaders, including three women, would be named soon, Hession issued arrest warrants for six men: the celebrated Big Pine rancher Major Percy Watson; Frank Spaulding, a Bishop businessman and secretary of the Owens Valley Property Owners' Protective Association; Walter Young, a Bishop rancher and Watterson associate; Fred Naphan, a former Owens Valley resident and stock buyer; Will Smith, a Bishop restaurant and pool hall owner; Perry Sexton, Sr., a former city employee and Lone Pine sawmill operator. The District

Attorney emphasized that these six men were only "drops in the bucket." The imminent "biggest roundup" would include highly placed public officials, members of the oldest valley families, and prominent community figures.[116]

As prosecutors and investigators fed the story to the newspapers, it became clear that the case rested on a confession by Perry Sexton, an outsider to the group centered in Bishop and the Protective Association. Indeed, Sexton had been involved in just one incident, the inconsequential sixth blast at Cottonwood Creek. With Sexton as the only cooperative eye witness, the prosecution's case was limited to a single incident, one that Sexton confessed to carrying out alone. His revealing testimony merely implicated the others in a conspiracy.

> Sexton, who has lived in Inyo County for twenty years, began his astounding story with the time he was employed as a watchman by the city at the intake of the Cottonwood power plant. He left the city's service April 9 or 10. A few days prior to this time he said he went to Bishop and had a talk with Mark Watterson at the Inyo county bank. "I owed a note at the bank," he related, "and the city owed me money. I told him that I couldn't pay the note, and Mark said he thought the city never would pay me. I told him I would shut off the water at the intake, and Mark said if you do that we'll give you all the time you want." Within a week after the time he had left the employ of the city, there was a meeting in Frank Spaulding's office in the Watterson Building at Bishop. Spaulding, Young, Naphan, and Watterson were present. "We talked about dynamiting, and that we were to do it at the aqueduct. We intended to blow Cottonwood first. For some reason they decided not to have that done until after the No-Name job. I said I wouldn't go on a job with anyone, that if I did a job I'd do it alone. Young and Watterson said it was up to me how to do the job." He told of another meeting at Spaulding's office on April 20, 1927. He said Young, Spaulding, and Watterson were there and that eight or ten sticks of dynamite were produced. "I saw it and handled it. The sticks were soft, but they said it was high-powered. Young and Naphan declared it was the powder that Major Watson had brought in."[117]

The detectives' report given to Hession is remarkably thin on corroborating testimony.[118] The Indian guards at No Name Syphon recognized none of the insurgents. Valley residents admitted to seeing cars and suspects traversing the highways at all hours, but that proved nothing. The largest source of alleged coconspirators was the Shelley Hill meeting, discussed by witnesses opposed to George Warren's exile; but that incident implicated people in the reparations campaign, not the bombings. Surveillance of Wilfred Watterson, Harry Glasscock, and

others in Los Angeles hotels turned up no meetings with city subversives, only with officials.

Months of investigation by scores of detectives produced just two
pieces of evidence against the dynamiters: the packing crates from Hercules Powder Company connecting Watson with the documented purchase of explosives, and the confession by Sexton, himself identified by
a "confidential source." Local speculation held that Sexton had been
plied with liquor and promises of reward money. In addition to the six
arrested, the Pyles Agency's report named forty-one suspects, most of
them activists in the Protective Association. Among those brought in for
questioning were Postmaster Arthur Shirley, Mark Watterson, ranchers
Fred Stockton and Frank English, Big Pine editor Harry Glasscock, and
businessmen Karl Keough and Elton Baker. None was charged, despite
promises of a "big parade." On the contrary, detective Pyles was threatened with bodily harm if he remained in the valley.[119] The investigation's meager results suggest that solidarity within the resistance movement held to the end.

It is plausible to suppose that the city and the Inyo district attorney
correctly identified participants in the bombings, if not their motives
and organizational base. The evidence implicating Major Watson in the
violence was undeniable, and he was also a well-known stalwart of the
Protective Association. Sexton's testimony sounds truthful, even if he
was offered inducements to give it. The city, moreover, put a number of
investigators to work on the case, and there is no reason to suggest that
they botched the job or invented a story (as was true, for example, in
explanations of the aqueduct occupation). Conversely, it was known
that the Protective Association, which included many of the alleged
bombers, had sanctioned other rough tactics in its frustration. Finally,
given that the bombings were group activities and were witnessed by
many people, one must wonder who else could have been responsible in
a community where there were few secrets.

The arrest and impending trial of the "Inyo Gang" enjoyed sensational newspaper coverage throughout the western states and in New
York City. Although the defense of the five movement men was financed
modestly by a fund raised from their neighbors (with Sexton represented separately), the publicity attracted a distinguished group of attorneys. Rex B. Goodcell, former head of the U.S. Internal Revenue
Service in Los Angeles and a gubernatorial candidate, headed the defense team, which included former Assemblyman Walter Little. Fresh

divided Bishop's small-town society. George Watterson had been estranged from his nephews for years, owing perhaps to business rivalries
in which George felt demeaned and, in Wilfred's evasive words, because
of "unfriendliness [that] dates back to a quarrel he had with my father
over forty years ago."[128] George married the sister of William Symons.
L. C. Hall's affections were rejected by one of the Watterson sisters. The
Wattersons stood at the apex of a squat social pyramid founded on the
Methodist Church, the Chamber of Commerce, and the Masonic
Lodge. Outsiders had reason to seek their own status attainments in
opposition to a movement controlled by the elite. Whatever local torments may have occasioned it, the split was significant less for any
competing values or meaningful numbers it represented than for the
wedge it opened to city power.

The second theory about social bases maintains that the resistance
movement represented rustics and drew its principal following from
them. This interpretation, too, began at the time of the aqueduct occupation. It was advanced by the Los Angeles Board of Public Service
Commissioners, who blamed the action on "the mental reactions of a
pioneer community . . . uninformed and unaccustomed to the ways of
the outside world."[129] Recent (and otherwise excellent) histories drop
the patronizing tone, but persist in describing movement supporters as
"the ranchers."[130] One exception is a thesis that noted the inconsistency
of a farmers' movement led by bankers and concluded it was the work of
Bishop businessmen with "very little participation from the farmers."[131]

A third interpretation of the social bases of the movement in the 1920s
is possible. Between 1908 and 1922 the valley occupational structure had
shifted moderately in the direction of upward mobility (table 8). Professional and managerial positions were more common, agriculture and
labor about the same, and skilled trades and mining slightly diminished.
Using a sample of 299 signatories to the petition for a referendum on the
irrigation district as representative of the protest movement,[132] one
detects a pattern of mobilization different from that of 1905. Support for
the protest movement was now drawn more uniformly from the entire
population. By contrast to the general population, agriculturalists, merchants, and professionals were moderately overrepresented among
movement supporters, while the trades and labor were underrepresented
(but less so than in 1905). The mobilized opposition was a cross-section
of the community; every occupational group was represented in proportions close to those of the general population.

The leaders of the 1920s movement are not so easily identified as those others in Los Angeles hotels turned up no meetings with city subversives, only with officials.

Months of investigation by scores of detectives produced just two pieces of evidence against the dynamiters: the packing crates from Hercules Powder Company connecting Watson with the documented purchase of explosives, and the confession by Sexton, himself identified by a "confidential source." Local speculation held that Sexton had been plied with liquor and promises of reward money. In addition to the six arrested, the Pyles Agency's report named forty-one suspects, most of them activists in the Protective Association. Among those brought in for questioning were Postmaster Arthur Shirley, Mark Watterson, ranchers Fred Stockton and Frank English, Big Pine editor Harry Glasscock, and businessmen Karl Keough and Elton Baker. None was charged, despite promises of a "big parade." On the contrary, detective Pyles was threatened with bodily harm if he remained in the valley.[119] The investigation's meager results suggest that solidarity within the resistance movement held to the end.

It is plausible to suppose that the city and the Inyo district attorney correctly identified participants in the bombings, if not their motives and organizational base. The evidence implicating Major Watson in the violence was undeniable, and he was also a well-known stalwart of the Protective Association. Sexton's testimony sounds truthful, even if he was offered inducements to give it. The city, moreover, put a number of investigators to work on the case, and there is no reason to suggest that they botched the job or invented a story (as was true, for example, in explanations of the aqueduct occupation). Conversely, it was known that the Protective Association, which included many of the alleged bombers, had sanctioned other rough tactics in its frustration. Finally, given that the bombings were group activities and were witnessed by many people, one must wonder who else could have been responsible in a community where there were few secrets.

The arrest and impending trial of the "Inyo Gang" enjoyed sensational newspaper coverage throughout the western states and in New York City. Although the defense of the five movement men was financed modestly by a fund raised from their neighbors (with Sexton represented separately), the publicity attracted a distinguished group of attorneys. Rex B. Goodcell, former head of the U.S. Internal Revenue Service in Los Angeles and a gubernatorial candidate, headed the defense team, which included former Assemblyman Walter Little. Fresh from the spotlight of the Watterson trial, Hession prosecuted for the county. In a courtroom packed with famous lawyers, wily bombers, and their vociferous supporters, the most terrified participant may have been the part-time justice of the peace, R. L. Patterson. Technically the proceeding was a preliminary hearing to decide whether a trial in Inyo County Superior Court was warranted. Under normal circumstances Independence Justice H. A. Piercy would have been responsible for conducting the hearing, but Piercy had been removed on a defense motion because he worked full-time for the city's aqueduct maintenance department as a tool sharpener; so Patterson got the call.

The trial introduced no new evidence. Hession covered Watson's purchase of explosives and called witnesses who had observed the defendants at various protest meetings. Revealingly, the district attorney represented participation in the popular resistance movement as providing motive and opportunity for the violence. A full day of Sexton's confession came as the intended coup de grace. Announcing that the defense would "clear up many of the problems of the Owens Valley," Goodcell signaled that he would attempt to put Los Angeles on trial. His closing speech asked, "Is there any crime in men, ground down under the heel of a great and powerful city, seeking justice? It seems to me that there has been an astute conspiracy born somewhere against the people of this valley."[120] Sexton's confession was attacked for inconsistencies, and his receipt of expense money from detectives was emphasized. The two-week trial ended with Justice Patterson unconvinced: "I did not believe the story of Perry Sexton."[121] Although Hession expressed great surprise, he chose not to exercise the option of issuing a new complaint. Arrested in three counties, Major Watson was never tried for involvement in any of the ten bombings that cost the city $250,000. The aqueduct raiders went free.

SOCIAL BASES AND CHANGE

Historical interpretations of the Owens Valley resistance, both popular and academic, have always misread its social composition and, to some extent, its purpose. One theory holds that the movement was split between naive moderates who failed to appreciate the city's benefaction and a radical fringe group that included anarchists, Wobblies, and vigilantes.[122] This interpretation began with self-serving claims by city officials that the Alabama Gates trespassers did "not represent the majority of the people of the Owens River Valley."[123] Despite their initial sympathy for the uprising, the major Los Angeles newspapers soon began to characterize its perpetrators as the "Inyo Gang," the "Aqueduct Mob," and "Aqueduct Outlaws" who "Should be Punished." The coverage was designed to blunt Owens Valley charges of injustice by associating the resisters with an anarchistic element distinct from the good pioneers who were prepared to sell to the city.[124] A 1950 book by Remi Nadeau (great-great-grandson of the 1870s Los Angeles freighter) popularized the incongruous idea that an Owens Valley chapter of the Ku Klux Klan was responsible for the property violence.[125] The reporters from Los Angeles had written about the late-night adventures of hooded men who roughly intimidated a few city sympathizers; Nadeau, reviving the rumor, concluded that the hooded men were Klansmen. Other evidence suggests that they were people from movement organizations and Masons who sometimes disguised themselves with hoods.[126] Contemporary reports reveal no radical fringe group and no evidence that a local KKK group ever existed.

There was a well-publicized split in the valley, but it was not a split between moderates and radicals. A small group gathered around William Symons, George Watterson, and L. C. Hall favored an agreement with Los Angeles. They hoped that the city would reward proffered land sales with concessions such as the construction of the reservoir demanded by the majority faction. The trio profited from their collaboration, particularly Symons, who had vast properties to sell and was in a strategic position to command good prices. As a major shareholder, Symons pressured his fellow property owners in the key sale of the McNally Ditch Company, which did as much as anything else to break the irrigation district's united front. The valley faithful resented the "traitors" and treated them badly. Yet the traitors represented at least twenty-seven, and perhaps eighty other citizens, judging from electoral opposition to the irrigation district. The minority faction also claimed legitimacy as defenders of the valley.

In an open letter to W. A. Chalfant,[127] which the *Inyo Register* did not publish, the group alleged that the Wattersons were in league with the speculative design of the former Los Angeles mayor, Fred Eaton, and that by holding out for a larger dam and storage reservoir, Eaton could sell his property and repay a bank loan. The proposition is debatable. The resistance movement stood for too many other positions that had little to do with speculation or Eaton. It is likely that some members of the minority faction made such accusations simply to justify their own profit making. But personal and status rivalries also divided Bishop's small-town society. George Watterson had been estranged from his nephews for years, owing perhaps to business rivalries in which George felt demeaned and, in Wilfred's evasive words, because of "unfriendliness [that] dates back to a quarrel he had with my father over forty years ago."[128] George married the sister of William Symons. L. C. Hall's affections were rejected by one of the Watterson sisters. The Wattersons stood at the apex of a squat social pyramid founded on the Methodist Church, the Chamber of Commerce, and the Masonic Lodge. Outsiders had reason to seek their own status attainments in opposition to a movement controlled by the elite. Whatever local torments may have occasioned it, the split was significant less for any competing values or meaningful numbers it represented than for the wedge it opened to city power.

The second theory about social bases maintains that the resistance movement represented rustics and drew its principal following from them. This interpretation, too, began at the time of the aqueduct occupation. It was advanced by the Los Angeles Board of Public Service Commissioners, who blamed the action on "the mental reactions of a pioneer community . . . uninformed and unaccustomed to the ways of the outside world."[129] Recent (and otherwise excellent) histories drop the patronizing tone, but persist in describing movement supporters as "the ranchers."[130] One exception is a thesis that noted the inconsistency of a farmers' movement led by bankers and concluded it was the work of Bishop businessmen with "very little participation from the farmers."[131]

A third interpretation of the social bases of the movement in the 1920s is possible. Between 1908 and 1922 the valley occupational structure had shifted moderately in the direction of upward mobility (table 8). Professional and managerial positions were more common, agriculture and labor about the same, and skilled trades and mining slightly diminished. Using a sample of 299 signatories to the petition for a referendum on the irrigation district as representative of the protest movement,[132] one detects a pattern of mobilization different from that of 1905. Support for the protest movement was now drawn more uniformly from the entire population. By contrast to the general population, agriculturalists, merchants, and professionals were moderately overrepresented among movement supporters, while the trades and labor were underrepresented (but less so than in 1905). The mobilized opposition was a cross-section of the community; every occupational group was represented in proportions close to those of the general population.

The leaders of the 1920s movement are not so easily identified as those in 1905, who gathered in a small citizens' committee. In order to identify these people for purposes of comparison and to discover who participated in the aqueduct seizure, a list of activists was developed that included local persons who led groups, took public positions, and authored published statements in opposition to city policies.[133]

No list of the insurgents at Alabama Gates survives; it is not known whether Sheriff Collins ever issued summonses in their names. No names of persons arrested appear in court records. In order to reconstruct a list of participants, two methods were employed. First, the names of some participants were obtained from the Los Angeles newspaper reports (Owens Valley papers mentioned no names, perhaps fearing to put colleagues in danger of legal prosecution). Second, a number of photographs of the occupation, taken by the newspapers, two local commercial photographers, and several amateurs, were enlarged and shown to elderly valley residents, who were asked to name any relatives or acquaintances appearing in the photographs. In combination, these procedures yielded the names of a dozen participants.

It seems safe to assume that the activists were also participants at the spillway; adding their names resulted in a list of 71 persons who may be reasonably designated leaders.

Leaders were drawn disproportionately from the upper occupational categories, as we would expect. Professionals and businesspersons comprised a large segment, but both the clerical-services category and agriculturalists were represented almost precisely in their proportions in the population. The trades and labor are sparse in this sample. Yet overall the two 1920s samples show a much more inclusive movement than that of 1905. Table 9 suggests that the movement's rank and file were not very different from the leaders in their socioeconomic characteristics. The leaders had larger land holdings, but the value of their property was not much greater. The pattern of relatively small landholdings with higher property values reflected the Bishop origins of the majority of the opposition.

Finally, to test the proposition that the aqueduct raiders constituted a separate faction of the resistance movement, the names of thirty-seven suspects, all of whom were men, were taken from the Pyles Detective Agency report. These included the six defendants, another eight who were questioned but not indicted, and twenty-three others named by witnesses as participating in angry meetings or traveling on valley roads when bombs were exploding. Inclusion in this list is not proof of individual responsibility in the bombings; rather, the sample provides a

TABLE 8.   OCCUPATIONAL STRUCTURE OF THE OWENS VALLEY AND PROTEST PARTICIPANTS, SELECTED YEARS

	Valley, 1908 (N = 1,250)[a]	Petition Signers, 1904 (N = 333)[b]	Citizens' Committee, 1905 (N = 10)[b]	Valley, 1922 (N = 1,954)[b]	Petition Signers (Irrigation District), 1922 (N = 299)[b]	Activists 1922–24 and Participants in Aqueduct Seizure, 1924 (N = 60)[b]
Professional	4%	4%	20%	7%	10%	15%
Commercial and managerial	5	5	0	8	14	28
Clerical and services	11	6	20	12	11	13
Farm and ranch	41	80	60	39	48	38
Skilled trades and mining	25	4	0	19	12	4
Labor	14	1	0	15	5	2
Total	100%	100%	100%	100%	100%	100%
Number of housewives	—	—	1	1,027	52	10
Number of retired persons	—	—	0	38	10	1

sources: Eastern California Museum, Index to the Great Register, Inyo County, 1908 and 1922; National Archives, petition "To the Right Honorable Secretary of the Interior of the United States," 1905; McClure 1925; petition for Formation of an Irrigation District, *Inyo Register*, Aug. 22, 1922; *Los Angeles Daily Times*, Nov. 17–22, 1924; interviews by author, 1980–84.
[a]In 1908 women did not have the vote and their exclusion from this enumeration produces some bias in the occupational structure. Moreover, the numerical total of male occupations in 1908 underestimates the economically active by approximately 150 due to missing data.

[b]The occupational distributions are computed without self-described housewives or retired persons. With no accurate guide to the types of work housewives performed, it is reasonable to assume that they were distributed throughout the occupations.

TABLE 9.   SOCIOECONOMIC CHARACTERISTICS OF THE OWENS VALLEY AND PROTEST
PARTICIPANTS, SELECTED YEARS

	Valley, 1900	Petition Signers, 1905	Citizens' Committee, 1905	Valley, 1920	Bishop, 1920	Petition Signers, 1922	Activists and Participants, 1924
Mean size of landholding (acres)	317	301	621	119	102	124	228
Mean value of town lots ($)[a]	—	—	—	865	1,116	1,654	1,732
Mean value of property assessment ($)	1,589	2,447	5,065	5,280	5,868	5,887	8,508

sources: Eastern California Museum, Inyo County tax assessment roll, 1900, 1920.
[a]Includes multiple holdings by individuals and represents, therefore, the average value in town property held by the subset of persons who are town residents. In 1900, prior to the incorporation of any municipalities, town lots were not assessed separately.

representative social profile of those persons thought to be involved in the violence. Proportionately, this group matches closely the leadership sample in table 8. Two-thirds of the suspected dynamiters were either ranchers (35 percent) or businesspersons (32 percent). The remaining one-third is divided equally among professionals, labor, public employees, and service workers. Individually, many of those who supported or participated in the aqueduct raids came from reputable sections of the resistance movement: Mark Watterson and Karl Keough from business, Frank Spaulding and Ben Leete from the Protective Association, Walter Young and Fred Stockton from the ranchers, and Postmaster Arthur Shirley. The protest movement was a single and solidary alliance embracing people from all walks of local life—a community movement that had superseded earlier class divisions. Violence and politics appeared not as the work of different factions but as alternating strategies of the unified resistance.

The revolt of the burghers that began in 1919 mobilized business and professional groups in the towns who, for the first time in local memory, made common cause with agrarian and working-class interests. Hard times encouraged the alliance. The drought of 1919 underscored the danger of competition for water between the Owens Valley and Los Angeles. Each side responded in ways that contributed to a climate of economic uncertainty—the valley with insurgency and the city with stepped-up property acquisitions. The valley's dramatic shift in protest mobilization from 1905 to 1924 demonstrates that an agrarian action was transformed into a community movement sustained by a broad class coalition and communal ethos. Diverse participants rallied with a political program and an organizational vehicle that innovatively embraced town and farm holders of water rights. Despite its boldly defensive acts of sabotage, the resistance movement advanced a moderate plan for mutual development with the city. Violence was used in hopes of favorably realigning negotiations.

The movement stood for the survival of Owens Valley communities and, in resonant ideological terms, the virtues of the "thoroughly American" frontier community. "Community" meant traditional pioneer values, the interdependence of town and farm, a continuation of 1900-style prosperity, especially for the commercial interests that led the revolt, and willing subordination to an equitable city patron. But Los Angeles held the stronger political hand and played it aggressively. The city wanted rights to all the water that could be channeled its way, and no higher political authority wanted to restrain the impulse. Bad publicity was a nuisance, but not an obstacle. Without federal or state intervention, local communities were simply overpowered—the local commercial interests and the Owens Valley Irrigation District badly mismatched against Los Angeles city-builders and the Department of Water and Power.

DECLINE

By 1925 the city had decided that the best security against drought and social unrest was simply to buy up as many farms and water rights as it could lay its hands on. City purchases rose to 450 in the following year.[134] By the end of 1926, Los Angeles controlled 90 percent of the valley's land and water. Purchases were temporarily suspended in 1927 as a sanction against reparation demands by the recalcitrant holdouts surrounding Bishop. Another peak in acquisitions came in 1931 with the completion of arbitration over fair value; but that record number included a high proportion of town lots, which contributed little additional land and water. Even the Wattersons sold their 1,200-acre ranch, in 1925, defending the decision as a way of raising cash to support the resistance and their many businesses operating in a depressed economy.[135]

The decisive blow to the 1920s movement came in August 1927, when the Wattersons' Inyo County bank failed. The brothers had been diverting bank funds to their flagging businesses, particularly a soda-processing plant and hot springs resort. The peculations were uncovered when the dissident faction, including their uncle and George Warren, filed for a state charter to open a new bank in the valley.[136] Because the filing automatically triggered a feasibility study by state bank examiners, it may have been that the Wattersons' opponents were more interested in exposing their financial dealings than in any opportunity afforded another bank in the depressed region. In any case, when State Superintendent of Banks Will C. Wood found the Inyo County Bank short by an estimated $800,000, its five branches were closed, wiping out virtually all of the savings of valley residents. Although the Wattersons submitted that the shortage was considerably smaller, they acknowledged the diversion, indeed justified it as essential to "keep the valley going" in the fight with Los Angeles. As records were sealed in five valley branches, a notice at the Bishop office indicated that it was temporarily closed "due to the destructive work carried on by Los Angeles city."[137]

Many local supporters agreed. As a measure of solidarity even at this late date, remaining property owners pledged $600,000 in collateral to cover the losses.[138] Although the sum mounted to $1.2 million, Wood indicated that it would not affect the investigation, and District Attorney Hession observed that he would seek indictments if crimes had been committed. The Wattersons tried to limit damage to the movement in a series of town meetings from Keeler to Bishop. "The Wattersons started their campaign this morning at a meeting at the Lewis Ranch, five miles north of Independence. The meeting at the Holland Ranch this afternoon was attended by about 200 men and women who seemed to be in sympathy with the bankers. They were told that the people of Bishop were standing by the Wattersons."[139] In the words of a sympathizer, "The Wattersons have carried everybody in the valley."[140]

In their defense the brothers explained that the bank suffered mainly from "frozen loans" to valley farms and businesses unable to make payments in the paralyzed economy. Deposits had run down at the same time the bank was buying land threatened by foreclosure to prevent further city purchases. Superintendent Wood refuted all of these explanations. Deposits had been constant over the past few years, profits were steady, and neither the bank nor the Watterson family had acquired new holdings within the last year. On the contrary, "indications were that the money was used to a large extent in speculative mining and mineral ventures in which the Watterson brothers were the chief shareholders."[141] Further probing showed that the bank's assets had been falsely overstated at the last routine visit of state auditors. The brothers were arrested on thirty-five counts of embezzlement and one of making false statements.

The towns became dispirited as the tragedy's effects were felt. Savings were lost, at least until the Wattersons could liquidate other assets for restitution and the examiners sorted out the financial tangle. Ready cash was in short supply. "Credit in the valley is destroyed and retail business has fallen away to nothing. Men who years ago with an eye to the future invested in insurance, today are turning in their policies or sending them to Los Angeles for loans. Others are selling their cattle. The men who have so long led the valley's fight against the water board's encroachment on their rights are crushed in spirit—and penniless."[142] A citizens' meeting on the eve of the Watterson trial denounced anti–Los Angeles violence and urged city officials to press forward with planned construction projects that would provide jobs.[143]

In court, the Wattersons attempted for the last time to battle the city in their own defense. Their attorney introduced the Los Angeles issue by "asking one witness if the money had not been used for supporting several companies during the war between Inyo County and the water board." But the judge forcibly ruled out this defense, saying "We are not trying the city of Los Angeles or the water board. This is a trial court and no war is involved."[144] There was no other defense. The jury and District Attorney Hession wept during his summation, which concluded that the bankers had violated the trust of their neighbors. The verdict was guilty and the Wattersons were sentenced to ten years in San Quentin State Penitentiary. Paroled after five years in 1933, they never returned to the Owens Valley.

The resistance movement collapsed with the twin failures of the bank and the reparations campaign. In February 1929, Los Angeles announced that it was willing to discuss a bloc sale of offered town lots throughout the valley. Each of the five towns selected two members to serve on the Committee of Ten charged with drafting a proposal for the city's consideration. Meanwhile, the DWP conducted its own survey to determine the value of property. Based on a formula of 4.5 times assessed valuation, the Committee of Ten arrived at a figure of $8 million. Los Angeles proposed $4.4 million. A conference in Bishop with the committee and the new mayor of Los Angeles compromised on $5.6 million. The package included 867 business and residential properties in five towns: Laws, Bishop, Big Pine, Independence, and Lone Pine. Of the total, 185 were businesses; Bishop gave up 75 businesses and 306 residential properties.[145] As might be expected, even the settlement dragged on in controversy. The deal struck in late 1929 was stalled for more than a year as Los Angeles scheduled a referendum on a bond issue to raise the money and tested the legality of the arrangement from the standpoint of the city charter. By early 1931, "indignant" meetings were being held in Bishop, and the governor ordered an investigation into the purchase delay.[146] Perhaps those measures helped. By far the largest number of sales in a single year took place in 1931. A final irony is that the bloc settlement, with allowances for lost livelihood, closely resembled proposals by the irrigation district that the city had refused seven years earlier.

By 1930 Bishop had lost 35 percent of its 1920 population (the total county loss was much smaller), and more would leave in the next few years. Laws and Big Pine gave up all appearance of being towns. The southern valley was less affected, with county government at Independence and trade at Lone Pine continuing. City acquisitions reduced the number of operating farms by 58 percent (see table 5). In the same period agricultural production fell by 84 percent as city-owned prop-

reorganization in the progressive era, however, emphasized urbanization, regional incorporation, and bureaucratic management exemplified
in the Reclamation Service and its Southern California surrogate, the
Los Angeles Department of Water and Power. For the Owens Valley,
this second phase of state incorporation was as traumatic as the first,
but its victims were now its former agents.

In the first step toward progressive reorganization, competition arose
between the local (Los Angeles) and national state in 1904, with conflicting bureaucratic designs for regional development. The Owens Valley welcomed incorporation under Reclamation Service management
and identified closely with its goal of agricultural efficiency. When the
federal plan was abandoned, an opening was created for opposition
mobilized around righteous claims to state patrimony. Owens Valley
citizens applauded Roosevelt's progressivism, and understood themselves to be its beneficiaries. Far from opposing the state, the settlers
shared its announced aims and wanted closer association with them. The
initial conflict of state bureaucracies provided local citizens a prima facie
case for claiming injustice. When the desired and, by their standards,
equitable plan for federal development was withdrawn as a result of city
machinations, citizens were handed an ideological weapon in the original
aims of the Reclamation Act. Ironically, the very process of incorporating the valley into a system of regional domination laid the foundation
for rebellion. Local protest relied on traditional organizing methods and
values, but they were readily adapted to new progressive ends.

In this way the Owens Valley uprising differed from populism and
agrarian unrest in peasant societies, although the three types are sometimes bracketed with the notion of "moral economy." The tradition-
inspired revolt in the Owens Valley took place within the framework of
state modernization and economic growth, not as a backward-looking
attempt to restore some precapitalist Eden or resist the penetration of
market forces. On the contrary, it sought fulfillment of the developmental promises that lured pioneers and spoke to western progressives.
Yet the rebellion was essentially about moral economy in the more
fundamental sense of "legitimizing notions . . . traditional rights and
customs that were supported by the wider consensus of the community."[151] The difference was that the rights and customs of settlers in the
American West were not precapitalist traditions but norms elaborated
in the nineteenth century of progress, incorporation, and the presumed
trickle-down benefits of capitalist development and state management.
The moral economy harmonized perfectly with the progressive promise

of efficient development on behalf of smallholders and small-town merchants, just as it clashed with the progressive means of bureaucratic
aggrandizement and urban bias.

The full meaning of the contradiction emerged slowly. The opening
agrarian protest was lost in 1906 as growing commercial interests in the
valley hoped for continued prosperity in a city alliance. From 1919
onward, city domination brought new hardships that threatened the
valley's very survival. A community rebellion developed under conditions that united all groups. Hardship visited the Owens Valley in the
form of drought, economic recession, and the city's acquisitive power.
Intervention, once construed as depriving only agrarian interests, became a generalized threat and was understood as such by a coalitional
response of social classes. The resistance movement built on these conditions in proactive strategies. Emboldened by community solidarity,
the rebels turned on the state by appropriating its means for their own
oppositional use. The law providing for irrigation districts was used
innovatively to create an organizational vehicle for purposes of legal
maneuver and insurgency. Public authorities and the courts were called
upon. Even illegal tactics were calculated to force the dispute into the
court of public opinion. As E. P. Thompson discovered regarding protest in eighteenth-century England, "Law has not only been imposed
upon men from above: it has also been a medium within which other
social conflicts have been fought out."[152] The popular movement in-
tervened in the running of the state, claiming a small public space and
using that to challenge state power on its own terrain.

The picnic at Alabama Gates symbolized a community mobilized to
confront the state. In the 1920s traditional picnics were transformed
into political conventions for organizing the irrigation district and for
rallying the movement. The irrigation district, which led the early struggle, was itself a strategic modern adaptation of the traditional ditch
companies paramount among the rustic democratic associations of the
nineteenth century. The moral economy was first aroused, then effica-
ciously adapted in a movement orchestrated by progressive values, notably prosperity within the design of regional incorporation. When the
strategy of demanding negotiation with the valley's organization,
backed up by political demonstration, failed to produce desirable results, traditional methods of popular justice were adopted by the aqueduct raiders. Yet once again, violence was meant to persuade, and it
succeeded in helping to create new alliances with state government and
liberal public opinion. Tradition energized modern political strategies

as the rebels tried to realign statewide coalitions. And through it all they continued using the courts as a level terrain on which to fight the city. Even after the towns and the popular movement had conceded defeat, lawsuits were pressed by diehard farmers (see chapter 6). In a harbinger of the struggles that would come decades later, forty-three remaining property owners successfully enjoined city ground water pumping in the early 1930s.[153]

The Owens Valley struggle differs from the theory of moral economy in which traditional conceptions of justice and styles of protest are rooted in precapitalist social relations or a "movement culture" sharply at odds with the larger society.[154] To be sure, the community revolt drew on all its traditional resources to engage directly the modern forces of state and market expansion. Tradition bequeathed viable sentiments and organizational forms. But as the maturing movement necessarily fashioned new "responses to novel situations which [took] the form of references to old situations," it also invented traditions.[155] An Indian legacy and ethnic diversity were submerged in the reappraised heritage of a "thoroughly American" community. Distinct stages and motives of resistance were collapsed in moral perceptions of a singular two-decade struggle for a way of life. And the purpose of rebellion was to reach an equitable agreement with the local state that would ensure mutual participation in development.

Theoretically, the Owens Valley case demonstrates that popular rebellions may take place within the precepts of state reorganization and regional incorporation, not only as reactions to those forces. The expanding and more inclusive state did not end popular revolt in 1905, but shifted its terrain. A new kind of struggle developed as constituents of the state fought from within over their political rights and the question of whom the bureaucracy should serve. The rebellion was no recrudescence of populism but a watershed of environmentalism. In that sense, it lends critical perspective to modern interpretations of western development. It shows that the American West was not the pliable object of federal bureaucratic domination and its instrumental rationality. The federal government and the city of Los Angeles entered the valley intent on creating Donald Worster's "Rivers of Empire—[a] hydraulic society of the West, increasingly a coercive, monolithic, and hierarchical system, ruled by a power elite based on ownership of capital and expertise [with people] organized and induced to run, as the water in a canal does, in a straight line toward maximum yield, maximum profit."[156] Yet local society rose against those efforts, drawing on traditions of cooperative organization, popular justice, and alternative values of community and prosperity. Even in decline they would not run in the city's traces.

For better or worse, in the 1920s the valley shared the economic ambitions of its urban patron and nemesis. The rebels aimed their struggle at political rights within the regional and national state apparatus. Their downfall was their opponents' superior political power. Frontier winners were modernity's losers. The Paiute canals now ran directly to the city, bypassing the dispensable pioneers who had trampled one society in hopes of stepping up to another. The expropriators had been expropriated, with the blessing of the state at each turn. If their illusions help explain their fate, no sense of superiority can be held by the modern observer. Their problem, how to preserve community and environment in the face of state-sponsored uneven development, offered no easy solution. Their dilemma was wrapped up in the costs of prosperity, and we are struggling with it still.

SIX

The Local World
Transformed

Decline was not defeat for the Owens Valley. Contrary to the rebellion's dire rhetoric, the valley never died, although its smaller hamlets perished and its economy slipped into a coma with the depression of the 1930s. Yet even in the worst of times the community persevered. Struggle lived on in dogged action and in embellished memory. The losing battle of the 1920s had proven local strategists right in at least one respect: Los Angeles was intractable, and any redressing action would have to come from higher governmental authorities beginning with the state legislature. Ironically, the campaign to create statewide public opinion in support of the valley's plight, having failed to win decisive results during the years of resistance, began to succeed with the movement's collapse. Indeed, far beyond generating sympathy, the Owens Valley story grew to legendary proportions in the years that followed, becoming a staple of popular culture and a political resource in its own right.

This chapter analyzes the transformation of both the material footing and the cultural sensibility of local society. In contrast to the American small town whose identity and political initiative may have been submerged in twentieth-century mass society, the Owens Valley maintained a keen sense of its destiny. That fact is surprising in light of generalizations from community sociology and the wave of changes that came in the generation after 1930.[1] The seeming paradox of how a new form of incorporation helped to consolidate local culture is precisely the question this chapter proposes to answer. Broadly, I argue that local culture was not homogenized as a result of welfare state interventions, but throve on reinterpretations of old injustices as it continued to wrestle with new developmental problems. This feisty nostalgia might have gone no further had it not been for political shifts at the national level that provided a new forum for traditional and reformulated environmental grievances. Local moral economy and the currency of state legitimacy took unexpected turns and headed back toward one another.

From the 1930s onward, small-town life and frontier culture came increasingly under the influence of metropolitan and national control. Welfare state expansion brought competition and conflict between the public bureaucracies involved in the management of western land, natural resources, and water. The changing organizational environment, coupled with the growing notoriety of the Owens Valley, elevated the local struggle to a new plane of political action and opened cracks for legal maneuver. At first the changes had little impact on local society at its lowest ebb under city domination around 1930. In their own words, the remaining residents agreed that they lived under "a practical colonial system."[2] As time went on, however, a reorganized local economy began to grow and to clash in new ways with the constraints of absentee ownership. As Los Angeles moved to consolidate and even extend its hold on the eastern sierra, it ran afoul of irrepressible community attachments and new laws for environmental protection. With encouragement from the courts, local partisans gradually succeeded in making the city accountable for its management of the valley. Local self-determination has not been restored to this day, but the continuing battle has brought it closer.

Beginning with the collapse of the rebellion, the issue became what kind of a colonial regime the city would attempt and have the capacity to maintain. Los Angeles now controlled the land and water, but not the people and their legal resources. Dissent persisted, limiting the city's powers to those of an owner and employer rather than an occupying authority. Modern local society was shaped by three related changes between 1930 and 1970. First, the valley moved from an economy of agriculture and local trade to a service economy fueled by tourism and public bureaucracies. Population turnover produced a new social structure in which a small but influential group of cattle-raising lessees found themselves often at odds with the expanding service enterprises and with public employees. Second, and paradoxically, as the community became increasingly dependent upon external economies, the legend of

its battle for autonomy grew in popular culture. New interpretations of
the water war not only lionized the defeated rebellion, but also legitimized the valley's continuing grievances in the eyes of lawmakers and
the general public. The legend became a political resource. Third, as the
local-metropolitan relationship was changing in material and symbolic
ways, the national state moved effectively toward new forms of inclusion. Where the progressive state had stressed conservation in the interests of efficient use of natural resources, the welfare state shifted
steadily toward environmental stewardship. By 1970 these three forces
would converge, with reorganized local interests drawing on legitimized
protest to demand environmental protection. To understand the modern environmental movement requires a full appreciation of how the
local world was transformed.

COLONY, CONFLICT, AND THE NEW SOCIAL STRUCTURE

Having acquired most of the farm land and town property in the Owens
Valley by the early 1930s, Los Angeles was faced with the unprecedented problem of how to manage its new colony. Two fundamental
considerations shaped its policy: the city wanted to maximize the water
supply available for its own use and minimize unfavorable publicity
that would hamper its image and operations. Avuncular studies of how
the Department of Water and Power (DWP) should manage its domain
revealed the city's preference for continued mass emigration as the best
solution for residents who wanted homes and jobs.[3] "Having just won
their war with the valley ranchers, the water and power commissioners
had little desire to reestablish their former adversaries on the lands the
city had bought."[4]

The city's preference, however, was firmly rejected by those who
intended to stay. A few town and farm proprietors simply refused to
sell out, even in the deluge of 1931. Others sold, but immediately turned
to leasing back their own or better-situated properties. Behind these
choices, of course, was the grim fact of a national depression that
limited migration opportunities. Many earlier émigrés had taken up
agricultural pursuits in California's Central Valley, which became the
destination of refugees from the dust bowl after 1933. The Inyo County
population dropped by about 500 during the late 1920s, with Bishop
suffering most of the loss; but in the following decade losses were
slowly recovered, bringing Inyo and Bishop to new highs (table 10).

TABLE 10.   POPULATION, 1920–1980

	Inyo County	Bishop	Indian Population, Inyo County
1920	7,031	1,304	632
1930	6,555	850	736
1940	7,625	1,490	943
1950	11,658	2,891	799
1960	11,684	2,875	519
1970	15,571	3,498	1,170
1980	17,895	3,550	1,609

SOURCES: *U.S. Census of Population, Fourteenth* (1920) to *Twentieth* (1980).

A population that would not disappear raised political problems. As we have seen, Los Angeles was blamed increasingly for its heartless destruction of the frontier community. Unsettling as this reputation was to the municipal ego (which had always relished its moral superiority over corrupt and sinful San Francisco), it also involved serious political costs. The state legislature had retaliated directly against Los Angeles in 1925 with the Reparations Act. Under pressure from continuing public sympathy with the valley residents, in 1931 the governor demanded prompt settlement of the city's delayed purchases, and the senate appointed a special committee to investigate its program of groundwater extraction, which was under siege in the courts. The legislature took a historic step to prevent any repetition of the Owens Valley expropriation by approving the County of Origin law, which prohibited exportation of water needed in one area for purposes of developing another. The Owens Valley experience, moreover, pushed state law toward the concept of the public's right to reasonable use of state water rather than that of the unfettered rights of riparian owners, such as Los Angeles had become.

As state government belatedly moved to support valley interests, local farmers began filing lawsuits to limit DWP groundwater pumping. In fact, legal redress had been part of the protest repertoire for a long time. The first suits challenging the city's right to dry up surrounding farms by pumping groundwater for export from DWP property had been filed in the early 1920s.[5] In 1928, before the bank failure and the

Dry Ditches. Miles of irrigation canals, dug by hand during the nineteenth century, are now abandoned, along with the land purchased by the city of Los Angeles and allowed to return to sagebrush. (Photo by the author.)

collapse of the movement, a number of Lone Pine ranchers sued to enjoin further pumping and sought money damages for impairment of their wells and their livelihoods.[6] Although city buyouts probably nullified some of these suits, as many as eight separate actions were pending at one time, and in a "bitterly contested" case involving twelve Lone Pine plantiffs the judge "ordered that the defendants (meaning Los Angeles and the water board) be restrained from diverting any waters pumped from underground . . . to places outside the watershed of the Owens River [and] from taking any of the surface waters of the Owens River in excess of quantities which the city [had] been taking prior to the period of five years preceding the court action."[7] Other suits were settled out of court.

The most celebrated groundwater case of the period began in 1931. Just two years after the demise of the resistance movement, a group of forty West Bishop ranchers convened a public meeting "to make a preliminary investigation as to the method and cost of bringing an injunction suit against Los Angeles to prevent the pumping by the city of the underground waters of the valley."[8] Calling themselves the North

Aberdeen School. The public school at Aberdeen once served as the hamlet's polling place and community center for an active farming area. (Photo by the author.)

Inyo Protection Association ("[D]ues in the new organization are but $2. . . . [T]he membership list is at Dusey's store and all property owners north of Tinemaha dam are invited to sign"), the group circulated a petition on the "irreparable damage" to their water supply, delivered it as a delegation to the board of supervisors' meeting, and urged the county to join them in a suit against DWP pumping.[9] In a protracted set of maneuvers, the city of Bishop (and the Hillside Water Company until its sale to Los Angeles) joined the ranchers' suit and, after many delays and DWP efforts to head off a trial, they won a permanent injunction in February 1934.[10] Coming at a low ebb of valley resistance, the victory not only revived local spirits but established a line of defense for those who remained on the land that city plans for the region's future would have to respect. With new water projects in the planning stages and other pumping cases threatening, it was now vital that the city quell resentment and appear as a benefactor. Ever alert to the political climate, Los Angeles chose the astute course of balancing its thirst for Inyo water with local concessions to maintain peace.

As the city began developing a strategy for managing Owens Valley lands, two plans were put forth by the board of water and power commissioners. The conciliatory first approach saw the city's charge as "a problem in regional planning" and recommended rehabilitating valley agriculture with water-conserving activities, particularly the established stock-raising and dairy industries.[11] The beguiling second alternative was to convert the valley into a vast sportsman's paradise and recreational playground—all in the interests of conservation, public benefit, and, not least, minimal water demand. Both plans had the advantage of appealing to local interests. Since the 1890s cattle ranchers had been a powerful group. Dreams of a sporting redoubt and a local tourist industry had begun even earlier when streams were stocked with trout and Los Angeles tourists in covered wagons were announced in the newspapers as a sign of economic progress.[12] In practical terms, however, both plans involved the city in negotiated commitments to local residents and both carried the portent of growth, which the city was bent on minimizing. The dilemma was irreconcilable within the requirements of political peace. Henceforth the city would be compromised by its own strategy.

The two management plans, rehabilitation and recreation, developed according to different timetables. Despite its many advantages, the sportsman's paradise was slow in coming. On one hand, it was not as free of population and water requirements as it first appeared. One representative of the Inyo-Mono Associates, a new organization for promoting local business, described the problem.

> Department of Water and Power people were dead set against having any more people coming to the valley. . . . [T]hey just didn't want the issue to come up of people saying "Well, now we need to have another gas station but we don't have any land to build a gas station on, so please, Mr. City of Los Angeles, won't you either lease us or sell us a corner lot?" Our largest problem was getting the Department of Water and Power people and the Los Angeles City Council people to recognize that this was a new day and that Los Angeles was growing and the Los Angeles people had to have recreation areas and that there wasn't any reason why they couldn't have it in the towns of the Owens Valley, except the City of Los Angeles wouldn't release any of the land.[13]

On the other hand, agricultural leases had two advantages that helped offset their water requirements. Farmers and stockraisers wanted them, often as a condition of selling property to the city. A number of transactions were arranged with this condition, even though the terms for the lessees were tough. Annual rents were considered high at 6 percent of the sale value, and the city refused to grant long-term leases and water allotments. Water could be canceled at any time. Land use was usually a year-to-year proposition and never on terms longer than five years. In the bargain, however, the seller received a cash settlement and paid no land taxes as a lessee. Judging from the constant number of farms maintained between 1930 and 1940 (218 and 228, respectively)[14] despite massive city purchases, we may assume that most remaining agriculturalists found leasing a satisfactory arrangement under the circumstances. The second advantage was on the city's side, in that rents more than offset its property taxes to Inyo County.

> The ability of the water and power commission to pursue any consistent program for development of the Owens Valley in the early 1930s was undercut by the increasing pressure it encountered from the mayor's office to turn an immediate profit on its properties. By forcing the abandonment of the once-productive farmlands in order to increase water deliveries to the aqueduct, the department was both reducing its revenues and increasing the share of Inyo County taxes it had to bear. . . . By leasing the land back to the Owens Valley ranchers, the department realized it could shift the entire burden of taxation on these properties to the leaseholders. In addition, the rents paid by the lessees would satisfy the mayor's demand for income to the city, while the policy as a whole would quiet the state legislature's concern for the treatment the ranchers had received at Los Angeles' hands.[15]

Leasing thus enjoyed priority among the city's management strategies in the early years; but the plans were later merged, and recreation took on greater local economic importance in the 1950s. In combination the two strategies had decisive effects on the evolving economy and social structure. Yet broadly conceived plans seldom cover all contingencies or work themselves out uniformly in particular groups and localities. Closer to the ground, the local economy and social structure were reshaped by policy changes in three areas: the Indian question, agriculture, and the service sector.

LAND FOR THE PAIUTE

By 1930 the Paiute population had fallen to a third of its preconquest number and comprised 11 percent of the county (see table 10). Always at the bottom of the socioeconomic scale, Indians suffered most from the economic collapse that followed the city's expropriation. White farmers and businesses also suffered losses, especially in the Bishop

area, but they sold their property to the city at good prices and some of
them remained on the farm lands or town lots as lessees. When city
purchases began in earnest during the 1920s, only about thirty Indians
had acquired private property (by purchase and a few successful homesteads). Nineteen of these sold out, five receiving city leases; and four-
teen remained as private owners.[16] In 1930, the Indian population of
between seven and eight hundred persons resided in 270 households,
the great majority of which (94 percent) neither owned nor leased
property and therefore depended on wage labor.[17] But farm labor,
which had been the principal source of Indian employment, virtually
disappeared under the city regime that favored water-conserving lease
arrangements. Stock raising assumed an even greater predominance
among agricultural activities and required less labor than field crops.

In testimony before a United States Senate committee investigating
Indian conditions across the country in 1932, a DWP official observed
that "the majority of the Indians are destitute, primarily from the lack
of a local labor market . . . a large number of them do not have
home-site allotments and are objects of charity." The official showed
little sympathy for the Indians' plight: "[T]o correct this condition it is
suggested that the Indians be moved from the Owens Valley to new
locations."[18] Tracing the developments that led to this sorry pass, he
also let slip the city's general objection to a continuing Indian presence.

> As the ranchers sold their holdings and migrated from the valley, the Indians
> have been left without homes, with the result that today a large percentage
> of the Owens Valley Indians are living in shacks, tents, wickiups, and hovels
> that generally are too small for the number of occupants, unsanitary, in vio-
> lation of the housing laws, impossible to properly heat in the winter, con-
> stituting not only a menace to the Indian, but to the entire population of
> Owens Valley, and particularly threatening contamination of local communi-
> ty water supplies and the municipal water supply for the city of Los Angeles.[19]

Eight hundred widely scattered Indians probably represented no
greater sanitation problem than the thousands of sheep and cattle that
leasing encouraged; it is more likely that the preference for Indian
removal stemmed from the city's broader strategy to depopulate the
valley. As the Senate inquiry suggested, a continuing Indian presence
risked more bad publicity—Native Americans within the city's ambit
suffering high unemployment at a time when the nation was attacking
the problem with welfare-state programs to relieve the effects of the

depression and with the Indian Reorganization Act of 1934, which endeavored to create permanent homelands.

An elaborate survey conducted in 1930 by DWP agents demonstrated just how bad Indian employment conditions had become. Among 270 households in the survey, only 95 had an employed head. In 19 cases both spouses were employed. The data are incomplete about the rest of the population: 14 households were designated as having no employment; 23 were headed by aged or dependent persons; and no evidence about employment was provided on the remaining 119 households, which were, however, interviewed for the survey and generated data about housing conditions. If we assume that no evidence means no employment, then only 35 percent of the households had one or more persons employed full-time or part-time. A slightly different calculation based on the number of all household heads and spouses (excluding the aged and dependent) who were employed yields a rate of 31 percent, although it does not reckon employed children in the household. Another survey item showed that only 19 percent of the sample could be assigned an occupation. Recalling that in 1880 fully 83 percent of the adult Indian population was employed (see chapter 2, table 1), it is evident that the transformation brought about by the city's purchase of the valley had reduced by more than one-half the sources of Indian livelihood.

Where the survey probed living conditions, the results were equally dismal. Half the households were headed by a single person, more often as a result of a spouse's death rather than divorce or marital separation. A minority lived in some kind of house, but 54 percent lived in a tent, a shack, or no shelter. Only 14 percent of 270 heads of household had some cash on hand, and among those the average was $823—perhaps the meager result of land sales to the city and savings from labor. In the view of those who conducted the survey, 20 percent of the Indian heads of household could be described as "progressive" or a "good worker"; another 17 percent were at least "self-supporting"; but the remaining 63 percent were either "irregular" (4 percent) or insufficiently impressive to earn a description. The principal investigator's own word, "destitute," effectively summarized the condition of at least two-thirds of the Indians.[20]

The city's preference for Indian removal met resistance, as had a similar plan in the 1870s, but this time from the Paiutes themselves rather than their white employers. John Symmes, a forty-year-old Indian from Independence who worked for the city, appeared before the Senate committee with a collectively prepared statement.

> We, the Indians of Independence Fort, Calif., Inyo County, say once we Indians had our ways and had own food and meat and we owned this valley—Owens Valley. When the white people come they took away everything from us and learned us how to work and we worked for them. Now they took the work from us, we are without work now. We want work to be given to us, we the Owens Valley Indians, right in Owens Valley.[21]

In the memory of local white residents and in some historical accounts, Los Angeles is credited with providing employment relief for the Paiutes beginning in the winter of 1931–32.[22] H. A. Van Norman, general manager of the DWP, made broader claims at the Senate hearings, saying "[W]e have employed Indians ever since we have been in the valley."[23] How many jobs were created is unclear. The DWP's own survey, taken in the spring of 1930, showed that only four Indians worked for the city. Although a deliberate policy of hiring Indians may have been conceived in the winter of 1931–32, at least some potential beneficiaries were unaware of it. Testifying before the Senate committee in September 1932, Billy Williams of Round Valley claimed "I have not worked one minute for the city of Los Angeles and I asked them for a job several times. They have lots of white men working around there cleaning ditches this spring and also all summer."[24] Other recollections agreed that the DWP was a ready source of employment for whites during the depression. "There was a time when anybody out of work could go to the department and get a good job. They didn't have to train themselves and position[s] didn't have to be justified too well."[25] Yet available data suggest that Los Angeles provided very little Indian employment. Indeed, beginning with the statement they prepared for the visiting senators, there is evidence that the Paiutes blamed the city for the loss of their jobs and took the bold step of demanding from members of Congress that new work be provided. They also made clear to city advocates of removal their "genuine native attachment for Owens Valley [and] their determination to cling there."[26]

In the interests of peace and a low profile, Los Angeles shelved the idea of Indian removal as "impracticable."[27] Moreover, as the depression years wore on and a reform administration took over the mayor's office, city policy shifted in the direction of enlightened self-interest. Separate federal grants in 1902 and 1912 had set aside 69,000 acres of Owens Valley land for Paiute homesites, most of it in a single tract of lava plateau north of Bishop. With the exception of a 360-acre reservation at the original site of Camp Independence and 93 acres adjacent to the towns of Bishop and Big Pine, the great majority of Indian land was worthless. Worthless, that is, for agriculture, but endowed with water rights under federal law, which required that the DWP supply water to widely scattered sites at some cost to its own conservation for export.[28]

Under the circumstances, efficiency-minded reformers in city government proposed a land exchange with local Paiutes and the Department of the Interior, whereby 2,914 acres of value only to the DWP were traded for 1,392 arable acres with first-class water rights—much to the Indians' benefit.[29] The Owens Valley Land Exchange, approved by an act of Congress on April 20, 1937, turned over 875 acres for a new reservation close to the center of Bishop, 280 acres in Big Pine, and 237 in Lone Pine.[30] The Paiutes at Camp Independence, scheduled to receive 120 acres, withdrew from the agreement before its completion, evidently suspicious of the city's intentions. This last fact is significant in connection with continuing Indian resistance. The reservation at Independence was "by far in the best financial and social condition,"[31] suggesting that only the more desperate settlements were ready to trust the white man. Although practical considerations prompted city action, including a reduction of taxes owed to Inyo County, the political implications were not ignored in a DWP report that credited the department with the responsible "discharge of a possible moral duty on the part of the City in assisting the Indians."[32]

CLIENT AGRICULTURE

The Land Exchange was but a piece of the city's welfare-state policy toward the valley that took shape in the 1930s. Even before the massive land purchases, the board of public service commissioners had employed a consulting agriculturalist to plan the valley's future under city control. In his report written in July 1925, Walter Packard urged as much resettlement as possible within the norms of water conservation, "to eliminate conflicts of interest which lead to misunderstandings and lack of harmony."[33] The leasing of agricultural lands was thus conceived early and implemented to facilitate the massive sales (with reparations waivers) that took place in the late 1920s. Most reports agree that once the resistance movement was broken, any rancher who wanted to stay on under a short-term lease arrangement was able to do so. Yet the city also made it clear that water for irrigation was scarce and subject to cancellation or reduction from year to year. These constraints meant that production of livestock and some alfalfa were the only rational choices for the farmer as, indeed, the Packard report had recommended.

After a decline during the years of rebellion, the amount of land in farms doubled during the 1930s (table 11). Most of this increase can be attributed to the program of city leasing. In succeeding decades, as the acreage devoted to sheep and cattle ranching expanded onto federal land, the number of farms dropped sharply, meaning that their average size and dollar value rose. Homesteads and cultivated fields of a few hundred acres were consolidated into cattle ranches of several thousand. The trend begun in the 1890s, which had divided cattle ranchers in the southern valley from persevering farmers in the north, now swept across the landscape. Hundreds of small-farm proprietors gave way to scores of agricultural managers who operated, but did not own, highly valued ranches.

The new class division separating lessee ranchers from wage earners, who were increasingly absorbed by public agencies including the DWP, introduced social and political cleavages. The valley's population began to divide into a large group of people forced to reorganize their lives under deteriorating economic conditions and a smaller, more powerful group of city clients who emerged as the beneficiaries of "practical colonialism." The second group, moreover, had the resources and interests that facilitated their control of local politics on behalf of their city patrons. Citizens in the nonagricultural majority were critical of the city-rancher alliance, judging it as both a source of exploitation and an obstacle to local development.

> The Department has subsidized the cattlemen, and as a result, they have never been willing to take a stand against the Department, even when they threatened to. Even in local issues, the Department used the cattlemen to defeat things that might tax DWP lands. They got the cattlemen to oppose a given issue by saying that if the tax goes on the land, then of course, their rental fees and their leases will be raised. So the cattlemen contribute very little to the economy of the country. They do lots of buying on the outside. They hire almost no employees and they contribute very little in Inyo County, and yet for years the cattlemen were the County Supervisors. They were the only ones that had the freedom to do it. People who would have been better qualified for supervisors were too busy in business or professional activities, making their own way, and didn't have time to devote to the politics of Inyo County. This, of course, really slanted the outlook of the

Red Mountain Fruit Ranch, 1920 and 1990. These two views, photographed from virtually the same spot, exemplify changes in the valley. The top photo, circa 1920, although taken in winter, shows a prosperous farm with several hundred acres of orchards. The one below, taken in June 1990, shows barely a trace of the farm, a grove of trees at the lower left kept alive only because they stand on a public campsite, and miles of devastation. (Courtesy of the Eastern California Museum.)

TABLE II.   AGRICULTURE, 1920–1980

	Number of Farms	Farm Acreage, Inyo County	Average Farm Size (acres)	Average Farm Value ($)
1920	521	140,029	269	28,687
1930	218	94,567	434	62,200
1940	228	183,564	805	30,142
1950	193	221,085	1,146	49,899
1960	104[a]	329,782	3,171	64,921
1970	90[a]	485,765	5,397	658,001
1980	80[a]	395,547	4,944	1,108,563

SOURCES: *U.S. Census of Agriculture, Fourteenth* (1920) to *Twentieth* (1978).
[a]U.S. Census of Agriculture changed reporting years to 1959, 1969, 1978.

county. It has resulted in a very exaggerated picture of the value of cattlemen in Inyo County, and the role they've played. Many of them wouldn't have made it, if it hadn't been for the cheap leases of the DWP as well as the similar situation on Bureau of Land Management and Forest Service lands.[34]

The city-rancher alliance, nevertheless, had its own tensions and by no means embraced all of the important local interests. When the DWP would get stingy with water allotments, stock raisers easily realigned with their town neighbors. Meanwhile, town businesses were also lessees, and thus in a position analogous to the ranchers, and the towns-people were urging that the city offer commercial and residential lots for resale to the public. Pressure for resale gathered as local businesses adopted one aspect of the city's own plan and pressed new opportunities in tourism.

THE SERVICE ECONOMY

Under the combined impact of the depression and city purchases, local economic activity hit bottom around 1930, stayed there for a few years, and then started the slow climb back. "People still had businesses, they had grocery stores and gas stations and clothing shops, and they were living off what little summer traffic came up to go fishing in the High Sierra and that type of thing."[35] As the leading center of population and commerce, Bishop had fallen farthest, but towns like Lone Pine expe-

Service Economy. Beginning in the 1930s, a service sector dependent mainly on visitors from outside the Owens Valley became the mainstay of the valley's economy. (Courtesy of the Eastern California Museum.)

rienced the 1930s much as they had the previous decade. The southern end of the valley

> had a cattleman's and tourist economy. That's about all. You had the stores that hired people that waited on the summer trade, and you had, oh, I'd say twenty or thirty pretty fair-sized cattle ranches and one or two very large cattle outfits. And eventually they got a little more water for raising alfalfa. You had quite a bit of mining still going on in those days—more dreamer's mining, I would say, but there was a lot of prospecting. The town of Darwin was still going with a big lead mill and had about a hundred or two hundred people working there. That kept some of the economy coming into Lone Pine.[36]

This description omits Lone Pine's glamor industry, the movies. Beginning in 1920, Hollywood studios used the Alabama Hills in the sierra foothills between Lone Pine and Independence as the location for several hundred B westerns and films with a British India motif, such as the classics *Lives of a Bengal Lancer* (1934), *Gunga Din* (1938), and *King of the Khyber Rifles* (1939). Russ Spainhower's ranch near Lone Pine rented horses and wagons to the film companies, and local residents were employed as extras. The work was irregular, of course, but it paid well, and companies followed so closely on one another that reservations had to be scheduled in advance for limited local hotel space. Walter Dow's sixty-five-room hotel on Main Street throve on the business. William Boyd was in town so often making Hopalong Cassidy pictures that he kept a cabin near Lone Pine. Tom Mix, as we have seen, threw his theatrical weight behind the Alabama Gates insurgency, inconsequential as both proved to be. The production of *Gunga Din* required "one of the largest location camps in the history of filmmaking. The climactic battle scene featured 1,200 [local residents as] extras, 400 horses, nine water buffalo, eight camels, and four elephants. . . . A small army of carpenters constructed a complete Hindu city [and] a tent city which housed 600 technicians and support crews for more than two months."[37] Pete Olivas, a local ranch hand who worked on the films as a wrangler and stuntman, recalled that "a lot of guys got a lot of work from the studios. They left a lot of money here."[38]

Business promoters throughout the valley began to fix their hopes for the future on the same qualities of Inyo County that attracted the film companies. Scenery, a playground for the southern metropolis, and outdoor sports all suggested complementary retail and service businesses. In the mid-1930s, an unlikely pair of newcomers assumed leadership for the valley's commercial development. Father John Crowley, the desert priest with a parish as large as his native Ireland, and Ralph Merritt, a recovering polio victim and former head of the Sun Maid Raisin Growers Association in Fresno, combined their efforts for economic recovery in a promotional organization called the Inyo-Mono Associates. With small cash subscriptions from merchants, they launched a campaign to attract investment and Los Angeles visitors to the valley's tourist opportunities. Crowley and Merritt recruited Robert Brown, a former English teacher at Big Pine High School with a journalism background, to head the Inyo-Mono Associates as a "publicity bureau." Brown felt he was successful at getting the metropolitan newspapers to carry articles in their sports sections about the abundance of fish and game in Inyo and Mono Counties. According to his account, "there were some very influential people in Los Angeles who were watching this struggle between the tiny community of people fighting for their life and the big outfits trying to hold onto the status quo." Oddly enough, the *Los Angeles Times* became a key ally when Brown persuaded its publisher "to get on our side and start needling the City a little bit."[39] If the *Times* was at odds with city government, however, that had less to do with any genuine sympathy for the valley than with metropolitan political infighting.[40] As the Inyo-Mono Associates cultivated one group of outside supporters, they encountered a division between the town merchants and the local interests aligned with the DWP.

> John Lubken was the largest cattleman in the country and also chairman of the Board of Supervisors. At this time John didn't like what we were trying to do in bringing the transients in because people would cut his fences and all that. He was not particularly for the program, although he was a smart and very able supervisor and realized that the economy had to be kept up by the merchants in the main streets of the town. One of the major store owners in Lone Pine was one of the Joseph boys. There were two drugstores; they were both active because they naturally got all the tourist business. There were also three or four restaurant owners. You would find a few businessmen who were soured and who didn't like life in general, who didn't think we were doing any good, who thought things were all going to hell in a handbasket and that it was all Los Angeles' fault, and this and that and the other, but really not very many. Of the major businesses in Lone Pine, we had good support, like I say, from the drugstore people, the grocery people, the hotel people, and anybody who would profit by getting more tourists into the county. They could see the results of what we were doing with the newspapers in Los Angeles because tourist travel picked up right away. There was a noticeable change in the cash register.[41]

As at various times in the past, valley groups were divided by the nature of their vertical ties to outside interests. By contrast to the years around 1900, however, the positions of farmers and merchants were now somewhat reversed. Agricultural interests, previously the defenders of local society, were now transformed and aligned with the city. Merchants, who once looked for salvation in external trade, were becoming the champions of community development.

The parallel may be extended further, because during each period the valley-city relationship was critically affected by the actions of the state—the federal government at the turn of the century and the State of California in the 1930s. The legislature, as we have seen, expressed its belated opposition to metropolitan expropriation of far-flung water supplies in the County of Origin statute of 1931, and state courts began deciding lawsuits in favor of valley claims against Los Angeles. More immediate results for the local economy were generated by the state's completion of a paved highway from the Mojave Desert to Lake Tahoe in the late 1930s. Contemporary research by geographer Ruth Baugh noted that "the significant element in today's economic life is the fact that the axis of the valley is the route of a major state thoroughfare."[42]

Among other indicators, she reports precious data from a "traffic census" showing that the 509 automobiles passing Bishop's main intersection in July 1924 had increased to 1,092 in July 1935. According to one estimate a million tourists visited the Owens Valley in 1940.[43]

> The opening of resorts on the east slope of the Sierra Nevada is bringing Bishop increased business. Bishop is the point of divergence of roads entering the recreation region. To help in serving the transient population eleven gas stations, five garages, four auto camps, one modern hotel, and a dozen or more cafes and other food dispensaries are distributed along the 1.2 miles of state highway upon which Bishop fronts. But the supplies purveyed to passing tourists are not valley products but are trucked in 300 miles from Los Angeles."[44]

The growing commercial and service economy put new pressure on the DWP to liberalize its management strategy, particularly as resurgent businesses fueled the campaign by Father Crowley for resale of town properties to merchant lessees. Bad public relations continued to hound the city's reputation both in the state legislature and locally. On occasion, glimpses of traditional popular justice appeared in the valley. The aqueduct was dynamited again in November 1931 during the mobilization against groundwater pumping. A new issue arose when the DWP occasionally demolished substandard housing on the abandoned plots it owned as a method of avoiding local taxes on improvements or the costs of the repair that would be required before any resale. The practice caused resentment among local residents, especially those who needed low-cost housing. "People get the idea that this [demolition] is just to make it hard on us . . . a lot of people would like to live in these shacks because of cheap rent."[45] Grievance and distrust prompted a new wave of arson on city-owned abandoned structures. As in the nineteenth-century firings of stores and haystacks, no arrests were made and residents disagreed as to the identity of the culprits. Some blamed dissident citizens; others speculated that the DWP had hired local agents to rid themselves anonymously of the structures[46]—a less likely conjecture because the city openly destroyed other buildings. The combination of economic growth, the local redevelopment campaign, and threatened protest explain the city's concessions to the resale initiative that followed.

Between 1938 and 1944, the city "sold by negotiation" 637 properties that, the DWP claimed, represented "more than 50% of the city-owned town lots" in all of Bishop, Big Pine, Independence, and Lone Pine. More were sold from 1947 to 1963, bringing the total to 1,083, or roughly 90 percent of all the city's holdings in Owens Valley towns.[47] A DWP report shows that during the same years, in addition to resales, over fifty leases and permits were granted for local recreational and public land uses, including the county fairgrounds, airports, churches, parks, hospitals, post offices, golf courses, a museum, a library, a California Institute of Technology test site, a University of California research station, a jail, and a parachute drop zone for a local club.[48] A resurgent spirit of local autonomy and the city's calculated conciliation led to repossession of the towns by residents and businesses, although the expanse of open land remained under DWP leases.

As tourism drooped with the onset of World War II, Inyo County received an alternative economic stimulant from an unwanted source. President Roosevelt issued Executive Order 9066 on February 19, 1942, requiring the internment of all Japanese Americans living on the west coast. Shortly afterward, the federal government notified the City of Los Angeles that 4,725 acres of DWP property would be appropriated for the first relocation center at the abandoned hamlet of Manzanar between Independence and Lone Pine. Arrangements for building and staffing the camp were begun by Assistant Attorney General (later Supreme Court Justice) Tom Clark, who established connections with the local DWP supervisor and Robert Brown of the Inyo-Mono Associates. Clark was astute enough to realize that local support would smooth the way toward establishing a camp for the now-vilified Japanese. Evidently on Brown's advice, Clark chose to work with a citizens' committee that included Brown as executive secretary of the Inyo-Mono Associates; its president, merchant Douglas Joseph; George Savage, owner of the Chalfant Press, which published the three major valley newspapers; Ralph Merritt, who in addition to his valley development work had been the federal food administrator for California during World War I and later comptroller of the University of California, and who would soon become the camp director at Manzanar; Inyo County Superior Court Judge William Dehy, a leader in the 1920s resistance movement; Dr. Howard Dueker; and lumber company owner R. R. Henderson of Lone Pine.[49] Acting through prominent organizations, the federal government confirmed a new leadership group in the valley, comprised mainly of people involved in commercial redevelopment work. Each generation seems to have its own Owens Valley Citizens' Committee, and the wartime volunteers used the name to suggest a civic responsibility for hosting the relocation camp.

Initially, local reaction to the proposed camp rekindled the odious nativism of the valley's nineteenth-century reaction to the Chinese.

Aroused by Pearl Harbor, the *Inyo Independent* published articles on the "Jap menace" in February 1942, including fantasized news of a Japanese plot to sabotage the Los Angeles water system.[50] The committee moved quickly to quell this mood.

> We had people from WCCA [Wartime Civil Control Administration] and the Army and the Attorney General's office come out and brief them [the community] very thoroughly, and then most of the members of the Owens Valley Citizens Committee would go out and talk to the Rotary Clubs and women's clubs and PTA and whatnot. We did this very fast [and] we had sort of a "let's wait and see" kind of support from most of the people. And we had ten or fifteen or twenty percent of the people who were violently against it.[51]

A key change of heart came from the publisher and co-opted committee member George Savage, whose alarmism of February shifted in March to the highroad of patriotism. In an editorial published in three valley newspapers, Savage now saw "History in the Making":

> These changes were not of our asking, but the military necessities of war brought war to our own doorstep in an unexpected manner. Thus we see that the people of Inyo County have a definite part to play in the American wartime effort. Let's do the job so that the eyes of the nation and the world will be focussed on the citizens of this county and outsiders will say that "there's a group of people who are tackling a most strategic international problem and doing a great job of it."[52]

Not everyone was persuaded. The rumor circulated that a vigilante militia was training for defense of the towns against possible attacks from camp escapees. Seeing the potential for commercial gain, twenty-two Lone Pine merchants asked that Japanese prisoners be allowed to shop in their stores, but they were abruptly chastised by a petition from five hundred citizens opposed to free movement of internees beyond their barbed-wire enclosure.[53] The racism that the Owens Valley shared with the rest of the country did not, however, present an obstacle to the commercial benefits that were bound to flow from ten thousand Japanese imprisoned in a county with a somewhat smaller population. Arguing for acceptance, the *Inyo Independent* foresaw agricultural renewal "for defense production [and] a large reservoir of labor" that might be applied to county public works.[54] Although neither of these possibilities was realized, "the opening of Manzanar did indeed bring the prosperity Savage and his colleagues had promised. Safeway, J. C. Penney, and Sprouse-Reitz opened branch stores to handle the increased commercial trade from the camp, and Savage himself began publishing the *Manzanar Daily Free Press.*"[55]

Most of the benefits fell to Lone Pine, the town closest to the camp. The owner of Hopkins Hardware Store recalled: "[I]t was a good commercial boom, I'll tell you that. I mean, that boosted the economy of our area here in Lone Pine immensely."[56] The strongest business surge came in the spring of 1942, when camp construction employed every available carpenter in the county and "it helped the lumber yards, for instance; many thousands of dollars worth of lumber was sold. And every business place in town was selling material out there, as well as in town."[57] The liquor dealers and cocktail lounge operators in Lone Pine and Independence were so popular with construction workers that camp contractors asked them to start closing at midnight to reduce absenteeism.[58] Although diversified trade slowed when the construction was finished, staple businesses continued to profit. "We had a drug store and market, and we'd run a truck daily to Manzanar."[59]

Although Manzanar has continued to draw visitors to the Owens Valley since its dedication as an historical landmark in 1973, its economic consequences were confined to the war years. Yet Manzanar illustrated two cosmopolitan influences on the changing local society. First, personal experience with what has become a national disgrace eroded some of the nativism that once pervaded the valley. The plaque that dedicates the site calls Manzanar a "concentration camp" and memorializes people who suffered "humiliation" and "economic exploitation" as a result of American "racism." If some local residents have trouble with the blunt words, in retrospect others have a keener appreciation for historical injustice than is typical of other California communities.[60] Second, from the time when "Lone Pine found itself just rolling in Uncle Sam's money,"[61] the valley has continued to depend economically on government payrolls in addition to the retail trade and services largely connected with tourism. Indeed, the major public employers, including the U.S. Forest Service, the Bureau of Land Management, the California Fish and Game Department, and the Los Angeles Department of Water and Power, are themselves linked indirectly with the tourist economy as an aspect of their responsibilities for managing natural resources.

It would exaggerate the socioeconomic changes of the 1930s through the 1950s to conclude that the Owens Valley prospered under city dominance or that anything like the ebullient mood of 1900 returned. People got by, most of them modestly and a few quite nicely on public leases. A new kind of inequality appeared, with a gap between wage employment in the service sector and control of large tracts of land. Public largesse had become the essential resource shaping the economy and social structure.

As oral histories suggest, the war years witnessed a surge in county retail sales and service receipts. The rate of increase county-wide slowed for retail businesses in the 1950s, but services in the county and all activities in Bishop increased dramatically in the same decade (tables 12 and 13). From 1958 to 1967 growth moved steadily upward, but the following decade saw a significant jump, with retail and service profits more than doubling. The rate of increase is sustained in recent figures. Census data by county for government employment at all levels only began to appear in published sources in 1960. At that time, 20 percent of the entire Inyo labor force was employed in public agencies. In tandem with expansion in other sectors, the labor force in government at all levels rose to 28 percent in 1970 and held at that level in 1980. In each of those decades the Inyo figure was ten percentage points higher than the average for all California counties.[62]

For the population as a whole, the significant changes in the structure of employment from 1930 to 1970 included a precipitous decline in farm owners, managers, and labor (from roughly 40 to 3 percent of the labor force). Nonfarm labor and operatives also declined from one-quarter to one-eighth of the employed population, while the trades held their own (16 percent). At the upper end of the occupational scale, the relative number of professionals remained the same (10 percent). The major shifts, therefore, took place in expanding retail sales, services, and public employment. In this respect Inyo County reflected national trends over the same period, a structural convergence with urban society that appeared for the first time at midcentury.

The economic revival accomplished by the 1970s did not boost all of the valley's citizens in equal measure. Paiutes, at the bottom of the nineteenth-century occupational ladder, had lost their conventional forms of employment in the transition from pioneer to modern society. Previous estimates suggest that perhaps two-thirds of the adult Indian population were unemployed in 1930. Although the change was gradual, over the next 50 years Paiutes improved their occupational standing without reaching full equality. In 1980, unemployment for all of Inyo County stood at 8 percent, while the level for Indians was 25 percent. Clearly some did not choose to work off the reservation. Those who did, however, found specialized niches that gave them less occupational mobility than whites experienced.

TABLE 12. COMMERCE AND SERVICES, INYO COUNTY, 1930–1982

	Retail Stores, N	Retail Sales ($ × 1,000)	Service Establishments	Service Receipts ($ × 1,000)
1930	127	2,865	—	—
1939	153	4,092	22	92
1948	195	14,934	51	479
1958	212	23,972	157	4,094
1967	244	37,848	189	5,963
1977	269	76,300	249	14,829
1982	264	129,670	—[a]	—[a]

SOURCES: *U.S. Census of Distribution*, 1930; *U.S. Census of Business*, 1939 to 1967; *U.S. Census of Retail Trade*, 1977 to 1982; *U.S. Census of Service Industries*, 1977 to 1982.

[a]Data available only for establishments with payroll.

TABLE 13. COMMERCE AND SERVICES, BISHOP, 1930–1982

	Retail Stores, N	Retail Sales ($ × 1,000)	Service Establishments	Service Receipts ($ × 1,000)
1930	—	—	—	—
1939	—	—	—	—
1948	73	7,794	24	268
1958	95	13,323	71	1,810
1967	125	22,896	91	3,262
1977	170	59,974	169	10,096
1982	171	94,747	—[a]	—[a]

SOURCES: *U.S. Census of Distribution*, 1930; *U.S. Census of Business*, 1939 to 1967; *U.S. Census of Retail Trade*, 1977 to 1982; *U.S. Census of Service Industries*, 1977 to 1982.

[a]Data available only for establishments with payroll.

The adult Indian population of Inyo County in 1980 numbered 970, with 566 in the labor force and 75 percent of those (422) employed. Indian women were almost as well represented in the labor force as men and had lower rates of unemployment (18 versus 30 percent). By contrast to the general county population, Indians were less represented in professional and managerial posts (13 versus 9 percent) and more in labor (7 versus 16 percent). Indian men worked in construction and mining, while women were conspicuous among cooks and motel maids. Yet the evidence suggests that Indians were gradually improving their occupational standing in the new economy. Thirty-six percent of all employed Indians worked for government (versus 28 percent of whites) and the service economy generally employed 51 percent of working Indians (versus 34 percent of whites). Indians were well represented among hospital, health, and education workers. Retail trade (19 percent) and mining (12 percent) follow service-sector employment at some distance. In summary, after one hundred years of wage work marked by the nadir of unemployment in 1930, Paiutes have returned to significant levels of participation in the labor force; although these are still below white levels, there is a marked trend toward integration in the locally expanding service economy and public employment.[63]

SUMMARY

In the fifty years following the valley's economic collapse under the weight of depression and city takeover in 1930, local society was steadily rebuilt and structurally transformed. Over five hundred modest farmers in 1920 were replaced by eighty cattle ranchers who managed, on average, five-thousand-acre ranches of city-owned land valued at over a million dollars each. The number working in agriculture had fallen to 3 percent of the labor force in 1980. Indians, once heavily employed in farm labor, had moved principally into low-level service jobs and public employment. Against these losses, however, a new commercial economy throve. The valley's current population is three times its 1930 size. Population growth reflects a significant expansion of retail trade and services, much of it linked to the new economy of tourism and recreation. Government agencies that maintain the towns and surrounding public lands comprise another pillar of the local economy. Tourism and public bureaucracy have transformed the valley, as a consequence of the region's subordination to urban expansion in Los Angeles. The new social structure, its class and political divisions, are products of state incorporation.

Nothing is produced in the Owens Valley today. City and federal workers mix with sports enthusiasts in the restaurants on Main Street. Motels and gas stations outnumber lodges and assembly halls. The valley's business consists of serving far-flung bureaus and visitors. Off Main Street, however, communities persevere—savoring their pioneer tradition and trying to put "the troubles" behind them. Try as they may, however, city domination cannot be forgotten or ignored as a condition of daily life. Usually they accommodate. At times, when the DWP tightens the screws, they fight back. By contrast to the rebellious 1920s, the Owens Valley in 1970 was a very different society, fortuitously prepared to fight with new weapons. Fewer local citizens had a taste for renewed struggle, and those who did were often newcomers. They had less to lose, yet circumstances were such that they would win more than their insurgent forebears.

SYMBOLS AND POLITICS

Paradoxically, as the Owens Valley economy and society steadily revived after 1930, the legend of its destruction grew even faster. The publicity that rebels in the 1920s had hoped would save their communities was reinterpreted and reproduced as California folklore and commercial fiction over the next half century—too late for some purposes, but not for others.

As the legend grew, historical accuracy inevitably suffered. Interpretations never entertained by the rebels themselves—such as conspiratorial intrigue behind city actions—were advanced in romantic and muckraking accounts. Dispassionate observers have properly exposed these "distortions," but few have moved on to analyze the nature and uses of the legend. The historian Abraham Hoffman speaks for many, including Los Angeles partisans, when he laments that a popular film about water and corruption based on the Owens Valley experience took liberties with the city's legitimate development efforts. "*Chinatown*, its excellent story supported by a distorted version of history, assures new misunderstandings. . . . [H]opefully the cause of history may be spared yet another contrivance manipulating time and events."[64] To hope for some impartial factual resolution of a highly charged political conflict now in its eighth decade not only seems quixotic but neglects the opportunity to analyze the cultural politics of the controversy—the manner

in which symbols, indeed distortions, have become part of the political
struggle. A distinctive aspect of this legend, moreover, is that in partisan
accounts and popular culture, "the Owens Valley controversy came to
be one instance in which the history of a conflict was not written by the
victors."[65] History became symbol, and symbolism played an essential
part in California water politics from the 1930s onward.

The legend, elaborated over some sixty years, appeared in two stages
divided by the watershed years of the late 1920s. A critical shift occurred at that time when the folkloric master theme changed from rural
romance to state intrigue.

Literary interpretations of Owens Valley society began appearing in
the 1910s, using the struggle over water rights as a backdrop for Western morality plays. With the valley's future still an open question, authors could write their own resolution and make their chosen protagonists responsible for the result. Peter Kyne's 1914 novel *The Long
Chance* is an engaging melodrama with overtones of Zane Grey's *Riders of the Purple Sage,* which appeared two years earlier. Kyne's hero,
Bob McGraw, an improbable combination of desert rat, clever lawyer,
and social reformer, is committed to outmaneuvering corrupt officials
in the state land office for the benefit of the toiling masses.

> I've cast my fortune in the desert of Owens river valley. I've cut out for
> myself a job that will last me all my life, and win or lose, I'll fight to a finish.
> I'm going to make thirty-two thousand acres of barren waste bloom and
> furnish clean unsullied wealth for a few thousand poor, crushed devils that
> have been slaughtered and maimed under the Juggernaut of our Christian
> civilization. I'm going to plant them on ten-acre farms up there under the
> shadow of Mt. Kearsarge, and convert them into Pagans. I'm going to create
> Eden out of an abandoned Hell. I'm going to lay out a townsite and men will
> build me a town, so I can light it with my own electricity. It's a big utopian
> dream. A few thousand of the poor and lowly and hopeless brought out of
> the cities and given land and a chance for life, liberty, and the pursuit of
> happiness; to know that their toil will bring them some return, that they can
> have a home and a hope for the future.[66]

McGraw succeeds, of course, by detecting "powerful private interests at
work in the state land office . . . aided by corrupt minor officials" who
were trying to grab land that they had "suddenly withdrawn from entry
and thrown into a Forest Reserve."[67] Kyne's plot uses familiar events,
but substitutes private speculators and dishonest bureaucrats for the
City of Los Angeles and Forest Service chief Gifford Pinchot, on one
hand, and the intrepid McGraw at the head of thousands of crushed

devils in place of the citizens' movement, on the other. The conflict is presented in nineteenth-century cultural themes that set capitalist greed, public corruption, urban exploitation, and Christian hypocrisy against rural virtue, grass-roots utopia, returns to honest toil, and philanthropy. Whatever distortions Kyne may introduce, his drama taps the cultural wellsprings of the 1905 protest movement. Rural probity, urban imperiousness, and all they entrain were the opposing symbols of the conflict and the meanings that fueled local action.

Mary Austin's more serious novel *The Ford* (1917) is similar to *The Long Chance* in important respects, despite a shift of moral responsibility to the settlers themselves and a jaundiced assessment of pioneer character. The story involves divisions within the valley between the strong and scheming land baron Timothy Rickart (after rancher Thomas Rickey) and the doleful farmers who, like Mary's own ineffectual husband, dream of one day "getting into something." The geographically repositioned valley of Tierra Longa is coveted by unsavory oil interests and city agents from San Francisco, who are taking options on land and water rights amidst local confusion over whether they are "government men representin' the Irrigation Bureau." Young Kenneth Brent uncovers Rickart's connivance in a land-grabbing plan to export water and endeavors to unite valley farmers in "common resentment [and] tribal solidarity," but fails. "The solitary, rural habit which admitted them to a community of beguilement could not lift them to a community of enterprise."[68] Austin is clearly evaluating the farmers' failure in 1905, attributing it to "their invincible rurality . . . how, by as much as they had given themselves to the soil, they were made defenseless against this attack on it."[69] They lacked any vision of an alternative to life on the land. "It isn't the Old Man's capital that the people of the valley are up against, so much as it is their *idea* of it, and their idea of the situation, or their lack of ideas. . . . The greatest common factor of the Tierra Longans was their general inability to rise to the Old Man's stature; they were inferior stuff of the same pattern."[70]

Both novels cast the legend in terms of class struggle—the rich, urban, and powerful bent upon dispossessing the humble poor. Although Austin's moral is equally critical of rural parochialism, neither author moves beyond individual actors motivated by stereotypical vices. Institutional actors and state designs were not yet evocative cultural themes; but that would soon change.

The integration of legend and politics began, as we have seen, with strategic efforts by the resistance movement to publicize its aims and win over public opinion throughout California. Noting that "the only weapon we have is publicity," Mark Watterson urged Mary Austin to write a partisan account for the Associated Press.[71] Although there is no evidence that Austin took the suggestion, the Wattersons successfully recruited metropolitan California newspapers to the cause. Court Kunze's impassioned twelve-part series in the *San Francisco Call* entitled "Valley of Broken Hearts"[72] was reprinted in the *Los Angeles Record,* and Burton Kniseley,[73] who edited that feisty opposition paper during the southland newspaper wars, was a constant ally.[74] The publicity campaign succeeded in at least two respects. Extended coverage of the Owens Valley struggle helped make it a statewide political issue, and public reaction was sympathetic even in Los Angeles, particularly in the wake of dramatic protests. Following the bank failure, the *Times* and *Record* found themselves in editorial agreement on the city's responsibility to help avert financial ruin in the valley.[75]

A big step from sympathetic news coverage to legend building occurred when the Wattersons began financing the Los Angeles civic reformer and publicist Andrae Nordskog. A man of varied talents, Nordskog began publishing the weekly *Gridiron* in Los Angeles after his phonograph record manufacturing firm failed in 1926.[76] Looking for bigger stories than excessive telephone rates and deficient city services, Nordskog traveled to the Owens Valley in June 1927 and immediately became an impassioned ally of Chalfant and the Watterson brothers. Before long the *Gridiron* was publishing denunciations of the city's water commissioners. Through his business connections, Nordskog carried the fight to a weekly radio broadcast and to civic groups—all of it subsidized by cash contributions from the Wattersons' bank, a fact that Nordskog tried unsuccessfully to hide.[77] The bank failure and the ensuing trial only intensified Nordskog's efforts to research and expose the injustice as he saw it. He next traveled to Washington, D.C., to research Bureau of Reclamation records in connection with the events of 1905 and their parallels to the new Colorado River project that would bring additional water to Southern California. The results of his study were presented in a long and, by all accounts, chaotic manuscript that Nordskog tried to publish—hounding Mary Austin and Los Angeles attorney and writer Carey McWilliams to provide a foreword that would sway New York publishing houses. On the podium or in print, Nordskog's faults included prolixity, self-importance, histrionics, and a tendency to misrepresent his hard-won evidence by overstating the conspiratorial aspects of the case. McWilliams was impressed with the revelations in his work, but found him tedious and "as a man, rather naive. N writes like a bond salesman with a yen to be a poet."[78] The manuscript, "Boulder Dam in Light of the Owens Valley Fraud," was never published.

Through an odd chain of circumstance, however, Nordskog's brief had a greater effect on subsequent events than anything written up to that time. As a result of his investigations, seeming expertise, and public visibility as a champion of water-management reform, in 1930 Nordskog was elected chairman of the Southwest Water League, an organization of forty-eight Southern California cities. With this organizational base, "a new opportunity for Nordskog to alert the public to Los Angeles' water aggressions came in early 1931 when the state senate adopted a resolution creating a special committee to investigate the city's actions in the Owens Valley. Nordskog was asked to testify before the committee."[79] With the legislature increasingly hostile toward Los Angeles, this investigation eventually led to the County of Origins law. In preparation for the hearings, Nordskog condensed the Boulder Dam tome into twenty-eight pages, which the committee, in an unusual act of assent, ordered published in the *Assembly Journal.* Under the official state seal, fifteen hundred reprints of Nordskog's *Communication to the California Legislature Relating to the Owens Valley Water Situation* were printed and mailed on request, at public expense. "Now, in the 1930s, critics of the actions of Los Angeles had what appeared to be a state-sponsored document supporting the view that it had all been a giant conspiracy."[80]

Carey McWilliams recommended to Mary Austin, and perhaps other critics, that she send for copies of the *Communication* and the Report of the Special Investigating Committee.[81] "They contain, in neatly digested form, all the pertinent facts about the Owens Valley steal."[82] But it was the popular book *Los Angeles,* published by journalist Morrow Mayo in 1932, that converted Nordskog's dense investigation into the stuff of popular legend. Mayo's breezy chronicle is best remembered for its chapter on "The Rape of the Owens Valley." Relying mainly on Nordskog, Chalfant, and newspaper sources, Mayo tells the story of how "a rich agricultural valley" was destroyed by the U.S. government for Los Angeles developers. Mayo's distinct contribution to folklore comes in the combination of a bludgeoning narrative with a sense of institutional action—a formula unknown in earlier writing on this history but resonant in the years of depression and the emerging welfare state.

> Los Angeles gets its water by reason of one of the costliest, crookedest, most unscrupulous deals ever perpetrated, plus one of the greatest pieces of engineering folly ever heard of. Owens Valley is there for anybody to see. The

City of the Angels moved through this valley like a devastating plague. It was ruthless, stupid, cruel, and crooked. It deliberately ruined Owens Valley. It stole the waters of Owens River. It drove the people from Owens Valley from their home, a home which they had built from the desert. It turned a rich, reclaimed agricultural section of a thousand square miles back into primitive desert. For no sound reason, for no sane reason, it destroyed a helpless agricultural section and a dozen towns. It was an obscene enterprise from beginning to end.

Today there is a saying in California about this funeral ground which may well remain as its epitaph: "The Federal Government of the United States held Owens Valley while Los Angeles raped it."[83]

Mayo's sexual symbolism had a sharp impact in the 1930s and, indeed, still carried force forty years later when a new citizens' movement would rally to "the rape of the Owens Valley." The countryside is now remetaphorized as feminine and nurturant, the city as masculine and brutal. Equally sadistic, the federal government helps subdue the victim. We have come a long way from 1905, when farm women like Lesta Parker turned to Uncle Sam's paternal justice on behalf of the common folk. In the emerging modern symbolism, violated citizens and rapacious institutions supplant wholesome pioneers building the West for the nation's benefit. Indeed, the masculine metaphor of conquering pioneer communities, their victory over nature and savages, is replaced by an agriculturally fertile feminine home. The symbolic shift transfigures the whole moral grammar. Mistreated pioneers deserve recognition, compensation, and fair play—the full rights of political citizenship. But violated innocents and home-makers demand vindication—restoration of their honor. Symbolically the modern struggle moved beyond politics to virtue.

It was a short step from Mayo's journalistic obloquy to novelistic social realism. *Los Angeles* supplied the plot for a series of books and films treating exploitation and the wages of avarice. Will Rogers helped advertise the Owens Valley story in his nationally syndicated column: "Ten years ago this was a wonderful valley with one quarter of a million acres of fruit and alfalfa. But Los Angeles needed more water for the Chamber of Commerce to drink more toasts to its growth, more water to dilute its orange juice, more water for its geraniums to delight the tourists, while the giant cottonwoods here died. So, now, this is a valley of desolation."[84]

Citing the inspiration of Chalfant and Mayo, Cedric Belfarge published *Promised Land* in 1938, a novel about the downfall of a family divided between Hollywood demoralization and federal fraud in the Ow-

ens Valley.[85] A John Wayne film of the same year, entitled *New Frontier,*
pits the homesteaders of New Hope Valley against the Irish construction
engineer for Metropole City's water project. After a wartime interval,
Golden Valley: A Novel of California by Frances Gragg and George
Palmer Putnam appeared in 1950.[86] Like the stories of Austin and Kyne,
this one centers on the Owens Valley and its infiltration by facsimiles of
Eaton, Lippincott, and Mulholland. When a fraudulently represented
reclamation project is revealed as a screen for the Los Angeles Aqueduct,
local citizens organize and threaten to dynamite the construction. Violence by land speculators matches bureaucratic peculation, but in the end
city and valley reach an accord, malefactors are purged, and settlers are
compensated for land lost to the reservoir and canal sites. As the repetition in these fictional works suggests, by midcentury the legend was
firmly entrenched in popular culture—the Owens Valley had become a
symbol of urban aggrandizement and bureaucratic malice.

Legend affected politics both directly and through the mediating
circumstances of statewide legal developments. In 1928, the legislature
had recommended a constitutional amendment calling for reasonable
use of state water resources as "the general welfare required."[87] Approved in a referendum, the reasonable-use doctrine was interpreted by
the courts as a mandate for conservation and the restraint of self-
interested parties, whether property-owning persons or governmental
bodies. "In the midst of these disputes stood the Owens Valley, a model
of the dangers of Mulholland's policy and an example of the need for
overhauling the state's outmoded water laws. . . . [By 1931] the memory
of the Owens Valley controversy had begun to haunt Los Angeles in the
halls of Congress as well as the State Capital."[88] Legislating against any
future expropriation of water required for the development of rural
counties, state lawmakers made a special point of adopting Nordskog's
views. The Owens Valley model would loom over the political struggles
that followed.

As adverse opinion mounted, Los Angeles followed the Wattersons'
lead and recruited its own publicists. Beginning in 1924, the city had
responded to newspaper accounts sympathetic to the rebels. In July of
that year, the *Municipal League of Los Angeles Bulletin* explained that
the Owens Valley "Revolt" was prompted by "the Wattersons [and
farmers] as land speculators"[89]—an interpretation that continues in
modern historical works, as we have seen. In December, *Fire and Water
Engineering* revealed "What Really Happened . . . No Justification for
the Mob's Action."[90] Over the following years, the DWP hired Don J.

Kinsley to write a series of exculpating tracts and published some of his work under such beguiling titles as *The Romance of Water and Power* ("A brief narrative revealing how the magic touch of water and hydro-electric power transformed a sleepy, semi-arid Western village into the metropolis of the Pacific") and *The Water Trail* ("The story of Owens Valley and the controversy surrounding the efforts of a great city to secure the water required to meet the needs of an ever-growing popula-tion").[91] Despite these efforts, Los Angeles was losing the propaganda war, in part because it lacked the sympathy due to the underdog and in part because its contradictory policy for managing the valley generated new disputes that received critical interpretations by public opinion.

The changing balance of forces is best illustrated by a simple lawsuit that burgeoned into major complications for the city. Stanley Pedder bought the Wattersons' Natural Soda Products Company in 1932 and began mining the dry bed of Owens Lake with newly installed pumps and equipment. When runoff from the heavy winter of 1936–37 strained the aqueduct's carrying capacity, DWP engineers dumped excess water into the old riverbed, eventually flooding and destroying the soda works. Pedder sued for damages and an injunction against future dumping. When a local jury awarded him $154,000, Los Angeles appealed to the state supreme court. That proved to be a mistake. To strengthen his case on appeal, "Pedder had persuaded the State Lands Commission to join his suit for the recovery of royalties the state had lost from the destruction of his works."[92] The high court's 1943 decision not only increased the damages award, but required the DWP to implement flood-control mea-sures in the future, thus interfering with its practice of keeping reservoirs full in case of drought. The courts, new ideas about water management, and public opinion were closing in on the city.

> Pedder went still further by suggesting that the city should be compelled to apply any water it could not use to the restoration of valley agriculture. The result was the enactment in 1945 of a new state statute prohibiting Los Angeles from wasting the water it derives from the Owens and Mono basins in any way. Although the city subsequently secured from the courts a limited right to waste excess water into Owens Lake under specified conditions, these restrictions resulting from the Natural Soda Products case represented the most severe limitations imposed on Los Angeles' operation of the aque-duct since [1906].[93]

Unchastened by growing opposition, the city retaliated against the valley with an announcement that its policy of negotiating land sales with extant leaseholders would be superseded by a policy of selling to the highest bidder. Local protest against the action was met with a rent hike at Christmas 1944. Once again, the California legislature responded, approving a bill by Inyo's Senator Charles Brown that required the city to give leaseholders first option on properties offered for sale. In addition, "[t]he uproar Los Angeles had fomented in the Owens Valley created problems for the city in Washington as well as in Sacramento."[94] A new controversy erupted in the U.S. Congress over previously approved bills that gave Los Angeles a right-of-way to extend the aqueduct northward into Mono County. Although the extension was built in 1940, Congress now refused to grant the city control of additional acreage for power plants as the original bills provided. "The controversy ultimately centered on distrust of Los Angeles,"[95] a mood that had spread through the interpenetrating realms of popular culture and practical politics.

The water wars between Los Angeles and the Owens Valley have inspired novelists, muckrakers, and film makers since the early years of this century. History and drama combine in accounts that have created a popular culture surrounding these events and have promoted a conspiratorial interpretation of the city's deeds. Most celebrated in the genre is Roman Polanski's 1974 film *Chinatown*. Robert Towne's brilliant screenplay takes great liberties with historical fact, yet forcefully portrays the Los Angeles power brokers in a manner consistent with the transformed legend. The whole story is moved to 1937, and the protagonists become unscrupulous city developers bent on acquiring the land of farmers in the San Fernando Valley, immediately adjacent to the city. Officials of the DWP collude with speculators by secretly dumping city water during a drought in order to win public support for a bond issue on dam and aqueduct construction. Meanwhile the farmers are cut off from irrigation water and forced into ruin, and their land is acquired for a pittance by a syndicate in the names of dummy buyers. The aqueduct will serve the ill-gotten land of the speculators and make fortunes for the cabal. Incest is an important subplot, carrying the sexual symbolism of rape further to the vile association of money and political power. Chinatown, the tarnished hero's police beat before he became a private eye, is a symbol of intrigue, deceptive appearances, and the futility of efforts to expose corruption. In one of the film's final lines a policeman comments: "You can't always tell what's going on in Chinatown." Attempts to reveal the scheme are discredited, and one is left with the understanding that Los Angeles was built on exploitation under the noses of a gullible public.

In fact, of course, the decisive events occurred from 1903 to 1906 and involved no conspiracy or contrived water shortage. City voters overwhelmingly approved repeated bond measures for aqueduct construction without the inducement of panic. A land syndicate of prominent business interests did purchase San Fernando Valley real estate for subsequent profit, but that was known and little regarded by the public, which shared in the spirit of boosterism. With the exception of Lippincott's double dealing and Eaton's unsuccessful speculation in the Owens Valley, officials of the DWP pursued mainly the aggrandizement of the agency and their own political position.

The significance of *Chinatown* is that despite factual inaccuracies it captured the deeper truth of the rebellion. Metropolitan interests appropriated the Owens Valley for their own expansionary purposes through the use of blunt political power. The film refueled the popular interpretation and may have energized the protest that returned to the valley in the 1970s. Los Angeles authorities are livid on the subject of *Chinatown*, knowing that the perceived "rape of the Owens Valley" is an albatross hung around the neck of anyone trying to ensure the city's water supply.

If, as Oscar Wilde suggested, life imitates art, one explanation is that art can become a force with which life must contend. Events surrounding the aftermath of *Chinatown* illustrate the proposition. In 1983, ABC Television and Titus Productions of New York produced a film for television based on the prize-winning screenplay *Ghost Dancing* by the freelance writer Phillip Penningroth. Set in "Paiute Valley," the teleplay begins with the elderly heroine, Sarah Bowman, dynamiting a reservoir in an effort to get arrested and call attention to the valley's destruction resulting from appropriation of its water. Sarah is outmaneuvered by the chief engineer of the unnamed city's water department. By persuading friendly local authorities not to make an arrest, the city avoids a public trial and avoids the effective defense planned by Sarah's adopted Indian daughter, who works for the district attorney's office. Although Los Angeles was never mentioned in the script (after changes made on legal advice), the reference was so transparent and the public relations effect so worrisome in the wake of *Chinatown* that the DWP refused to grant permission for filming on its Owens Valley property. When filming *Chinatown*, the film makers had told the city that they "were doing a detective story set many years ago, so they had no idea what was going on."[96] Los Angeles did not intend to be burned again. *Ghost Dancing* was filmed in Utah, and much of its impact was neutralized by censorship.

But life had not finished its imitation. A new controversy erupted in the midst of negotiations over a permanent agreement to settle disputed water rights and strengthened the hand of local hardliners. Following reports on Bishop radio and cable television, six hundred residents signed a petition condemning Los Angeles for intimidating ABC. The county board of supervisors agreed and unsuccessfully urged the film makers to reconsider shooting on privately owned property in the valley.

The Ghost Dance was a nineteenth-century Paiute ritual that was intended to cause the disappearance of whites and the restoration of Indian land. While the teleplay endeavored to adapt the symbol for modern political purposes, Los Angeles hoped to quell the Owens Valley legend. The DWP acknowledged its fear of copycat aqueduct bombings that might be inspired by the film, but local observers saw more to the censorship. Inyo County Administrator John K. Smith observed: "Most of what they're doing now has nothing to do with getting water to Los Angeles. From here on in, it's all psychological damage to keep us down and make people forget what the valley used to look like."[97]

Yet the effects of the now-celebrated legend and each new controversy that recalled it worked in the opposite direction. The 1920s protest movement and the subsequent urban domination became part of a living history. Popular culture not only depicts nostalgically the lost world of local society, but recreates potent symbols for modern use.

STATE TRANSFORMATION AND ENVIRONMENTALISM

As the old style of city domination faltered in the Owens Valley, the expanding federal welfare state adopted a more influential role in the management of western lands. The New Deal drew rural areas into a plan for national reorganization and recovery. Federal conservation work, for example, became an essential means of depression relief by providing employment and restoring land damaged by drought, erosion, and flood. Never had so many programs and bureaus affecting rural society been created so rapidly: the Soil Conservation Service, the Civilian Conservation Corps, the Grazing Service, the U.S. Fish and Wild Life Service, the Rural Electrification Commission, and the short-lived National Resources Planning Board. The Bureau of Reclamation expanded with projects such as Grand Coulee Dam and the California (Central Valley) Aqueduct, while the Forest Service pressed reforestation and commercial tree farming.[98]

The implications of state transformation for western society centered on expanded public responsibility. Federal agencies increased in size and administrative scope. The Taylor Grazing Act, for example, permanently closed federal lands to settlement and gave the Grazing Service, or Bureau of Land Management (BLM) after 1946, authority to create grazing districts, issue permits, collect fees, and generally manage public lands, ostensibly for purposes of conservation. Local jurisdictions and the individual states were superseded in some important respects. The decisive relationships in the West were increasingly those between ranchers and BLM land managers or between farmers and Bureau of Reclamation water allocators. Naturally, the new arrangements varied widely by region.

In the Owens Valley, the welfare state and local society were joined in important ways that interacted with the changing pattern of city domination. The first and most direct effect of a new state presence came in the federal contribution to expanding public employment, particularly by the Forest Service and the Bureau of Land Management. From a narrow and underfinanced institution at the turn of the century, government became the major valley industry. During the depression the local impact of various forms of federal relief, including employment with the Civil Conservation Corps, were gratefully noted.[99] Organizationally, moreover, federal agencies suffused the asymmetrical relation of city and county. Manzanar and the Paiute land exchange demonstrated in bold strokes how decisions taken in Washington could precipitously alter the local economy and social climate. As the amount of acreage—almost all of it leased—expanded five times over from 1930 to 1970 (see table 11), the Forest Service and the BLM joined Los Angeles as potent landlords. In the combined Inyo and Mono basins, Los Angeles owned or controlled under federal withdrawals 39 percent of the land. "But 52 percent of the total land area, lying principally within the Inyo National Forest, fell under the jurisdiction of federal agencies whose acquiescence in the city's programs could no longer be taken for granted."[100] Equally significant, a majority of the recreational sites and watersheds tapped by the city were located on federal land.

As the scope of federal intervention in the valley spread after 1930, local fortunes were increasingly determined by interagency dealings. In some instances, such as the land exchange, Washington and Los Angeles cooperated to their mutual benefit. At least as often their interests were in conflict, particularly as the growing legend of city callousness put pressure on congressional representatives. When the titans clashed, however, local ambitions were not necessarily trampled. Meekly at first, valley interests participated in a three-way relationship, and later they would exploit critical opportunities to reclaim a measure of local autonomy.

The previously mentioned right-of-way conflict was the first engagement in a new kind of struggle. In 1944, Los Angeles applied to the Department of the Interior for control of additional land in Mono County on which to construct court-ordered flood control facilities. Local opposition came from Mono County officials, who feared becoming "another Owens Valley" and from Bishop merchants, who argued that new withdrawals of land from the public domain would stall the recreation-based commercial revitalization they were enjoying. Although the DWP offered assurances that the project would not affect prevailing lease arrangements, Inyo's Senator Brown scoffed at the value of city promises. Brown rallied support in the state senate for U.S. Congressman Clair Engle's efforts to nullify the original right-of-way acts; and the State Lands Commission joined the fray, asking the Department of the Interior to cede the land to its control. A fight in Congress between Engle (a future U.S. Senator for California) and Los Angeles Congressman (soon to become Mayor) Norris Poulson ended in stalemate, but the city was forced to build its new facilities without the land it wanted. In the broad current of political change, Los Angeles could no longer count on the federal support it had enjoyed since the Reclamation Service awarded it sovereignty over the Owens Valley in 1906. After forty years, "the Water and Power Machine had been broken."[101]

For the first time since settlement in the nineteenth century, the New Deal and its legislative aftermath brought state-sponsored development to the Owens Valley. New and revamped federal agencies generated employment and recreational opportunities, expanded rangeland, and, most important, constituted a public authority alternative to the DWP that introduced new approaches to old conflicts. These effects were windfalls to local groups, however, not the results of their own mobilization or empowerment through the exploitation of federal resources. That would change as the welfare state entered the field of environmental protection in the 1960s.

For all its programmatic initiative and expanded sense of public stewardship, Franklin Roosevelt's New Deal resembled Theodore Roosevelt's progressivism in that both construed conservation as a stimulant to rational economic growth. Scientific resource development, aided by state coordination initiated at the turn of the century,[102] shaded into bureaucratically driven economic recovery in the 1930s.[103] "Sustained yield and public stewardship had replaced exploitation, but the goal of management, both public and private, was still economic gain."[104] The New Deal, and subsequently wartime mobilization, unleashed a frenzied period of natural resource extraction, the methods of which would soon be lamented by environmentalists. BLM land was leased for the strip-mining of coal, and the Forest Service allowed contracts for the clear-cutting of timber in national reserves.[105] Through subversion of the Reclamation Act's 160-acre limitation, federal water projects subsidized the rise of corporate farming, which made extensive use of chemical fertilizers, pesticides, herbicides, and salt-leaching irrigation.[106] Yet, if federal resource development was often a direct agent of environmental despoliation, it was just one contributor to the ecological costs of advanced production, consumption, and technology.

Even in the halcyon years of American production following World War II, environmental degradation was a growing concern among scientists and groups such as the International Union for the Conservation of Nature and Natural Resources, founded in 1948.[107] Their jeremiads were ignored or trivialized as unsophisticated failures to appreciate technology's capacity to solve the problems of its own making. Official statements took a similar line, as in the influential Paley Commission Report on Materials Policy of 1952, which argued that by contrast to "the hairshirt concept of conservation," efficient exploitation of the environment was "compatible with growth and high consumption."[108] Resistance to environmental protection ran much deeper than propagating misinformation. Repeated recommendations, by the Hoover Commission of 1949 and Senator Murray of Montana in 1959, that the Department of the Interior be overhauled or overseen in the interests of resource preservation met with broad congressional opposition. "A major obstacle to reorganization of the Interior Department has been the political strength of the Corps of Engineers. It is widely known though seldom explicitly stated that the Corps of Engineers is a major source of pork barrel projects for congressmen and of subsidized water projects for widely dispersed and vociferous local interests."[109]

The Owens Valley was an early victim of environmental destruction. The elimination of farms and natural waterways destroyed vegetation, deprived wildlife, and converted large portions of the Owens Lake into a dust bowl. One of the most vivid memories of Manzanar internees was the "billowing flurry of dust and sand churned up by the wind through Owens Valley."[110] Although the city adopted palliatives such as a reserve for migrating elk, any real restoration of the natural and settled environment that required local application of city-bound water would depend upon a basic alteration in relations between the occupying authorities. In one respect valley citizens had initiated such change by obtaining injunctions from state courts against groundwater pumping in the early 1930s.

Changes at the federal level would require similar empowerment of environmental interests. As state-centered theorists argue in connection with related policy questions, the deeply rooted political economy of environmental exploitation would only be slowed by an equally formidable transformation of party alignments in Congress and of the state's capacity for reform.[111] The political opportunity arose in the decade of the 1960s. John Kennedy's presidential campaign and the Democratic Party platform endorsed Senator Murray's bill calling for a cabinet-level Council of Resource and Conservation Advisors. Once elected, Kennedy appointed Stewart Udall as secretary of the interior. Udall's 1963 book *The Quiet Crisis* (with a foreword by Kennedy), appearing on the heels of Rachel Carson's widely read *Silent Spring,* seemed to signal a new public commitment to environmental protection. When Kennedy was given the opportunity to press the Murray bill in Congress, however, "as President he abandoned this approach," deciding instead to create an advisory committee and ordering a National Academy of Sciences study on the scope of federal research and planning related to environmental issues.[112] Nevertheless, the National Academy report proved a "major breakthrough"[113] with its recommendation of a natural resources group within the federal government, adding prestige to the environmental legislation that had been "introduced into every Congress during the nineteen sixties. Under the Kennedy administration, the nation had moved somewhat indecisively toward a policy for the environment."[114]

During the Johnson administration, both the environmental movement and congressional action picked up speed. Johnson's New Deal roots and his encouragement of participatory politics dovetailed with the mobilization of independent groups concerned with nuclear fallout, pollution, and other environmental hazards. From 1963 to 1969, twenty government and congressional reports were published, culminating with the Senate's *National Environmental Policy.*[115] In congressional sessions of the late 1960s, "more than thirty-five bills were introduced," including one proposing "that each person has a fundamental and inalienable right to a healthy environment."[116] Senator Henry Jackson of Washington took the lead in consolidating the sundry initiatives into legislation that built on Murray's early efforts. The New Deal legacy was evident in Jackson's bill calling for the creation of a Council of Environmental

Quality that "traced directly to the model of the Employment Act of 1946, which established the Council of Economic Advisors."[117] As it became clear that a major piece of legislation was in the offing, congressional pulling and pushing centered on whose committee powers would be enhanced or endangered. The forceful statement of environmental rights was abandoned and a détente arranged between Senators Jackson and Muskie, both presidential aspirants, who headed respectively the Interior and Public Works Committees. Although Richard Nixon prevailed in the 1968 presidential election and initially opposed the legislation, mounting public concern and Jackson's imposing position in the Senate won the president's pragmatic approval.

The National Environmental Protection Act (NEPA), which became law on January 1, 1970, embodied three major elements: the establishment of a Council on Environmental Quality to advise the president, a declaration of national environmental policy, and the creation of an "action-forcing mechanism" requiring all federal agencies to evaluate the environmental impacts of their programs. Ironically, the final provision, which was destined to have the greatest legal and political effects, was the least considered in the policy-making process. "Environmental Impact Statements (EIS) were invented in response to the anticipated administrative indifference or outright hostility toward the environmental council and the environmental policy statement, [yet the bill's specific] language combined with environmental activism have served to transform the impact statement process into a tool for 'external,' public participatory policymaking."[118]

With NEPA in 1970, the idea of environmentalism was expressed for the first time as public policy. The idea's provenance was straight out of the New Deal, and, at least in germ, it radically extended welfare-state responsibilities. Yet the initiative for these changes came from deep within the political system—from Democrats in the executive branch and Congress who were seeking to build their own political bases on an incipient issue, with little more than acquiescence from three presidents. Public concern was clearly an element in the thinking of these political entrepreneurs, but the environmental movement had not yet discovered its name or the common interests among antinuclear groups, clean-air advocates, and nature lovers. Earth Day in April 1970, which began to forge these alliances, was itself facilitated by the attention NEPA generated. Focusing on administrative detail and potential opposition, Congress set in motion more than it had bargained for or could control when the implications of environmentalism were seized by a diverse public. Immediately states, including California, adopted parallel laws, and the courts arrived at surprising interpretations, such as retroactive application of environmental protection. Even the diminutive Owens Valley was alert to what it all might mean for the perennial struggle.

CONCLUSION

From the suppressed citizens' rebellion to the emergence of environmentalism, a pioneer community in the Owens Valley was socially and economically incorporated into urban society. Economic renovation based on government and retail services catered to cosmopolitan needs, but it also nourished a new pattern of local interest and small steps toward the occupational integration of white and Indian societies. Economic dependency invited political domination to the extent that local constituencies were divided by city power. But even at its lowest ebb local society refused acquiescence to city authority. Resistance simmered in the grudging language of "practical colonialism," flared in lawsuits and rare political challenges, and generally evolved into a culture of moral opposition. Locally fashioned or adopted from abroad, new symbols feminized the valley's virtue and made its defense a question of honor. As legend outran local innocence and city arrogance, it became a tangible resource for mobilizing action. The rights of myth makers and censors were contested politically in the national limelight, enlivening mundane bureaucratic battles. And finally, in the midst of material and symbolic realignment on the regional level, the welfare state was gradually enveloping the administration of western lands.

The pattern of local initiative and resistance to incorporation in the Owens Valley would appear an exception to the rule of "political surrender to mass society" observed in North American community studies.[119] Although I doubt the validity of such a rule, it is revealing to draw some comparisons with the classical study by Arthur Vidich and Joseph Bensman of the small, upper-New-York-state town of Springdale, where the decline of local initiative was first analyzed in detail. Like many American small towns, Springdale had gone into decline in the twentieth century and its local institutions had collapsed, until in the 1940s regional industry and the possibility of commuting to jobs brought newcomers who combined with older residents to produce a heterogeneous community with politically ambivalent attitudes toward mass society—the source both of America's economic strength and of its social problems. Springdale gave up its political autonomy because the community was poor and segmented, and outside agencies were available to provide costly services without dire penalty such as expropriation of local property or resources. "The village board in Springdale accepts few of the powers given to it. Instead, it orients its action to the facilities and subsidies controlled and dispensed by other agencies and, by virtue of this, forfeits its own political power. Solutions to the problems of fire protection are found in agreements with regionally organized fire districts. The school district . . . is financed primarily by grants-in-aid from the state."[120]

In the Owens Valley a strong civil society had always provided local services, and that tradition was actively employed in modern political struggle. When the region suffered economic decline, community solidarity persisted rather than collapsing as in Springdale. As William Cottrell says about the desert railway town that he initially believed would die after the advent of the diesel locomotive, instead "collective effort to secure the ends shared by most community members became more significant as the loss of jobs continued. . . . Those left behind as others moved on realized more completely how the survival of each depended on the acts of the others, and values that contributed to the survival of the community began to move up relative to those emphasizing the primacy of private profit."[121] Then, of course, Bishop and the surrounding towns were not simply embraced by metropolitan sprawl, but directly threatened with destruction—the elimination of business, private property, livelihood, water, and population. By the time these threats became most severe and a political response was required, the Owens Valley had already acquired the necessary experience and repertoire of action in its frontier and agrarian struggles. Finally, local action rather than capitulation to metropolitan society was slowly made possible and legitimized by changes on the national political scene. If there are more causal factors here than can be sorted out in the two-case comparison, there may nevertheless be suggestive evidence for the core idea that collective action is explained by the interplay of culture and the state.

Fifty years ahead of its time, the Owens Valley resistance movement anticipated environmentalism and even helped to generate its legal underpinnings in California. When the environmental movement emerged from political entrepreneurship at the national level, local agitators were attentive to its implications. Perhaps at long last the state had, inadvertently, taken their side.

SEVEN

The Environmental Movement

A new rebellion swept the Owens Valley during the fifteen years that followed Earth Day and the proclamation of a national environmental movement in 1970. Locally, the movement was new in some respects and a continuation of the old resistance in others. Citizens organized to fight the expansionary policies of Los Angeles, which they believed were again aimed at destroying their communities and the natural environment, by resurrecting the water wars of the 1920s in symbol and strategy. Once more, the valley created traditional citizens' committees to circulate petitions, lobby state and federal representatives, press lawsuits, and, in moments of exasperation, to wreak popular justice on city property. Yet in key respects the movement of the 1970s differed from its predecessor. It was, foremost, a legal struggle orchestrated by state and federal environmental legislation and conducted chiefly within bureaucratic arenas. Second, county government shared with citizen groups the responsibility for waging the struggle; insurgent leadership passed back and forth over several stages of the conflict. And finally, this time they won. That is, short of ousting the Department of Water and Power or reclaiming full self-determination, they won most of the major legal battles and forced Los Angeles into an agreement that demanded accountability to local authority.

By means of longitudinal analysis it is possible not only to follow a seemingly defeated movement through its dormancy to rekindled success, tracing both phases to their antecedents, but also to explain the different outcomes. Much of what we know from the rich literature on social movements is based on studies of their rise and fall within a circumscribed historical period—why, for example, populism flourished regionally in the 1880s but succumbed nationally in the following decade. This is perfectly appropriate when movements do indeed end or reappear in totally new forms. In many instances, however, movements that appear new actually revitalize old ones and move forward in ways that depend on the past. When this is the case a longitudinal analysis is capable of addressing a broader range of issues: What is involved in claims that a movement is either new or continuous with the past? What is the meaning of movement success and failure if later victories depend on earlier defeats? How is the legacy of a movement effectively transmitted to its successors? How are we to compare causal explanations of movement outcomes in one period with those of another when later conditions include earlier results—when, that is, the events compared are not independent? Longitudinal analysis is equipped, at least, to detect and deliberate these questions.

The resistance movement of 1904 to 1928 was not so much defeated as arrested—pressed down like a coiled spring. An evolving local culture kept its spirit alive, and the emerging national environmental ethos provided the link between perennial grievances and contemporary opportunities. Movement continuity was further encouraged by the city's decision to construct a second aqueduct and by the project's ill effects that duplicated exactly fifty years later the valley's desiccation of the early 1920s. The strongest evidence for continuity, however, comes from the actions and interpretations of participants in the new movement themselves. Although the valley's population and socioeconomic structure were thoroughly reconstituted by 1970, the renewed protest mobilized in customary ways and defined its purpose in a language resonant with the lessons of experience. Part of its success lay precisely in drawing political attention to problems created in the past and left as unresolved anachronisms in a new age. The new movement's challenge was to win legal support for its moral case, which had changed symbolically but continued to focus on the politics of domination. In local parlance, the central problem was still "colonialism" or "historical domination," and the solution lay in developing new principles and means of self-determination.

Environmentalism provided the vehicle for a revitalized local movement. As a group, Owens Valley citizens were not philosophical environmentalists in 1970. Their mobilizing grievances had to be translated into the new idiom and their action repertoire realigned with new claims of legitimacy. Although that was accomplished in short order, and led directly to a series of local victories, it would be simplistic to explain the new movement exclusively in terms of the opening provided by national and state legislation. Rather, the change can be explained only by a complex set of intersecting forces in local society, culture, and the state. The local movement was not given an opportunity—it had to make one.

NEW EXPLOITS AND ECOLOGISTS

In 1959, the federal government and Los Angeles separately embarked on courses that would collide in the Owens Valley. While Washington moved toward a National Environmental Protection Act with Senator Murray's plan to overhaul the Department of the Interior, the city began plans for a second aqueduct. The second "barrel" would run alongside the original transmission line, including its 1941 extension to the streams feeding Mono Lake, increasing overall capacity by roughly 40 percent (the estimates varied; an average estimate was that the new barrel could deliver 210 of the maximum export goal of 666 cubic feet per second). The project was originally pegged at a cost of $91 million. Although Los Angeles faced no shortage of water, there was mounting pressure to build a second aqueduct, stemming from the very imperiousness with which the city had met its previous needs.

Three institutional circumstances combined to recommend the plan. First, as a founder of the Metropolitan Water District (MWD) that imported its supply from the Colorado River, Los Angeles discovered itself using proportionately less water than other member communities in Southern California, but contributing a majority of the taxes supporting the district. Other problems loomed, such as an Arizona lawsuit before the U.S. Supreme Court seeking a greater share of Colorado River water; but essentially Los Angeles wanted independence from the MWD. Second, in 1956 California hydrologists learned that the Department of Water and Power was actually exporting far less than the total available water in the Owens Valley. "This revelation prompted the legislature in 1959 to direct the [California] Department of Water Resources to prepare a detailed investigation of how the water Los Angeles left behind could be more efficiently applied to the economic development of the valley."[1] Once again Los Angeles faced the old political imperative of retaining control and maximum discretion while satisfying critics that its policies were beneficent. Finally, economic

transformation in the valley had brought two decades of political quiescence. The city no longer feared local resistance and, in the beginning
at least, it was reasonable not to.

Construction of the second aqueduct from 1963 to 1970 was greeted
by a thoughtful local response. Far from any repetition of the 1905
attempts to block the project, Inyo County supervisors sought an agreement with Los Angeles that would assure the future of recreational
projects, continued irrigation of 20,000 acres, restoration to the public
domain of federal land withdrawn but not used for city projects, and a
limit on groundwater pumping.[2] Successful lawsuits in the 1930s, as we
have seen, and the important groundwater protections won by the private owners of 640 acres on the alluvial Bishop cone in the 1940 Chandler Decree,[3] combined with the city's water surplus to end groundwater
production for export from 1935 to 1960.[4] To service the second barrel, the DWP initially projected a modest rate of groundwater pumping
(89 cubic feet per second), but as time went on estimates doubled, and
from 1970 to 1972 the actual rate increased from 140 to 200 cubic feet
per second.

The first organized protest of the environmental era, in spring 1970,
was only indirectly related to the aqueduct expansion and groundwater
pumping. California's U.S. Senators Cranston and Murphy introduced
the Inyo-Mono Land Exchange Bill (Senate bill 3191) late in 1969 for
the purpose of providing the city with new authority superseding the
public-land and right-of-way concessions granted in the 1930s. The
Forest Service and the Bureau of Land Management would grant Los
Angeles thousands of acres in Inyo and Mono Counties for expanded
water collection and electrical power generation. In exchange, the city
would turn over 308 acres for residential development in the towns of
Lone Pine, Independence, Big Pine, and Lee Vining. At a public hearing
on the bill in Lone Pine, members of the newly organized Committee to
Preserve the Ecology of Inyo-Mono voiced two objections: behind the
land exchange was a "water giveaway," and the terms of the bill suggested that the city intended to construct fossil-fuel or nuclear power
plants in the valley. Mrs. Francis Chitwood, who headed the committee,
explained that they favored the land exchange but insisted that Congress
write into the bill "absolute protection of all foreseeable water needs and
a guarantee of the ecological future of Inyo and Mono Counties."[5]

Confident of its support in Washington, the DWP was in no mood to
deal seriously with this insubordination. Dissent could be quieted with
a blunt reminder of power and patronage. The DWP's resident chief

Los Angeles Aqueduct. The aqueduct as it appears from the highway bridge between Lone Pine and Independence. At this point the gravity-driven water is in a man-made canal connecting the original Owens River bed to the point at which the concrete aqueduct channel begins, leading finally to an iron pipe. (Photo by the author.)

engineer suggested to the Lone Pine Chamber of Commerce that water supplied to town properties at a flat rate would eventually have to be metered. Too much water was being wasted by domestic users made indifferent to real costs by generous subsidies. The recreational Diaz Lake south of town would no longer be filled with water diverted from the aqueduct. The engineer suggested that "the chamber take the matter up with the county soon so it can receive budgetary consideration."[6] Whatever the city's explanation for delivering this bad news in the midst of the land exchange controversy, citizens saw it as a reprisal aimed at dividing local groups. With county supervisors still on record in support of the land exchange and the city's wedge driven between business and environmental interests, a new fight was on.

The Committee to Preserve the Ecology of Inyo-Mono, based in Lone Pine, began to cultivate a broader following. It circulated its views valley-wide, and it changed its name to reflect these ambitions. Under the banner Concerned Citizens of the Owens Valley (the second of three

groups to use that name; the first was concerned with local development in the 1940s) the ecologists made their debut at a meeting of the
board of supervisors in October. A variety of speakers for the committee urged the board to reconsider Senate bill 3191. Realtor John P.
"Mac" Davis said the county should draft its own master plan for
development and should assert its justified claims on water for the
valley's use, rather than having to accept the patronizing consequences
of the city's agenda. Local Native Americans joined white citizens in a
political initiative for perhaps the first time (Paiutes had withdrawn
from joint reparations claims in 1927); Michael Rogers, who headed
the Paiute-Shoshone tribal trustees, "feared drying up of the Owens
Valley, air pollution through fossil fuel plants, and the fact that such
legislation would be a national precedent harmful to the ecology of the
nation." Aubrey Lyon of Bishop's Izaak Walton League observed that
the bill was in conflict with the state constitution and "could override
decrees such as the Chandler decree dealing with pumping of the Bishop
Cone, [leaving the] Owens Valley as a dust bowl and a biological
desert."[7] The supervisors were convinced, and voted to reconsider their
position and hold public hearings.

The Concerned Citizens of Owens Valley (CCOV) now began a
publicity campaign designed to win over the general public and the
supervisors. From October through December 1970 the CCOV ran a
series of ads in local newspapers aimed at the land-exchange bill:

RAPE OF OWENS VALLEY CONTINUES

> We are just concerned citizens like yourselves who only wish to protect
> our homes and valley from the grasp of the monopolistic, dictatorial De-
> partment of Water and Power.
>
> We, as concerned citizens, have no axe to grind. HOWEVER: this may not
> be the case with a FEW OF YOUR GREEDY BUSINESSMEN who are concerned about
> a FAST BUCK TODAY and not concerned about tomorrow.
>
> In SB 3191 and HR 15426 there are two phrases that give away the
> Rights of the people forever: (1) Gives the DWP the right to water—NO
> MATTER HOW OBTAINED. (2) Gives the DWP the right to raise and lower water
> tables WITHOUT ANY LIABILITY FOR DAMAGE IT MIGHT CAUSE.
>
> Rumors, started and spread by DWP puppets, split this valley in the 20's
> so they could gain control of the land and water—REMEMBER—THE DWP
> WANTS ONLY WATER—PEOPLE ARE EXPENDABLE.[8]

Other ads under the same heading stressed the environmental damage
that stemmed from sustaining the aqueduct and called for a master water
plan developed in collaboration with California and federal agencies.

Fellow citizens were urged to write their congressional representatives and to show up at the next supervisors' meeting.[9] The campaign interwove old and new themes. Violation of the valley begun in the 1920s could be reversed if misinformation was exposed and local divisions averted.

The appeal worked. Senator Cranston withdrew his sponsorship of the bill as public opinion came forward on the CCOV side. Local support for the land exchange dwindled to Lone Pine business interests, which were under pressure from the DWP and destined to receive the largest share of residential and recreational development (110 of the total 308 acres) under the terms of Senate bill 3191. In a "supercrowded" meeting of the board, with Los Angeles television cameras looking on, the supervisors voted four to one to rescind their support for the land exchange (Lone Pine's representative sticking with the business minority). An estimated 90 percent of the audience endorsed the board's decision.[10]

The CCOV relished this defensive victory and soon decided to take the initiative with Los Angeles and their own county officials. Fifty-five men and women representing the committee made an unscheduled appearance at the board of supervisors' meeting in January 1971, demanding action to reduce the amount of water going to Los Angeles. The volume of groundwater pumping in 1968 and 1970 was high by the standards of the mid-1960s, and the operation of the second aqueduct beginning in July 1970 meant that exportation would accelerate—as, indeed, production from wells alone rose from 48 cubic feet per second (cfs) when the second barrel opened, to 232 cfs in 1972.[11] Aubrey Lyon, the committee's ecological specialist, called the board's attention to the effects of desiccation and suggested that Inyo explore state laws permitting the regulation of water export by local ordinance.[12] The CCOV presented a proposal, simultaneously published in local newspapers, that (1) reminded the officials that their own efforts had produced no favorable response from Los Angeles, (2) called for a master plan following state and federal statutes, (3) proposed that Los Angeles offer a plan containing "reasonable public checks and balances" on water management, and (4) announced the fundamental objective of ending "historical domination."[13]

The supervisors were caught off balance by this new assertiveness, with little to say beyond defending their previous efforts and inviting the CCOV to try its luck in Sacramento. On reflection, however, county officials noted the group's praise for their new position on the land exchange, and they warmed to its proposal, which clearly had mobilized favorable opinion. By June the supervisors affirmed a "county watershed and management plan," which drew on the CCOV proposal, and they traveled to Sacramento for meetings with legislators, DWP officials, and the state water resources agency. Inyo's entourage included the full board, the district attorney, the county administrator, the mayor of Bishop, and a representative from the citizens' committee. Rising to a new mission, the supervisors saw themselves as "represent[ing] the people of Inyo and speak[ing] for the millions of people who demand the preservation of the natural environment."[14]

By now Los Angeles appreciated the wisdom of entertaining environmentalism, especially as it flourished in the sometimes troublesome state legislature. The DWP prepared a water and land management plan for state and county officials that began by emphasizing the city's rights to underground and surface water, but went on to concede that: (1) pumping should observe "safe limits"; (2) irrigation, wildlife, and recreational facilities must be protected; and (3) a third aqueduct would be "impractical." On the question of exactly how these objectives would be ensured, however, the department stated that it "cannot legally agree to arbitrarily restrict or cut back on the aqueduct flow or groundwater production. . . . [T]his is a matter of water rights and neither the state nor the county can require that the Department cut back on these flows."[15] Negotiations over the next nine months showed the city unwilling to compromise its near-monopoly of power over land and water use. The environment enjoyed a good deal of approving rhetoric, but when the DWP was pressed about priorities it noted that sufficient water was available to meet them all. As county officials continued to insist on a real plan, the city got tough again in August 1972 by announcing increases in groundwater extraction that would bring both aqueducts to capacity.

Inyo's last attempt at moral suasion came from the supervisors in September. In a letter to the DWP they disputed the city's right of unlimited export and, with growing interest, identified environmental quality as the standard against which all other uses must be evaluated. The direct challenge to city authority was without precedent since Teddy Roosevelt's decision in 1906. The supervisors wanted an absolute limit on export and a plan stating that Owens Valley needs came first. "The whole purpose of a Water Management and Protection Plan for the Owens Basin is to make a legal definitive decision as to how much water is necessary for the future growth of the Owens Valley . . . and to guarantee the enhancement of the Valley's environmental quality. All water surplus *after* these needs have been identified may be considered as water available for export to the city of Los Angeles."[16] This represented a radical shift from the supervisors' diffident reception of the Committee to Protect the Ecology of Inyo-Mono less than two years earlier; and their new principle of "Inyo first" went further toward self-determination than anything proposed in the years of rebellion.

The city's response was predictably arrogant. The supervisors' effort to upset long-settled questions about water rights deserved no reply beyond turning up the pumps. Inyo officials probably expected that and were ready with a new initiative. In November 1972, Inyo filed suit against the mayor of Los Angeles under the California Environmental Quality Act (CEQA). The city, it was charged, had never filed an environmental impact report on the second aqueduct.

What led to the resurgent spirit of self-determination? The explanation begins with the legacy of struggle, now close to the core of local culture and never far from consciousness. The irritants of city domination, even among a new class of economic interests, were nevertheless a constant and do not explain the timing of the environmental revolt. Proximate causes start with the degrading effects of accelerated groundwater pumping. As the water table went down, stately cottonwood trees began to die, spots of greenery shriveled, irrigated acreage shrank, and the dust thickened.

> By 1972 two years of heavy pumping had dried up the valley's most popular and ecologically significant springs. The artesian wells along Mazourka Canyon Road, from which Independence townfolk had for years taken fresh water, stopped flowing; and the vibrant plant and animal community at Little Black Rock Springs was destroyed. The people of Inyo also noticed a dramatic increase in the frequency and intensity of dust storms during the windy winter months. Prior to the pumping, the relatively high water table in the valley supported water-loving plants which gave color and protection to the valley's desert soils.[17]

As a longtime resident observed, "We've always had dust storms, ever since DWP dried up Owens Lake and turned it into an alkali pit, but it got worse."[18]

With the National Environmental Protection Act and its California counterpart now at the center of the domestic political stage, Owens Valley residents were quick to associate their grievances with the broader movement's legitimacy. Environmentalism provided new principles regarding the ownership and use of natural resources, new rights,

Department of Water and Power Property. Fenced portion of the aqueduct at Lone Pine. The sign advises: These waters are part of the municipal water supply of the City of Los Angeles." The list of restrictions (no swimming, etc.) that follows is punctuated by bullet holes. (Photo by the author.)

and new public responsibilities. Among the valley's changing population there were new residents especially keen on environmental protection. George Seielstad, a radio astronomer at the California Institute of Technology Research Station, who narrowly missed being elected the valley's U.S. Congressman in 1974, believed that the city had "no reservation or hesitation concerning the complete destruction of a scenic resource."[19] Mary De Decker, a well-recognized botanist who had lived in Independence since 1935, became an activist in the environmental struggle. Speaking of Los Angeles, she explained:

> I feel that they have been very high-handed in their attitude of demanding and taking the water. They feel they have a right to the water because they own the land. Well, there is much of the land they don't own, and pumping affects any land in the basin. It affects the air, which they don't own. It will, in time, affect climatic conditions which they certainly don't own. They have had a narrow viewpoint focusing on getting water to Los Angeles. Everything is not only centered around that viewpoint, but they have tried to control the situation to force that on everybody else. That is where I've rebelled.[20]

Finally, the environmental movement began to integrate citizens and officials around the merged objectives of local autonomy, environmentalism, and the economic future based on recreation and services. The initiative came from a small band of ecologists who enjoyed little favor in official circles until they demonstrated both the originality and the popular appeal of their proposal. Once the supervisors were convinced, however, the loosely formulated CCOV proposal was transformed into bold public policy. Environmentalism was the effective vehicle for this new coalition, but it was by no means the heartfelt sentiment of all participants. The founders of the CCOV were ecologists with credentials, and public opinion readily associated local issues with environmental degradation. But the potency of environmentalism owed much to its capacity to absorb long-standing grievances against city domination. The alloyed character of the new movement became clear as time went on, when supporters of the struggle against Los Angeles vigorously opposed the use of valley land for wildlife preserves and opposed growth limitations that would restrict economic development. Environmentalism in the Owens Valley stood for both more and less than the ecological agenda. It embraced a variety of interests united by the overarching desire for local autonomy.

THE SUIT

Inyo officials now took the lead, notably county administrator John K. Smith and Frank Fowles, who was appointed district attorney not long after moving his law practice to Bishop from Vallejo, California. With the approval of the board of supervisors, it was Fowles who filed *County of Inyo v. Yorty* (Sam Yorty was the mayor of Los Angeles) in 1972, claiming that groundwater extraction had caused irreparable harm to the environment.

The plaintiffs asked the Inyo County Superior Court to enjoin any further groundwater extraction until Los Angeles submitted an environmental impact report (EIR) on the effects of pumping, as required by CEQA. With "Independence drying up, more pumping going on," and no help from the state Water Resources Board, Fowles and Smith saw their action as one of "public officials doing their job. CEQA gave us a golden opportunity to get LA to do what we had wanted the state to do all along, to make a report on planned [water] use."[21] The idea of suing Los Angeles under CEQA had occurred to Inyo officials in September 1972, when the California Supreme Court ruled in *Friends of Mammoth v. Board of Supervisors of Mono County* that government agencies as well as private developers were required to submit environmental impact statements.[22] Environmentalism was beginning to provide effective tools for legal practitioners. As Fowles noted with an aplomb never previously expressed in struggles with the big city, "We know all the department guys by their first names. They're good guys. Their job is to take our water so Los Angeles can keep on growing, and they do it supremely well. Our job is to keep our valley from drying up completely."[23]

As Fowles had hoped, by mutual agreement with Los Angeles the suit filed in Inyo County was transferred to the Sacramento Superior Court, where it would eventually come before the California Court of Appeal for the Third District. Fowles believed that the panel of three appellate judges, particularly Judge Frank Richardson, would be sympathetic. The key point of the Inyo suit was that the operation of the second aqueduct, constructed prior to CEQA, should nevertheless fall within its coverage since pumping and its damaging effects continued to the present. Los Angeles "responded with disbelief that the operation of its project could be bound by strictures of a law which had not even been imagined when work began on the second aqueduct, and which still had not taken effect by the time the new system was placed in service. But the city had not reckoned with the attention this new conflict with the Owens Valley would prompt in the Third District Court of Appeal in Sacramento."[24] In January 1973, without deciding on the substance of the case, the Sacramento Superior Court agreed with Los Angeles to the extent of refusing to issue a temporary injunction against continued pumping while the trial went forward. Fowles appealed that decision. "The court of appeal did not issue the injunction that the county requested. Instead on February 26 it took an action of far greater magnitude and significance: the appellate court elected to treat the county's request for an injunction as a claim for final relief on the merits, and boldly assumed the duty of adjudicating the claim on its own."[25]

In June 1973, the Court of Appeal ruled in favor of Inyo and ordered that Los Angeles must prepare an EIR examining both the potential environmental damage from the pumping program and feasible alternatives. Groundwater pumping would be restricted in the interim (although the court subsequently relaxed the initial limitation of 89 cfs). Over the next three years Los Angeles dragged its feet on the EIR, producing several drafts that neglected tough issues, all the while pressing the court to approve more pumping while the study was in progress. The DWP created a local advisory committee to assist in preparing the EIR, but failed to include its evidence of environmental deterioration in draft reports aired at public meetings. Local experts who participated were soon disillusioned, concluding that the city only wanted to blunt their opposition and had no intention of producing an objective report.[26]

If Los Angeles was losing on the legal front, it still could work the levers of local control in an effort to divide the movement. When Inyo sought a court order that the first EIR be withdrawn as inadequate, the DWP reacted in September 1974 by announcing the immediate cessation of all its water deliveries to agricultural and recreational users—a gesture the city frankly called "educational."[27] The appeals court promptly ordered restoration of the service. In the months that followed, water and electrical power rates were increased. Water meters were back on the agenda by the end of 1975. The city announced that commercial metering would begin in March 1976 and that it would study the need for residential meters. Meanwhile the DWP indicated that a revised EIR would be ready in the spring. The issues were intentionally conflated—pushed by pending lawsuits and pumping restrictions, the city pushed back by reducing the supply and raising the cost of water for agricultural, recreational, commercial, and domestic use.

STRIKES AND VIOLENCE

The decision to install commercial water meters caused a furor. The city was proposing not only to intrude further into the operation of local enterprises but also to charge local clients at rates equivalent to those paid by Los Angeles residents, whose water was transported hundreds of miles. The action replacing flat-rate with metered billing was justified as a water conservation measure, although the estimated saving was minuscule. Only three-tenths of one percent of the total export volume was consumed by all commercial and residential uses—and even that figure was based on the city's estimates, which residents hotly disputed.

The controversy focused on southern valley towns, because Bishop had installed its own municipal water system at the time of incorporation in 1903, prior to the city's intervention. The DWP provided water service to two hundred commercial users in Laws, Big Pine, Independence, and Lone Pine. In January 1976, a crowd with "no kind words for [the] DWP" met the board of supervisors and requested that commercial users be included in the three-year postponement of metering granted to residential consumers.[28] Los Angeles promptly denied the request. The county government, itself a commercial user under the metering plan, took the offensive. District Attorney L. H. "Buck" Gibbons, Fowles's successor, filed suit to enjoin the rate increase on the

grounds that it was exorbitant, unauthorized by the state Public Utilities
Commission (PUC), and in violation of CEQA. When the court denied
the county's request for a temporary injunction while the case was
pending, Inyo acted unilaterally to the same end by refusing to pay any
water bills above the old flat rate and depositing the difference in an
escrow account. The county government embarked on a ratepayer's
strike against the DWP.[29]

The city's actions were now interpreted as punitive responses to the
valley's exercise of independence—an impression the city sometimes encouraged. The circumstances of the new struggle were recreating the
traditional formula for popular justice, as broad mobilization combined
with a growing perception of injustice and the frustrating results of legal
methods. The city's water system had been the target of violence in May
and September 1975, when rancor over groundwater pumping erupted—
in the May incident, locks and control devices were broken on a DWP
control gate on the Owens River, north of Bishop; in September some
insulators on a DWP power line were shot out, resulting in a power
failure.[30] During the metering controversy of early 1976, the DWP
neglected to fill Diaz Lake at the recreational park south of Lone Pine.
This time the vandals who took charge demonstrated skill and purpose.
"The gate had apparently been opened with a blow torch and the water
had run into the lake for about 12 hours before the flow was discovered
by a DWP employee. The lake had been down to 16 inches but with this
illegal influx it is estimated that there will be enough water in the lake
to last through June and make it safe for boating activities."[31] The city
moved quickly to quell any new outbreak of violence. The oversight was
explained as a result of county "confusion" over responsibility for maintaining the lake; but the DWP restored water delivery.[32]

But the new insurgency was not so easily quieted. A culture of popular justice persisted in the use of symbols and in the protest repertoire.
The legal avenue of dissent now dominated the valley agenda, but city
peevishness elicited supporting acts of property violence. The mood of
the 1920s was rekindled in one essential respect—citizens believed that
the city's methods were unjust. If unprincipled tactics could be used
against them, then they could understand, if not always approve of,
protest in kind. On September 16 violence returned to the Alabama
Gates after a forty-eight-year respite. Once again, front-page news and
pictures in the *Los Angeles Times* reported:

> An explosion near Lone Pine ripped apart a spillgate on the Owens Valley
> aqueduct early Wednesday morning forcing a shutdown of the system that
> brings Los Angeles nearly 80% of its water.

Alabama Gates, 1990. The refurbished site of the aqueduct occupation and the location of various bombings from 1924 to 1976. The control house and spillway are located just a mile below the beginning of the concrete channel section of the aqueduct. (Photo by the author.)

The Los Angeles Department of Water and Power, which owns the aqueduct and which has been in a heated dispute with Owens Valley residents over an increase in underground pumping, said the system would be closed for two days. . . . The explosion stirred memories of dynamite blasts that damaged the aqueduct during the 1920s. . . . No official was ready to say that the latest incident was related to the current uproar over a DWP project to step up the amount of water being pumped from underground.

Emotions have reached a high level with residents and farmers who lease from DWP fearing that the entire Owens Valley will become a barren wasteland.[33]

When the blast was traced to two local youths, the city concluded it was a random act of vandalism. The interpretation not only ignored local unrest and symbolism, but neglected to connect the Alabama Gates explosion with the coincident assault of a dynamite-carrying arrow on the statue of William Mulholland (the DWP's chief engineer at the time of the 1905 protest) in a Los Angeles park.[34] Echoing the valley mood, Aubrey Lyon reflected, "When I read about it, I thought about the Boston Tea Party. Those people are recognized now as patriots. Well, maybe a hundred years from now these fellows will be patriots too, but right now the paper calls them vandals. I don't blame anyone for trying to protect their resources, but I do think we should do it by legal means."[35]

Indeed, the main struggle still lay in the courts. Inyo retained the legal counsel of Antonio Rossman, a young water expert from Northern California, to assist District Attorney Gibbons, and together the lawyers carried the original suit through three additional stages and established the principle of public regulation of proprietary water rights. In successive rulings the appeals court held that: CEQA applied to public projects with effects continuing after the law's enactment in 1970 (*Inyo I*); the city's EIR had to satisfy the panel of judges (*Inyo II*); the first EIR produced by the city was an "egregious misrepresentation" of the environmental impact of groundwater pumping as requested in the original decision (*Inyo III*), and the city's second effort at an EIR was a "sham" (*Inyo IV*).[36] All told, eleven major lawsuits were brought against the city's program of water production in the Owens Valley.[37] Los Angeles won a few concessions; the court ruled that pumping should not be held to the level (89 cfs) prevailing at the time of CEQA's enactment and subsequently allowed increases, to 149 cfs and then to 178 cfs.

A serious drought throughout California in 1977 worked to the city's advantage in the appeals court and in negotiations with Inyo officials. City strategists saw the drought as an opportunity to remind political decision makers of the vital public service provided by the DWP. Extralegal pressures to lift the court injunction on groundwater pumping could be exerted statewide and locally. Los Angeles first sought assistance from its sister Metropolitan Water District of Southern California (MWD) in negotiations with the state Department of Water Resources. At a meeting with the governor, MWD representatives suggested that the city could help relieve water shortages in the Central Valley if the Inyo pumping restrictions were set aside. State Senator Walter Stiern described the proceedings: "At the recent meeting held in the Governor's office on the drought situation—this was an emergency thing and hastily called—I could not believe my ears when I heard the legal arm of the Metropolitan Water District state to the Governor that if he would interfere or intervene with the injunction that Inyo County has with the City of Los Angeles that the city could in turn send more water north."[38] The MWD next informed the Central Valley's Kern County that a water entitlement of 80,000 acre feet could be turned over for agricultural use if officials in Kern and Inyo could agree to co-operate on drought relief. Kern County officials hastened to Bishop, urging their counterparts to ease up on the DWP. Los Angeles simultaneously asked the appellate court to allow pumping at the aqueduct's capacity rate of 315 cfs. Inyo supervisors rejected the plea from their Kern colleagues, noting angrily that "the various maneuvers added up to a colossal effort by the DWP to get Inyo to relent."[39] Los Angeles should try water conservation and other sources of supply before attempting to purloin Inyo's small gains.

The city also applied pressure to an array of local interests. Irrigation water was withheld from normal spring deliveries to ranchers. Crowley Lake levels fell as more storage water was released to the aqueduct. Bishop business interests reacted sharply to the commercial implications for the popular fishing spot and filed a strongly worded lawsuit charging the DWP and MWD with conspiring to manipulate public concern during the drought. For its ordinary residential clients in the southern valley, the DWP suggested insouciantly that water meters installed at the department's expense would further the conservation effort.[40] Although the court initially held to pumping limitations and ordered the DWP to restore water deliveries to the ranchers, by July drought and politics produced a reversal; the court granted the city's request for increased pumping to 315 cfs until April 1978.[41]

One odd consequence of the drought was an incipient split between Inyo officials and the citizens, who had firmly supported the public initiative since the initial lawsuit of 1972. As the drought demanded closer collaboration among agencies, the state Department of Water Resources offered to mediate an agreement between Inyo and Los Angeles.[42] The supervisors were ready to approve "an independent study of the Owens Valley to determine its management that will yield the proper amount of groundwater extraction for export after first protecting the environment."[43] The county reasoned that the recent gains in court, although in the form of temporary injunctions, might be converted into permanent guarantees of local control. The city would welcome an arrangement that returned their discretionary powers, bottled up in the appeals court for the past five years. An out-of-court settlement might also avoid the EIR requirement. The delays and the sketchiness of the draft EIRs clearly indicated that the DWP wanted to evade a full analysis of the second aqueduct. As everyone knew, the effects had been harmful, but to admit that to the court under CEQA would have obligated the city to explore "feasible alternatives" to extraction from the Owens Valley (such as conservation in Los Angeles)—alternatives the city considered worse than protracted legal maneuvering. The parties came to negotiations with opposing motives and were very far apart on the purpose of an independent study; but their willingness to talk about an agreement annoyed the Inyo rank and file.

A resurgent popular movement began to organize in mid-1978, after the Los Angeles Board of Water and Power Commissioners had voted to install approximately 850 residential water meters in Laws, Big Pine, Independence, and Lone Pine, communities in which the city serviced a total of 2,500 households.[44] Opposition appeared immediately from civic groups and local government. The Independence Civic Club, already on record against metering and city claims of excessive local water consumption, began to hold public debates.[45] Inyo County had sued to stop the installation, saying that the DWP was not yet in conformance with CEQA and that no EIR had been accepted documenting the effects of its own consumption.[46] That suit, like its predecessor that tried to stop commercial metering, was unsuccessful.

As the meters were being tuned up, residents were sent "projected bills," purportedly to familiarize them with the concept of metering, previously unknown in the valley. The recipients suspected that intimidation was the real purpose. Lilian Nelson claimed that her projected bill for forty-five days was $560. "Everybody was getting bills like that. They were trying to scare people out. I can't figure any other reason . . . except wanting to intimidate people here into leaving."[47] When the actual bills began arriving they were more realistic, but they still represented increases over the previous flat rates on the order of one thousand percent—bills of $8 to $10, for example, rose to $60 or $100.[48] A retired woman in Big Pine unable to afford a $52 water bill asked her neighbors, "[S]hall we take this sitting down or shall we fight?"[49] Most of them already had made their decision to fight and were considering the question of means.

Popular justice appealed to a few; new acts of sabotage and arson were perpetrated on city facilities. The following list describes the new wave of property damage in the late 1970s and early 1980s.

Source of Report	Description
Inyo Independent, May 8, 1975	Locks and control devices broken on DWP control gate on Owens River north of Bishop
Inyo Independent, Sept. 11, 1975	Insulators on DWP electrical lines shot out, causing power failure

Source of Report	Description
Inyo Independent, May 20, 1976	Aqueduct gate opened by blow torch to fill Diaz Lake for recreational use
Inyo Independent, Sept. 16, 1976	Alabama Gates spillway bombed
Los Angeles Times, Sept. 17, 1976	Dynamite stick attached to arrow fails to explode at Mulholland Statue in Los Angeles
Inyo Independent, May 15, 1979	Insulators shot out at Southern California Edison site, causing power failure in Bishop
Inyo County News-Letter, June 29, 1979	Shack and platform at DWP well between Big Pine and Independence fired
Inyo County News-Letter, June 29, 1979	House, barns, and shop on DWP lease at Lone Pine fired
Inyo Independent, Nov. 15, 1979	Two men in possession of explosives arrested for shooting out insulators on DWP high-voltage line
Inyo Independent, Mar. 13, 1980	Bomb threat at DWP offices
Inyo Independent, June 12, 1980	City meter reader run off with use of a gun
Inyo Independent, July 30, 1981	DWP skiploader parked near office destroyed by fire of suspicious origin
Inyo Independent, Aug. 8, 1984	DWP power boat on Mono Lake exploded in suspicious circumstances

A visiting writer reported:

Yesterday in Lone Pine all the talk was about the Molotov Cocktail some-body had hurled into the Independence office of the Los Angeles Department of Water and Power, and none of the good citizens I heard on the street expressed anything but regret that it hadn't burned the place to the ground. [After encountering an armed and bellicose man on a backroad] two days later, in the *Inyo Register* news office, I overheard a couple of reporters talking about the DWP pump somebody had shot to pieces down along the aqueduct between Big Pine and Independence. The damage done, one of them said, was increased by the use of armor-piercing shells. No wonder my man was a bit curt. Molotov cocktails? Armor-piercing shells? And windows smashed in DWP cars and trucks? Bags of concrete poured into water meters? The Owens Valley water war, cold since 1927, was obviously heating up again.[50]

The Concerned Citizens of Owens Valley was reactivated by Lilian Nelson and Lois Wilson, who organized a petition drive garnering "more than 1000 signers" and a series of protest meetings. The new CCOV attracted a different membership, with little recollection of the defunct land exchange and little sense of organizational continuity. Environmental issues were secondary to the offensiveness of the city's control extended literally into people's homes. The group was more vocal and gregarious, less given to planning—they were "seeking any kind of relief including the formation of community or county water boards with powers to shape their own destinies."[51] Populism pervaded their mood and strategy.

In the midst of this uproar the board of supervisors unveiled a draft agreement with the DWP that provided for a "five-year operational study" as the potential basis for a mutually acceptable management plan and allowed for pumping at the high-side rate of 200 to 250 cfs during the period of study.[52] Capacity crowds turned out at a series of public hearings on the draft agreement. A train of speakers spoke against the agreement, citing familiar arguments about EIRs, dust, and dried-out habitats and linking those environmental issues to the immediate metering problem. Pumping should be reduced, not increased, they argued. Why make a concessionary agreement when Inyo was winning in the courts? "No one spoke in favor of signing the DWP-Inyo agreement. Some suggested that the Inyo case be the subject of a CBS-TV '60 Minutes' program. There was strong talk that if the supervisors couldn't cope with the matter, then the people should take the matter into their own hands. Both meetings got emotional at times, with some suggesting a recall of the entire board of supervisors."[53]

The Concerned Citizens chose independent action by calling a meter strike against the DWP. In the months that followed, the CCOV organized demonstrations and invited Los Angeles television reporters, circulated petitions, picketed DWP offices in Independence, followed meter readers on their rounds, packed public meetings, printed bumper stickers ("Flat Rate Only" and "Let's Stop the Damn Water Pumps"), and generally showed a flair for guerrilla theatre. At a protest party in Big Pine they dyed sheets red and cut ribbons to mark sites of pumping damage. Withering trees along the highway were tied in black mourning ribbons for the benefit of passing tourists and DWP trucks. "Vandalism against city-owned equipment and facilities in the Owens Valley increased, and valley residents took to hissing whenever an official Department of Water and Power vehicle passed by, with the result that many department officials by the late 1970s were traveling in unmarked cars."[54]

The meter strike urged valley customers to pay only the original flat-rate sum in response to inflated DWP bills. When the department threatened to shut off service to delinquent customers, the strike faltered; but some persevered. Louis Statham of Lone Pine offered to provide free water from his own well and started looking for a tanker truck. Protesters accompanied the city workers assigned to turn off residential water. The tactics succeeded in drawing sympathetic national attention to their cause. In a two-part feature on California water issues, the *Wall Street Journal* reported how the owner of the Big Pine General Store, Connie Johnson, "used a chrome-plated Colt .45 revolver a year ago and chased away a department worker who threatened to turn off Johnson's water."[55] Frivolous as some of the protest methods seemed to the more dignified residents and the lawyers, Los Angeles was embarrassed by the publicity. Metered billing was delayed, and strikers were later given hearings to dispute the accuracy of bills while their water service continued. A crackdown on residential strikers risked advertising that the county had not paid its meter bill for three years. The city simply outlasted the meter strike. The CCOV was good at publicity, but had no appealing plan for a long-term solution. Municipal ownership was advocated at one point and later recanted, perhaps because it would be costly and technically involved and would need to be decided by the supervisors, who were pursuing other avenues. The CCOV called off its strike in May 1980 and took its unsatisfied grievances back to conventional politics.

THE POLITICS OF AGREEMENT

Popular protest had affected Inyo officials, who moved in a more assertive direction following criticism of the first draft agreement. Stricter pumping limits written into a revised draft led Los Angeles to reject that plan. In response, Inyo filed a new suit with the appeals court, charging

the city with unnecessary delays; and the board of supervisors began
public hearings on the CCOV proposal to purchase town water systems. The public ownership idea collapsed when the CCOV, still wary
from the last agreement, filed a petition in which 155 signers charged
that they had little sense of the purchase agreement's contents and what
they did know suggested needless concessions such as dropping the
water-metering suits. The county, never enthusiastic about purchasing
and operating the water system, had a better idea.

THE LOCAL ORDINANCE

Nearly two years earlier, special counsel Rossmann surprised a meeting
on the latest draft EIR by announcing that the county was looking into
the legality of a local ordinance to regulate groundwater pumping.[56]
The idea reappeared in spring 1980 as a carefully researched proposal
for a ballot measure. The county had made impressive legal gains during the 1970s. As Rossmann observed, "by use of its injunctive power,
the court demonstrated that the county, although not holding any water
rights of its own, could nonetheless effectuate restraints on Los Angeles's proprietary water rights."[57] Important as the principle obviously
was, the original question of the rate at which Los Angeles could extract
groundwater was left open pending an EIR. Interim rates invoked by
the court said nothing of what would happen if Los Angeles finally
submitted an acceptable EIR. In the aftermath of the drought these
issues were absorbed in a statewide study and a governor's commission
on groundwater regulation. Although the commission's final report
failed to generate any definitive legislation, the process helped bring Los
Angeles and Inyo into negotiations, joined by public agencies with jurisdictions in the valley. As the governor's commission on groundwater
completed its work with no legislative result, Inyo County was left in
limbo over whether and how city pumping could be regulated. From the
commission's deliberations, Rossmann drew "two important conclusions: 1. even a so-called vested groundwater right can be redefined by
a police power licensing and permitting program, and 2. the California
Legislature has not yet exercised that power to the exclusion of regulation by local authorities."[58] Inyo County asked Rossmann to write an
ordinance, consistent with existing state law, that would allow local
regulation of groundwater. The idea promised a major breakthrough,
comparable only to the original 1972 lawsuit.

The Ordinance to Regulate the Extraction of Groundwater within the Owens Valley Groundwater Basin was released for public review in April 1980. If placed on the ballot by the board of supervisors and approved by voters, the law would (1) establish a county water department with a director appointed by the supervisors, (2) create a citizen-advisory water commission, (3) require all groundwater extractors to obtain permits from the water department, (4) require fees for permits, and (5) impose civil and criminal penalties for unlawful extraction. The law's stated purpose, to provide "the maximum long-range benefit of the environment," demonstrated its direct descent from CEQA and the national environmental movement.

Public hearings on the proposed ballot measure drew a divided response. Ranchers and other city lessees opposed the plan. As Tom Fogarty of the Anchor Ranch explained, "our contract with DWP says anything the county does in the way of regulations that cost them (DWP) is passed on to the rancher." Supporters of the citizens' movement, however, were overjoyed. Speaking for the environmentalists, Mary De Decker said: "[A] great step has been taken by Inyo County that should have been done long ago." Flora Nash of the League of Women Voters emphasized that the measure "gives us the opportunity to choose LOCAL CONTROL."[59]

As support for the ordinance gathered, Los Angeles moved to head off a public referendum. When the city announced it would sue to keep the measure off the ballot, a county lawyer remarked: "I hope they do sue. That will assure its passage."[60] The DWP proposed reopening discussions on the management agreement it had previously rejected, but new talks went nowhere. The mood in Inyo was too confident for the conventional leverage to work, particularly when the California Supreme Court denied the city's request to remove the ballot measure. District Attorney "Buck" Gibbons ebulliently mixed his metaphors, calling the effort an "unprecedented colonial venture, a regrettable assault by a feudal landlord." By election time in November 1972 the ordinance, now described as Inyo's Declaration of Independence, was a sure winner. Local voters approved the measure by a margin of 76 percent—greater even than the 71 percent given the former grand marshal of Bishop's Mule Days Parade, Ronald Reagan.

The city's regime of "practical colonialism" was never the same afterward. Los Angeles was now losing on two fronts and was in palpable danger of having its discretionary power over the use of Owens

Valley water usurped by the courts or the county. Initially the city
responded with a combination of sanctions and goodwill gestures.
Lease fees were raised, as promised, and the DWP filed a new lawsuit to
invalidate the local ordinance. Los Angeles charged that under the state
constitution Inyo had no right to interfere in the municipal affairs of a
chartered city (by extracting water on its own land) and, in an ironic
twist, that the local ordinance violated CEQA because no environmental impact study had been completed on its effects. At the same time,
however, Los Angeles offered commercial lots in Bishop for sale and
announced a "general policy of getting out of the landlord business, at
least in the towns."[61]

Inyo adopted the same strategy of thrust and parry. When Los Angeles ignored the new local ordinance, a county crew stopped the drill-
ing of a DWP well that had not obtained a permit. Yet the county
decided to end its meter strike early in 1981, with an agreement
whereby the money held in escrow would be used to pay the $38,000
differential between the flat and metered rates since 1976, but without
penalties or interest. The parties were gradually moving toward an
agreement, owing in large part to the city's realization that dealing with
local officials was preferable to the alternatives.

THE BATTLE FOR MONO LAKE

Any understanding of Inyo's environmental movement during the
1980s requires an appreciation of the contemporaneous developments
in Mono County, where the water war had opened on yet another front.
The much publicized campaign to save Mono Lake has a history intertwined with political movements in the Owens Valley. Mono Lake is a
unique natural formation, a saline body of water with no outlet that
nevertheless supports an ecological network of bird and water life. As
early as the 1920s, the DWP began thinking about a sixty-mile northward extension of the aqueduct to the streams feeding Mono Lake near
the town of Lee Vining. The public first took notice of the plan in 1929,
when the city started acquiring right-of-way land and water rights by
requesting congressional withdrawals from the public domain and by
initiating condemnation proceedings. By 1931, the small settlement
around the lake had organized its own Mono Basin Land Owners'
Protective Association to protest against the city's preference for condemnation of the desired land rather than straightforward purchase.
Mono residents had a "vivid memory of 25 years of bitter struggle in

which property owners in the Owens River Valley have had to fight for their rights."[62] Eventually the DWP bought large tracts, and in 1933 it unveiled its plan to tunnel under Mono Basin and divert water to the Owens River from the creeks feeding Mono Lake.[63]

The city was slow to exploit this new capacity after completion of the pipeline in 1941. In the early years just one-third of the city's annual entitlement was diverted, and streams continued flowing into the lake, although its level was dropping slowly. As in the Owens Valley, the situation changed abruptly in 1970 with the completion of the second aqueduct. The amount being exported from Mono County doubled within a few years.[64] From 1941 to 1981, the level of Mono Lake dropped 46 vertical feet, one-third of the loss occurring after 1970; the surface area receded from 90 to 60 square miles.[65]

Although declining lake waters concerned local resorts, the problem received little public attention until 1974, when David Gaines, a biologist from the University of California at Davis, undertook an inventory of natural areas in Mono County for the California Natural Areas Coordinating Council. Gaines had worried about the lake's decline for several years, and his first systematic investigation caused sufficient concern to enlist the support of students from Davis and Stanford University in a successful application for a grant from the National Science Foundation in 1976.[66] Before long these scientists and environmentalists produced evidence showing the chain of natural depredation that resulted from stream diversions: as the lake level dropped, salinity (already greater than that of the ocean) doubled from 5 to 10 percent; higher salinity threatened the survival of the brine shrimp and flies that provided the diet of California seagulls and several species of migratory birds; a recently exposed land bridge to one of the lake's islands gave coyote predators access to the nesting grounds of birds; various species of birds and wildlife were endangered; and the receding shoreline exposed salt deposits, resulting in noxious dust storms. These discoveries by the students were subsequently disputed by DWP researchers, but they were corroborated by a congressionally mandated National Academy of Sciences study published in 1987.

Environmental activists from the beginning, Gaines and about ten of his associates founded the Mono Lake Committee in 1978. In contrast to citizen groups in the Owens Valley, the Mono Lake Committee was not the result of a local initiative or protest tradition. It was a pure expression of the new environmental movement nationwide and in California, although it is also true that Gaines took inspiration from the

Owens Valley struggle, stayed in close contact with developments there
through his biologist friends, and, in the opinion of the committee's
present director, felt that saving Mono Lake depended on the same
principle of "citizens asserting rights to the protection of their own
resources."[67] In an effort to mobilize supporters and resources, Gaines
traveled a circuit of Audubon Society and Sierra Club meetings with his
own slide-show presentation and research evidence. The grassroots effort proved remarkably successful at raising money, enlisting committee
members, publicizing the cause, and building strategic organizational
alliances.

Equally astute in state politics, the Mono Lake Committee approached the county's representatives, who convinced the Department
of Water Resources to sponsor an Inter-Agency Task Force to study
Mono Lake. The task force (including representatives from Water Resources, the Department of Fish and Game, the Bureau of Land Management, the Forest Service, Mono County, and the Los Angeles Department of Water and Power) held public hearings and issued a report
in 1979 with the endorsement of all parties save the DWP. The rest of
the task force firmly supported the Mono Lake Committee's position
that there was a present danger to the regional ecosystem, and they
suggested that Los Angeles could reduce by 85 percent the amount of
water diverted from the lake if it made a conservation effort equal to
what it had recently achieved in the 1977–1978 drought. Although bills
attempting to regulate the diversion of water from Mono Lake were
defeated in the state legislature in 1979 and 1980, the same body succeeded in creating the Mono Lake Tufa State Reserve in 1981, and
Congress followed suit in 1984 by establishing the Mono Basin National Forest Scenic Area—both acts helping to preserve the lake's surroundings if not its water.[68]

All these achievements were a direct result of the research, public
relations, and political work of the Mono Lake Committee and its
allies. The time was right for the committee, and its volunteer staff of
educated young people, including many naturalists and lawyers, knew
the ropes of liberal politics. The committee also had a genius for publicity. "Save Mono Lake" bumper stickers began appearing all over the
state during the 1980s; later there were other slogans ("Don't Owenize
Mono") and applications—for example, toilet stickers ("I Save Water
for Mono Lake"). In well-publicized bucket brigades, hikers and jog-
gers carried water from Los Angeles to replenish the lake, while bike-
a-thon participants carried symbolic vials. Mono Lake was featured on

the cover of *Life* magazine in July 1981, and in articles appearing in *National Geographic, Smithsonian,* and *Audubon.* A visitor's center was established at Lee Vining, marked by an official-looking, state-installed road marker; it attracted a steady stream of curious tourists, who passed through in the summer months—including many Europeans who had read about the lake and seen pictures of its dramatic tufa towers (once submerged spires of salt deposits). On its tenth anniversary, the committee counted 18,000 members (one-third from Southern California) and had a yearly budget of $700,000.[69]

By far the most telling accomplishment of the Mono Lake Committee and its allies, however, was a series of court decisions that steadily reduced the city's proprietary rights in favor of the public interest. After more than a decade of continuous legal maneuver, the history of these suits requires a volume of its own (and, indeed, is the subject of the committee's unfinished *Field Guide to Mono Lake Lawsuits.* Yet, as they affected developments in the Owens Valley, two stages were crucial. In 1979, a coalition of environmental groups, organized by the Mono Lake Committee and including the National Audubon Society, Friends of the Earth, the Los Angeles Audubon Society, and several residents of Lee Vining, sued the DWP. They claimed that Mono Lake was a public trust, which Los Angeles had no right to destroy. In law, the public-trust doctrine derived from the need to protect navigable waterways from obstruction by private property rights. "During the California gold rush, the doctrine was often used to stop hydraulic miners from filling up rivers with silt. . . . A 1971 California court declared that the doctrine should apply to the preservation of lands in a natural state for the purposes of scientific research and the protection of wildlife and air and water quality."[70] To the strategists inside the Mono Lake Committee, these and other extensions of the public-trust doctrine suggested that it could also be applied to preserving a flow of water into the lake sufficient for the public's use of the resource.[71]

The suit was transferred through several courts; the plaintiffs' claims were rejected by the Alpine County Superior Court; and the plaintiffs appealed to the California Supreme Court. In February 1983, the high court declared: "Mono Lake is . . . a navigable waterway. The beds, shores, and waters of the lake are without question protected by the public trust. The streams diverted by the DWP, however, are not themselves navigable. But, drawing on precedents from California mining cases, [the court] concluded that the public trust doctrine . . . protects navigable waters from harm caused by diversions of nonnavigable tributaries."[72] Although the supreme court made no decision on the actual allocation of water, merely calling for a balancing of DWP and public interests, the decision was a huge victory for the environmental movement. If the public-trust decision was the first legal breakthrough for Mono Lake, the second came in a series of water-allocation cases from 1984 to 1988, in which DWP diversions were enjoined and stream flows were ordered restored for the protection of fish as well as the lake habitat.[73] The lawsuits continue to this day, but it is clear that the principle of preserving Mono Lake for the public against destructive proprietary use has been established.

The extensive publicity generated around Mono Lake and the public trust decision came at a critical time for the DWP-Inyo negotiations on a joint management agreement. After February 1983 it was clear that the city's share of Mono water would be limited by the courts, and that court injunctions would govern the DWP's discretion over aqueduct operation at virtually all of the sources of supply. By reaching an interim agreement with Inyo, the city could relieve the legal siege by getting the appeals court out of its affairs, at least temporarily. The Mono Lake campaign significantly improved the chances of a victory in the Owens Valley.

STAGES OF AGREEMENT

Over the next four years, organized valley citizens, county officials, and the DWP alternately fought and negotiated about the terms of an agreement. Leadership changed hands and alliances shifted, although the characteristic pattern found Inyo negotiators trying to develop terms acceptable both to militant citizens and to conservative city representatives. The intricacies are best summarized in three stages: initial impasse, creation of the mechanisms, and the final showdown.

The first stage was a premature effort by the supervisors to use the threat of passing the local ordinance as leverage for city concessions on the old idea of a master plan. The new draft agreement, the second in a series, resembled the 1979 five-year operational study, and it met a similar fate. In May 1981, city and county negotiators offered a plan for public consideration. The DWP would drop its lawsuit against the local ordinance, finance a three-year study of groundwater management costing $840,000, limit pumping during the first year of the study to the court-ordered 149 cfs, and agree not to raise lease fees. Inyo would shelve the local ordinance for three years, dismiss its suit seeking to require Los Angeles to produce a new EIR, and abandon its recent split-roll property tax system whereby the city was assessed at higher rates than private owners.[74] As concerned citizens were quick to point out, the draft agreement was one-sided. Inyo was giving up its legal victories, at least temporarily, for a city-sponsored study with no foreseeable outcome. At "emotion packed" public hearings with the CCOV and civic groups "supervisors were condemned for selling out, for giving away gains earned over a period of years and for taking the side of a vocal, militant minority in making any agreement with the DWP which did not include victory for the county in water meter complaints and the groundwater pumping ordinance." The minority here was the ranchers, who praised the supervisors for heading off a threatened 24-percent rise in lease costs. But leaseholders were outnumbered. Enid Larson, a valley native and history enthusiast, was applauded when she observed that "if the supervisors approved this agreement their names would rank with that of J. B. Lippincott as someone who sold out the county."[75] The supervisors not only reversed their position, but affirmed that the local ordinance would not be compromised in any future negotiations. "A crowd estimated at more than 150 persons broke out in cheers and applause."[76]

The second stage stretched over the next two years, although talks resumed at once. Los Angeles applied pressure with water-rate increases, drawing a hostile response from local officials and the CCOV, but the city was chastened by an appellate court's rejection of its second EIR. The necessity of preparing a third report was a motive for compromise. The newly established county water commission began formulating terms for an agreement consistent with the local ordinance and informed by professional consultants. City pumping would be locally prescribed, and the limits would be adjusted if the DWP took "mitigation measures" to reverse environmental damage. A revised agreement endorsed by the supervisors in mid-1982 complicated matters by introducing a land exchange and joint hydroelectric development into the basic tradeoffs (that is, the lawsuits, split-roll taxation, and the study). This time even the county's top strategists, such as special counsel Rossmann and the recently retired administrator Smith, denounced the plan.

Several false starts served the useful purpose of identifying the essential elements of any agreement that would succeed locally. In July 1982 the supervisors indicated that they were not interested in an agreement that ignored the local ordinance, but would welcome a study conducted by the state Department of Water Resources and the United States Geological Survey (USGS). The new Inyo County Water Department was already engaged in environmental studies and in need of additional financial support. The city now had an opening—it would help finance the larger independent study if pending legal cases were put on hold. Early in 1983, just as the public-trust decision was announced, city and county came together on a five-year study jointly financed by the DWP ($350,000 in the form of a grant to Inyo), the USGS ($400,000), the State of California (a $200,000 grant), and the county ($200,000). Los Angeles was relieved and expressed a new mood of cooperation. Thirty-one town parcels were offered for private sale, and a city official admitted that the installation of water meters had been a "bad mistake."[77] With the collaborative study underway, a general agreement was imminent—or so it appeared until two new difficulties developed.

The local ordinance was ruled unconstitutional in the Superior Court in July 1983. Although the decision could be appealed, it weakened the county's negotiating position. Inyo officials reasoned that it was preferable to get what they could in the agreement already well along than to press for more, with the risk of losing an appeal and along with it all the political gains since 1980. At the same time, however, the citizens' movement was increasingly dissatisfied with the agreement under discussion.

The third stage was a final showdown between Inyo citizens and the county government. After long negotiations, the supervisors, legal counsel, and professionals connected with the Inyo Water Department were united behind a draft agreement produced in the wake of the joint study. The elaborate plan contained twenty-one provisions divided into sections on pumping, enhancement and mitigation projects, and litigation. The agreement's key feature was joint management of water. County Counsel Dennis Meyers noted, "That's historical because they've [DWP] never allowed anyone to manage what they feel is their own water. It is a historical step." Frank Fowles, who helped start it all in 1972, remarked, "I never expected to see the day when the city would agree to let someone else help it manage water in the Owens Valley."[78] The agreement would run for five years unless either party served notice to end it. A standing committee with representatives from the county and the DWP would set yearly pumping quotas, unless they were unable to agree, in which case a previously agreed-upon table pegging extraction to the spring runoff would be used. The city would rotate pumping from various underground fields to spread its effects. In dry years the city would look to the MWD for supplementary supplies, and both governments would practice conservation. Valley water rates were rolled back to 50 percent of those prevailing in 1983, and lease charges were guaranteed against increase. As stipulated by the local ordinance, permits for new wells would have to be obtained from the county. Los Angeles continued to finance the USGS study, and the county kept $540,000 in taxes collected through the disputed split-roll system. During the period of the agreement the county would not appeal the decision invalidating the local ordinance and would put on hold its challenge to the city's second EIR. The appeals court limit on pumping, set at 149 cfs, would be replaced by provisions in the agreement. And finally, the city would pay for 19 enhancement and mitigation projects, ranging from watered alfalfa fields and swimming holes to revegetation and restoration of the Owens river below the aqueduct intake.[79]

The CCOV at first called the agreement a "very good start," but its members turned to blunt opposition as they studied it. One problem, they felt, was that the agreement had been reached in secret negotiations with the city and that the subsequent public meetings merely presented a fait accompli. More important, court protections were being abandoned and the DWP was being allowed to pump too much water. The agreement failed to spell out enforcement procedures. In stormy hearings, the CCOV urged modifications that would allow the lawsuits concerning the local ordinance and the EIR to continue; set a definite pumping limit at the court-imposed rate of 149 cfs; roll back water rates further, to those of premetering days; and create an independent arbitration board to settle any differences between the city and the county. The CCOV position was supported in one aspect or another by the League of Women Voters and environmental groups, although the agreement also had popular support from the Inyo County Cattlemen's Association and a fair number of individuals who thought that it was the best deal they could get.

The CCOV had been flagging since its glory days of the meter strike. After the county government seized the initiative with the local ordinance, concerned citizens were increasingly cast in the role of critics who turned up at public hearings and supervisors' meetings to oppose early and dubious agreements. In November 1983, opponents of the current agreement who had been using the CCOV name met at the home of Bill and Barbara Manning to form a new organization. Among the twelve people at the charter meeting of the Advocates for Repre-

sentative Government, the name of which was soon changed to the
Owens Valley Committee (OVC), were Ellen Hardebeck and Flora
Nash of the League of Women Voters, attorney Kenny Scruggs and
journalist Benett Kessler (both women), botanist Mary De Decker, engineer Vince Yoder, and Bishop's Episcopal Father Christopher Kelley.
Manning, a retired engineer, and his associates agreed that a campaign
against the new agreement required more professional methods than
those of the CCOV—more expertise on legal and environmental issues
and less rabble-rousing. In the months that followed, the OVC confronted the Inyo supervisors as professionals and urged modifications in
the agreement. When the supervisors countered with the observation
that most valley residents supported the agreement, the OVC conducted
its own telephone survey, which showed that only 9 percent favored the
plan, 41 percent opposed it, and half of the 273 registered voters polled
were undecided.[80] The OVC worked closely with Kessler and John
Heston, who used their local radio station, cable TV channel, and
radical *Inyo County News-Letter* to oppose the agreement. In Manning's words, "We were fighting our own government."[81] Rallying
OVC support in an open letter to the recently merged *Inyo Register and
Independent*, Father Kelley reminded supervisors that Los Angeles was
responsible for "the rape of the Owens Valley."[82]

The OVC was winning converts to the position that the agreement
needed enforcement mechanisms, firm pumping limitations, and continuation of the lawsuits. The advisory committee to the county water
department voted to side with the OVC and reject the pending agreement. The supervisors noted the opposition and modified the agreement
by adding a bail-out provision that would allow either party to terminate
the arrangement. Although that failed to satisfy critics, the supervisors
decided in November to approve the "draft concepts" and forward them
to Los Angeles for the next review. The local battle continued into early
1984. Now the OVC charged that the supervisors had violated state law
(the Brown Act) by holding their deliberations with the city in secret
meetings. The Inyo County grand jury agreed, but an effort to place the
proposed agreement on the ballot was squelched by the board. New
hearings were scheduled when the document was returned with revisions
from Los Angeles and presented to the public in final form.

The final showdown in March 1984 found the OVC as strongly
opposed as ever. Ten problems with the agreement were cited in a
published statement, the gist of which was the claim that the "DWP gets

everything it could not get from 12 years of litigation"—that the court-imposed restrictions would be set aside, that the pumping limits in the agreement were too high, that control would be placed in the hands of a technical group, that loopholes left no means of enforcing such terms as the conservation of water in Los Angeles, that Inyo would be given no control over surface water, and that the standards of environmental protection were not explicit.[83] Greg James, director of the county water department, replied that Inyo's legal advantage was not being given up, only set aside during the period of the agreement. Any time that the county wanted to terminate the plan, or after its expiration, the lawsuits could be reactivated. Concerning pumping limits, he noted that the mitigation projects and other protections (such as well rotation) in the agreement would prevent environmental damage. Judging from the sample of audience opinion at public hearings in Bishop and Lone Pine, the OVC was ahead in the debate.

> The Bishop meeting, punctuated at times with jeers, was the more acrimonious of the two hearings. Father Christopher Kelley said the agreement was "morally defective and so was anyone who signed it." Speakers at both hearings were overwhelmingly opposed to the proposed pact. Groups represented who opposed the agreement included the League of Women Voters of the Eastern Sierra, the Owens Valley Committee, and local chapters of the Native Plant Society, the Audubon Society, and the Sierra Club. But most opposition came from individuals and much of that opposition was directed at the pumping table. Several people said they could support the agreement if the table was removed. The agreement did draw support.[84]

As the water war reached its eightieth anniversary, the fight over an agreement witnessed a first: Owens Valley citizens threatened to sue their own government if the settlement was approved. The board of supervisors responded again by meeting with the OVC and environmental groups, but without success. The OVC held out for continued court jurisdiction over water extraction and its environmental effects, the very circumstance Los Angeles was most determined to eliminate. Inyo officials talked about dropping the controversial pumping table from the agreement, but decided instead to change the termination clause by reducing the time stipulated for giving notice. The supervisors unanimously approved the agreement in late March and sent it to Los Angeles, where it was promptly endorsed by the board of water and power commissioners and the city council.

Approval of the agreement came as no political surprise. After years of negotiation, the supervisors and county officials had developed a commitment to the process. Some wanted to be remembered for finally bringing peace to the historical controversy. Others simply wanted to end the conflict with the concessions already won. As a participant, county administrator John K. Smith understood the logic of the negotiating process: "Two political bodies sit down and try to negotiate out lawsuits and misunderstandings and try to bury the hatchet, so to speak, so they can get about their business without continually haranguing each other."[85] The supervisors' dealings with the opposition suggested, as even the OVC survey showed, that perhaps half the public found the intricate debate too difficult to evaluate, and some of the others favored an agreement. The OVC was capable and well organized, but the supervisors doubted that it represented the majority. Oppositional politics in this final phase had shifted to legal interpretations and technical questions that rallied less popular fervor as discussions wore on. The waning of demonstrations and acts of violence is a valid indicator of public acceptance, however ambivalent or just plain weary it may have been. Finally, everyone knew that the agreement was a victory—that the continuing debate focused less on whether there would be a settlement than on whether the city could be trusted or whether more guarantees could be extracted. For the supervisors it was time to act.

The OVC was not finished, however. Making good its threat to sue if the agreement was approved, the OVC claimed in the Superior Court that the agreement itself required an EIR under the California Environmental Quality Act. When the court ruled against it, the OVC appealed to the Third District Court of Appeals in Sacramento. Because Los Angeles was still under a court injunction limiting pumping and requiring an EIR, the appeals court was faced with approving an agreement that the parties hoped would replace the court's authority. But the OVC hearing produced a dramatic and unexpected result. The court approved the agreement but retained jurisdiction. The agreement would substitute for the court-imposed pumping limitations during its five-year term, but at the end of that period the court would review the results, to be reported in the form of an EIR and a new management plan. The OVC had won a major victory for Inyo by establishing a principle that the city certainly did not want and the county had feared to demand.

Final court approval in 1985 institutionalized the conflict rather than ending it. The joint groundwater management study under USGS, begun in 1983, went forward and was subsequently extended so that its expiration date would coincide with that of the five-year agreement on June 30, 1990. During the five years, the DWP and the county water department worked closely on technical questions of water management, environmental assessment, and the implementation of enhancement and mitigation projects. Although they remained adversaries in broad political terms, they developed a collegial relationship in technical areas, particularly as they began to develop the terms of a second agreement.

The public debate was reopened in 1989 on a second, long-term agreement to follow on the expiration of the first. In preliminary form, the new plan would continue indefinitely, with Inyo and Los Angeles jointly filing an EIR finally to satisfy the appeals court. With that step the issue would be removed from the court's jurisdiction. The county would receive a number of customary gifts, including more enhancement and mitigation projects, the sale of more city land in or near towns, no increase in lease charges, a lease-purchase plan to transfer ownership of the town water systems, and a tidy $1 million per year for the general fund, in addition to financial assistance for studies, maintenance, and projects. The major innovation was to eliminate any formula-based pumping limit and instead to link extraction to soil moisture and vegetation growth. Inyo botanists would monitor the health of plant life in a sample of ecological zones, and moisture sensors planted in the soil would automatically shut off pumps when the water table dropped below the requirements for viable desert plant life.[86]

Hearings before the board of supervisors in the spring of 1989 were spirited, but drew no organized opposition. Individuals insisted on including a definite pumping ceiling and a commitment to the restoration of habitats, particularly at Owens Lake, where dust storms were getting worse according to Keeler residents. Some of the old fire reappeared in talk of a recall election if the agreement failed to include firm protections; but far from opposing the agreement, critics pressed to strengthen it. Supporters felt that joint management, a measure of local control, and environmental awareness were now established achievements of the local struggle. Critics acknowledged these changes, but noted that through them all, Los Angeles has continued taking the water while the valley has become drier, dustier, and more desolate since the second aqueduct began operation. The agreement might end that downward spiral, but they wanted assurances.

After revisions to tighten the language, the permanent agreement was accepted by all official parties in August 1989. Newspapers from *Toiyabe Trails* (published by a chapter of the Sierra Club) to the *New York*

Times announced that the historic water war was over.[87] That conclusion was premature. One year later the joint EIR was still unfinished, and many local activists were withholding judgment on the results of the DWP-county collaboration until the document received close scrutiny. Meanwhile, in the throes of a new drought, a small group of dissidents had organized as the People Who Love the Valley, taken ads in the local paper, and obtained seven hundred signatures on a petition calling on supervisors to repudiate the entire agreement and return to pre-1970 pumping levels or face a recall campaign. Official assurances can be expected, and the appeals court will still have to approve any permanent accord; but history would lead us to expect that peace is contingent on a general belief that justice is being done in local society.

INNOVATION AND CONTINUITY

The environmental rebellion of 1970–1984 was less a new movement than a continuation of the original water war, which collapsed in 1928 but did not die. The second phase of the struggle built on both the achievements and the lessons of defeat drawn from the 1920s. First, the original movement was culturally elaborated after 1930, becoming the salient feature of civic consciousness and providing symbols that were called upon explicitly in the mobilization that began in 1970. Second, resistance strategies begun during the first phase, such as lawsuits over groundwater pumping, were continued during the latency period from 1930 to 1970, and they nourished the arrested spirit of local autonomy. Third, the rebellion of the 1970s used environmentalism to attain perennial aims—local control and economic development in tandem with the city.

Based on a continuing tradition, the environmental rebellion was nevertheless distinct in many ways. Like its predecessor, it began with depredations stemming from the urban growth and incorporation. But the second aqueduct appeared in the midst of national concern for environmental protection. If the Reclamation Act of 1902 provided valley interests with encouraging rhetoric about western development, NEPA and CEQA gave them tools for self-defense. A small group of environmentalists introduced these ideas into a local conflict over a land exchange and its implications for greater water extraction. Before long environmental protection was not only embraced by county officials, but creatively pursued in the 1972 lawsuit that, in its many extensions, finally shifted the balance of power away from Los Angeles. The state had given Inyo officials the legal means for a struggle that they took up to "do their job as public officials" and not as environmentalists. Speaking about county officials, the veteran environmentalist Aubrey Lyon noted that "when they started, they couldn't have cared less for the environment, but that was the only legal argument they could give. Now they have begun to realize that this is something important."[88] Among local environmentalists, "most of these ideas came from new people of course."[89]

From 1972 onward, the struggle was a joint enterprise of citizens and local government—an alliance, however troubled, that did not exist in the 1920s and might indeed have been pointless, given the weakness of county government at that time. If the alliance was stormy at some times, it came together as a united front at others and was generally the medium through which policies concerning Los Angeles had to pass. Its leadership alternated: citizens began the new rebellion, but stepped aside when the first lawsuit was filed; they returned in 1976, when the DWP cut back on water supplies and instituted commercial metering, in 1979 with the residential meter strike, and in 1982 to protest the final agreement. The county responded to each mobilization by moving closer to the citizens' position and taking a harder line in city negotiations. Without the popular movement, county officials would have settled for far less, judging from their readiness to enter agreements that the citizens successfully opposed. But the county also took a militant stand at times, with lawsuits, its own meter strike, and the critical local ordinance. The struggle was often carried forward by a citizen-government alliance, although the decisive arena was public. "It is a conflict waged between governmental agencies, sustained by public funds, attended by battalions of consultants and expert witnesses, and aimed ultimately at achieving an enforceable regulatory compromise."[90]

City countermoves punctuated each stage of the struggle. On one hand, the DWP offered incentives for a settlement, conceding some points (such as rate rollbacks and ownership of the town water systems) and initiating others (such as property resales). On the other hand, the city resorted to clear reprisals, calling them educational measures, to divide local interests and squelch dissent. Water for recreational use was withheld, lease and water rates were increased, countersuits were filed, ranchers and business groups were intimidated, and meters were installed. But reprisals did not work. The groups most subject to city pressure were too small (for example, the ranchers) or drawn more strongly to valley aims (such as the businesspeople). Not only did the city's tactics fail to make converts, they often energized the opposition. Popular justice now routinely answered spiteful measures with arson, dynamite, and property damage, particularly during peak periods of popular mobilization—over a ten-year span, nearly every reported act of violent protest listed on pages 258–59 occurred in two periods of heated controversy, 1975–1976 and 1979–1980. As in the clamorous and well-publicized meter strike, the city learned that it had made a "bad mistake."

The success of the popular movement deserves closer examination in view of the limitations its predecessor met in the 1920s. For purposes of a direct comparison of the social bases of the two movement phases, methods similar to those discussed in chapter 5 were developed for the second phase. Rank-and-file participation was inferred from the sample of 155 persons who signed the petition in 1980 requesting that the board of supervisors not proceed on an agreement with the DWP.[91] This petition effectively spanned two stages of the modern movement, coming at the transition from the meter strike to the final battle over an agreement. Leadership of the citizens' movement was judged from a sample of 39 officers of the Concerned Citizens of the Owens Valley (in 1970 and 1976) and the Owens Valley Committee.[92] As we saw in chapter 5, the popular revolt of the 1920s had grown from an agrarian, class-based constituency to a broadly representative community movement. Its leadership reflected a slightly higher socioeconomic status, but similar breadth.

A distinctive pattern of participation characterizes the popular movement of 1980 (table 14). Rank-and-file petition signers generally resembled the county population in their occupations, but with fewer professionals and working-class persons (such as craftsmen, foremen or operatives) and more in the category of proprietors, managers, and officials. Slightly more than 70 percent of movement supporters came from three occupational groupings: proprietors, managers, and officials; technical, sales, and clerical personnel; and service workers. The census figures did not include homemakers and retired persons, self-designations used by about 25 percent of the petition signers. In order to maximize comparability with the general population, retired persons who signed the petition were classified occupationally when they volunteered their former employment. Moving from the abstract census categories to concrete jobs, petition signers had a characteristic occupational profile. Most frequently they worked as motel managers, county clerical workers, owners of small businesses (often of gas sta-

TABLE 14. OCCUPATIONAL STRUCTURE OF INYO COUNTY
AND PROTEST GROUPS, CIRCA 1980

	Inyo County (N = 7,875)	Petition Signers, 1980 (N = 103)	Concerned Citizens and Owens Valley Committee (N = 39)
Professional persons	10.1%	3.9%	30.8%
Farmers and farm managers	0.4	1.0	0
Proprietors, managers, and officials	10.5	28.2	23.1
Technical, sales, and clerical personnel	27.5	23.3	2.6
Craftsmen and foremen	16.2	3.9	2.6
Operatives	10.0	1.0	0
Service workers	20.7	19.4	7.7
Farm laborers	2.9	0	0
Nonfarm laborers	4.0	2.9	0
Homemakers	—	14.6	30.8
Retired persons	—	1.9	2.6
[Retired but classified by previous occupation]		[12.6]	[23.1]
Total	102.3%	100.1%	100.2%

SOURCES: *Twentieth U.S. Census of Population,* "Characteristics of the Population," part 6, "California" (table 177); Inyo County, petition to the board of supervisors, June 2, 1980; interviews by author; unpublished survey by the Eastern California Museum.

tions and tourist shops), housewives, volunteers in community groups, restaurant and grocery personnel, teachers, and an assortment of service workers (from hairdressers and waitresses to bank employees). In summary, the rank and file came mainly from the distinct commercial-services economy that grew up from 1930 to 1970.

Leadership of the citizens' committees was even more sharply defined. Slightly more than 60 percent of committee officers were professionals and homemakers. Adding proprietors, managers, and officials to those two categories shows that 85 percent of the leaders were working or retired professional persons (many of them teachers, scientists, and engineers), small business owners, and homemakers (typically also activists in civic associations).

Main Street, Bishop, 1990. Bishop's modern economy is dominated by motels, service stations, restaurants, and shops, plus the headquarters for a number of federal, state, county, and Los Angeles governmental agencies. (Photo by the author.)

In summary, the popular movements of the 1920s and 1970s were built on separate social bases—different cross-sections of the public. This difference is not explained by population change alone. The movement in the 1920s fairly represented the county's population of the time at both the rank-and-file and leadership levels; whereas in the 1970s the movement drew disproportionately from the commercial and service sector, while the leadership was even more concentrated on working and retired professionals, homemaker–civic activists, and business pro-prietors. The sophistication of this group increased its effectiveness in dealing with county officials. Contrary to conventional expectations, the earlier, more representative movement was defeated—temporarily perhaps, but for the lifetime of its supporters—and the later, more professionally specialized movement succeeded. The success and failure of each of the movement phases, of course, was not solely due to their strategies and personnel. A key point of comparison, nevertheless, is that the environmental movement made effective use of its professional skills. Political changes in California and the nation provided an open-ing, but these opportunities did not affect the Owens Valley until state intervention was forced by inventive local action.

RESULTS

The fate of the Owens Valley, initially posed as a dire issue in 1904, is a topic of spirited discussion in town meetings today. The almost ninety-year struggle is not finished, although a permanent agreement promises to replace the limbo of court jurisdiction that reigned for the benefit of local interests from 1972 to 1990. Whether the new agree-ment will actually reverse the environmental damage suffered by the valley, or simply create a more subtle form of "practical colonialism," time will tell. For the present, the results of the long water war deserve reflection. The question is simple: did the struggle succeed? The answer is not so simple.

The argument against a local victory points out that city domination continues despite court injunctions and mutually acceptable manage-ment plans. The DWP still owns the land it acquired during the 1920s, with the exception of town lots resold privately; and the extraction of surface water and groundwater continues pretty much at the city's convenience. Local opposition comes and goes; the DWP lasts forever. Institutional aims are persistent over time, protest groups' memories are short. Los Angeles is rich by Inyo standards, easily able to divert a small fraction of DWP revenues generated in the Owens Valley to palliative measures and financial assistance to local government. County officials have traded environmental protection for short-term operating funds. Mitigation projects are little more than showcases along the highway—a few hundred acres of irrigated alfalfa or pasture, for example, in the midst of many thousands of acres barely sustaining sage brush. Environmental quality has declined since the second aqueduct, a point acknowledged even by supporters of the new agreement and in the city's disingenuous second EIR.[93]

My conclusion is different. The struggle has succeeded—sometimes only defensively, often in small ways, but generally with significant gains across a range of indicators that reflect the viability of local society. The argument for failure is valid in many respects, but it suffers from an exclusive focus on physical conditions. If social and political considerations are included in the evaluation, another more nuanced conclusion is supported—gains, under the circumstances, if not victory.

First, and fundamentally, the Owens Valley has never been dominated by Los Angeles. Local opposition has been virtually continuous since the city's appearance in the valley. In 1906 and again in 1928, the DWP attained considerable power over the valley's physical resources and political life, but little legitimacy. Power and domination have to be distinguished; the first refers to the probability that a party in a transaction will realize its own will even against resistance, whereas the second implies acceptance of that power as legitimate according to traditional or legal standards.[94] Domination in this sense did not succeed, despite the city's extensive power. And even that power has been the object of successful challenges that range from protest violence to legal disputes. Los Angeles maintains significant power over the valley's physical environment and a weighty presence in local society, but its power is contested and its domination repudiated. Against the realities of power, an equally obvious legacy of the long conflict is the highly participatory style of Inyo County politics. The city's supposed domination has nourished a continuing tradition of citizen mobilization and involvement in public affairs, a tradition routinely observed by the county government, which holds town meetings up and down the valley when major issues are being considered. Reflecting on the environmental movement, the author of the local ordinance concludes that "Inyo's greatest achievement [is] the renaissance of self-respect and self-determination."[95]

Second, the environmental movement finally succeeded in attaining the objective of the first revolt by placing the city-county conflict under the jurisdiction of a higher and independent authority. Rebels in the 1920s tried every way they knew to force intervention by the governor and state legislature, but only through the exploitation of modern state and federal law (CEQA and NEPA) has the environmental movement been able to realign the authority relations governing the valley. The

EIR lawsuit broke the city's monopoly of power by introducing the appeals court into county policy-making, and the local ordinance broke the city's monopoly of knowledge by creating expertise in a new county agency and, eventually, in the research of state and federal (USGS) departments. Environmentalism now sets the standard for policy debates, and the evidence on environmental effects is more objective. If knowledge is power, as Michel Foucault says, then power over the valley's future is more broadly shared.[96] Administration of the city's system of water and power has been demystified—insouciantly analysed by ecologists and citizens' committees.

Third, many of the concessions won through public relations pressures and negotiated agreements have produced tangible improvements in local life. Property resales, the subject of a local campaign in the 1930s and a means of blandishment by the city from the 1960s onward, have helped reestablish citizen ownership and control of town life. If the commercial and services economy depends on city vacationers and governmental agencies, it is thriving nevertheless. Los Angeles may have used the Paiutes for public-relations purposes in the 1937 land exchange, but the result was a boon for Indians formerly deprived of a decent home. The Paiute community today is actually increasing as registered tribal members return to the valley. If they are still restricted to the lower occupational ranks, statistical evidence suggests their gradual integration in public employment. For the general population, cost-of-living increases have been dampened by rate rollbacks and city subsidies to county government. Los Angeles and the federal government bear the costs of maintaining the recreational facilities that attract many local business patrons. Agriculture continues on city leases with more stable rates and fewer threats. If many of the enhancement and mitigation efforts funded by the city are window dressing, the cumulative effect of more than twenty projects at least provides some public amenities (such as parks, restored waterways, museum improvements, and tree planting) at no cost to Inyo taxpayers; and these projects have the potential for significant improvement should the DWP accept its share of responsibility for the dust pollution at Owens lake.[97]

Nevertheless, the critics are right in one important respect. The physical environment is not improving and is not likely to as the result of the agreement. Enhancement and mitigation projects are far too limited to restore the valley's springs, vegetation, and wildlife habitat to anything approximating pre-1970 conditions. The principle of the agreement is

Keeler Swimming Club, 1990. Once a center of ore processing, Owens Lake cargo-boat shipping, and the railroad terminus, Keeler is now virtually abandoned. The few remaining residents suffer from dust storms coming off the dry lake bed. (Photo by the author.)

that things should not get worse; but the standard against which getting worse will be measured (by soil-moisture sensors and microscopic sections of surviving leaf area on desert plants) is itself retrograde: the valley's condition in the early 1980s following years of low precipitation and high pumping. The agreement settles for too little by way of environmental restoration.

Finally, we must recall that the revolt that began in 1904 and flowered in the 1920s had one overriding purpose, to "save the communities of the Owens Valley." That has been accomplished, despite the city's preference that the towns wither away or devolve into sparsely populated recreational redoubts making few demands on city services and having no influence on their management. In 1928, Los Angeles thought it had won the water war; by 1982 it badly wanted a compromise. Surveying the valley today, the Watterson brothers might be stunned by its desolate landscape, but impressed by the fulfillment of their main objective: the communities survive and prosper in partnership with the city. Of course, goals change with time. Local leaders want more today, and they have made a case for their ambitions that the courts have supported. Perhaps they will make further progress toward restoring a verdant ecology. So far, they have maintained their communities and developed a healthy tradition of local control, while other rural areas around the state and nation have been swallowed up by urban expansion. A final irony is that while the Owens Valley struggled for survival, an abundant water supply allowed Los Angeles to grow beyond manageable limits, with air pollution, congestion, and all the sprawling problems that attend unregulated urban expansion. Belatedly, the city wants the growth control it once imposed on its hinterland.

CONCLUSION

Longitudinal comparison of the resistance and environmental movements must recognize, first, their continuity, and second, the compromised nature of their victories and defeats. The environmental movement depended on the achievements and the legend of the community revolt. Also, protest in the 1920s achieved results that are mistakenly associated only with the movement of the 1970s. The community rebels were not naive about the importance of state and federal support or strategic use of the courts. On the contrary, they tried to appropriate those resources for their movement, and sometimes succeeded. Before environmental legislation existed, they used state water law to create a new, publicly empowered protest vehicle, the irrigation district. They publicized their struggle and won the support of statewide public opinion. They filed and won lawsuits, although the scope of those actions, based on the law of the time, was limited to enjoining city operations in small areas. The community rebels understood the importance of alliances with state political officials. They established a presence in state politics, enabling the passage of important statutes; these did not save the Owens Valley from city acquisition—but not for want of trying. Conversely, when the state appeals court ruled in favor of Inyo in the original 1972 lawsuit and its direct successors, it was deciding new questions of California water law in a context shaped in important ways by the Owens Valley revolt of the 1920s and by doctrines that favored regions of origin for metropolitan water supplies.

The critical difference between the arrested community revolt and the successful environmental movement was the result of a *combination* of cultural elaboration, movement strategies, and changes in the state that incorporated environmentalism in its political and legal forms. After 1970 the state provided an opening that did not exist previously for mobilized, professionalized, and politically astute local movements. Opportunity, therefore, made a big difference. But that fact alone is too simple an explanation. The environmental movement won important gains because the community revolt preceded it, creating a culture and political conditions that the next generation could use in its own circumstances to turn the opportunity into a local reality.

EIGHT

State, Culture, and Collective Action

From the conquest of the native Paiute bands by pioneer settlers in the 1860s until the agreements on its environmental management in the 1980s, local society in the Owens Valley has experienced three regimes and transformations orchestrated by its relationship with the state. Under the aegis of an expansionary state, settlers and indigenous people created a pioneer society from 1860 to 1900 that worshiped prosperity but saw few of its fruits. The progressive state reorganized local, regional, and national relationships from the turn of the century until 1930 in a new form of incorporation that ensured the city's development but generated a protracted period of community rebellion in the Owens Valley. From the Depression until the present, the welfare state first rehabilitated a defeated local society on a new economic foundation in tandem with the program of national recovery, and later inadvertently gave the valley the means to reclaim some of its autonomy through the environmental movement.

The constitution of local society, however, is far more than an imposition or small-scale reflection of the national state. On the contrary, it is the evolving product of multiple influences—the people, the economy, natural resources, intermediate levels of state authority, local accommodation to some broader designs, determined resistance to others, and, perhaps above all, collective action founded on cultural meaning. Action takes place within social structures that forcibly shape experience, yet people live in local societies where particular customs, exigencies, and choices mediate structural constrains. On the ground people construct their lives in consciously meaningful ways that cannot be read from state-centered directives any more than they can be deduced from modes of economic production. The basic question for this concluding chapter, therefore, is how to explain the nature and transformation of collective action in a theoretically coherent fashion that joins structure, consciousness, and action.

When one looks to western U.S. history for a theoretical interpretation that meets these requirements, few reliable guides are to be found. Judging from the Owens Valley saga and its general similarities to other western localities, described in chapter 1, most classical interpretations are factually mistaken or causally misspecified. Far from living in Tocqueville's world where "society has no existence," western settlers and Indian laborers built a distinctive civil society on the narrow footing of local government and the broadly complementary base of voluntary association. The individualism described by Turner and Tocqueville was more an expression of isolation and necessity among smallholders than a preference of those people—who, within the limits of austerity, developed collective means of law enforcement, public service provision, irrigation, and economic union. Independence, or the independent invention of society postulated by Royce, hardly describes settler communities whose subsistence depended on public land grants, coerced labor, the provisioning and police power of federal troops, and the ideological support of an expansionary state. The frontier, moreover, was not the exclusive creation of white settlers. Conquest did not eliminate Native Americans from subsequent history or marginalize them in a role of minority contributors to economic and cultural development.

Just as the life of the frontier is misconstrued in epochal interpretations of western history, so the alleged demise of local societies at the hands of economic incorporation and bureaucratic domination is overdrawn in recent "conflict" interpretations.[1] Incorporation under the organizational tenets of the progressive and welfare states meant many things, some of which were gratefully embraced and others effectively resisted. The form and extent of incorporation into the capitalist market varies across local societies according to their resource or commercial attractions and the degree to which communities like the Owens Valley that lie along the course of aqueduct "rivers of empire" may refuse being "organized and induced to run, as the water in a canal does, in a straight line."[2]

Epochal theories of western development, whether predicated on consensus or conflict, are of little use because they pose the wrong questions. Instead of asking why individualism flourished on the frontier, for example, the results of this study suggest that the proper question is: Why did civil society govern some important activities but not others? Instead of puzzling over why communities are systematically incorporated into a dominant economy and culture, the question is, Why does incorporation differentially affect various aspects of local life, and why is it sometimes actively resisted? The approach pursued here does not attempt to find the theory that fits (or is tested by) the Owens Valley experience, but the reverse: it asks what the historical study contributes to a theoretical understanding of the relationship between the state, culture, and collective action. As Arthur Stinchcombe suggests, "one does not apply theory to history; rather one uses history to develop theory."[3] The history produced in this study can be used to develop theory, as Stinchcombe further suggests, by making analogies between practices or institutions described here and similar ones revealed in other historical monographs devoted to the study of collective action by, for example, European artisans or Third World peasants. "(T)he analogy . . . consists of the actions of people or, more exactly, the causal texture of their actions," and similar causes provide the basis for general interpretations—theory—developed from deeply understood cases. In this conclusion, I shall explore Stinchcombe's proposition that we may find good theory "in exactly the opposite place from where we have been taught to expect it, [that is, in] *a causal interpretation of a particular case*" and through analogies between cases.[4]

Let us be clear, first, about what is to be explained. Collective action is the problem. Generally, I want to explain the nature of the different forms of community organization and protest mobilization that characterize the three historical periods; the differences in their origins, participatory styles, ambitions, and consequences; and the processes of their transformation in a longitudinal perspective. Specifically, what explains the differences between the action and accomplishments of the pioneer society, those of the community rebellion, and those of the environmental movement?

Broadly, pioneer society in the late nineteenth century created the civil institutions for meeting the local requirements of economic production and a rudimentary social order, but was incapable of mounting any social movement aimed at redressing the problem of dependent development. Civil society produced the co-operative irrigation companies; a government assisted by vigilantes for law enforcement and by public subscription for infrastructure; protestant associations that built the moral apparatus of schools and lodges; and a paternalistic order founded on masculine affiliation and on control of Indian labor. The code of popular justice defined the limits of civil society. Where law and the moral order lacked the power of collective sanction, the rough morality of retributive justice took over in the tacitly accepted practices of arson or other property violence. White and Indian societies coexisted in a tensely coercive arrangement, although the exploitation of Indian labor was tempered to some extent by the Indians' resistance and their autonomous management of tribal affairs. Although the complementary responsibilities of government and civil society were gradually extended and popular justice was slowly confined to special circumstances, pioneer society never really rose to efficacious political action.

The problem of dependent development was readily apprehended, but the attempted solutions were anemic. The settlers tried what they could. Petitions were circulated from the earliest days asking for market access to the mines on public roads and asking for retention of the army post, which provided scarce cash for local agricultural products. State and local officials were urged to act, and the county did, belatedly, attempt to tax the mines and open them to trade. Local committees were formed to explore new trade opportunities (merchants and teamsters thought about their own freight line to Los Angeles) and to persuade the railroad to build its line through the towns. All of these actions merely pleaded for someone else's consideration, and none of them succeeded. The one major exception was the Farmers' and Producers' Cooperative Union, created in 1886 for centralized processing and direct marketing as a local expression of the Populist Movement. Although the union became the largest local corporation and prospered for many years, the model did not extend beyond agricultural producers. Populist methods were employed in limited areas, but the Owens Valley as a whole did not take up the Populist Movement as an ideology or as a vehicle for addressing the problem of dependent development.

Political mobilization was rare, and collective action proved ineffective for several reasons. Farmers and merchants disagreed on many issues (for example, imports, traveling herds of sheep, liquor sales) and blamed one another for the lack of economic progress. Government was weak and preoccupied with law enforcement, particularly the suppression of Indians and regulation of the liquor trade. Leadership was rare, and what did exist was also divided, pursuing separately populist methods in agricultural marketing or the expansion of town commerce—enterprises that conflicted with one another at some junctures.

At bottom, pioneer society was ideologically self-defeating. Collective action that might come to grips with dependent development could not be conceived within the tenets of frontier culture. Borrowed pieces of populism inspired cooperative marketing, but not a unified offensive of farmers and merchants against the trade monopoly. Settlers congratulated themselves on their modest achievements, assumed paternalistic superiority over their Indian labor, grudgingly envied the mine owners who denied them markets, and ultimately blamed the lack of development on a deficient spirit of enterprise among their fellows. Something was bound to happen if they kept doing what they had been doing; prosperity was around the next corner. Collective action was fragmented along class lines (such as farmer versus merchant) and status group lines (such as gender or ethnicity); it was limited, mainly civic, and at its best, populist.

The Progressive Movement promised a solution to local underdevelopment through scientific conservation, reclamation, organizational efficiency, and economic centralization. Farmers and merchants in the Owens Valley were "alive to the importance of progressive things" and saw Teddy Roosevelt as an advocate of their own western vision. Maybe this movement was the something that had been "bound to happen" for so long. It appeared that prosperity had arrived with the Reclamation Service and the new markets at the mines, which boomed in the first few years of the twentieth century. Rebellion took root, first as agrarian class protest and later as an inclusive community movement, when the promise of progressivism was betrayed. Collective action developed from petitions and pleas to the federal government by an insurgent coalition of social classes capable of innovative organization, political maneuver in the field of state power, public relations, and mass action. The community rebellion drew heavily on pioneer society for its methods of mobilization (such as petitions, town meetings, and festivals), for the tactics of popular justice, and for the energizing legitimacy claimed by those who had "built the West." Yet new ideologies were also developed in the struggle. Pioneer society was reconstructed as a heritage of rural virtue and solidarity—rather than paternalism, developmental inaction, and social control by arson. Prosperity supposedly existed in an imagined past before Los Angeles came along to usurp the verdant fields, abundant harvests, and bustling commerce. Under a common threat, social classes became one community; town and country became one valley. Culture was evolving to lend new meaning to the troubled present.

Collective action built on tradition, used it effectively in mobilization, and then moved on from reactive to proactive efforts. In contrast
to an earlier supplicating defense of local interests, the distinctive features of the community rebellion were its innovative ability to appropriate the means of state authority for its own purposes in the irrigation
district and its attempt to realign the losing battle with Los Angeles on
the broader terrain of state politics by engaging the courts, the state
legislature, and public opinion. The rebellion failed mainly because the
city could overpower, or at least stalemate, alliances in the wider arena
while continuing to wear down the rebellion's local supporters, who
began selling out in the paralyzed economy, and while undermining the
rebellion's institutional base in the bank. Collective action was relatively united across classes, community based, and politically proactive;
but it lacked firm external anchorage and allies.

Arrested rather than defeated, the community rebellion of the 1920s
persevered in the courts and acquired a legendary stature, replacing the
pioneer tradition as the centerpiece of local culture. From the 1930s
onward, to speak of the Owens Valley in California parlance was to
evoke memories of rural recusants pitted against callous city promoters,
night-riding dynamiters, and western patriots, as portrayed in novels
and the motion pictures produced in the rebels' own locale. The legend
was savored in proportion to the disappearance of its subjects. The
welfare state and Los Angeles's need for a recreational preserve transformed the valley into a new economy of tourist and governmental
services. Remarkably, the major towns lived on, even throve, despite the
city's antipathy to demands on its water and its preference for managerial free rein. The aims of city policy in the valley shifted between
depopulation and recreational development, and in concrete form both
policies conflicted with the public-relations image that Los Angeles
needed to foster to avoid interference from state courts, state agencies,
and the legislature. Owens Valley symbolism threatened serious political repercussions. Why else did the nation's largest public utility worry
about the movie *Chinatown*?

The National Environmental Protection Act and its California counterpart, the Environmental Quality Act (CEQA), rekindled local ambitions for self-determination. The local environmental movement began
modestly with a small group of bona fide environmentalists who used a
routine land-exchange proposal as the occasion to register complaints
about groundwater pumping, dust, dying plant life, disappearing
springs, and the overall decline of environmental quality. As local gov-

ernment gradually came around to environmentalism, the movement's capacity to absorb perennial issues within a new and federally backed context of legitimation became apparent. Before long, the struggle of nearly seventy years' standing had been recoded as an environmental problem. Just as state water law was used imaginatively in the 1920s to create the irrigation district as a public political vehicle, now CEQA was used for inventive post factum claims in a lawsuit against the city's second aqueduct—claims that challenged the city's whole program of water production and environmental management.

Collective action in the environmental movement combined features of its nineteenth- and twentieth-century predecessors with new methods. It began as a citizens' initiative and, although the decisive battles were legal and electoral, citizens exercised critical leadership at successive stages including the final one, in which they won more than their own government dared to ask. Yet at other times local officials, attorneys, and technical experts led the fight and attempted to reconcile citizen militance. Popular justice returned during periods of frustration and city reprisal, wreaking minor damage and achieving major publicity. The protest repertoire included other elements from the 1920s such as petition drives, concerned citizens' committees, mass meetings up and down the valley, noteworthy popular participation, delegations to Sacramento and Los Angeles, and publicity. The environmental movement drew adherents from the core service economy, and its leadership came from the relevant professions. Collective action mobilized the key population and economic groups, citizens and officials, behind a decisive legal battle and a social movement led by experts that succeeded, unlike the previous movements, by forcing the struggle onto state political terrain and holding it there, despite city efforts to settle it outside the reach of constraining state authority.

In summary, collective action across the three periods was transformed from fragmented class and status-group action to community rebellion and, ultimately, to a social movement. Group action in civil society met the exigencies of frontier life within limits that excluded patently political initiatives in the form of programmatic claims on higher authorities for an organized constituency—save for a circumscribed populist initiative. Fragmented class and status-group action was transformed by incorporation, which at once bound valley fortunes to the designs of urban expansion and betrayed the moral economy of progressivism as it was understood in the rural areas that hoped for an equal part in progress. Ironically, the fearsome welfare state provided the legal means whereby a new social movement absorbed and extended the historical practice of collective action.

Rebellion was replaced by a social movement in Charles Tilly's sense of "a sustained series of interactions between national authorities and persons successfully claiming to speak on behalf of a constituency lacking formal representation in the course of which those persons make publicly-visible demands for changes in the distribution of power, and back those demands with public demonstrations of support." Tilly's definition, intended to mark a watershed in early nineteenth-century British history, also captures the transformation of collective action in the Owens Valley—a "collective-action repertoire [that] underwent two fundamental changes: first parochial and patronized forms gave way to national and autonomous forms; second, the creation of a national social movement became the way to accomplish a set of political ends."[5]

In the Owens Valley, the fragmented class and status-group action of the nineteenth century pursued parochial ends, such as a piece of the market provided by the mines or a railway through the towns, and success or failure was measured in terms of patronage. Autonomous actions such as the Farmers' and Producers' Cooperative Union or Indian self-policing were exceptions to that pattern. Community rebellion represented a transition. Unlike the fragmented group action, it made demands for a constituency lacking formal representation within the city's regime of absentee ownership and management, and it backed those demands with public demonstrations—which, however, aimed at inclusion within the city's economic and political ambit rather than autonomy. The rebellion did not become a full-fledged social movement; this was not attained until the 1970s, when the Owens Valley aligned itself with a national program and demanded, for the first time, a change in the distribution and exercise of power—local control given substance and legitimacy in the new environmental law. By contrast to the incipient social movement of the 1920s, moreover, the environmental movement was a sustained series of interactions between the national and, especially, State of California authorities and local actors, who succeeded in making legitimate claims for their constituents when their demands were upheld by the courts.

The Owens Valley struggle became a social movement through a series of actions over half a century, which came to fruition when the dispute was brought within the ambit of the state and national authorities. In one vital respect, however, the Owens Valley did not follow the pattern Tilly discovered, in which "the interests and organization of ordinary people shifted away from local affairs."[6] On the contrary, this study shows how a combination of expanding state authority and so-cial-movement action can intensify local interests and provide them with new means of expression. National and local interests and orga-nization are not necessarily zero-sum relationships. Local issues can generate interest in national policies; organizational initiatives at the national level, such as environmentalism, may acquire vitality by sub-suming local passions. New forms of collective action such as the social movement may expand a repertoire that includes elements of traditional rebellion, which occasionally return in revealing circumstances. The transformation of collective action is historical and evolutionary.

The theoretical problem is now more tractable: to explain the trans-formations of collective action in local society, from fragmented group conflict through community rebellion to social movement, in a general interpretation that may allow comparisons with other times and set-tings. The context in which the problem appears is that of local society resting on a particular population and economic foundation shaped by the state. Collective action is generated from local needs and aspira-tions, particularly in conflicts between the state, the economy, and dis-tinctive forms of social organization. Local action responds to these forces, but it does so from its own standpoint, through its own lens of cultural meaning and motivation. The state, collective action, and cul-ture compose the interacting medium in which local society is con-structed and reconstructed. It remains to show the constitution of each element and the ensemble formed by their interplay.

STATE AND SOCIETY

An initial and compelling discovery of this study is the manner in which the state shapes the basic contours of local society and punctuates its transformation. If the proposition is unsurprising in an era of the ad-vanced welfare state, it went unrecognized in the classic interpretations of western U.S. history, which looked to frontier individualism as the wellspring of national character and institutions. Instead, we find that pioneer society was predicated and elaborated on the mechanisms of state expansion. Epochal shifts in the organization of local society, moreover, followed periods of crisis and reorganization of the state such as the Progressive Movement and the New Deal. A recent text, for example, notes about conquest and race relations that "[t]he involve-ment of the federal government in the economy and the resulting dependence, resentment, and deficit have become major issues in American history and in contemporary politics, and the American West was the arena in which an expanded role for the federal government first took hold."[7]

Indeed, modern interpretations of the American West have come close to a complete inversion of the classical artesian metaphor. Two related interpretations have been advanced concerning the effects of state expansion, one emphasizing political domination and the other economic incorporation. Writing in 1953, Wallace Stegner traced the origins of the welfare state to federal agencies created in the late nineteenth century to chart and manage the western public domain. "The concept of the welfare state edged into the American consciousness and into American institutions more through the scientific bureaus of government than by any other way, and more through the problems raised by the public domain than through any other problems."[8] Stegner's argument, intended as a corrective and an appreciation of the reciprocal relationship between western and national institutions, has lately been turned to a forceful reading of state domination. Donald Worster's bold reinterpretation of the American West draws heavily on the Frankfurt School: the idea from Herbert Marcuse that "technological rationality" constitutes the key depoliticizing force in a one-dimensional "society without opposition"[9] and, particularly, Karl Wittfogel's claim for a historically invariant association between the water-management technology of "hydraulic societies" and political systems of "total power."[10] Worster argues that the modern metaphysic of "instrumental reason" forged an alliance of federal bureaucracy and capitalist agriculture to form a vast regional empire based on publicly subsidized irrigation systems. Worster's analytic and moral concerns focus on how these "rivers of empire" distort social organization. There is "a kind of order underlying this jumbled, discordant West, though it is not in the main the order of nature or of landscape aesthetics or of closely integrated community life. The hydraulic society of the West, in contrast, is increasingly a coercive, monolithic, and hierarchical system, ruled by a power elite based on the ownership of capital and expertise."[11]

The second, and closely parallel, interpretation draws on European social history, emphasizing the incorporation of the countryside into capitalist market relations sustained by state designs and subsidies. By drawing local economies into expanding national markets, incorporation threatens the autonomy of independent producers and local merchants through competition, wedges profit-taking middlemen between farmers and distant consumers, dictates demand and prices, monopolizes distribution, imposes alien standards, and generally dissolves the lineaments of local communities. In David Thelen's portrait of Missouri populism, "[t]he new order seemed constantly to invent new ways of stripping Missourians of their familiar forms of social, economic, and psychological security as increasingly it forced them to compete with others in order simply to survive. As everything seemed to become a commodity to be bought and sold, people could no longer rely on families, friends, churches, political representatives, or communities to provide the support they had depended on in the past."[12] Although Thelen goes on to document the diverse paths that Missourians took to resist incorporation, their powerlessness and their eventual defeat testify to the economic, political, and cultural domination of corporate society. Developing a general interpretation of America since the Gilded Age, Alan Trachtenberg similarly argues "that economic incorporation wrenched American society from the moorings of familiar values, that the process proceeded by contradiction and conflict. The corporate system in business, politics, and cultural institutions engendered opposing views, however inchoate and incomplete that opposition remained."[13]

There is much to be admired in these modern interpretations. They bring the state back in, as a general framework and as an agent working through historically specific bureaucratic forms. They temper the usual exceptionalism of U.S. historical interpretation by placing our experience within a broader process of capitalist-market and welfare state expansion. They permit us to see parallels in the American West between the causes and consequences of, for example, commercialized agriculture in Great Britain or dependent development in the Third World. As Steven Hahn and Jonathan Prude argue, "comparisons such as these might also shed new light on the nature and meaning of political conflict in the United States. Without pushing comparisons too far, there is much to be learned from rural resistance to the incursions of the market and state, from popular hostility to enclosures and related agricultural 'reforms,' and from those moments when local peasant unrest grew into larger rebellions."[14] The chapters on frontier society and dependent development provide support for this conjecture.

Yet part of what we learn from the Owens Valley story is to doubt the sweeping claims made for the pressures toward domination and incorporation. Worster's conception of hydraulic society does not apply to the irrigation technologies of the Indians or the settlers. However much Los Angeles may have aspired to a "coercive, monolithic, and

hierarchical system ruled by a power elite," the local community vigorously resisted it, steeled its resolve rather than caving in to technological reason, and eventually reduced the city's power to dominate the
valley's economy and society. In the Weberian terms Worster only selectively borrows, "value rationality" coexisted with the "instrumental
rationality" illegitimately forced on community tradition.[15] In addition
to local opposition, conflicts within the state from the county to the
federal level belied any monolithic or hierarchical system. The California government opposed the city's imperial ways in the Owens Valley,
and the federal government took back for environmental protection
some of what it had given the city in progressive reform. If, however,
Worster's argument, like Stegner's, is simply to stress the important
influence of the state and of water projects in western U.S. history, then
it has considerable bearing on the Owens Valley.

Similarly, the economic and political incorporation of the Owens
Valley is a key process that helps explain its conquest, its frontier society, and its modern transformation. Yet incorporation represents only
one side of a fierce dialectic with local society. Taken alone, its effects
are easily overgeneralized. The form of incorporation varies by time,
region, resources, community organization, and the economic and political instruments employed. Initially, the Owens Valley was incorporated for its mineral wealth in a pattern of dependent development that
neglected, rather than dispossessed, local agriculture and commerce.
Economic incorporation in this form paradoxically helped to unify the
local community, rather than dissolving it in market relations. A dis-
tinguishing feature of frontier social organization was the manner in
which local society itself incorporated Indian labor as a condition of
subsistence and of paternalistic culture. Incorporation as it affects local
social organization, therefore, not only takes different forms, but works
at different levels. In the early years of city intervention, political incorporation was welcomed by town and commercial interests as the
fulfillment of local ambitions that progressivism promised. As that
promise faded and incorporation through city ownership expanded,
rebellion flourished, never yielding to ideological co-optation. The market incorporation of Missouri farmers and merchants followed a different course, marked by traditional forms of resistance and ending in
defeat; and Colorado towns resisted monopoly capital in different ways
according to the organizational strength of local labor or capital, both
forms of local organization finally losing to external intervention.[16] The

point here is to begin to identify some of the circumstances that explain such differences.

The theory of incorporation usefully stresses resistance, but typically in the form of heroically doomed expressions of a local tradition over-awed by a hegemonic national culture. The Owens Valley demonstrates other possibilities: first, that resistance may persevere despite defeats and may even win in the long term; and second, that local tradition may actually coincide with the ideological program of incorporation. This was true of frontier society and in the early progressive years. The expressed aims of town progressives were incorporation into the capi-talist market and submission to the city's suzerainty, not a wrenching break from traditional moorings. And that was so because local tradi-tion enshrined values, such as prosperity, that also featured in progres-sive ideology at the national level—itself rent with contradictions. Re-bellion arose not from incorporation per se, but from what people called "colonial" incorporation—from the perceived injustices of co-erced land sales, paralyzed credit, refusal to negotiate with the people's organization, violence by the city, and sheer arrogance. Finally, incor-poration is a theory of a single and decisive transformation whose effects persist ever after. In the Owens Valley, the effects of incorpora-tion changed dramatically from the dependent development of its eco-nomic form in the expansionary state to the recovery and empowerment of its political form in the welfare state. Incorporation proved to be a continuing, even reversible, process with different forms and effects over time.

Just as broad interpretations of domination and incorporation reso-nate with some of the themes in this study, so recent work on the state complements the local perspective investigated here. Two issues dem-onstrate this complementarity: the relation between different levels of the state, and the process of state transformation. Max Weber defined the state as "a human community that (successfully) claims the monop-oly of the legitimate use of physical force in a given territory . . . a compulsory association which organizes domination" based on the le-gitimacy of tradition, charisma, and law. Modern states are rationally organized, principally on a legal basis and in bureaucratic form, having developed through "expropriation of the autonomous and 'private' bearers of executive power [in] a complete parallel to the development of the capitalist enterprise through gradual expropriation of the inde-pendent producers."[17] The modern state is embodied in public bureau-

cracy—in government—but is constituted as the exclusive legitimate
authority. As Alan Wolfe puts it, "that thing called government can
only do what it is supposed [to do] if behind it is an apparatus responsible for the reproduction of the social system within which the government operates. That other thing, which cannot in fact be directly
touched or seen, is the state."[18] For present purposes, this means that
the state is fundamentally a relationship of legitimate domination,
which is expressed increasingly (as the state appropriates private powers) through rational bureaucratic organizations, or government in a
broad sense. The state exists at many levels, across localities and institutions, wherever the relationship of legitimate domination occurs.
State transformation involves changes in that relationship in the man-
ifold sense of the territory, organizations, and social arenas that are
subject to successful claims of state domination. In a mundane sense,
the state is extended and transformed when new powers are legitimately
claimed by a progressive or welfare state as well as when citizens create
organizations with a legitimate public mandate (such as an irrigation
district) or successfully represent their grievances (such as environmental degradation) as matters under state authority.

In this study, changing state relationships have proven critical to the
development of collective action, particularly the interplay of the local
and the national state. Pioneer society in the Owens Valley developed
during the nineteenth century under an American state that was insti-
tutionally weak whether judged by the range of functions it performed
or by its executive capacity. The state sought to promote, but not to
regulate, national development.

> It maintained the currency, funded the national debt, collected the customs,
> registered patents, and—what was most important—assisted in the transfer
> of public lands and natural resources to private hands and thereby played a
> key role in the conversion of the vast continental inheritance into commod-
> ities for commercial exploitation. Yet because of the extraordinary abun-
> dance of the hinterland, this distributional activity involved little ongoing
> regulation or allocative choices, and thus required little in the way of a
> national state apparatus.[19]

When faced with the demands of conflicting interests—agriculture and
industry, or slave and nonslave states—the federal government re-
treated from direct involvement in the economy. It relied on compromises with the states of the union or rewards to mass mobilizations and
political parties. Patronage dispensed by mobilized parties became the
medium of government, and intense competititon for spoils led to po-

litical stalemate. Government was "reduced to gift giving" and the courts were left the job of supervising conflicts in a "state of courts and parties."[20]

By the 1880s, however, that state had drifted into a crisis marked by the Populist uprising, massive labor unrest, electoral realignment, financial panic, and business interests seeking a more active regulatory role for the federal government. The Progressive Movement appealed to a broad and loosely allied public drawn from business, industrial capital and labor, the urban middle class, professional reformers, and generally all those who stood against corruption, political machines, ethnic politics, and agrarian unrest.

> The proponents of administrative expansion spoke to all who were fearful of socialists and agrarian radicals but were, at the same time, uncomfortable with making stark choices between support for industrial capitalism and support for democracy. Constructing a national administrative apparatus held a dual potential for promoting the further development of the private economy and providing new rights and guarantees to the average citizen. Packaged in the rhetoric of "good government," the rise of the professional public servant in America merged hopes for a responsible new democracy with hopes for a responsive political economy. The bureaucratic remedy represented at once a narrowing of the political alternatives and an obfuscation of the distinctions among them. By transforming ideological conflicts into matters of expertise and efficiency, bureaucrats promised to reconcile the polity with the economy and to stem the tide of social disintegration.[21]

Progressivism within the state addressed the crisis haltingly with the methods at its disposal. The new administrative state was not produced overnight or as a straightforward response to class power. Skowronek argues that the social forces urging change represented no single or unambivalent mandate; change had to come from the instrumentalities of the preexisting state, and the transformation had to be worked out in a process of state-building subject to its own conflicting forces. "In the early twentieth century, this preestablished order gave way to expanding administrative power and internal government confusion. The result was the halting development of a new state that institutionalized governmental disarray as it spawned new kinds of services and supports for a burgeoning industrial society."[22]

State transformation in the New Deal inherited some of the progressive disarray and followed analogous paths. The American welfare state responded to economic crisis on behalf of a broad political coalition, yet with methods fashioned from a preexisting apparatus. Theda Skocpol and Kenneth Finegold argue that the path and consequences of national recovery depended on party alignments and the state's capacity to carry out new programs. The National Industrial Recovery Act (NIRA) failed, not for want of social force and party support, but because the historically noninterventionist state was incapable of industrial planning and conflict management. An irony of the autonomous state-making process, however, was that the very failure of the NIRA left industrialists weakened and helped bring about gains to labor—the subsequently enacted Wagner Act far exceeded what business and the president had previously opposed.[23]

Recent theory and research based on the state-building approach of Skowronek or the state-and-party-centered analysis of Skocpol and Fine-gold have the virtue not only of bringing the state into the analysis of historical transformation but also of demonstrating its unique influence on the results. The historical process, moreover, receives its deserved attention with the emphasis on preexisting structures and their para-doxical role as both the means and the obstacles to change. Serendip-itous findings spring from the approach, as in the analysis of how defeat can lead to victory. Substantively, this work complements the study of local society. Analyses of the weak state in the nineteenth century help explain why collective action in the Owens Valley was limited to frag-mented class and status-group struggles. That is, beyond whatever local limitations impeded action, the state failed to extend to the citizens the organizational means and legitimate rights with which they could claim wider responsibility for and public intervention in their problems. The state did not regulate development, and it offered no avenue for re-dressing the consequences of dependent development. The expansion-ary state simply gave gifts, such as an army post or a land office, and special pleading was the only recourse against the threatened with-drawal of those gifts. Local enthusiasm for the progressive state is ex-plained more fully from this standpoint. Not only did town leaders in the Owens Valley readily identify with the progressive coalition and ideology, but the whole community welcomed its institutional interven-tion in the form of the Reclamation Service. State expansion in this form initially promised a solution to development problems and later legiti-mated the collective action that protested the abandonment of federal plans. If Teddy Roosevelt sacrificed the Owens Valley for political al-liances with urban reformers in Los Angeles, progressive ideology and bureaucratic instruments nevertheless provided a model that inspired a new form of local community action. Similarly, state transformation in the New Deal introduced bureaucracies that led the valley's economic recovery and also rechanneled its collective action. Like the legislation benefiting labor that Skocpol and Finegold analyzed, the National Environmental Protection Act emerged from an intrastate struggle, yet produced the means and legitimacy for social-movement action far beyond the expectations of its supporters.

If state theory complements the study of local society, the converse is also true. The state as a relationship, in Weber's meaning, exists at all levels of society—if, indeed, *levels* is not a misleading term for the human community and its compulsory organization that increasingly appears in all spheres of social life. State theory has confined itself too exclusively to the organizations of government at the national level, neglecting state relationships as they are fostered and experienced in other settings. As I have emphasized, people live much of their lives in local society, which includes its own expressions of the state and mediates the effects of federal and regional governments. In the Owens Valley, people alternately embraced some policies of the federal government; resisted others of national and regional origin, by drawing on cultural tradition and state mechanisms such as the courts and agencies; and struggled directly with the state to alter the dominance relationship. Local society provides a unique vantage point from which to observe conflict and accommodation among the many forms of state authority, and also that authority's limits, marked by resistance and the repudiation of its claims to legitimacy. Only in activities surrounding the issue of dominance on the ground is the state relation fully illuminated. The question of legitimacy is finally decided in the interaction of state coercion, facilitation, acceptance, opposition, and use.

State theory, of late, has been obsessed with Marxism, particularly the issue of whether the state is a mere instrument of class power and capitalist development, in the vein of Worster's critical theory, or an autonomous actor, in Skowronek's state-building theory or Skocpol's state-centered theory. The latter approaches are more plausible and nuanced, but they suffer from a mirror-image problem. Skowronek, for example, is so intent on demonstrating the intrastate origins of national policy that the welter of social, economic, and cultural influences on the state are folded into a barely analyzed set of "pressures" that act mainly to delimit the more "pivotal" state-building process—itself the result of a "scramble" rather than a coherent relational pattern.[24] Certainly there is more to understand about the state than its relative autonomy from class forces. Skocpol's recent work develops this argument and

takes it in a fruitful analytic direction. If it is vital to bring the state back
in, that "does not mean that old theoretical emphases should be turned
on their heads: Studies of states alone are not to be substituted for
concerns with classes or groups; nor are purely state-determinist arguments to be fashioned in the place of society-centered explanations. The
need to analyze states in relation to socioeconomic and sociocultural
contexts is convincingly demonstrated in the best current work on state
capacities."[25] Skocpol names two complementary approaches and
briefly implies a third. The state is more than an arena of contention, it
is also an ensemble of organizations that act in their own right; this has
been the focus of state-centered work, which now needs to be emended
with "a new theoretical understanding of states in relation to social
structures."

> On one hand, states may be viewed as organizations through which official
> collectivities may pursue collective goals, realizing them more or less effec-
> tively given available state resources in relation to social settings. On the
> other hand, states may be viewed more macroscopically as configurations of
> organizations and action that influence the meanings and methods of politics
> for all groups and classes in society.[26]

This welcome reconceptualization, nevertheless, still relies on the
idea of states as organizations rather than that of the state in its most
general sense as itself a relationship of domination that takes different
organizational forms over time. At least one way in which a more
holistic understanding can proceed is to see the state as a relationship
and then examine the forms in which it is extended and resisted. One of
the premises of state-centered theories is that they represent the state as
more than a mere "arena within which economic interest groups or
normative social movements contend."[27] Although that is doubtless
true, recent state theory has too quickly passed over the point. One key
aspect of the state relationship is precisely how this arena is defined—
the political process in which it is extended, resisted, or claimed by
contending actors.

In the Owens Valley, the expansionary state subsidized development,
but it provided no arena in which people could participate or submit
claims to redress dependency. The progressive state expanded the public
arena through agencies such as the Reclamation Service and by legitimizing conservation and scientific development. When the reclamation
project was dropped in favor of the regional state in Los Angeles, local
protest pleaded for restoration of federal intervention and pounded the

theme of that intervention's legitimacy by contrast to urban exploitation. Abandoned by the federal government, the community rebellion in the 1920s was distinguished precisely by its attempt to appropriate state authority by creating a legal organization representing the valley (the irrigation district), by seeking the intervention of California public actors (the governor, the militia, and the legislature), and by placing the conflict before state courts. The rebellion collapsed, in important part, because the state failed to expand its jurisdiction to encompass the conflict. At bottom the struggle centered on widening the arena of state responsibility.

Welfare state expansion from the 1930s onward brought welcome recovery and a new basis for economic life. Extended state responsibility for environmental protection in the 1970s introduced a new source of legitimacy to the old struggle; and, in contrast to the progressive state, the welfare state provided the legal means by which local political entrepreneurs could align their fight with federal authority in opposition to the regional state. In a direct parallel with the community rebellion, the struggle of the 1970s and 1980s centered on the local strategy of placing the conflict in the state courts under the mantle of environmentalism, and on the city's strenuous attempts to avoid that arena.

The Owens Valley experience parallels the accomplishments of progressive coalitions that Elisabeth Clemens interprets as redefining the public realm. "Many of these newly organized groups . . . sought to use state agencies to solve problems that had been defined as private responsibilities and, thereby, laid the foundations for the modern American welfare system."[28] Clemens's cross-sectional comparison of progressive movements in Washington and Wisconsin mirrors the longitudinal shift in the Owens Valley. Washington's progressive movement was based on a radical populist alliance of agrarian and industrial communities—an antimonopolist and antistatist reform movement. Wisconsin workers and farmers formed an alliance in community or "lodgelike" organizations rather than radical new ones, framed their agenda in terms of public policy, and achieved reform results while Washington remained mired in conflict. "Wisconsin's farmers and laborers were able to ally on the basis of their common acceptance of state institutions as mechanisms for meeting or brokering the demands of interest groups."[29] The Owens Valley evolved from Washington's model in 1905 to Wisconsin's in the transition to rebellion and social movement—and the latter strategy successfully altered the state in both places by widening its arena. The analogy between the Wisconsin movement and the Owens Valley movement lies in the causes for the political strategy of redefining the public realm: in each case an ideologically unified coalition confronted well-developed public agencies on their own terrain.

In the Owens Valley, local efforts succeeded under the welfare state because the legitimate means for their expression became available. Collective action at each stage worked within the strategies that were defined by or could be made acceptable to the state. Yet the relationship between state forms and social movements is reciprocal—action also transforms structure. The social-movement strategy worked because it exploited implicit contradictions between different levels and aims of the state; for example, the contradiction between modern environmentalism and progressive public utilities.

The results of this study support a relational conception of the state, with implications extending well beyond theories of state-centeredness and states as organizations. The image here is closer to the dual character of the state described by Nicos Poulantzas: the union of domination and struggle.

> [P]opular struggles traverse the State from top to bottom and in a mode quite other than penetration of an intrinsic entity from the outside. If political struggles bearing on the State traverse its apparatuses, this is because they are already inscribed in that state framework whose strategic configurations they map out. *Of course, popular struggles, and power in general, stretch far beyond the State:* but *insofar* as they are genuinely political, they are not really external to the State. Strictly speaking, popular struggles are inscribed in the State not because they are exhaustively included in a totalizing Moloch-State, but because the State bathes in struggles that constantly submerge it.[30]

If Poulantzas's observation describes the modern condition, then the Owens Valley is characterized by its growing envelopment by state and struggle. The struggle, feeble and indemnified under the expansionary state, was transformed and further "inscribed in the State" by progressive reorganization and New Deal recovery. Much of the actual effort of the community rebellion and social movement lay in urging this fact on public authorities by exploiting the opportunities offered by contradictions within the state and those offered by newly legitimized forms of protest. The long struggle succeeded, as comparisons with analogous studies suggest, under conditions of regionally developed state agencies, a local coalition oriented toward the public arena, and a movement ideology superseding local divisions.

The analysis suggests several related propositions: that the state is defined in some key respects by its arena, that conflict is embodied in state organization, that contradictions between levels and principles provide leverage for change, and that legitimacy is a critical resource for mobilizing and effecting that change. The state in modern society is both a relationship of domination and an invitation to protest.

CULTURE AND IDEOLOGY

The question of legitimacy pervades the foregoing analysis of state and protest. On one hand, the state is defined as a human community and a compulsory organization that successfully claims legitimate domination. In Weber's treatment, under the modern state these claims rest on rational-legal principles that evolve from cultural tradition. As Phillip Corrigan and Derek Sayer argue, state forms are cultural and cultural forms are state-regulated. The state is not an object but "an exercise in legitimation [and] a bid to elicit support" for domination, which succeeds to the extent that it constructs cultural justifications.[31]

On the other hand, challenges to the state, whether as resistance or redefinition of the public realm, also claim legitimacy from tradition, law, the conflicting tenets of the state itself, or some combination of all these. This two-way influence of culture is neatly illustrated in the Owens Valley history. State forms were presented as the means for achieving the American cultural heritage—conquest fulfilled the destiny of Puritan civilization, and progressivism promised developmental completion of the intrepid pioneer initiative. From below, local culture mobilized and defined the aims of collective action that alternately embraced, resisted, and actively challenged state designs. Alongside the state, therefore, culture is a key term in the explanation of collective action. Yet, like the idea of the state, culture requires some explaining of its own before it can be brought to bear effectively on this material.

The definition of culture offered in chapter 4 and drawn from Clifford Geertz provides a useful start. People operate in "webs of meaning" of their own construction, and culture consists of those webs. "Culture, here, is not cults and customs, but the structures of meaning through which men give shape to their experience."[32] The analysis of culture is a search for meaning in the activities and interpretations of experience that people construct for themselves—the symbols people use to explain their lives. Geertz goes on to distinguish culture and

ideology as concerning, respectively, taken-for-granted social values
and the aims of conscious action.

> The function of ideology is to make an autonomous politics possible by
> providing the authoritative concepts that render it meaningful, the suasive
> images by means of which it can be sensibly grasped. It is, in fact, precisely
> at the point at which a political system begins to free itself from the imme-
> diate governance of received tradition . . . that formal ideologies tend first to
> emerge and take hold. The differentiation of an autonomous polity implies
> the differentiation, too, of a separate and distinct cultural model of political
> action. . . . It is when neither a society's most general cultural orientations
> nor its most down-to-earth, "pragmatic" ones suffice any longer to provide
> an adequate image of political process that ideologies begin to become cru-
> cial as sources of sociopolitical meanings and attitudes.[33]

Geertz's insights have been usefully extended in recent writing. Ann
Swidler argues that although the stress on meaning helps to break away
from older notions of culture as a repository of ultimate values that
direct action, it tends to emphasize description more than causal explanation. Swidler proposes an alternative analysis of culture based on
three propositions:

> First, it offers an image of culture as a "tool kit" of symbols, stories, rituals,
> and world-views, which people may use in varying configurations to solve
> different kinds of problems. Second, to analyze culture's causal effects, it
> focuses on "strategies of action," persistent ways of ordering action through
> time. Third, it sees culture's causal significance not in defining ends of action,
> but in providing cultural components that are used to construct strategies of
> action. . . . Action is not determined by one's values. Rather action *and*
> values are organized to take advantage of cultural competencies.[34]

Aram Yengoyan further develops the culture-ideology distinction in the
context of class and political domination. Ideology is less a subdivision
of culture (as it is for Swidler) than a complementary process. "The
major difference between culture and ideology is that while culture is a
set of conscious and unconscious givens or ontological axioms which
are not questioned by participants, ideologies are willfully developed
paths of explanation which in theory are consciously developed through
reasoned and rational action. It is the ideological domain which
emerges in and through group or class interest as a means of providing
unity to the body politic under rapidly changing situations." For present
purposes, Yengoyan usefully demonstrates how ideologies reinterpret
traditional symbols for use in political struggles, "how they are re-

metaphorized and the kinds of social targets they are aimed at in terms
of power and hegemony," and how the resonant description of the
"invention of tradition" by Hobsbawm and Ranger is absorbed in these
theoretical terms.[35]

The "new country" of the American West produced in a short time
a culture distinguished by its meaningful integration of contradictory
forces: state sponsorship and risk-taking pioneers, indigenous society
and a diverse settler population, austere material conditions and dreams
of prosperity, civil society and an ethic of individualism, uneven development and the idea of progress. Frontier culture borrowed less, from
its Indian and Spanish forebears, than it destroyed. If pioneer society
adapted Paiute irrigation technology to more intensive use, that society's material underpinnings were military occupation and public land
distribution. The result was an economy of smallholders dependent on
state patronage, coerced labor, and marginal participation in mining
and transportation. Paternalism formed the local link in a pattern of
nested dominance that connected the bullion kings and railroad mag-
nates to the Indian field hands. Between those extremes, settler society
legitimated its role as making a heroic contribution to extending civilization and developing the land. The capitalists owed the settlers more
consideration than they received—access to mining markets and afford-
able rail service to the towns; yet the settlers generally accepted their
disadvantage, admired the tycoons, and only wished that they were
capable of similar exploits—"inferior stuff of the same pattern" as
Mary Austin described the envious settlers. The valley's wounds were
self-inflicted, they averred, the natural consequence of a deficient spirit
of enterprise in their fellows—in the farmers' lack of competitiveness if
they were merchants, or in the merchants' irrational marketing if they
were farmers. Class antagonisms dissolved, not in solidarity against
capital, but in complaints both about Indian lassitude and about Indian
wage demands.

Paternalistic culture at once fortified and burdened local society.
Suppression of the Paiute ensured labor for irrigation, harvesting, road
building, and domestic service, but it also encouraged reciprocal obligations. Labor was scarce, and skilled Indians could command wages
nearly equivalent to those of white workers. Labor mobility and opportunities in the subsistence economy endowed the Paiutes with effective leverage on wages and income supplements such as marginal land
and garden plots. Conditions of labor control were ameliorated by the

threat and practice of malingering, resistance, sabotage, or simply walking away from the harvest. Indians learned the efficacy of arson from the ambivalent role of popular justice in white society.

The law and order of civil society were similarly compromised. Although Indians were effectively restricted from homesteading and land ownership, and even terrorized in occasional incidents that genuinely outraged whites, they also successfully claimed and defended certain rights. The whiskey trade justified vigilante police power but also exposed the moral corruption of white society. The threat of a new Indian uprising, combined with the inability of civil society to restrain white drunkenness and whiskey selling, enabled the Paiutes to institute self-governance in the limited areas of intratribal policing and intergroup peace negotiation. Indian testimony was gradually accepted in white courts. Although escalating wage rates tempted whites to believe that the whiskey trade was a problem of Indian affluence, they were too deeply chagrined to deny that the vendors were white; that whites physically abused Indians, particularly Indian women; and that the whites were unable fully to regulate the moral order. Paternalism generated a culture of narrow legitimacy and anguished exigency that weighed on everyone. As Eugene Genovese says about American slavery, it "bound two peoples together in bitter antagonism while creating an organic relationship so complex and ambivalent that neither could express the simplest human feelings without reference to one another. . . . [Paternalism] grew out of the necessity to discipline and morally justify a system of exploitation." It imposed reciprocal obligations in which Indians, like slaves "found an opportunity to translate paternalism itself into a doctrine different from that understood by their masters and to forge it into a weapon of resistance. . . . In this as in so many other ways, the racism of the whites worked against them; but they regarded these expensive inconveniences as necessary evils and bore them doggedly."[36]

Paternalism on the fronteir was complicated further by the relationship of ethnic minorities and women to the peculiar pattern of domination. Mexican miners and settlers enjoyed the tolerance and fellowship of white society, lending a kind of cosmopolitanism to their segregated communities and providing a buffer with Indian society through Hispanic marriages in both directions. Opprobrium was reserved for the Chinese, who were less essential to the valley labor force and who threatened commercial competition. Frontier culture was a masculine creation in the sense of temporal and social priorities—built around the needs of predominantly male early residents and patriarchal farm families. Army barracks, mining camps, ditch companies, vigilance committees, and saloons provided the social forms in which business was done and sociability enjoyed. As the number of women grew, their essential place was in household production on isolated farms, their conviviality only in occasional town socials, and their organizations auxiliary to male-dominated churches, lodges, and civic associations. Women met the unattended needs for schools and the arts, but they suffered paternalism in what Mary Austin called their "paralyzing impuissance" or in ostracism for defiance, such as Austin herself earned.

Paternalistic culture endowed the rigors and vices of frontier life with a characteristic meaning. Pioneering was a civilizing and developmental mission. People came to make their fortunes in a game legitimately governed by the natural laws of economic competition. Hard work was their chosen lot and the Indians' necessary purgatory. Paternalism justified class and gender stratification. Its vices were deemed necessary and appropriate or, when that was impossible (as in the abuse of Indian women), they were rhetorically denounced as outrages alien to the community. Prosperity, just over the horizon, would prove that it was all worth the toil. The country had to boom sometime. Penury would yield somehow to pluck and perseverance, not to illegitimate protest. In a crisis, farm families embraced populism as a means of economic cooperation and, perhaps, gender equality, but the ideological appeal did not overcome class divisions. Paternalism burdened its agents as much as its subjects, fostering at the same time a modest subsistence and a competent if rudimentary civil society. Frontier hardiness and the virtue of pioneer women were celebrated in proportion to the pains of austerity and impuissance. Prosperity was the justifying end, the meaning of their veiled sin and vaunted sacrifice.

Frontier culture hailed progressivism in the theory and person of Teddy Roosevelt. Locally, farmers and merchants called themselves progressives, but they found themselves on the losing side of the politics aimed at ingratiating urban reformers. When the city's intervention began to threaten their property and livelihood, people drew on frontier culture for strategies of protest. They revitalized populist organizational forms, the moral claims of rural virtue opposed to urban greed, the nation's debt to the pioneers, and newly legitimated claims on the progressive promise of reclamation. As the struggle evolved from agrarian class action to community collective action, a locally fashioned progressive ideology attacked "colonialism" and played on its contradiction of national principles. Tradition was invented, or selectively reinterpreted, to legitimate the growing rebellion. A marginal economy was recalled as agricultural bounty and commercial bustle; class conflict and popular justice were remembered without irony as "thoroughly American community." These were the achievements now being sacrificed by the city—and sacrificed senselessly, because the ideologically progressive valley communities wanted nothing more than an equitable share in regional development, which they accepted should be led by Los Angeles. In the 1920s, just as in the 1870s, popular justice raged to the extent that civil politics failed. Traditional arson was strategically modernized by Major Watson's bomb squad.

With the arrest of the movement and political quiescence, the 1930s saw the disappearance of progressive ideology, yet saw a surprising elaboration of the Owens Valley legend in popular culture—a new and picaresque interpretation of the community rebellion that would transform local culture and thrive in the renewed struggle. The language of the 1920s, centered on the "destruction of pioneer community," was remetaphorized as the "rape of the Owens Valley." The valley's fate was no longer the result of a knockdown fight between hardy frontiersmen and city villains, but a violation of feminine virtue, the seduction of innocence. Coined in temporary defeat during the 1930s, the rape metaphor germinated in local culture until the 1970s, when it was neatly incorporated as a protest slogan in the new environmental ideology.

Environmentalism, like progressivism at an earlier time, captured the local problem in an apposite and fertile ideology. As the new movement of the 1970s sought to define itself and legitimate its claims, it became clear that the old struggle, the rape of the Owens Valley, had always been an environmental problem. The ideological groundwork was prepared in all of the abuses to the social and natural environment that now could be subsumed in the strategic question of groundwater pumping. Environmentalism not only absorbed and recoded the perennial struggle, it provided the legitimate strategic means and purpose for renewed action in the mode of environmental politics. The new ideology creatively adapted culture to action, as Swidler and others argue.

Yet there was something more significant about the role of ideology, about the way it became the issue rather than simply a tool for framing it. As William Sewell argues about the forces that shape revolution, ideology "must be understood as constitutive of the social order."[37] That is, the struggle came to center on the ideology, and the ideology informed a new set of institutional practices for addressing environmental problems. The political battle was fought over what the heritage of the valley actually comprised—whether it was a harmonious environment raped by urban aggrandizement or a semidesert turned into a recreational paradise by city beneficence. The question of what that environment had been and how it reached its modern form not only obsessed local romanticism and city propaganda but also set the agenda for a long line of increasingly academic histories in search of an even-handed answer. The peculiar praise and vilification heaped on popular renditions of the story (such as the row over *Chinatown*) signify the stakes involved in the cultural interpretation of what the Owens Valley experience actually means and, therefore, what we are to do about it and similar cases. The intensity of the ideological struggle derives precisely from the realization that different institutional practices will follow depending on which interpretation prevails. The political struggle is finally about the alternative metaphors for what happened.

Theoretical discussions of the relationship between culture and ideology tell us little about the general conditions under which protest action is legitimated. Geertz observes too generally that ideologies emerge when neither culture nor pragmatic experience suffice to provide an "adequate image" of the political process, and Swidler notes somewhat tautologically that "unsettled times" call for new and meaningful strategies.[38] These observations are not especially informative about social conditions generally, and neither includes specifically local or protest-group influences. A useful analogy to the persevering tradition of protest in the Owens Valley comes from Miriam Golden's analysis of how Italian workers have been able to mobilize continuously on the basis of a radical socialist tradition over a period in which other European labor movements have been co-opted by parliamentary reformism. Ideological orientations developed in earlier movements have been perpetuated and reformulated for new struggles because political reforms failed to improve the conditions of labor and because historical memory kept radical aims alive. "Ideological form is generated by historical memory. . . . [T]he daily mechanisms of this transmission . . . include the perpetuation of myth, ritual, rhetoric, and habit, the conscious handing-on of organizational tradition, savored and saved up, even in the worst of times, to await the re-emergence of appropriate times. The stability of local political traditions [offers] a means of endurance."[39] Ideological form in the Owens Valley shifted across the three periods of state transformation, but the parallels with the Italian labor movement are strong in the application of historical memory, stable local traditions, a geographical base, continuing protest even in the worst of times, and the saving of dissent for another day.

Similarly, Golden captures the central and proactive role that ideology plays in new movements. "When ideology is not merely used to legitimate but is the basis for practical applications—when chunks of a formative historical experience are re-enacted, with whatever modifications—such applications become institutionalized and serve as vehicles into the future. . . . When used to invent and innovate on the basis of a historical event perceived as experience, historical memory is displaced onto the future in the form of codified practice."[40] In some ways, political protest in the Owens Valley during the 1920s and 1970s re-enacted historical experience, just as new forms of collective action, particularly the social movement, were created to meet new circumstances. Drawing on the parallels, we may hypothesize that ideologically informed protest recurs when reforms fail and depredations return. Collective action is then made possible when oppositional groups persist, historical memory is nurtured in the "daily mechanisms" of local tradition, and new ideologies appear that provide concrete, meaningful alternatives. In short, protest reappears in response to new troubles because the memory of its efficacy is kept alive in culture and is programmatically activated by ideology. This explains, conversely, the preoccupation with history and popular culture in the tumultuous Owens Valley. Culture changes as the ideologies constructed in current struggles absorb certain elements of tradition and as meaningful new interpretations supplant those of an earlier time. Frontier culture in the Owens Valley, for example, was subordinate but significant in the community rebellion, and both of those traditions informed the modern spirit of local autonomy. In both cases, of course, the new ideologies of progressivism and environmentalism respectively subsumed and redirected cultural themes.

If historical memory explains how traditional protest recurs under given conditions, then the question remains, Why does legitimacy fail, thereby calling forth ideological challenge? From the standpoint of culture and ideology, that is, What precipitates protest? Legitimacy, as the right to command, in Weber's terms, is more or less successfully claimed by the modern state on the basis of law and tradition. Protest, particularly in the form of social movements, challenges legitimacy, which means that it challenges law and its relationship to tradition. Why? In the Owens Valley, a community rebellion in the 1920s and a social movement in the 1970s disputed both the legitimacy of state policy generally and its managerial implementation by the regional state in Los Angeles. At bottom the dissenters claimed that an injustice had been done, that the state at various levels had betrayed its own lawful promises in the Reclamation Act and NEPA. The expropriation of the valley and its subsequent exploitation denied local development and self-determination, rights assured in tradition and law. The injustice was gross and palpable. The city prospered handsomely with valley water while the valley became a poor colony serving tourists, whose relish for the valley's time-warped western quaintness added insult to injury. Local claims of injustice were invigorated by clear and accumulating contradictions in practice: in 1905 by the conflict between reclamation and city intervention; in the 1920s between state law (the irrigation district, counties-of-origin legislation, and reparations) and city power; in the intervening years by the inconsistencies of welfare-state recovery and city schemes for depopulation; and after 1970 in the bold contradiction between environmental protection and water exportation.

The failure of legitimacy in the Owens Valley bears a striking similarity to E. P. Thompson's analysis of rebellion provoked by the British state when it expropriated forest commons during a period of state reorganization in the early eighteenth century. Walpole's government attempted to consolidate the new regime by dispensing patronage in the form of game parks for the nobility and positions in the "forest bureaucracy" for their retainers. Local "blacks," yeoman farmers and artisans who violated the new preserves by night with blackened faces and prompted the infamous Black Acts, defied the state by continuing their common uses of the forest (hunting, sod cutting, cultivation), striking back with property violence (cutting fences and dams), and righteously defending their actions in the local courts. The Owens Valley parallel lies not only in a similar imposition of the state and in a protest based on local tradition, but more fundamentally in the limits of legitimacy and the reappropriation of law for its traditional purposes.

> It is inherent in the especial character of law, as a body of rules and procedures, that it shall apply logical criteria with reference to standards of universality and equity. It is true that certain categories of person may be excluded from this logic. . . . But if too much of this is true, then the consequences are plainly counterproductive. Most men have a strong sense of justice, at least with regard to their own interests. If the law is evidently partial and unjust, then it will mask nothing, legitimize nothing, contribute nothing to any class's hegemony. The essential precondition for the effectiveness of law, in its function as ideology, is that it shall display an independence from gross manipulation and shall seem to be just. It cannot seem

to be so without upholding its own logic and criteria of equity; indeed, on occasion, by actually *being* just. . . . The forms and rhetoric of law acquire a distinct identity which may, on occasion, inhibit power and afford some protection to the powerless. . . . [S]uch law has not only been imposed *upon* men from above: it has also been a medium within which other social conflicts have been fought out.[41]

In the two hundred years between the Black Acts and the rape of the Owens Valley, not only did the state become stronger and more reliant on legitimacy, but dissenters acquired more skill and historical memory about how law could be used for challenging the contradictions of legitimacy. The contradictions between local conditions and state policy, which might have been rationalized in the progressive era, became, as Thompson put it, too gross to legitimize in the era of environmentalism. The fight was always about injustice, culturally defined with reference to law and tradition. But the feeling of injustice grew after 1970 with the intersection of the environmental movement and local desiccation. Environmentalism provided the modern medium in which to fight out the social conflict on legal terrain—to inhibit power and protect the powerless.

Ideology affects collective action through a variety of forms, ranging from its emergence out of the cultural backdrop as political prescription to its constitutive role in a transformed social order. Although few ideologies evolve through the full cycle, conceiving a spectrum in this way has the advantage of emphasizing the contingencies that lie between the emergence and the institutionalization of political alternatives. In the Owens Valley, a populist ideology grew out of frontier culture; it appealed to one segment of the population and supported parochial action, but never spread beyond the farmer-producer and the local horizon. Subsequently, and cumulatively, progressive ideology moved further along the spectrum by unifying the entire community in a movement that won the belated support of state authorities; and environmentalism actually reconstituted the social order locally and at its state center. The historical analysis reveals the conditions under which ideology contributed to these changes—the persistence of historical memory, contradictions in policy, and the failure of legitimacy. Under these conditions, ideology transforms culture and the state by imparting direction and momentum to collective action.

COLLECTIVE ACTION

I have traveled the long route to a discussion of collective action because theorizing on the subject must be informed by historical interpretation of the state and culture. Over the last two decades, the study of collective action has made important strides; it has shown that social protest is not an aberrant or pathological expression of strain in an otherwise integrated society but a normal and strategic political response to perceived injustices. Such progress, however, has also brought formulaic applications in which action is supposedly explained by invoking exiguous models of rational choice and resource mobilization or by merely identifying a conflict between preexisting moral traditions. A more complete explanation is necessary, one that links collective action to its origins in cultural beliefs about legitimate rights and in the contexts of state authority. My aim is less to fault singular or parsimonious theories of collective action than to attempt a broader historical sociology of the phenomenon. Indeed, I shall not review all of the theories in the field, but shall focus on those that seem most promising to an explanation of historical action and social transformation. I propose to build on the theories of resource mobilization developed mainly by sociologists[42] and those of moral economy preferred mainly by historians.[43] I shall argue that these interpretations, although not consistent with each other, capture important aspects of the Owens Valley experience and contribute to a more general synthesis incorporating state and culture.

Before embarking on that discussion, a prefatory comment about rational-choice theory will help to clarify what follows. Since the publication of Mancur Olson's influential book *The Logic of Collective Action,* the term has been associated with a neo-utilitarian form of explanation variously referred to as public-, social-, or rational-choice theory. These are economic models that explain collective action on the assumption (of methodological individualism) that groups usually behave in the manner of rational individuals making choices on the basis of economic self-interest. The generalizability promised by this approach has led some authors to treat it as a stark and compelling alternative to sociological explanations.[44] In brief, rational-choice theory holds that, beyond small groups, individuals will not participate in collective or cooperative action for the attainment of public goods (that is, goods from which individuals cannot be excluded, such as improvements in air quality) unless motivated to do so by some form of coercion or selective incentive. The reason for such seeming perversity is plain rationality: individuals will receive the same benefit whether or not they devote their own effort to attaining the collective good, and they will suffer no sanction, in large and anonymous public settings, for being free riders. Romantic illusions about moral economy or community solidarity are belied by the cold realities of factionalism, threat, opportunistic alliance, and political bargaining, which, on closer examination, explain whatever collective action does take place.[45]

Rational-choice theory encounters two problems when applied to the subject of this study: lack of empirical fit, and reification. In the Owens Valley, a participatory civil society provided public goods for relatively large groups of settlers without evidence of coercion or selective incentives. The cooperative ditch companies, to be sure, were a special case, organized for purposes of economic production. But voluntary efforts provided schools, roads, law enforcement, fire protection, social welfare, and civic events or festivals, all on a relatively unselfish basis as far as the evidence reveals—perhaps because these public-goods-providing activities were simultaneously the occasions of social life and fellowship in an austere world. Although one might argue that frontier communities were essentially small or close-knit groups capable of exerting coercive pressures to ensure conformity, in fact they included fair-sized, socially heterogeneous populations in which certain kinds of conflict occurred routinely. The widespread practice of arson as social control is most revealing in this respect, because it was aimed not at coercing stubborn collective action but at settling individual disputes that lay beyond the scope of civic institutions. There is nothing especially romantic about the notion of a normative order that addressed in different ways the problems of collective goods and internecine conflict—the first by means of civil society and the second by informal social control. Nothing in the historical record suggests that social participation was ever an issue; conversely, the only thing resembling awareness of a free-rider problem was the occasional lament that high rates of population turnover reduced the numbers that stayed on to "build up the country."

During the community rebellion, collective action ran high, with petitions, meetings, the organizing of an irrigation district and election of its officers, the popular aqueduct occupation, and, later, campaigns of violence. In each instance, the pattern was a high level of participation, overwhelming support for the rebellion, and a small opposition group—which, indeed, suffered attempts at coercion, but they had no apparent success. No doubt there were free riders in the crowd waiting to see which way the struggle would go, but the defectors who sold their property to the city did not prevent collective action or constitute the main obstacle to the rebellion's success. Most people remained loyal to the resistance movement as long as they could hold out financially, even when their self-interest would have dictated another course, such as breaking ranks with the irrigation district sooner or not participating in costly efforts to preserve the valley. And even after selling out, many of them remained on leased land and housing to continue the struggle for local autonomy along with their neighbors who never sold.

Similarly, the environmental movement never lacked for participants, and those who joined in collective action (petitions, meetings, organizations, the local ordinance campaign and election, demonstrations, lawsuits, violence) displayed a variety of interests. Some, particularly among the leaders, were dedicated environmentalists and others were converted to the belief that environmental protection was in their interest. Many, particularly among the rank and file, were service-sector workers and entrepreneurs who had an economic interest in preserving the valley's natural environment (to encourage tourism, for example). Yet perhaps the largest single incentive for participation was local pride—identification with the legendary Owens Valley, contempt for "practical colonialism," and a vigorous urge to achieve local autonomy and control over the valley's own resources. Each of these interests was important in varying degrees over time, and all were embedded in a set of social and cultural relationships. In all three periods, the combination of hardship and the meanings and purposes generated by culture and ideology provides the most telling explanations for collective action.

The second problem in applying rational-choice theory is that of reification. Interests, as Mark Granovetter argues,[46] are embedded in social relations in a manner that renders narrow and arbitrary any effort to isolate economic motives from others involved in collective action, such as principle, pride, or passion. Even more idiosyncratic is the equation of rationality with self-interest, which suggests that action in the collective interest is somehow not rational. Greater insight in this regard can be derived from Max Weber's types of rationality, which include formal (or instrumental) rationality, based on expectations about people and the environment that figure as conditions or means in the attainment of the actor's own ends; and value rationality, governed by a belief in the value of something for its own sake.[47] Value-oriented action may be no less rational than self-seeking. Rational-choice theory forces unrealistic alternatives on the analyst who sees collective action as both rational and inspired by values that go beyond self-interest, values that are economically relevant and socially rooted. Formulated in this way, the question then becomes one of explaining the conditions under which value rationality and material interest interact in shaping action. Moreover, the free-rider question becomes no longer a logical problem but an empirical question. The evidence from this study supports the conclusion that "[t]he more social are choices, the less useful is a social-choice theory based on individuals and their preferences."[48] Having reached such a conclusion in connection with the Owens Valley case, I was reassured to discover that recent writing on rational-choice theory has recognized that any explanation of collective action must incorporate social norms or community values.[49] Returning, then, to questions of resource mobilization and moral economy, a more complete explanation of collective action may lie in an integration of approaches around the idea of value rationality.

The theory of resource mobilization is admirably explicit. Social groups routinely suffer grievances arising from diverse sources in the normal course of political and economic events. By themselves, however, neither the frequency nor the intensity of hardship and discontent explain the incidence of redressing action. Some groups may suffer chronically and severely yet never protest, while others act on mild or transient grievances. The key to explaining collective action lies in the interaction of the group's ability to mobilize and the structure of opportunity it confronts. Resource-mobilization theory specifies "a multifaceted model of social movement formation . . . emphasizing resources, organization, and political opportunities in addition to traditional discontent hypotheses."[50] Charles Tilly broadens the aims of the theory to encompass varied forms of collective action (defined as "people acting together in pursuit of common interests") and examines two models and their interaction. On the "capacity side," collective action depends on the organization, interests, and mobilization of a group. Yet collective action invariably entails costs that affect capacity. On the "opportunity side," therefore, collective action is a function of power, repression, and opportunity or threat.[51]

Although resource-mobilization theory is formulated at a very general, even axiomatic, level, it has three valuable features. First, the models identify sets of key considerations and their potential interactions in ways that allow for the development of hypotheses. Tilly recognizes that the models are static in their initial formulation; he sees the next challenge for the theory as being to set them in motion, and especially to determine how past action changes the conditions under which mobilization, interest, organization, and opportunity interact in subsequent action. Second, the approach has intuitive appeal. Only a little critical reflection is sufficient to show that political action is not linked monotonically with hardship, that improving conditions may dispose people to protest as readily as worsening conditions. Resource-mobilization theory provides a plausible account of these contingencies. Third, it generates fertile and theoretically distinctive propositions. Craig Jenkins, for example, reasons that "the formation of movements is linked to improvements in the status of aggrieved groups, not because of grievances created by the 'revolution of rising expectations' but because these changes reduce the costs of mobilization and improve the likelihood of success."[52] Resource-mobilization theory effectively describes certain key features of the Owens Valley study. Local interests were shaped by the agrarian economy and commercial development, giving rise to distinctive forms of class organization. Mobilization and organization were intimately linked; for example, the citizens' committees and the irrigation district mobilized new and effective popular alliances just as an aroused population generated new organizational forms. Opportunities introduced by progressivism and environmentalism provided the essential conditions for successful action.

Despite these advantages, however, resource-mobilization theory has at least four limitations, illustrated in the Owens Valley study. First, the theory is overly general—less an explanatory scheme of testable contingencies than a high-level descriptive model of purposive action. The examples just cited prove that cases of collective action can be described in terms of resource mobilization, but the theory does not explain much about why mobilization occurs and opportunities are seized. A valid description is useful, but it raises an additional problem: in Tilly's own words, "to integrate the purposive and causal analyses." Although Tilly observes that "in principle, it should not be hard" to accomplish that integration, it is not so easy in practice, and its actual realization is deemed a challenge for the future.[53]

This raises the second difficulty: how the theory deals with change. Tilly links the twin problems of explanation and change by suggesting that the purposive-causal integration may be accomplished with longitudinal analyses. "We might try to do it by gradually building time into the basic mobilization model: showing, for instance, how a contender's collective action at one point in time changes the conditions which are relevant to the next round of action."[54] The suggestion is inviting, but its development takes a different direction. When Tilly turns to the analysis of change, he introduces the idea of a repertoire of collective action, the set of means that a group has for making claims on individuals and other groups. Yet repertoires change as a result of broad historical causes such as state-making and capitalism, not from the chemistry of mobilization and opportunity, which, indeed, become mediating factors in a more general explanation. Tilly deals directly with changes over time in the conditions that shape action, but does not redraw the static models to show what they would look like, or hypothesize, at some second or third time following earlier actions. This is precisely the question raised by the Owens Valley study, and one I have begun to answer by showing, for example, how community revolt affected the conditions in which the environmental movement became possible.

A lucid example of how resource-mobilization theory addresses the problem of change is Jenkins's study of farm workers and their successful unionization in the mid-1960s following two decades of frustrated struggle. Success in the later period is explained, on one hand, by new coalitional strategies and a somewhat higher level of protest action and, on the other hand, by changes in the political environment that weakened the growers opposing unionization, brought liberal and civil rights groups to the aid of farm workers in the turbulent 1960s, and encouraged the State of California to implement legislation governing growers and unions. The second set of changes was decisive: "The key to this dramatic success was the altered political environment within which the challenge operated. . . . The dramatic turnabout in the political environment originated in economic trends and political realignments that took place quite independently of any 'push' from insurgents."[55] Snyder and Tilly provide a similar analysis of disturbances over a 130-year period in France and conclude that openings created by the struggle over political power at the national level are a better predictor of collective violence than is hardship.[56] These studies pose an interesting irony for resource-mobilization theory. Change results from new configurations on the "opportunity side," not from new mobilization strategies shaped by earlier group struggles and not, therefore, from any demonstrated effect of mobilization on opportunity.

The Owens Valley case presents a different pattern, one that solves the foregoing riddle of mobilization and opportunity. Mobilization strategies capitalized on the past, changed significantly, and played a key role in helping to precipitate new opportunities. Environmentalism, for example, was certainly a change in the political environment that "took place quite independently of any push from [the local] insurgents," but NEPA and CEQA did not generate a successful local environmental movement until Owens Valley insurgents made their own opportunity by seizing upon these statutes, creatively applying them to the local problem, and struggling in the courts for more than a decade to ensure that the statutory protections would be applied to their case. Oddly, resource-mobilization theory singles out the importance of time, but neglects to build it into the basic model. When longitudinal changes are addressed in research, their effects curiously belie the interactive model—changes on the structural or opportunity side simply lift the lid on the same old style of mobilization, which succeeds now because it is less repressed, not because it is more resourceful by dint of past experience and historical memory. In the Owens Valley case, the theory is incomplete or misleading in several respects. One of the central determinants of mobilization is what has happened on earlier occasions. New opportunity structures reshape mobilization strategies in addition to simply lifting restraints on old ones. And new movements make opportunities rather than merely inheriting them.

The third difficulty is that resource-mobilization theory seldom comes to grips with the state in its concrete and changing forms or as a contextualized relationship of legitimacy. The theory hypostatizes a polity that affects mobilization through its variation along universal dimensions, from repression to facilitation, or from the threat of claims on contenders to vulnerability in the face of their challenges. The image is flat—one kind of state that acts as the giver or taker of the resources that enable collective action. As we have seen in this study, the role of the state in collective action not only is more variegated, it also changes in its scope, arenas, legitimacy, incorporative ambition, and regulative responsibility—and these changes create new possibilities for action and repression. The expansionary state subsidized western development but provided no ideological bases or statutory mechanisms for challenging uneven development and its contradictions. Progressivism broadened the scope and authority of the state, creating at once greater domination and legitimate grounds for protest. It was not the same polity with the same dimensions or range of resources available to contenders as the expansionary state. Jenkins has noted this problem, suggesting that "the future of resource mobilization theory lies in . . . extending the basic polity model to deal with a broader variety of regimes," and Pierre Birnbaum, in a more ambitious theoretical account, proposes "to interpret the many forms of collective action in terms of the type of state involved."[57]

Tilly's work has undertaken that extension, yet in ways that subsume the theory of mobilization within the broader compass of a historical theory of capitalism and state making. In one of his initial moves in that direction, Tilly explained the rise and decline of European food riots as a consequence of how policies on the production and distribution of food were shaped by the exigencies of state making under capitalism. Food riots appeared in early modern Europe not as a response to hunger, but in tandem with policies to assure the subsistence of new populations dependent on the expanding state: armies, bureaucracies, and growing cities. These policies, aimed at state consolidation with the support of new social class alliances, included favoring claims on the land by large producers (for example, enclosure), forcing producers into the market through taxation, regulating imports, reorienting distributional patterns, and many more. Collective action in the varied forms of food rioting (price riots, blockage, retribution) rose in response to these policies, just as they eventually subsided as state and commercial interests steadily undermined the framework of peasant life.[58] In this theoretically cogent account, interests, mobilization, repression and all the rest appear in the chain of reasoning, but as intervening factors orchestrated by the demands of state making under capitalism.

The fourth difficulty with resource-mobilization theory concerns the role it assigns to beliefs, which is essentially no role at all. Once again, Tilly sees the problem and hopes that it can be handled down the line, after the basic models and their permutations have been worked out. Although Weber's concerns deserve a place in the scheme, "the model does not directly represent the effects of beliefs, customs, world views, rights, or obligations. Instead, in the elementary version, it assumes that [all these] affect collective action indirectly through their influence on interest, organization, mobilization, and repression. This assumption, and others like it, will need attention later on."[59] Later on, however, although customs and rights occur in Tilly's accounts of historical contention, they do not enter the models or inspire new ones. The notion of collective rights arises in the analysis of protest, but we get no explanation of where rights come from, whether they belong in the models, or what their status is as exogenous forces that affect the models. It is questionable, moreover, whether the role of culture (that is, rights, beliefs, and customs) in social protest is adequately treated when culture is seen as something that interests and organizations mediate, rather than something that is prior to and more fundamental than the terms within the models.[60]

The Owens Valley study supports the latter view of culture. The interplay of culture and ideology precede particular mobilization strategies, give meaning and purpose to group organization, and determine the interests, organization, and mobilization methods available to a population or community. We have seen this plainly in the culturally fashioned forms of organization that took root in the frontier economy, first as fragmented group action and later, through ideological and cultural elaboration, as agrarian protest, community rebellion, and social movement. The interests of pioneers were modest by contrast to those of early twentieth-century farmers and merchants, not so much because their needs changed as because their culture changed in response to progressivism. Interests and organizational forms are conceived within a cultural framework that, as it changes, makes new forms possible. Rebellion and organized forms of resistance could not be conceived within the meanings of civil society. This does not mean that interests, organization, and mobilization are unimportant in collective action, but that their changing forms are a result of cultural elaboration. In this respect, the causal connections in the standard resource-mobilization theory are either incomplete or misspecified.

Recognition of the problem has come slowly. Resource-mobilization research has focused on particular kinds of contenders or social-movement gains over a limited period of time—why farm workers successfully unionized in a new political environment or why the Southern Farmers' Alliance failed as its leadership became oligarchical and entered electoral campaigns remote from members' needs.[61] Tilly usefully reformulates the problem by asking how collective action changes over longer periods of time—when and under what conditions the social movement appears in history as part of an action repertoire, for example. The study of repertoires turns away from a search for "universal forms [which will not] take us very far [and] draws us into thinking about the cultural settings in which [concrete] forms appear."[62] A population's repertoire of collective action includes not only organization and repression but also standards of justice, daily routines, and accumulated experience of past action. Yet even here, a causal role for culture remains elusive. The fact that repertoires are associated with culture does not tell us where standards of justice come from, how they affect the state and the economy, or whether culture is a causal force or simply a setting. To the extent that culture is discussed as anything more than local color, additional assumptions are required that are not made explicit in the theory's framework.

In a new departure for resource-mobilization theory, Tilly's comprehensive study of the changing action repertoires in France over the past four hundred years employs the twin processes of capitalist development and national state making as fundamental causal mechanisms. Major shifts in the protest repertoire, "from relatively parochial and

patronized [such as food riots and machine breaking] to relatively national and autonomous [such as strikes and social movements]" are
traced to the centralizing effects of capital and of bureaucratic states.[63]
This is an impressive empirical demonstration, but it is accomplished
with two moves that should be noted. First, the general theory of resource mobilization is reduced to a set of categories for analyzing the
effects of historical change on collective action in its varied concrete
forms. This, I believe, is an appropriate move, and the results are consistent with those of the present study—although the least developed
part of Tilly's study is the precise connections between capitalism, the
state, and action. Second, the new theory of a changing repertoire of
collective action assigns no essential role to culture, despite earlier intentions to include this in longitudinal models. This, I believe, is a
limitation—one that may be rectified through detailed studies of cases
like the Owens Valley, showing how culture and ideology affect state
formation and provide key resources for transformative action.

To summarize, resource-mobilization theory contributes something
to the explanation of collective action. The elements of mobilization
(such as interests or organization) and opportunity (such as repression
or power) certainly must be seen as interacting. Recent longitudinal
research suggests the possibility of relating mobilization and opportunity to the processes of state formation and capitalist development. And
short of any solution to the question of the role of culture, there is at
least an awareness that action is culturally formulated. Yet resource-
mobilization theory fails to address explicitly the decisive impact of the
state and culture on changing forms of collective action. Neglect of the
state can be remedied if the theory is cast in the more limited role of
mediation between historical change and protest action, rather than
attempting to gloss history in overly general claims for the polity. As for
the role of culture, the Owens Valley case demonstrates at least three
essential links between culture and collective action that deserve attention in a more complete theory. First, historical experience, particularly
when it is about previous struggles, under certain conditions is elaborated in legend and historical memory. As popular culture, this experience can become an important resource in its own right for mobilizing
participation, publicity, and support from certain authorities in jurisdictional conflicts. Second, ideology produced in the conflict of culture
and change (in the form of state expansion or capitalist development,
for example) makes politics possible, in the sense of providing specific
action strategies that have meaning for dissenters—informing their

choices by indicating a concrete plan and higher purpose. Third, through persistent action ideologies may become constitutive parts of the social order to the extent that they shape new institutional arrangements—and so may provide bases for future action. Historically, then, culture and ideology help actually to define the interests, organizations, power relations, and sundry elements of resource mobilization. In that sense, they are more than additional factors explaining collective action; they are features of the world that give action its meaning.

It is at this juncture that the theory of moral economy comes into play as the most determined effort to link collective action and culture. Beginning in E. P. Thompson's work, moral economy has developed as an emendation of Marxian theories of class formation and action. Thompson's project has been to show how class and class consciousness take shape as cultural forms that embody standards of rights and obligations. "We cannot understand class unless we see it as a social and cultural formation, arising from processes which can only be studied as they work themselves out over a considerable historical period. . . . Class consciousness is the way these experiences are handled in cultural terms: embodied in traditions, value-systems, ideas, and institutional forms."[64] Class action proceeds from interests, to be sure, but interests themselves and the aims of action are conceived in ideas about legitimacy. The moral economy is comprised of traditional "legitimizing notions," beliefs that inspire action, which people understand as "defending traditional rights or customs . . . supported by a wider consensus of the community."[65] Thompson's most complete statement on moral economy and action comes in a study of food riots: "[G]rievances operated within a popular consensus as to what were legitimate and what were illegitimate practices in marketing, milling, baking, etc. This in its turn was grounded upon a consistent traditional view of social norms and obligations, of the proper economic functions of several parties within the community, which, taken together, can be said to constitute the moral economy of the poor. An outrage to these moral assumptions, quite as much as actual deprivation, was the usual occasion for direct action."[66]

The cultural approach to class formation and collective action represented by Thompson and other European social historians has had an enormous impact on reinterpretations of U.S. working-class history and, more recently, on studies of rural transformation.[67] In the latter field, Lawrence Goodwyn's analysis of the Populist Movement rejects earlier theories based on economic hardship or status anxiety and locates the impetus to the mass mobilization for grassroots democracy in a "movement culture" propagated in regions of increasing farm tenancy by traveling lecturers and by cooperative marketing practices.[68] Following Thompson's lead in a somewhat different direction, Scott McNall interprets the rise and decline of populism as a class-based movement that was created by rural Americans threatened by exploitative market relations, but that was soon appropriated by business and political interests because its rapid growth outran its ability to consolidate a coherent class organization and ideology.[69] The moral economy appears, in name or spirit, in most of these interpretations. It is used explicitly in the studies of Southern Populism by Steven Hahn and Robert McMath, who challenge Goodwyn's account of the diffusion of populist institutions by showing that a moral economy of small producers predated the itinerant Alliancemen in "'habits of mutuality' born of a premarket economy shaped by a powerful and persistent sense of community."[70] Similarly, David Thelen's Missouri study of populist resistance to market expansion, ranging from social banditry to consumer revolt, locates the wellspring of collective action in a "moral tradition" of folk memories, mutual security, and mutual aid.[71]

In the Owens Valley, culture, class, and collective action developed generally along the lines Thompson indicates. Farmers and merchants formed distinctive, and sometimes antagonistic, social classes based on the cultural norms of, respectively, settling the land with productive homesteading and opening the country to commercial enterprise. Class divisions stemming from conflicting ideas about rights and obligations were manifested in disagreements as to imports, the liquor trade, and the responsibility for weak markets. Class action for farmers consisted of organizing a cooperative union; for merchants it consisted of allying with teamsters to open new markets. Yet, if the classes were sometimes divided by their legitimizing notions and their actions, more often they were united by the stronger cultural premises of paternalism, manifest destiny, and the laissez-faire economy. The moral economy was defined by the assertion of the right of both classes to a share of state patrimony and an opportunity to compete for mining markets and rail service; and by both classes' acknowledgment of an obligation to civilize the Indians, maintain public order, and perfect a spirit of enterprise. Acceptance of these standards confined the farmers' and merchants' collective action to civic pursuits and petitions, just as it ruled out rebellion against uneven development. Like Kansas populists, "they wanted, in short, a capitalist system with none of the abuses of that system."[72] Moral economy is not synonymous with recusancy.

Yet all that changed. The Owens Valley did rebel, and it went on to create a social movement challenging the system of incorporation. On one hand, the change resulted from the combined impact of urban incorporation and progressive reorganization, whose depredations provided a new basis for legitimate claims on the state. Progressivism, like the welfare state that followed, was also a cultural change. On the other hand, local culture fashioned a new understanding of rights and obligations that grew out of the sense of community and superseded limiting class initiatives. Collective action, begun as agrarian protest, was transformed through class alliance to a revolt in the name of community—and was later transformed again to a social movement based on an ideological elaboration of the new culture. As Craig Calhoun concluded in his reanalysis of the Thompsonian argument, not class but "community was the crucial social bond" unifying people for collective action.[73]

Key to this change was a moral economy that evolved from Thompson's "traditional view of social norms and obligations" to legitimizing notions that invented and merged tradition with new rights. This process is a direct parallel to Calhoun's analysis:

> The conception of a moral economy to which somewhat differently focused appeals were made did not come directly from any prior state of virtuous relations among men. . . . [Rather,] from trying to make common sense of their communal experiences, they created their idealized vision of the moral past. It is because tradition was shaped in this way, by present experience as well as by "real" history, that [people] could interpret their grievances in terms of the disruption of a traditional way of life.[74]

The Owens Valley case suggests a further alteration of the concept of moral economy, implied by its connection to the state—a relationship that is diffuse in Thompson's analysis but is highlighted by this comparison. Thompson grounds the moral economy on community standards about the proper functions of the various parties to economic transactions, determined by traditional norms defining legitimate or illegitimate practices. But there is another dimension to the moral economy, one that makes its popular origins more complex. When the actors in the food riots described by Thompson judged the market practices of grain dealers to be illegitimate, they did not simply appeal to traditional community norms, they appealed to the law and to the officials charged with its enforcement. Thompson shows that, often, before food rioters engaged in direct action they petitioned local magistrates to enforce laws intended to supply the poor with a subsistence by regulating food markets. These laws were established in the sixteenth century by the Crown and Parliament and were regularly enforced until the 1630s; after that time they fell into disuse. The traditional norms embedded in the eighteenth-century moral economy originated in the legislation of a paternalistic government of the sixteenth century. Local magistrates were called upon to apply the law; when they were unable to do so, the populace enforced it themselves. In order to legitimate their rebellious actions, English rebels appealed to standards of good government and fair law enforcement, from which present officials had allegedly fallen away. Usually the protesters presented themselves as supporting long-standing traditions of an idealized monarchical government; they thereby claimed to be loyal to the monarch while attacking corrupt officials and intermediary powers.

The moral economy of the Owens Valley was clearly founded on a similar interweaving of tradition and law. The protest repertoire included petitioning and appealing to authority or law from the earliest date; these efforts typically preceded illegal or direct action. Tradition was recalled, and invented, in a form that included principles of state formation and law—the rights of homesteading settlers or the developmental promises of progressive reform, for example. The moral economy was vividly expressed in Lesta Parker's letter to Teddy Roosevelt: a loyalist appeal, "in the name of the Flag, the Glorious Stars and Stripes," to the chief executive to act in defense of the agrarian, smallholder values for which the Republic stood, and against the corrupt dealings of officials (Lippincott) and intermediary powers (the DWP). In its reformulations in the 1920s and 1970s, the moral economy continued to build not only on a growing tradition and legend, but also on newly enacted laws.[75]

In the Owens Valley a traditional moral economy, developed initially within the contraints of civil society, was adapted in two major stages, at each juncture adding to its mobilizing force and its relevance for collective action. First, the austere pioneer heritage was reinvented under progressivism as one of harmony and prosperity. The state now had the obligation not merely to subsidize western development, as expected in the period of expansion, but to protect and advance it with incorporation. When that failed to occur in the 1920s, the moral economy was elaborated further, its elements reordered to stress heroic struggle, violation, environmentalism, and legal claims against abusive power. Tradition was brought to bear at each stage, and it helped people to make sense of the ideological present in which new rights and grievances were defined. Collective action always proceeded from this moral economy, which was made more pertinent, not less, by its adaptation to change. Current uses of the concept of moral economy fail to appreciate this process of continuous development. As Raymond Williams says, "this is where the idea of a 'traditional' order is most effectively misleading. For there is no innocence in the established proprietors at any particular point in time. . . . [C]ommunity only became a reality when economic and political rights were fought for and partially gained."[76] This reformulation of moral economy, capturing its roots in the state as well as in community tradition, its past and present, provides the link between culture and collective action that is missing in other theories, such as the theory of resource mobilization.

A THEORETICAL SYNTHESIS

I have argued that it is appropriate to develop a theoretical explanation of collective action based on a longitudinal case study and its analogies to other experiences of social protest. This study combines a portrait of historical change in the patterns of collective action with a detailed account of how meaning and strategy are fashioned in local communities. The problem to be explained, therefore, is how communities respond to broader changes in society and, specifically, how collective action is transformed over time. The explanation should not be primarily concerned with the many and varied causes of social protest or the methods by which social movements recruit members and devise organizational strategies for maintaining their participation.[77] Michael Useem properly cautions that "general theories dealing with social movements often encounter serious explanatory problems because of the great diversity in their subject's social origins. . . . Inclusion of qualitatively different types of movements under the rubric of social movements . . . had led to excessively abstract concepts and theories which explain everything or nothing."[78] Rather than proposing a general model of the development of social movements, this study addresses the historical changes in the relationship between a local community and modern society that explain the changing forms of collective action, including the emergence of social movements.

In modern society, collective action is increasingly shaped and surrounded by the state. No explanation of popular protest can ignore the
state's integral part in determining the motives, means, purposes, and
legitimation of contention. The state plays this part because of its expanding power as a relatively autonomous administrative bureaucracy
and its collateral purposes of promoting and regulating economic
growth. While individuals and corporations pursue the accumulation of
surplus, the state endeavors to generalize its own claims to legitimate
domination; these two purposes are often in conflict.

The state suffuses modern society in three analytically distinct ways:
through expansion of its administrative capacity and coercive power,
through incorporation of social groups and geographical communities,
and through reorganization of the social relations of domination that
sustain the state as a compulsory association. In these ways, the state
simultaneously provides new opportunities for power and profit and
generates grievances concerning the unevenness of development—the
winners are those who are positioned to take advantage of legal and
economic opportunity, and the losers those whose lives and resources
are sunk in an earlier socioeconomic organization. Expansion of the
state's administrative and coercive power shifts power away from autonomous groups and local communities and places it in the hands of
corporations, bureaucracies, and those with privileged access to state
agencies. With incorporation, autonomous groups and communities are
brought under the state's dominion in a process that denigrates and
supersedes parochial forms of institutional authority. Finally, reorganization of the relations of domination substitutes new standards of legitimacy, based on formal or instrumental rationality in place of the
value rationality and tradition of nonbureaucratized communal societies. The expanding influence of the state along each of these axes
generates conflicts over the new forms and agents of domination—
conflicts that are articulated by the moral economy and are at once
material, political, and cultural.

The general process of expansion, incorporation, and legitimation of
the state does not proceed smoothly or inexorably toward the triumph
of instrumental reason and a "society without opposition." Analyses of
technological rationality and state-centered theories prove misleading
to the extent that they focus on the hegemonic ambitions of the state,
neglecting its difficulties in ensuring obedience or coping with resistance
and challenges to state power. Claims to legitimate domination are
successful only when they are recognized, and state rule is vulnerable

insofar as it generates grievances with the potential for action. Conflicts arise because the state cannot always harmonize political and economic interests within and across various levels, from local and regional governments to the federal center. The state is faced with the delicate task of serving particular class and political interests while maintaining legitimacy based on its claim to serve the general interest. Its advance, moreover, threatens to destabilize established patterns of social order.

Viewed in historical perspective from above, the state "raised unprecedented problems of how to maintain or even establish the obedience, loyalty, and cooperation of its subjects or members, or its own legitimacy in their eyes. The very fact that its direct and increasingly intrusive and regular relations with its subjects or citizens as individuals became increasingly central to its operations tended to weaken the older devices by which social subordination had largely been maintained."[79] And viewed from below, the new form of domination is a social relationship requiring not only the acceptance but also the active participation of citizens. "[T]he state increasingly defined the largest stage on which the crucial activities determining human lives as subjects and citizens were played out. . . . The state was the framework of the citizens' collective actions, insofar as these were officially recognized. To influence or change the government of the state, or its policy, was plainly the main objective of domestic politics, and the common man was increasingly entitled to take part in it."[80] The combination of required participation and growing legal entitlements in state forms opened the way for alternative action.

The contradictory effects of state expansion and uneven development set up a dialectic between the state's claims on behalf of domination and its vulnerability to challenge—a tension that rests ultimately on legitimacy and, therefore, on the premises of moral economy. Political systems derive their authority from cultural values and evolve by adapting those values to the exigencies of changing historical circumstances—notably, in the modern state, the exigencies of rationalizing economic growth and political centralization. At bottom, legitimacy is a cultural claim, and the state is an exercise in legitimacy. Culture as received tradition is usefully contrasted with ideologies—that is, explicit principles and programs elaborated in contentious situations, which make it possible to act purposefully. Ideology links the concrete means and transformative purposes of collective action to its traditional moorings. Indeed, ideologies arise in material and political struggles as means of refitting traditional values to the legitimation of action under emergent conditions. The distinctive task, and the test, of ideology is to demonstrate that contemporary grievances constitute an *injustice* defined by contradictions between culture and the depredations involved in the new conflict.

Collective action takes many forms in modern society; it gains political significance to the extent that it moves from fragmented class and status-group conflicts to communal alliances, and ultimately to social movements that challenge some aspect of the state's claim to legitimate domination. Beyond describing this transition from local and patronized to national and autonomous, a theory of collective action should explain the conditions under which the change is likely to occur. It should explain, moreover, the circumstances, such as appeared in the Owens Valley, in which local forms of resistance do not disappear with a growing orientation to the state, but on the contrary increase and energize the broader aims of the social movement. Local conditions, as much as the contradictions of state reorganization, provide the key to ideological and organizational means for challenging the state. Social movements thrive to the extent that they are capable of embracing and generalizing local perceptions of injustice.

The essential conditions under which class and community actions are transformed into social movements are those developments that result in the claims of dissenters becoming generally recognized, by participants in the protest and by key sectors of the society, as legitimate. When this is accomplished, it takes place through a set of contingent events. The expansion, incorporation, and reorganization that rationalize the state and the economy are justified culturally. That is, they are claimed to promote perennial values by means of a new order of things—a progressive program or a new deal that will bring to fruition stalled promises. The dominant ideology, however, is not uniformly interpreted, nor is it in the sole possession of potential winners in the new order; it may also be understood as an expression of the rights and legitimate aspirations of potential losers.[81] By its very nature, legitimacy is sought by many claimants. As the practical implications of political and economic reorganization become clear, contesting claims begin to take shape—not least because of new entitlements attending state change.

Social protest, then, effectively challenges the claims of legitimate domination to the extent that (1) traditional communities and aggrieved groups possess a distinct, viable culture; (2) they construct an ideology relating that culture to palpable, group depredations of clear authorship; (3) protest groups are able to mobilize relatively free of repressive sanctions; (4) the protest ideology appeals to and provides a redressing role for organized constituencies; and (5) dissent appropriates the legitimating principles and institutional means of the oppressive regime, demonstrating on state terrain that the grievance is an injustice and thereby turning the intended domination into a legitimation of the aims of the oppressed. Under these conditions, social movements are likely to appear and succeed by sustaining legitimized counterclaims to the dominant ideology and by attracting external support from groups with related grievances, both from civil society and within the state. Alliance and claims of injustice turned against the state make the movement. Successful social movements are distinguished by their ability to force their case into the state's arena for a broader hearing on the issue of justice, although they seldom win all that they hope.

CONCLUSION

Over 130 years of postconquest history in the Owens Valley there is a general correspondence of state forms and collective action patterns. The expansionary state fostered action by status groups (whites, Indians, Protestant sects) and social classes (farmers, merchants, mine owners, and workers), but it also limited such action to circumscribed purposes. The state provided the essentials for settlement (land, police power, and minimal government), but little more. Civil society was the noteworthy achievement of settlers and Indians; it consisted of voluntary institutions and practices for meeting public responsibilities (schools, vigilance committees, tribal councils) and building an economic infrastructure (ditch companies, public-subscription roads). Popular justice filled the vacuum left by the modest capabilities of civil society. The repertoire of protest action was limited to town meetings and citizen committees that petitioned the powerful (mine owners, the railroad, the state government) but made no demands because they possessed no means to give force to their demands. The exceptional farmers' cooperative union and tribal self-government were born of unusual hardship, succeeding within the group but providing no precedent for coalitional action. As resource-mobilization theory would have it, pioneer society lacked the organizational means for collective action aimed at that society's central problem, uneven development; and that lack was partly the result of the expansionary state's failure to provide either promise or opportunity. But the limitations on action were to a large extent self-imposed. Against their own interests, settlers accepted the rights of the bullion kings and railroad barons to pursue maximum gain, and envied their ability to do so; they plaintively suggested that the powerful should have more civic interest, but saw no obligation for them to do so. Progress would take care of the settlers in the long run, as it had already done for the beneficiaries of uneven development, provided only that they keep the enterprising faith. That was their moral economy and their humble lot.

The progressive state transformed the American West by simultaneously incorporating it into the restructuring of national politics and intervening regionally with a promise of conservation, meaning efficient economic development. The promise was expressed in a reform ideology that westerners understood and endorsed, a new institutional apparatus (including the Reclamation Service), and an obligation that the state assumed in the political bargain. Here was the means by which long-cherished dreams of progress would be realized in practice—the settlers' right was linked to state responsibility. In 1905, when local hopes for reclamation were sacrificed to urban development, a limited protest was registered, mildly expressed in the old repertoire of committees, petitions, and agrarian class action. The community as a whole kept the progressive faith, accepting the idea that incorporation had its costs and that its tide would raise local fortunes along with those of Los Angeles. The pattern was finally broken in the 1920s, when acute hardship combined with an adjudged betrayal of the progressive promise. Interests were threatened, to be sure, but the mobilization of community rebellion as a new action in the repertoire drew its energy and inspiration from a deeply felt injustice. The moral economy was elaborated—traditional rights and current state obligations were fused with real and invented tradition. The Owens Valley fought in the name of "thoroughly American" values. Thompson's words echo the rebellion's rhetoric: "[A] way of life was at stake for the community."[82] Organization followed. The irrigation district and the reparations committee innovatively fashioned a new form of collective action designed to engage the state on its own terms, indeed to constitute the community as a legal entity of the state. The protest movement was wrapped in questions of legitimacy, from the state's alleged betrayal to the appropriation of the state's organizational and legal means of redress. What people believed about justice led them to risk repression and make opportunities, not merely to calculate them before deciding whether to act. The rebels made rational choices at many junctures, particularly in political maneuvers and legal strategies. But, had the calculation of rational interests been the only principle of action, the struggle would have ceased in 1927 when the battle was lost, or in the early 1930s when reparations were denied. Instead, an arrested movement persevered while a legendary culture grew for use in the next round. The strength of moral-economy theory lies in this apprehension of agency, of people making their own history because value choices sometimes take precedence over self-interest.

The welfare state supported the valley's recovery from expropriation and depression, introducing in the process a new economic and social structure. New interests found themselves alternately in conflict and in cooperation with what they called the city's "practical colonialism." The federal and California governments provided the foundation for a reorientation of collective action centered on bureaucratic politics, legal challenge, and, as environmentalism grew nationally, a social movement. But the change had historical precedent, and traditional protest methods carried on. Resistance in the 1920s displayed some features of a social movement, failing only to engage national authorities; and popular justice was as much in evidence in the 1970s as in the 1870s. What changed was the mix and the thrust. The successful environmental movement began in 1970 with a small band of citizens who organized a new coalition of professionals, small business people, public employees, and service sector workers, all threatened, as in the 1920s, by a sharp increase in depredations to the environment. Over fifteen years, committees of concerned citizens alternately pressed local government to take stronger positions and ceded leadership to their representatives in legal initiatives, electoral challenges, and negotiations with the city. An alliance of popular and official interests took shape locally, animated by the perception of illegitimate domination.

Environmentalism legitimated the movement and in many ways redefined its aims and action strategies. Given all the changes that followed the arrest of the community rebellion, however, it is remarkable that local culture continued to drive the social movement. Historical memory provided its symbols; explicit comparisons were drawn with city abuses and resistance in the earlier period. Community was reinvoked as a unifying bond and a value to be defended. The concept of the rape of the Owens Valley captured an idealized past and merged neatly with the new environmental ideology. Traditional protest tactics were employed, down to arson and bombing. Most distinctively, perhaps, local legend had become popular culture—a potent resource for challenging city domination where it was vulnerable: in its own contradictions, in state politics, and in the national standards of environmental protection. The environmental movement succeeded, at least partly, because hardship and historical memory mobilized local society for a legitimate fight, the state provided a key opening with environmental legislation, and the city made itself vulnerable by its high-handedness. Yet if those circumstances were conducive to the movement's success, the actual victory was won by local citizens who pressed their claims well beyond what state environmental law envisioned or the city wanted to concede. In the end, people made their opportunities by and for self-determination. In modest ways, they remade their lives.

As interpretation, this study attempts through the longitudinal analysis of one case to show that the past of the western United States is not an isolated patch of picaresque history, but fertile terrain for the elaboration of general ideas about the conquest of indigenous peoples, state intervention in the economy, uneven capitalist development, and rebellion. In the opening chapter, I argued that the Owens Valley is an appropriate microcosm within which to develop the interpretation. I believe that such an interpretation improves on conventional approaches that dwell on idealized notions of frontier uniqueness or generalize in all directions from populism and its demise with incorporation. Any case I have made for this interpretation relies on the strength of the explanation of how state and culture interact with collective action as the decisive agent of change.

California's eastern sierra is an unlikely setting in which to discover the workings of such large forces. The Owens Valley is a small place, sparsely populated by ordinary people whose historical experience is marked as much by meanness as by courage. Without its water and its proximity to Los Angeles, that history would have gone unremarked. At first glance it is merely a local society gone the way of many other rural redoubts in urban society. At second glance it is a special story about water and power. Looked at from the outside, the Owens Valley means water; for those who live there it is a community shaped in many ways by a culture that gave rise to a fight over water, a fight to defend and advance a way of life. As that story unfolds analytically, it gets as troublesome for imperious social theories as the rebels were for the ruling assumptions of urban society. However much local society is invaded by the state and by exogenous social forces, it continues to affect the lives of people on the ground in ways that sometimes resist and often reconstitute those influences. Like the city of Los Angeles, social theory and historical interpretation cannot rest content that local action will follow predictably the assumptions of domination fashioned from above. All this, perhaps, is unsurprising until its implications are developed. State and dominion are not things that sit on top of social actors, but relationships that are sustained by legitimacy, that are changed as much by cultures and movements that germinate in local settings as by structural forces. States and domains change in important part because local people challenge them on the basis of culturally fashioned claims.

Notes

Archival collections are abbreviated in the notes:

CSHS   California State Historical Society Library, San Francisco

CSL   California State Library, Sacramento, California Collection

ECM   Eastern California Museum, Independence, California

HEH   Henry E. Huntington Library, San Marino, California, Special Collections

HP   Hession Papers, private collection of Bill and Barbara Manning, Big Pine, California

IC   Inyo County Records

MABL   Museum of Anthropology, Bancroft Library, University of California, Berkeley, Ethnological Documents

LRM   Laws Railroad Museum, Laws (Bishop), California

NA   National Archives, Department of the Interior, Owens Valley Project 527

OVC   Owens Valley Committee Records, private collection of Bill and Barbara Manning, Big Pine, California

UCLA   University of California at Los Angeles Library, Special Collections

CHAPTER 1

1. Austin 1974 (originally published in 1903).
2. Austin 1932.
3. Worster 1985; Reisner 1986.
4. Williams 1958, p. 104.
5. Gutman 1966.
6. Lloyd 1986.

7. Williams 1958, p. 37.

8. Paul 1988; Bartlett 1974; Faragher 1986; Limerick 1987; Hine 1973, 1980.

9. Stinchcombe 1978, p. 1.

CHAPTER 2

1. Von Schmidt, quoted in Chalfant 1933, p. 122.

2. Wilke and Lawton 1976, p. 19.

3. *Los Angeles Star,* Aug. 27, 1859, quoted in Chalfant 1933, p. 126.

4. Wilke and Lawton 1976, pp. 19–20.

5. Bettinger 1984, p. 1.

6. Lawton et al. 1976, p. 15.

7. Steward 1934b, p. 236.

8. Steward 1938, p. 50. (Bishop Creek changed its name to Bishop when it incorporated in 1903.)

9. Chalfant 1933, p. 166.

10. Steward 1930.

11. Steward 1934b, p. 248.

12. Lawton et al. 1976, p. 27.

13. Ibid., p. 37.

14. Chalfant 1933, p. 123.

15. Ibid., p. 29.

16. Pearce 1988, p. 70.

17. Quoted in Chalfant 1933, p. 172.

18. MABL, Mattie Bulpitt. The original text of these oral histories is by the interviewer as rendered through an interpreter. Unusual grammar and spellings are in the original.

19. Chalfant 1933, chaps. 12–21; McGrath 1984, chap. 2.

20. McGrath 1984, p. 28.

21. Quoted in ibid., p. 24.

22. MABL, Edith Dewey.

23. Ibid., Ben Tibbitts.

24. Ibid., Mattie Bulpitt.

25. Ibid., Hank Hunter.

26. Ibid., Mary Rooker.

27. Ibid., George Robinson.

28. Ibid., John Shepherd.

29. Ibid.

30. Ibid., Ben Tibbitts.

31. *Visalia Delta,* quoted in Chalfant 1933, p. 179; emphasis added.

32. MABL, Ben Tibbitts.

33. Ibid., Susie Westerville.

34. Ibid., Edith Dewey.

35. J. H. P. Wentworth, quoted in Chalfant 1933, p. 195.

36. Sauder 1988, p. 6.

37. Hall 1986, p. 397.

38. Knight 1978, p. 7.

39. Jacobson 1984, p. 160.
40. Hurtado 1988, p. 69.
41. Ibid., pp. 161, 165.
42. MABL, George Robinson.
43. Quoted in Chalfant 1933, p. 178.
44. Ibid., pp. 226, 231.
45. Hurtado 1988, pp. 161, 165. See also Knack 1987 for similar wage rates and employment of Indian labor in nearby Las Vegas during the 1890s.
46. *Inyo Independent,* June 8, 1872.
47. Ibid., June 15, 1872.
48. MABL, Ben Tibbitts.
49. Ibid., Mary Cornwell.
50. ECM, oral histories, Birdie Yandell.
51. Earl 1976, p. 41.
52. *Saga of Inyo County,* pp. 15, 19.
53. Calhoun 1984, p. 31.
54. Doyle 1934, pp. 152, 156.
55. ECM, oral histories, John Shuey.
56. Ibid., Augustus Cashbaugh.
57. *Inyo Independent,* Apr. 24, 1875.
58. Ibid., Sept. 12, 1885.
59. ECM, oral histories, Augustus Cashbaugh.
60. MABL, Joe Lent.
61. *Saga of Inyo County,* pp. 117, 191, 200; ECM, oral histories, Louis Serventi.
62. ECM, Mulholland ledger.
63. *Inyo Independent,* Aug. 22, 1885.
64. Ibid., Mar. 1, 1873.
65. Ibid., May 3, 1873.
66. Ibid., June 14, 1873.
67. Ibid., Mar. 20, 1875.
68. Ibid., Apr. 17, 1875.
69. Ibid., June 10, 1876.
70. MABL, Mary Cornwell.
71. Ibid., Jennie Cashbaugh.
72. *Inyo Independent,* Oct. 2, 1875.
73. ECM, Inyo County tax assessment roll, 1885.
74. Leys 1975, p. 171. For complementary discussions of modes of labor control see Wolf 1959, 1982; Ranger 1985; McMichael 1984; Stern 1988; and Wallerstein 1989.
75. *Inyo Independent,* Oct. 16, 1875.
76. Ibid., Sept. 11, 1875.
77. Ibid., Sept. 26, 1870.
78. Ibid., July 19, 1879. See chapter 3 for a discussion of the Indians' role in a broader pattern of retributive arson.
79. *Inyo Independent,* June 2, 1887, and also July 26, 1873.
80. Scott 1985.
81. Chalfant 1933, p. 29.

82. Rogin 1987, p. 138.
83. Chalfant 1933, p. 229.
84. MABL, Mary Harry and Ben Tibbitts.
85. Steward 1934a, p. 425.
86. *Saga of Inyo County,* p. 183.
87. CSHS, Mary Austin letter.
88. *Saga of Inyo County,* p. 182.
89. ECM, oral histories, W. G. and Martha W. Dixon.
90. CSHS, Minnie C. Randolph letter.
91. *Inyo Independent,* Aug. 29, 1870.
92. Ibid.
93. Ibid., Dec. 30, 1870.
94. Ibid., Apr. 3, 1873.
95. MABL, Joe Lent.
96. *Inyo Independent,* May 23, 1874. The practice was complicated, and certain extenuating circumstances were recognized; cf. *Inyo Independent,* Sept. 9, 1876.
97. *Inyo Independent,* Apr. 5, 1873.
98. Ibid., Nov. 10, 1877.
99. UCLA, Bynum oral histories, Harriet Bulpitt interview.
100. *Inyo Independent,* Feb. 21, 1874.
101. Ibid., Aug. 15, 1874.
102. Austin 1932, p. 267.
103. ECM, oral histories, A. A. Brierly. See also CSHS, Mary Austin letter; and *Inyo Independent,* July 6, 1878, and Jan. 23, 1886.
104. *Inyo Independent,* Dec. 14, 1872.
105. Ibid., Mar. 21, 1874.
106. Ibid., Oct. 10, 1874.
107. Ibid., Sept. 18 and Oct. 16, 1875.
108. *Inyo Register,* July 25, 1901.
109. *Inyo Independent,* Oct. 3, 1885.
110. Chalfant 1933, p. 228.
111. Steward 1934b, p. 321.
112. *Inyo Independent,* Nov. 10, 1877.
113. Ibid., Sept. 5 and 12, 1885.
114. MABL, Joe Lent.
115. Steward 1934b, p. 238.
116. Pearce 1988, pp. 4–5.
117. Ibid., p. 4.

CHAPTER 3

1. *Dependency* is understood here in the sense employed by the more analytical, and less polemical, students of international development such as Dos Santos 1970 and Cardoso and Faletto 1979.
2. Hogan 1985, 1990; Limerick 1987; Worster 1985. For a review of the critical writings see Athearn 1986, chap. 6.
3. Turner 1920, p. 37; see also Tocqueville 1958 and Boorstein 1973.

4. Royce 1886, p. 1.
5. Pearce 1988, p. 49.
6. Whitman 1955 (1881), p. 197.
7. Tocqueville 1958, 2:104.
8. Tocqueville 1958, 1:53–54.
9. Ibid., 1:266, and Turner 1921, p. 2.
10. Tocqueville 1958, 1:30.
11. Royce 1886, pp. 374, 501.
12. Boorstein 1973, p. 1.
13. Hine 1980, p. 32.
14. Smith 1950.
15. *Saga of Inyo County*, pp. 98, 57.
16. ECM, oral histories, John Shuey.
17. *Saga of Inyo County*, pp. 114, 148, 177, 182.
18. Yonay 1977, p. 23.
19. UCLA, Bynum oral histories, Anne Nelligan interview.
20. Austin 1932, p. 243.
21. On the "California dream" that attracted immigrants during these years, see Starr 1973.
22. *Saga of Inyo County*, p. 172.
23. Doyle 1934, p. 17.
24. *Saga of Inyo County*, p. 173.
25. Ibid., pp. 155, 186.
26. Ibid., pp. 149–150.
27. Austin 1974 (1903), p. 166.
28. Ibid., p. 171.
29. Sauder 1988, p. 7.
30. ECM, oral histories, John Shucy.
31. Earl 1976, p. 41.
32. *Inyo Independent*, Sept. 5, 1870.
33. *Saga of Inyo County*, pp. 116, 155–158.
34. ECM, oral histories, Mrs. Robinson.
35. *Saga of Inyo County*, p. 116.
36. ECM, oral histories, Augustus Cashbaugh.
37. Calhoun 1984, p. 64.
38. *Saga of Inyo County*, p. 122.
39. ECM, Bishop Creek general merchandise store ledger.
40. Chalfant 1933, p. 278.
41. Nadeau 1977; Likes and Day 1975.
42. Nadeau 1977, pp. 34, 80.
43. Ibid., p. 78.
44. Ibid.
45. Likes and Day 1975, p. 44.
46. *Inyo Independent*, Nov. 30, 1872.
47. Ibid., Oct. 12 and Nov. 18, 1872.
48. Ibid., Oct. 12, 1872.
49. Ibid., Dec. 9, 1876.
50. Ibid., Feb. 21, 1880.

51. Ibid., June 11, 1881.
52. Ibid., Feb. 18, 1882.
53. Chalfant 1933, p. 212; Schumacher 1962, p. 190.
54. *Inyo Independent,* Sept. 2, 1882.
55. Sauder 1988, p. 13 and fig. 5; Gates 1979.
56. Sauder 1988, p. 15.
57. *Inyo Independent,* July 27, 1889.
58. Ibid., May 11, 1889.
59. Ibid., Apr. 4, 1890; Feb. 13, 1891.
60. Ibid., May 18, 1889; *Eleventh* (1890) *U.S. Census of Population.*
61. *Inyo Independent,* Feb. 13, 1891.
62. Ibid., Feb. 27, 1891.
63. Ibid., Mar. 6, 1891.
64. Ibid., Mar. 16, 1889.
65. Sauder 1988, p. 11.
66. *Eleventh* (1890) and *Twelfth* (1900) *U.S. Census of Population.*
67. Sauder 1988, pp. 23–24.
68. Weber 1958.
69. *Inyo Independent,* Nov. 3, 1883.
70. Sauder 1988, p. 25.

CHAPTER 4

1. Chalfant 1933, chap. 22.
2. Calhoun 1984, p. 49.
3. *Inyo Independent,* Jan. 22, 1876.
4. Ibid., Dec. 22, 1877.
5. Ibid., Oct. 24, 1870.
6. Chalfant 1933, p. 327.
7. *Inyo Independent,* May 25, 1872.
8. Ibid., Feb. 5, 1876; Oct. 27, 1877.
9. Ibid., Jan. 22, 1876.
10. Ibid., Apr. 4, 1877.
11. Ibid., May 26, 1877.
12. Ibid., May 1, 1875.
13. Ibid., July 21, 1877; Feb. 16, 1878.
14. Ibid., July 14, 1887.
15. Ibid., June 23, 1883.
16. Ibid., Apr. 11, 1871; Mar. 29, 1884.
17. Ibid., Dec. 27, 1873; Dec. 25, 1875; Dec. 29, 1871.
18. Weber 1958, chap. 12.
19. Dumenil 1984, p. 109.
20. *Inyo Independent,* Feb. 24 and Mar. 16, 1872.
21. Ibid., July 23, 1870; Dec. 22, 1877.
22. Ibid., Aug. 10, 1872.
23. Ibid., July 6, 1872; Feb. 5, 1876.
24. Ibid., Apr. 20, 1872; Oct. 6, 1877; Dec. 5, 1890.
25. Ibid., Feb. 5, 1876; May 19, 1883.

26. Mowry 1951; McWilliams 1973.
27. *Inyo Independent,* Jan. 5, 1878.
28. Ibid., Apr. 20, 1889.
29. Ibid., Feb. 16, 1889.
30. *Inyo Register,* Feb. 25, 1886.
31. Ibid., Mar. 11, 1886.
32. Ibid., July 18, July 25, and Aug. 22, 1901.
33. *Inyo Independent,* Sept. 26, 1874.
34. Ibid., May 7, 1881; Apr. 28, 1883; Nov. 4, 1882.
35. Ibid., Sept. 24, 1896.
36. Ibid., Dec. 30, 1882; Sept. 22, 1883.
37. Abbiatecci 1978; Hobsbawm and Rude 1968; Thompson 1975; Sharp 1980.
38. *Inyo Independent,* July 13, 1872.
39. Ibid., Mar. 7, 1885.
40. Ibid., July 19, 1879.
41. Ibid., July 21, 1877.
42. Ibid., Aug. 18, 1877.
43. Ibid., Aug. 17, 1878.
44. Ibid., June 15, 1878.
45. Ibid., May 3, 1879.
46. Ibid., Apr. 5, 1879.
47. Ibid., July 22, 1876.
48. Ibid., Jan. 5, 1900.
49. Ibid., Aug. 17, 1878.
50. Ibid., Aug. 26, 1882.
51. Ibid., July 1, 1876.
52. Ibid.
53. Lingenfelter 1986.
54. *Inyo Independent,* June 6, 1902.
55. ECM, Bishop Creek general merchandise store ledger.
56. *Inyo Independent,* Sept. 23, 1876.
57. Ibid., Dec. 22, 1877.
58. Ibid., July 6 and 13, 1878.
59. Ibid., Jan. 19, 1894.
60. Ibid., Mar. 2, 1894.
61. Ibid., Mar. 9, 1894.
62. Ibid., May 7, 1881.
63. Ibid., May 6, 1883.
64. Ibid., July 20, 1894.
65. Ibid., Dec. 28, 1894.
66. Black 1983.
67. Thompson 1975, p. 227.
68. *Inyo Independent,* Oct. 9, 1875.
69. Ibid., Apr. 10, 1875.
70. Ibid., Apr. 17, 1875.
71. Clifford and Marcus 1986.
72. Geertz 1973, pp. 5, 30.

73. Austin 1932, pp. 284–85.

74. Ibid., p. 271.

75. *Saga of Inyo County,* p. 165.

76. *Inyo Independent,* Mar. 30, 1894.

77. Ibid., May 27 and May 6, 1871.

78. Doyle 1934, p. 335.

79. Austin 1932, p. 281.

80. Saxton 1971.

81. *Inyo Independent,* Aug. 1, 1885.

82. *Inyo Register,* Mar. 11 and 25, 1886.

83. *Inyo Independent,* Feb. 6, 1886.

84. Ibid., Mar. 18, 1904; *Saga of Inyo County,* p. 181.

85. *Inyo Independent,* June 13, 1874.

86. Ibid., Feb. 13, 1875.

87. HEH, McWilliams to Austin, Feb. 3, 1906.

88. *Inyo Independent,* Nov. 13, 1903; Apr. 1, 1904.

89. *Statement of the Vote.*

90. Steinbeck 1979 (1952), p. 285.

91. Melville 1954 (1857), chap. 26.

92. See, e.g., Athearn 1986; Hall 1989; Hahn and Prude 1985; Limerick 1987; Trachtenberg 1982; Worster 1985.

93. Bogue 1960.

94. See, e.g., Hine 1980; Faragher 1986.

95. Hogan 1990.

96. Hogan 1985, p. 35.

97. Hogan 1990, p. 14.

98. Ibid., p. 16.

CHAPTER 5

1. *Statement of the Vote* 1900.

2. Ibid. 1904.

3. Wiebe 1967.

4. Lingenfelter 1986.

5. Chalfant 1933, p. 320.

6. Likes and Day 1975, p. 59.

7. *Inyo County, Anno Domini 1912,* p. 22.

8. Ibid.

9. *Inyo, 1866–1966,* p. 27.

10. ECM, Inyo County tax assessment rolls.

11. *Inyo County, Anno Domini 1912,* p. 24.

12. Sauder 1988, fig. 5.

13. *Inyo County, Anno Domini 1912,* p. 49.

14. Ibid.

15. ECM, real estate listings.

16. One basic promotional document was issued circa 1910 in long and short, illustrated and plain versions by the county board of supervisors and the Owens Valley Chamber of Commerce under the titles *A Few Facts about the*

Famous Owens Valley, Inyo County and the Famous Owens River Valley, Inyo County California, and *Inyo the Peerless.*

17. *Inyo County California.*
18. *California Prices Received by Farmers.*
19. Stegner 1982, p. 334.
20. Ganoe 1931–32; Lilley and Gould 1966.
21. Hayes 1959.
22. Bright 1984, pp. 149–51.
23. Lilley and Gould 1966, p. 71.
24. Wiebe 1967.
25. Skowronek 1982, pp. 165–66.
26. Charles Fletcher Lummis, quoted in McWilliams 1973 (1946), p. 128.
27. Kahrl 1982, pp. 13–14.
28. Hoffman 1981, p. 68.
29. Kahrl 1982, p. 48.
30. Ibid., pp. 43, 53.
31. Clausen, quoted in Kahrl 1982, pp. 53–54.
32. Chalfant 1933, p. 339.
33. NA, petition "To the Right Honorable Secretary of Interior."
34. *Inyo Register,* Aug. 11, 1905.
35. NA, petition.
36. NA, Austin to Roosevelt.
37. NA, Dehy to Roosevelt.
38. *San Francisco Chronicle,* Sept. 3, 1905.
39. NA, Parker to Roosevelt.
40. Stedman-Jones 1983, p. 95.
41. ECM, Index to the Great Register.
42. Of 380 petition signers, occupational data exist for 333 on the petition itself or in the Great Register.
43. The data for the "citizens' committee" in fact cover five persons of the nine-member committee (occupational data on the other four were unavailable), plus six other persons who took public positions, as documented in newspaper accounts of town meetings and in letter-writing campaigns. These eleven persons are assumed to represent the protest's leadership by virtue of having achieved public recognition of their position in the committee or of their opinions.
44. Kahrl 1982, p. 142.
45. Quoted in ibid., p. 140.
46. Kahrl 1976, p. 11.
47. Kahrl 1982, p. 138.
48. Wiebe 1967, pp. 190–91.
49. Starr 1985, p. 275.
50. Aqueduct construction camps suffered arsonist attacks, but the reports are insufficient to judge motive—whether, for example, they arose out of labor disputes or were citizen sabotage. *Inyo Independent,* Feb. 19, 1909.
51. Kahrl 1982 provides excellent coverage of these details.
52. ECM, *Los Angeles Aqueduct Investigation Report,* 1912.
53. *Inyo Register,* June 12, 1919.

54. Ibid., June 19, 1919.
55. IC, author's tabulation of sales based on property deeds.
56. Baugh 1937, p. 27.
57. *Inyo Register,* Dec. 28, 1922; Aug. 9, 1923.
58. Ibid., Aug. 9, 1923.
59. Ibid., Aug. 16, 1923.
60. *Inyo Independent,* Jan. 5, 12, and 19, 1924.
61. Ibid., Aug. 30, 1924.
62. Ibid., Mar. 1, 1924.
63. McClure 1925, pp. 38–39.
64. Ibid., pp. 40, 43.
65. *Inyo Independent,* May 24, 1924.
66. Ibid., July 5, 1924.
67. Starr 1990, p. 159. See also Lavender 1972, pp. 352–53; Reisner 1986, p. 97.
68. IC, author's tabulation of sales based on property deeds.
69. *Inyo Independent,* July 12, 1924.
70. Ibid., Oct. 25, 1924.
71. Ibid., Nov. 15, 1924.
72. *Literary Digest,* Dec. 6, 1924.
73. *Los Angeles Daily Times,* Nov. 20, 1924.
74. ECM, Eaton telegram.
75. *Los Angeles Daily Times,* Nov. 20, 1924.
76. McClure 1925, p. 10.
77. *Inyo Register,* Dec. 4, 1924.
78. IC, author's tabulation of sales based on property deeds.
79. Ibid., May 25, 1922.
80. McClure 1925, pp. 20–21.
81. Hoffman 1981, p. 172.
82. Kahrl 1982, pp. 287, 291.
83. HEH, Watterson to Austin, Dec. 18, 1924.
84. HEH, Chalfant to Austin, Nov. 8, 1932.
85. Tilly 1978, pp. 151–59.
86. *Inyo Register,* June 12, 1919.
87. McClure 1925, p. 22.
88. *Inyo Register,* Aug. 16, 1923.
89. *Los Angeles Evening Express,* May 24, 1924.
90. *Los Angeles Examiner,* May 28, 1924.
91. *Los Angeles Daily Times,* May 23, 1924.
92. *Los Angeles Evening Express,* May 24, 1924.
93. Ibid., Aug. 28, 1924; *Los Angeles Daily Times,* Aug. 31, 1924.
94. Nadeau 1976; Delameter 1977.
95. *Facts Concerning the Owens Valley Reparations Claims.*
96. Ibid.
97. *Los Angeles Daily Times,* Apr. 5, 1926.
98. *Los Angeles Examiner,* Apr. 6, 1926.
99. Ibid., May 14, 1926.
100. *Los Angeles Record,* May 13, 1926.

101. *Los Angeles Daily Times,* April 13, 20, and 22, 1927.

102. *Sacramento Union,* Mar. 29 and 30 and Apr. 3, 1927.

103. *Los Angeles Record,* June 14–22, 1927.

104. Ibid., July 16, 1927; *Los Angeles Daily Times,* July 19, 1927.

105. *Los Angeles Examiner,* Mar. 9, 1928.

106. *Los Angeles Daily Times,* May 7, 1927.

107. *Los Angeles Record,* May 16, 1927.

108. *Los Angeles Daily Times,* May 29, 1927.

109. *Los Angeles Record,* May 16, 1927.

110. Ibid., June 21, 1927.

111. Ibid., July 12, 1927.

112. Ibid., July 2, 1927.

113. HEH, Watterson to Nordskog, July 6, 1927.

114. *Los Angeles Daily Times,* July 6, 1927.

115. *Los Angeles Spartan News,* July 28, 1927.

116. *Los Angeles Daily Times,* Feb. 23, 1928; *Los Angeles Evening Express,* Feb. 23, 1928; *San Pedro News,* Feb. 24, 1928; *El Centro Press,* Feb. 24, 1928.

117. *Los Angeles Examiner,* Mar. 13, 1928.

118. HP, detectives' report.

119. *Los Angeles Daily Times,* Feb. 23, 1928.

120. *Los Angeles Daily Times,* Mar. 19, 1928.

121. *Los Angeles Examiner,* Mar. 20, 1928.

122. Nadeau 1976; Hoffman 1981.

123. *Los Angeles Daily Times,* Nov. 17, 1924.

124. *Los Angeles Examiner,* Nov. 19 and 20, 1924.

125. Nadeau 1976; Hoffman 1981.

126. This interpretation is supported by an interview with Augustus Cashbaugh (June 12, 1984), and also by the well-known Masonic ties of many resistance leaders such as Chalfant and the Wattersons.

127. "Open Letter" in Delameter 1977, pp. 38–40.

128. HEH, Watterson to Franklin, Oct. 9, 1926.

129. Quoted in Kahrl 1982, p. 298.

130. Kahrl 1982, Hoffman 1981.

131. Delameter 1977, p. 51.

132. On August 17, 1922, the *Inyo Register* published a list of 430 signatories to a petition calling for a referendum on the irrigation district. Approximately 80 names were duplicates, and no socioeconomic data were found on another 50 in the Great Register and the tax assessment rolls, leaving a sample of 299.

133. For example, from documents reprinted in McClure 1925.

134. IC.

135. Nadeau 1976, p. 79; Hoffman 1981, p. 191.

136. *Los Angeles Record,* Aug. 15, 1927.

137. *Los Angeles Examiner* and *Los Angeles Daily Times,* Aug. 5, 1927.

138. *Los Angeles Daily Times,* Aug. 11 and 13, 1927; *San Francisco Chronicle,* Aug. 12, 1927; *Los Angeles Record,* Aug. 16, 1927.

139. *Los Angeles Examiner,* Aug. 13, 1927.

140. *Los Angeles Record,* Aug. 12, 1927.

141. *Los Angeles Daily Times,* Aug. 13, 1927.

142. *Los Angeles Record,* Aug. 18, 1927.

143. *Los Angeles Daily Times,* Sept. 26, 1927.

144. *Inyo Register,* Nov. 3, 1927.

145. *Los Angeles Daily Times,* Aug. 25, 1929; *Inyo Register,* Sept. 19, 1929.

146. *Inyo Register,* Jan. 24, 1931.

147. Baugh 1937, p. 30.

148. Chalfant 1933, p. 406.

149. Austin 1917, p. 242.

150. Ibid., p. 95.

151. Thompson 1971, pp. 78–79; see Hahn and Prude 1985 for the more general usage.

152. Thompson 1975, p. 267.

153. *San Francisco Examiner,* Feb. 18, 1930.

154. Hahn and Prude 1985; Goodwyn 1976.

155. Hobsbawm and Ranger 1983, p. 2.

156. Worster 1985, p. 7.

CHAPTER 6

1. See, e.g., Vidich and Bensman 1958, Stein 1960, Warren 1972.

2. Lyon in Delameter 1977, pp. 1–28.

3. *Survey of the Condition of Indians.*

4. Kahrl 1982, p. 351; Kelly in Garrett and Larson 1977.

5. See chapter 5, n. 61.

6. *Inyo Independent,* May 19, 1928.

7. Ibid., May 4, 1929.

8. Ibid., Feb. 7, 1931.

9. Ibid., Apr. 4 and 11, 1931.

10. Ibid., Oct. 20 and 27 and Nov. 3, 1933; Feb. 9, 1934.

11. Dykstra 1928.

12. *Inyo Independent,* May 9, 1885; Mar. 9, 1900.

13. Brown in Garrett and Larson 1977.

14. *Fifteenth* (1930) and *Sixteenth* (1940) *U.S. Census of Agriculture.* See table 11 later in this chapter.

15. Kahrl 1982, pp. 351–52.

16. *Survey of the Condition of Indians,* p. 15260; Kahrl 1982, p. 354; Ford 1930.

17. Ford 1930 estimated the Indian population at 784, while the U.S. Census reported 736; Ford counted 270 households.

18. *Survey of the Condition of Indians,* p. 15231.

19. Ibid., p. 15235.

20. Raw data from Ford 1930, compiled by the author.

21. *Survey of the Condition of Indians,* p. 15199.

22. Kahrl 1982, p. 356.

23. *Survey of the Condition of Indians,* pp. 15219–20.

24. Ibid., pp. 15212–13.
25. De Decker in Delameter 1977, pp. 1–51.
26. *Survey of the Condition of Indians,* p. 15259.
27. Ibid., p. 15231.
28. Kahrl 1982, p. 356.
29. Walter 1986.
30. Clark and Porter n.d.
31. Ford 1930, p. 12.
32. Quoted in Kahrl 1982, p. 359.
33. Packard 1925.
34. De Decker in Delameter 1977, pp. 1–47.
35. Brown in Garrett and Larson 1977, p. 20.
36. Ibid., pp. 27–28.
37. Mitchell 1986, pp. 14–15.
38. Ibid., p. 20.
39. Brown in Garrett and Larson 1977, p. 22.
40. Ryan 1968; Van Valen 1977.
41. Brown in Garrett and Larson 1977, p. 28.
42. Baugh 1937, p. 30.
43. Kahrl 1982, p. 364.
44. Baugh 1937, pp. 30–31.
45. De Decker in Delameter 1977, p. 63.
46. Brierly and Partridge in Delameter 1977.
47. *Recreation and Other Public Uses of the City of Los Angeles Lands in the Owens Valley–Mono Basin Area.*
48. Ibid.
49. *Inyo Independent,* Mar. 20, 1942.
50. Ibid., Feb. 13, 1942.
51. Brown in Garrett and Larson 1977, p. 33.
52. *Inyo Independent,* Mar. 20, 1942.
53. Kahrl 1982, p. 369.
54. Quoted in ibid., p. 368.
55. Ibid., p. 369.
56. Hopkins in Garrett and Larson 1977, p. 47.
57. Brown in Garrett and Larson 1977, pp. 127–28.
58. *Inyo Independent,* Mar. 20, 1942.
59. Joseph in Garrett and Larson 1977, p. 78.
60. Garrett and Larson 1977.
61. Brown in Garrett and Larson 1977, p. 35.
62. *U.S. Census, County and City Data Book* 1967, 1972, 1983.
63. *Twentieth* (1980) *U.S. Census of Population.*
64. Hoffman 1978, pp. 179, 191.
65. Kahrl 1982, p. 319.
66. Kyne 1914, p. 115.
67. Ibid., p. 119.
68. Austin 1917, p. 381.
69. Ibid., pp. 432, 384.
70. Ibid., pp. 403–4.

71. HEH, Watterson to Austin, Dec. 18, 1924.
72. *San Francisco Call,* Apr. 24–May 3, 1924.
73. HEH, Watterson to Kniseley, Nov. 24, 1926.
74. Ryan 1968.
75. *Los Angeles Record,* Aug. 20, 1927.
76. The discussion of Nordskog relies on Hoffman 1981, chap. 7.
77. HEH, Watterson to Clausen, July 8, 1927.
78. HEH, McWilliams to Austin, Jan. 27, 1930, and n.d.
79. Hoffman 1981, p. 226.
80. Ibid., pp. 227, 228.
81. Cited in Kahrl 1982, p. 329.
82. HEH, McWilliams to Austin, June 22, 1931.
83. Mayo 1932, pp. 245–46.
84. Quoted in ibid., p. 241.
85. Belfrage 1938.
86. Gragg and Putnam 1950.
87. Miller 1973, p. 33.
88. Kahrl 1982, pp. 302, 394.
89. *Municipal League of Los Angeles* Bulletin, July 15, 1924.
90. *Fire and Water Engineering,* Dec. 17, 1924.
91. Kinsey 1926, 1928.
92. Kahrl 1982, p. 377.
93. Ibid., pp. 378–79.
94. Ibid., p. 381.
95. Ibid., p. 383.
96. *Los Angeles Times,* Calendar section, Apr. 3, 1983.
97. Ibid.
98. Petulla 1977.
99. E.g., *Inyo Independent,* Sept. 8, 1933.
100. Kahrl 1982, p. 388.
101. Ibid., p. 386.
102. Hayes 1959.
103. Coyle 1957; Reisch 1976.
104. Dreyfus and Ingram 1976, p. 245.
105. Petulla 1977; Udall 1963.
106. Worster 1985; Reisner 1986.
107. Caldwell 1970.
108. Quoted in Schnaiberg 1980, p. 381.
109. Wandesford-Smith 1970, pp. 210–11.
110. Houston and Houston 1973.
111. Skocpol 1980; Skocpol and Finegold 1982.
112. Caldwell 1970, p. 173.
113. Wandesford-Smith 1970, p. 213.
114. Caldwell 1970, p. 174.
115. Ibid., pp. 264–66.
116. Ibid., p. 97.
117. Dreyfus and Ingram 1976, p. 248.
118. Ibid., pp. 251, 258.

119. Vidich and Bensman n.d., p. 100; Stein 1960.
120. Vidich and Bensman n.d., pp. 101, 221.
121. Cottrell 1972, pp. 79, 72; Cottrell 1951.

CHAPTER 7

1. Kahrl 1982, p. 406.
2. Ibid., p. 414.
3. Ostrom 1953, chap. 5; Kahrl 1982, pp. 401–2.
4. *Final EIR.*
5. *Inyo Independent,* Mar. 19, 1970.
6. Ibid., Aug. 6, 1970.
7. Ibid., Oct. 22, 1970.
8. Ibid., Nov. 19, 1970.
9. Ibid., Nov. 5 and Dec. 10, 1970.
10. Ibid., Nov. 12, 1970.
11. *Final EIR.*
12. *Inyo Independent,* Jan. 21, 1971.
13. Ibid.
14. Ibid., June 10, 1971.
15. Ibid., Nov. 18, 1971.
16. Ibid., Sept. 7, 1972; emphasis added.
17. Rossman 1978, p. 203.
18. Quoted in Stegner 1981, p. 65.
19. Quoted in Morgan 1976, p. 109.
20. De Decker in Delameter 1977, pp. 1–51.
21. Interview with author, Sept. 25, 1987.
22. Andrews 1973; *Inyo Independent,* Nov. 30, 1972.
23. Morgan 1976, p. 417.
24. Kahrl 1982, p. 417.
25. Rossmann 1978, p. 205.
26. De Decker in Delameter 1977.
27. Kahrl 1982, p. 418.
28. *Inyo Independent,* Jan. 29, 1976.
29. Ibid., Dec. 2, 1976.
30. Ibid., May 8 and Sept. 11, 1975.
31. Ibid., May 20, 1976.
32. Ibid., May 27 and Aug. 26, 1976.
33. *Los Angeles Times,* Sept. 16, 1976.
34. Ibid., Sept. 17, 1976.
35. Lyon in Delameter 1977, pp. 1–40.
36. Rossmann and Steel 1982.
37. *Inyo Independent,* July 7, 1981.
38. Ibid., Feb. 24, 1977.
39. Ibid., Mar. 17, 1977.
40. Ibid., Apr. 4 and 21, 1977.
41. Ibid., July 28, 1977.
42. Ibid., June 9, 1977.

43. Ibid., July 14, 1977.
44. Ibid., June 29, 1978.
45. Ibid., May 4, 1978; Jan. 11, 1979.
46. Ibid., July 27, 1977.
47. Stegner 1981, p. 66.
48. Kahrl 1982, p. 428.
49. *Inyo Independent,* June 7, 1979.
50. Stegner 1981, pp. 60–61.
51. *Inyo Independent,* June 28, 1979.
52. Ibid.
53. Ibid., July 5, 1979.
54. Kahrl 1982, p. 426.
55. *Wall Street Journal,* Feb. 4, 1981.
56. *Inyo Independent,* Nov. 16, 1978.
57. Rossmann and Steel 1982, p. 924.
58. Ibid., p. 925.
59. *Inyo Independent,* Apr. 17 and Oct. 23, 1980.
60. Ibid., Aug. 28, 1980.
61. Ibid., Jan. 29, 1980.
62. Ibid., Nov. 2, 1929; Jan. 17, 1931.
63. Ibid., July 7 and Aug. 25, 1933.
64. Steinhart 1980, pp. 113–14.
65. Gaines 1981, p. 25.
66. Chasan 1981.
67. Martha Davis, interview with author, Aug. 15, 1990.
68. Mono Lake Committee 1989.
69. Roderick 1989.
70. Steinhart 1980, p. 124.
71. Guy 1982; Hoff 1982.
72. *National Audubon Society v. Superior Court* (1983). Reprinted by Mono Lake Committee; the quotation is from p. 29.
73. Kahrl 1988; *Mono Lake Newsletter* 1990.
74. *Inyo Independent,* May 7, 1981.
75. Ibid., May 7, 1981.
76. Ibid., May 14, 1980.
77. Ibid., Feb. 3, Mar. 3, and Mar. 31, 1983.
78. Ibid., Aug. 11, 1983.
79. Ibid., Oct. 20, 1983.
80. OVC, records.
81. Interview with author, Apr. 1989.
82. *Inyo Register,* Oct. 20, 1983.
83. Ibid., Mar. 7, 1984; OVC, records.
84. *Inyo Register,* Mar. 16, 1984.
85. Ibid., July 15, 1982.
86. *Concepts for a Preliminary Agreement.*
87. *Toiyabe Trails,* Oct.–Nov. 1989; *New York Times,* Sept. 25, 1989.
88. Lyon in Delameter 1977, pp. 1–54.
89. Partridge in Delameter 1977, pp. 1–115.

90. Kahrl 1982, p. 431.
91. IC, Petition.
92. OVC, records.
93. *Final EIR.*
94. Weber 1958, chap. 7; Weber 1978; Bendix 1962, chap. 9.
95. Rossmann 1978, p. 217.
96. Foucault 1980.
97. *Water Reporter,* Jan. 1989.

CHAPTER 8

1. See, e.g., Trachtenberg 1982; Worster 1985. The consensus and conflict approaches are compared in Hogan 1990.
2. Worster 1985, pp. 6–7.
3. Stinchcombe 1978, p. 1.
4. Ibid., pp. 20–21 (Stinchcombe's emphasis).
5. Tilly 1981, p. 6.
6. Tilly 1986, p. 395.
7. Limerick 1987, p. 28.
8. Stegner 1982, p. 334.
9. Marcuse 1964, pp. 2–3.
10. Wittfogel 1957.
11. Worster 1985, p. 7.
12. Thelen 1986, p. 44.
13. Trachtenberg 1982, p. 7.
14. Hahn and Prude 1985, p. 14.
15. Weber 1978.
16. Thelen 1986; Hogan 1990.
17. Weber 1958.
18. Wolfe 1974, p. 149.
19. Bright 1984, pp. 121–22.
20. Ibid., p. 138; Skowronek 1982, pp. 39–46.
21. Skowronek 1982, pp. 165–66.
22. Ibid., p. 166.
23. Skocpol and Finegold 1982.
24. Skowronek 1982, p. 169.
25. Skocpol 1985, p. 20.
26. Ibid., p. 28.
27. Ibid., p. 4.
28. Clemens 1988, p. 1.
29. Ibid., p. 24.
30. Poulantzas 1978, p. 141 (Poulantzas's emphasis).
31. Corrigan and Sayer 1985, pp. 3–9.
32. Geertz 1973, p. 312.
33. Ibid., pp. 218–19.
34. Swidler 1986, p. 273.
35. Yengoyan 1989, pp. 11–12, 21.
36. Genovese 1972, pp. 3, 5–7, 40.

37. Sewell 1985, p. 61.
38. Geertz 1973, p. 219; Swidler 1986, p. 278.
39. Golden 1988, pp. 22–23.
40. Ibid., p. 25.
41. Thompson 1975, pp. 263–67.
42. Jenkins 1983; Tilly 1978; McCarthy and Zald 1977; Gamson 1975; McAdam 1982; Obershall 1973.
43. Thompson 1966, 1971; Hahn and Prude 1985.
44. Olson 1965.
45. Popkin 1979; Taylor 1988; Hechter 1987.
46. Granovetter 1985; Reddy 1987.
47. Weber 1978, pp. 24–26, 85–86; Levine 1981; Kalberg 1980.
48. Calhoun 1982, p. 211.
49. Elster 1989; Taylor 1988.
50. Jenkins 1983, p. 527.
51. Tilly 1978, pp. 98–99.
52. Jenkins 1983, p. 532.
53. Tilly 1978, p. 229.
54. Ibid.
55. Jenkins and Perrow 1977, pp. 263, 266.
56. Snyder and Tilly 1972.
57. Jenkins 1983, p. 549; Birnbaum 1988, p. 10.
58. Tilly 1975.
59. Tilly 1978, p. 58.
60. Robertson 1988.
61. Schwartz 1976.
62. Tilly 1978, p. 143.
63. Tilly 1986.
64. Thompson 1966, pp. 10–11.
65. Thompson 1971, p. 78.
66. Ibid., p. 79.
67. Gutman 1966; Frisch and Walkowitz 1983; Hahn and Prude 1985.
68. Goodwyn 1976.
69. McNall 1988.
70. Hahn 1983; McMath 1985, p. 207.
71. Thelen 1986, p. 205.
72. McNall 1988, p. 306.
73. Calhoun 1982, p. 7.
74. Ibid., p. 43.
75. Sharp 1980, and personal communication to the author.
76. Williams 1958, pp. 50, 104.
77. Useful work of this kind does continue, however; e.g., Snow et al. 1986.
78. Useem 1975, pp. 5–6.
79. Hobsbawm and Ranger 1983, p. 264.
80. Ibid., p. 265.
81. Abercrombie, Hill, and Turner 1980.
82. Thompson 1966, p. 548.

Bibliography

UNPUBLISHED PRIMARY SOURCES

California State Historical Society Library, San Francisco. [Cited as CSHS.]
    Austin, Mary. Letter, n.d.
    Randolph, Minnie C. Letter, February 18, 1907.
California State Library, Sacramento. California Collection. [Cited as CSL.]
    Original schedule of the Ninth U.S. Census. 1870.
    Original schedule of the Tenth U.S. Census. 1880.
Eastern California Museum, Independence, California. [Cited as ECM.]
    Bishop Creek general merchandise store ledger.
    Eaton, F. Telegram to Karl Keough, November 19, 1924.
    Index to the Great Register [of voters], 1908–1922.
    Inyo County tax assessment rolls, 1882–1930.
    Meysan, Charles. Store ledger and business letters.
    Mulholland, Charles. Ranch and business ledger.
    Oral histories. Taped and transcribed interviews with A. A. Brierly, Augustus
        Cashbaugh, W. G. and Martha W. Dixon, Louis Serventi, John Shuey,
        Birdie Yandell, Mrs. Robinson.
    Real estate listings for the Homeseekers Bureau. [Leaflet.]
Henry E. Huntington Library, San Marino, California. Special Collections.
    [Cited as HEH.]
    Chalfant, W. A. Letter to Mary Austin, November 8, 1932. AU Box 6.
    McWilliams, Carey. Letters to Mary Austin: February 3, 1906; no date;
        January 27, 1930; June 22, 1931. AU Box 16.
    Watterson, Mark. Letter to Mary Austin, December 18, 1924. AU Box 22.
    Watterson, Wilfred. Letter to Nelson Franklin, October 9, 1926; to Burton
        Knisely, November 24, 1926; to Isabel Watterson, June 23, 1927; to An-

drae B. Nordskog, July 6, 1927; to J. C. Clausen, July 8, 1927. FAC 805
and 806.

Hession Papers. Private collection of Bill and Barbara Manning, Big Pine, California. [Cited as HP.]

Inyo County Records. [Cited as IC.]
Petition to the Inyo County Board of Supervisors, June 2, 1980.
Record of deeds. County Recorder's Office.

Laws Railroad Museum, Laws (Bishop), California. [Cited as LRM.]
Cashbaugh, Augustus. Local history notebooks and early maps of Bishop.

Museum of Anthropology, Bancroft Library, University of California, Berkeley.
Ethnological Documents. [Cited as MABL.]
Interviews with Mattie Bulpitt (91.8), Jennie Cashbaugh (91.2), Mary Corn-
well (87.1), Edith Dewey (91.4), Mary Harry (92.3), Hank Hunter (85.4),
Dee Lacy (212.7), Joe Lent (91.1, 104.3), George Robinson (209.3), Mary
Rooker (93), John Shepherd (212.2), Ben Tibbitts (92.3), Susie Westerville
(208.2, 209.1).

National Archives, Washington, D.C. Department of the Interior, Owens Valley
Project 527. [Cited as NA.]
Austin, S. W. Letter to Theodore Roosevelt, August 4, 1905. Record Group
48.
Dehy, William D. Letter to Theodore Roosevelt, August 18, 1905. Record
Group 115.
Parker, Lesta V. Letter to Theodore Roosevelt, August 15, 1905. Record
Group 115.
"To the Honorable Secretary of the Interior." [Citizens' Committee letter,
August 9, 1905.] Record Group 115.
"To the Right Honorable Secretary of the Interior of the United States."
[Petition, 1905.] Record Group 115.

Owens Valley Committee Records. Private collection of Bill and Barbara Manning, Big Pine, California. [Cited as OVC.]

University of California at Los Angeles Library. Special Collections. [Cited as
UCLA.]
Bynum, Linley. "Reminiscences of Inyo County." Oral histories. 1952–1954.
Transcribed interviews with Harriet Bulpitt, Anne Nelligan.

REPORTS AND PUBLISHED PRIMARY SOURCES

Austin, Mary. 1905. "The Owens River Water Project." San Francisco Chronicle, September 5.
———. 1932. Earth Horizon: Autobiography. New York: Houghton Mifflin.
Calhoun, Margaret. 1984. Pioneers of the Mono Basin. Lee Vining, Calif.:
Artemisia Press.
California Prices Received by Farmers for Farm Commodities, 1908–1960.
1961. Sacramento: California Department of Agriculture.

Clark, Douglas, and E. A. Porter. N.d. "General Report of Owens Valley Land Exchange." City of Los Angeles, Department of Water and Power.

Concepts for a Preliminary Agreement between the County of Inyo and the City of Los Angeles and Its Department of Water and Power on a Long Term Groundwater Management Plan for the Owens Valley. 1989. Inyo County Water Department.

Delameter, C. Ellis. 1977. "The Owens Valley, City of Los Angeles Water Controversy: An Oral History Examination of the Events of the 1920's and 1970's." M.S. thesis, California State University, Fullerton.

Doyle, Helen MacKnight. 1934. *A Child Went Forth: The Autobiography of Dr. Helen MacKnight Doyle.* New York: Gotham House.

————. 1939. *Mary Austin: Woman of Genius.* New York: Gotham House.

Earl, Guy Chaffee. 1976. *The Enchanted Valley and Other Sketches.* Glendale, Calif.: Arthur Clark Co.

El Centro Press, February 24, 1928.

Facts Concerning the Owens Valley Reparations Claims. 1925. City of Los Angeles, Department of Water and Power.

A Few Facts about the Famous Owens River Valley. [c. 1910.] Independence, Calif.: Inyo County Board of Supervisors.

Final EIR: Increased Pumping of the Owens Valley Groundwater Basin. 1979. City of Los Angeles, Department of Water and Power.

Ford, A. J. 1930. *Owens River Valley, California, Indian Problem.* City of Los Angeles, Department of Water and Power.

Garrett, Jessie A., and Ronald C. Larson, eds. 1977. *Camp and Community: Manzanar and the Owens Valley.* Fullerton: California State University, Japanese Oral History Project.

Inyo County and the Famous Owens River Valley. [c. 1910.] Independence, Calif.: Inyo County Board of Supervisors.

Inyo County California. [c. 1910.] Bishop, Calif.: Owens Valley Chamber of Commerce.

Inyo County California, Anno Domini 1912. 1983. Bishop, Calif.: Bishop Chamber of Commerce in cooperation with Chalfant Press. Reprint.

Inyo, 1866–1966. 1966. Bishop, Calif.: Inyo County Board of Supervisors and Chalfant Press.

Inyo Independent, 1870–1930.

Inyo Register, 1885–1988.

Inyo the Peerless. [c. 1910.] Bishop, Calif.: Owens Valley Chamber of Commerce.

Literary Digest, December 6, 1924.

Los Angeles Aqueduct Investigation Report. 1912. Los Angeles Department of Water and Power. Memos.

"The Los Angeles Aqueduct Seizure—What Really Happened." 1924. *Fire and Water Engineering.* December 17.

Los Angeles (Daily) Times, 1905–1990.

Los Angeles Evening Express, 1924–1930.

Los Angeles Examiner, 1924–1930.

Los Angeles Record, 1924–1930.

Los Angeles Spartan News, 1924–1930.

McClure, W. F. 1925. *Owens Valley–Los Angeles: Report Made at Request of Governor Friend Wm. Richardson Following the Opening of the Alabama Hills Waste Gates of the Aqueduct by the People on November 16, 1924.* Sacramento: State of California.

Municipal League of Los Angeles Bulletin, July 15, 1924.

New York Times, September 25, 1989.

Packard, Walter E. 1925. *Report on the Agricultural Situation in Owens Valley, as It Relates to the Agricultural Development of Lands Belonging to the City of Los Angeles.* City of Los Angeles, Department of Public Service.

Recreation and Other Public Uses of the City of Los Angeles Lands in the Owens Valley–Mono Basin Area. 1967. City of Los Angeles, Department of Water and Power.

Sacramento Union, March 29–April 3, 1927.

Saga of Inyo County. 1977. Covina, Calif.: Taylor Publishing Co.

San Francisco Call, April 24–May 3, 1924.

San Francisco Chronicle, September 3, 1905; August 12, 1927.

San Francisco Examiner, February 18, 1930.

San Pedro News, February 24, 1928.

Statement of the Vote, 1882–1926. Sacramento: California Secretary of State.

Steward, Julian H. 1934a. "Two Paiute Autobiographies." *American Archaeology and Ethnology* 33:423–38.

———. 1930, 1934b, 1938: See under Secondary Sources.

Survey of the Conditions of the Indians in the United States. Part 29, California. 1932. 72d U.S. Congress, 1st Session.

Toiyabe Trails, October-November 1989.

United States Census, County and City Data Book, 1967, 1972, 1983.

United States Census of Agriculture. Tenth (1880), *Eleventh* (1890), *Twelfth* (1900), *Thirteenth* (1910), *Fourteenth* (1920), *Fifteenth* (1930), *Sixteenth* (1940), *Seventeenth* (1950), *Eighteenth* (1959), *Nineteenth* (1969), and *Twentieth* (1978). Washington, D.C.: Government Printing Office.

United States Census of Business. 1939, 1948, 1958, 1967. Washington, D.C.: Government Printing Office.

United States Census of Distribution. 1930. Washington, D.C.: Government Printing Office.

United States Census of Population. Ninth (1870), *Tenth* (1880), *Eleventh* (1890), *Twelfth* (1900), *Thirteenth* (1910), *Fourteenth* (1920), *Fifteenth* (1930), *Sixteenth* (1940), *Seventeenth* (1950), *Eighteenth* (1960), *Nineteenth* (1970), and *Twentieth* (1980). Washington, D.C.: Government Printing Office.

United States Census of Retail Trade. 1977, 1982. Washington, D.C.: Government Printing Office.

United States Census of Service Industries. 1977, 1982. Washington, D.C.: Government Printing Office.

Wall Street Journal, February 4 and 5, 1981.

Water Reporter [Inyo County], December 1988 and January 1989.

Wilke, Philip J., and Henry W. Lawton, eds. 1976. *The Expedition of Capt. J. W. Davidson From Ft. Tejon to the Owens Valley in 1859.* Socorro, N. Mex.: Ballena Press.

SECONDARY SOURCES

Abbiatecci, Andre. 1978. "Arsonists in Eighteenth-Century France: An Essay in the Typology of Crime." In *Selections From the Annales: Economies, Societies, Civilizations,* edited by Robert Foster and Orest Ranum, 4:157–79. Baltimore: Johns Hopkins University Press.

Abercrombie, Nicholas, Stephen Hill, and Bryan S. Turner. 1980. *The Dominant Ideology Thesis.* London: George Allen and Unwin.

Andrews, Robert, Jr. 1973. "Aftermammoth: Friends of Mammoth and the Amended California Environmental Quality Act." *Ecology Law Quarterly* 3 (Spring): 349–89.

Athearn, Robert G. 1986. *The Mythic West in Twentieth Century America.* Lawrence: University Press of Kansas.

Austin, Mary. 1917. *The Ford.* Boston: Houghton Mifflin.

———. 1974. *The Land of Little Rain.* Albuquerque: University of New Mexico Press. (Originally published in 1903.)

Bartlett, Richard A. 1974. *The New Country: A Social History of the American Frontier, 1776–1890.* New York: Oxford University Press.

Baugh, Ruth E. 1937. "Land Use in the Bishop Area of Owens Valley, California." *Economic Geography* 13(1): 15–34.

Belfrage, Cedric. 1938. *Promised Land.* London: Victor Gollancz.

Bendix, Reinhard. 1962. *Max Weber: An Intellectual Portrait.* Garden City, N.Y.: Anchor Books.

Bettinger, Robert L. 1984. "Native Land Use in the White Mountains: Archeology and Anthropology." Manuscript. University of California, White Mountain Research Station.

Birnbaum, Pierre. 1988. *States and Collective Action: The European Experience.* Cambridge: Cambridge University Press.

Black, Donald. 1983. "Crime as Social Control." *American Sociological Review* 48 (February): 34–45.

Bogue, Allan G. 1960. "Social Theory and the Pioneer." *Agricultural History* 34 (January): 21–34.

Boorstein, Daniel J. 1973. *The Americans: The Democratic Experience.* New York: Random House.

Bright, Charles C. 1984. "The State in the United States during the Nineteenth Century." In *Statemaking and Social Movements: Essays in History and Theory,* edited by Charles C. Bright and Susan Harding. Ann Arbor: University of Michigan Press.

Caldwell, Lynton Keith. 1970. *Environment: A Challenge to Modern Society.* Garden City, N.Y.: Anchor Books.

Calhoun, Craig. 1982. *The Question of Class: Social Foundations of Popular*

Radicalism during the Industrial Revolution. Chicago: University of Chicago Press.

Cardoso, Fernando Enrique, and Enzo Faletto. 1979. *Dependency and Development in Latin America*. Berkeley: University of California Press. (Originally published in Spanish in 1971.)

Chalfant, W. A. 1933. *The Story of Inyo*. Rev. ed. Bishop, Calif.: Chalfant Press.

Chasan, Daniel Jack. 1981. "Mono Lake vs. Los Angeles: A Tug-of-war for Precious Water." *Smithsonian* 11 (February): 42–51.

Clemens, Elisabeth S. 1988. "Redefining the Public Realm: Progressive Coalitions and Social Policy in Wisconsin and Washington, 1890–1915." Paper presented at annual meeting of the American Sociological Association, Atlanta, August.

Clifford, James, and George E. Marcus. 1986. *Writing Culture: The Poetics and Politics of Ethnography*. Berkeley: University of California Press.

Corrigan, Philip, and Derek Sayer. 1985. *The Great Arch: English State Formation as Cultural Revolution*. London: Basil Blackwell.

Cottrell, W. F. 1951. "Death by Dieselization: A Case Study in the Reaction to Technological Change." *American Sociological Review* 16 (June): 358–65.

———. 1972. *Technology, Man, and Progress*. Columbus, Ohio: Charles E. Merrill Publishing Co.

Coyle, David Cushman. 1957. *Conservation: An American Story of Conflict and Accomplishment*. New Brunswick, N.J.: Rutgers University Press.

Dos Santos, Theotonio. 1970. "The Structure of Dependence." *American Economic Review* 60 (May): 231–36.

Dreyfus, Daniel A., and Helen M. Ingram. 1976. "The National Environmental Policy Act: A View of Intent and Practice." *Natural Resources Journal* 16(1): 243–62.

Dumenil, Lynn. 1984. *Freemasonry and American Culture, 1880–1930*. Princeton: Princeton University Press.

Dykstra, Clarence A. 1928. "Owens Valley: A Problem in Regional Planning." *Community Builder* (February).

Elster, Jon. 1989. *The Cement of Society: A Study of Social Order*. Cambridge: Cambridge University Press.

Faragher, John Mack. 1986. *Sugar Creek: Life on the Illinois Prairie*. New Haven: Yale University Press.

Foucault, Michel. 1980. *Power/Knowledge: Selected Interviews and Other Writings, 1972–1977*. Edited by Colin Gordon. New York: Pantheon.

Frisch, Michael H., and Daniel J. Walkowitz, eds. 1983. *Working-Class America: Essays on Labor, Community, and American Society*. Urbana: University of Illinois Press.

Gaines, David. 1981. *Mono Lake Guidebook*. Lee Vining, Calif.: Kutsavi Books.

Gamson, William. 1975. *The Strategy of Social Protest*. Homewood, Ill.: Dorsey.

Ganoe, John T. 1931–32. "The Origin of National Reclamation Policy." *Mississippi Valley Historical Review* 18.

Gates, Paul W. 1979. *History of Public Land Law Development*. New York: Arno Press.

Geertz, Clifford. 1973. *The Interpretation of Cultures*. New York: Basic Books.

Genovese, Eugene. 1972. *Roll Jordan Roll: The World the Slaves Made*. New York: Random House.

Golden, Miriam A. 1988. "Historical Memory and Ideological Orientations in the Italian Workers' Movement." *Politics and Society* 16 (March): 1–34.

Goodwyn, Lawrence. 1976. *Democratic Promise: The Populist Moment in America*. New York: Oxford University Press.

Gragg, Frances, and George Putnam Palmer. 1950. *Golden Valley: A Novel of California*. New York: Duell, Sloan and Pearce.

Granovetter, Mark. 1985. "Economic Action and Social Structure: The Problem of Embeddedness." *American Journal of Sociology* 91 (November): 481–510.

Gutman, Herbert G. 1966. *Work, Culture, and Society in Industrializing America*. New York: Random House.

Guy, Martha. 1982. "The Public Trust Doctrine and California Water Law: *National Audubon Society v. Department of Water and Power.*" *Hastings Law Journal* 33 (January): 653–87.

Hahn, Steven. 1983. *The Roots of Southern Populism: Yeomen Farmers and Transformation of the Georgia Upcountry, 1850–1890*. New York: Oxford University Press.

Hahn, Steven, and Jonathan Prude. 1985. *The Countryside in the Age of Capitalist Transformation: Essays in the Social History of Rural America*. Chapel Hill: University of North Carolina Press.

Hall, Thomas D. 1986. "Incorporation in the World System: Toward a Critique." *American Sociological Review* 51 (June): 390–402.

———. 1989. *Social Change in the Southwest, 1350–1880*. Lawrence: University Press of Kansas.

Hayes, Samuel P. 1959. *Conservation and the Gospel of Efficiency: The Progressive Conservation Movement, 1890–1920*. Cambridge: Harvard University Press.

Hechter, Michael. 1987. *Principles of Group Solidarity*. Berkeley: University of California Press.

Hine, Robert V. 1973. *The American West: An Interpretive History*. Boston: Little, Brown.

———. 1980. *Community on the American Frontier: Separate But Not Alone*. Norman: University of Oklahoma Press.

Hobsbawm, Eric, and George Rude. 1968. *Captain Swing: A Social History of the Great English Agricultural Uprising of 1830*. New York: Pantheon.

Hobsbawm, Eric, and Terence Ranger, eds. 1983. *The Invention of Tradition*. Cambridge: Cambridge University Press.

Hoff, Jeff. 1982. "The Legal Battle Over Mono Lake." *California Lawyer* (January): 28–58.

Hoffman, Abraham. 1978. "Fact and Fiction in the Owens Valley Water Controversy." Los Angeles Westerners Corral, *Brand Book* (no. 15) 179–92.

————. 1981. *Vision or Villainy: Origins of the Owens Valley–Los Angeles Water Controversy.* College Station: Texas A & M University Press.

Hogan, Richard. 1985. "The Frontier as Social Control." *Theory and Society* 14(1): 35–51.

————. 1990. *Class and Community in Frontier Colorado.* Lawrence: University Press of Kansas.

Houston, Jeanne Wakatsuki, and James D. Houston. 1973. *Farewell to Manzanar.* New York: Bantam Books.

Hurtado, Albert L. 1988. *Indian Survival on the California Frontier.* New Haven: Yale University Press.

Jacobson, Cardell K. 1984. "Internal Colonialism and Native Americans: Indian Labor in the United States From 1871 to World War II." *Social Science Quarterly* 65 (May): 158–71.

Jenkins, J. Craig. 1983. "Resource Mobilization Theory and the Study of Social Movements." *Annual Review of Sociology* 9:527–53.

————. 1985. *The Politics of Insurgency: The Farm Workers' Movement in the 1960s.* New York: Columbia University Press.

Jenkins, J. Craig, and Charles Perrow. 1977. "Insurgency of the Powerless: Farm Worker Movements (1946–1972)." *American Sociological Review* 42 (April): 249–68.

Kahrl, William L. 1976. "The Politics of California Water: Owens Valley and the Los Angeles Aqueduct, 1900–1927." *California Historical Quarterly* 55 (Spring): 2–25.

————. 1982. *Water and Power: The Conflict over Los Angeles' Water Supply in the Owens Valley.* Berkeley: University of California Press.

————. 1988. "A Fine Kettle of Fish for Los Angeles." *Sacramento Bee,* June 19.

Kalberg, Stephen. 1980. "Max Weber's Types of Rationality: Cornerstones for the Analysis of Rationalization Processes in History." *American Journal of Sociology* 85 (March): 1145–79.

Kinsey, Don J. 1926. *The Romance of Water and Power.* Los Angeles: City of Los Angeles, Department of Water and Power.

————. 1928. *The Water Trail.* Los Angeles: City of Los Angeles, Department of Water and Power.

Knack, Martha C. 1987. "The Role of Credit in Native Adaptation to the Great Basin Ranching Economy." *American Indian Culture and Research Journal* 11(1): 43–65.

Knight, Rolf. 1978. *Indians at Work: An Informal History of Native Labour in British Columbia in 1858–1930.* Vancouver: New Star Books.

Kyne, Peter B. 1914. *The Long Chance.* New York: H. K. Fly.

Lavender, David. 1986. *California: Land of New Beginnings.* Lincoln, Nebr.: Bison Books. Reprint. (Originally published in 1972.)

Lawton, Harry W., Philip J. Wilke, Mary De Decker, and William M. Mason. 1976. "Agriculture among the Paiute of Owens Valley." *Journal of California Anthropology* 3 (Summer): 13–50.

Levine, Donald N. 1981. "Rationality and Freedom: Weber and Beyond." *Sociological Inquiry* 51(1): 5–25.

Leys, Colin. 1975. *Underdevelopment in Kenya: The Political Economy of Neo-Colonialism, 1964–1971.* London: Heinemann.

Likes, Robert C., and Glenn R. Day. 1975. *From This Mountain—Cerro Gordo.* Bishop, Calif.: Chalfant Press.

Lilley, William, and Lewis L. Gould. 1966. "The Western Irrigation Movement, 1878–1902: A Reappraisal." In *The American West: A Reorientation,* edited by Gene M. Gressley. Laramie: University of Wyoming Press.

Limerick, Patricia Nelson. 1987. *The Legacy of Conquest: The Unbroken Past of the American West.* New York: Norton.

Lingenfelter, Richard E. 1986. *Death Valley and the Amargosa: A Land of Illusion.* Berkeley: University of California Press.

Lloyd, Christopher. 1986. *Explanation in Social History.* Oxford: Basil Blackwell.

Marcuse, Herbert. 1964. *One-Dimensional Man: Studies in the Ideology of Advanced Industrial Societies.* Boston: Beacon Press.

Mayo, Morrow. 1932. *Los Angeles.* New York: Alfred Knopf.

McAdam, Douglas. 1982. *Political Protest and the Development of Black Insurgency, 1930–1970.* Chicago: University of Chicago Press.

McCarthy, John D., and Mayer N. Zald. 1977. "Resource Mobilization and Social Movements: A Partial Theory." *American Journal of Sociology* 82 (May): 1212–41.

McGrath, Roger D. 1984. *Gunfighters, Highwaymen, and Vigilantes: Violence on the Frontier.* Berkeley: University of California Press.

McMath, Robert C., Jr. 1985. "Sandy Land and Hogs in the Timber: (Agri)Cultural Origins of the Farmers' Alliance in Texas." In *The Countryside in the Age of Capitalist Transformation: Essays in the Social History of Rural America,* edited by Steven Hahn and Jonathan Prude, pp. 205–29. Chapel Hill: University of North Carolina Press.

McMichael, Philip. 1984. *Settlers and the Agrarian Question: Foundations of Capitalism in Colonial Australia.* Cambridge: Cambridge University Press.

McNall, Scott G. 1988. *The Road to Rebellion: Class Formation and Kansas Populism, 1865–1900.* Chicago: University of Chicago Press.

McWilliams, Carey. 1973. *Southern California: An Island on the Land.* Salt Lake City: Peregrine Books. Reprint. (Originally published in 1946.)

Melville, Herman. 1954. *The Confidence Man.* New York: Hendricks House. (First published 1857.)

Miller, Gordon R. 1973. "Shaping California Water Law, 1781 to 1928." *Southern California Quarterly* 55 (Spring): 9–42.

Mitchell, Jim. 1986. "They Went Thataway." *Sierra Life* (July–August): 8–21.

Mono Lake Committee. 1989. *Mono Lake: Endangered Oasis.* Position paper.

Mono Lake Newsletter. 1990. Lee Vining, Calif.: Mono Lake Committee. [Compendium of articles on Mono Lake Lawsuits.]

Morgan, Judith, and Neil Morgan. 1976. "California's Parched Oasis." *National Geographic* (January): 98–127.

Mowry, George E. 1951. *The California Progressives.* Berkeley: University of California Press.

Nadeau, Remi. 1976. *The Water Seekers*. Santa Barbara, Calif.: Peregrine, Smith. Reprint. (Originally published in 1950.)

―――. 1977. *City-Makers: The Story of Southern California's First Boom*. Corona del Mar, Calif.: Trans-Anglo Books.

National Audubon Society v. Superior Court. 1983. Opinion of the Supreme Court of California. Reprinted by the Mono Lake Committee.

Obershall, Anthony. 1973. *Social Conflict and Social Movements*. Englewood Cliffs, N.J.: Prentice-Hall.

Olson, Mancur. 1965. *The Logic of Collective Action*. Cambridge: Harvard University Press.

Ostrom, Vincent. 1953. *Water and Politics: A Study of Water Policies and Administration in the Development of Los Angeles*. Los Angeles: Haynes Foundation.

Paul, Rodman W. 1988. *The Far West and the Great Plains in Transition, 1859–1900*. New York: Harper and Row.

Pearce, Roy Harvey. 1988. *Savagism and Civilization: A Study of the Indian and the American Mind*. Berkeley: University of California Press. (Originally published as *The Savages of America*, 1953.)

Petulla, Joseph M. 1977. *American Environmental History: The Exploitation and Conservation of Natural Resources*. San Francisco: Boyd and Fraser.

Popkin, Samuel L. 1979. *The Rational Peasant: The Political Economy of Rural Society in Vietnam*. Berkeley: University of California Press.

Poulantzas, Nicos. 1978. *State, Power, Socialism*. London: New Left Books.

Ranger, Terence. 1985. *Peasant Consciousness and Guerrilla War in Zimbabwe: A Comparative Study*. London and Berkeley: James Curry and the University of California Press.

Reddy, William M. 1987. *Money and Liberty in Modern Europe: A Critique of Historical Understanding*. Cambridge: Cambridge University Press.

Reisch, Anna Lou. 1976. "Conservation under Franklin D. Roosevelt." In *The American Environment: Readings in the History of Conservation*, 2d ed., edited by Roderick Nash, pp. 147–51. Reading, Mass.: Addison-Wesley.

Reisner, Marc. 1986. *Cadillac Desert: The American West and Its Disappearing Water*. New York: Viking.

Robertson, Roland. 1988. "The Sociological Significance of Culture: Some General Considerations." *Theory, Culture, and Society* 5: 3–23.

Roderick, Kevin. 1989. "Selling a Lake." *Los Angeles Times*, September 24.

Rogin, Michael Paul. 1987. "Liberal Society and the Indian Question." In *Ronald Reagan, the Movie and Other Episodes in Political Demonology*, pp. 134–68. Berkeley: University of California Press. Originally published in *Politics and Society* 1 (May 1971).

Rossman, Antonio. 1978. "Water for the Valley." In *Deepest Valley*, rev. ed., edited by Genny Smith, pp. 202–17. Los Altos, Calif.: William Kaufman.

Rossmann, Antonio, and Michael J. Steel. 1982. "Forging the New Water Law: Public Regulation of 'Proprietary' Groundwater Rights." *Hastings Law Journal*. 33 (March): 903–57.

Royce, Josiah. 1886. *California, from the Conquest in 1846 to the Second*

Vigilance Committee in San Francisco: A study of American Character. Boston: Houghton, Mifflin.

Ryan, Marian L. 1968. "Los Angeles Newspapers Fight the Water War, 1924–1927." *Southern California Quarterly* 50 (June): 177–90.

Sauder, Robert A. 1988. "Patenting the Arid Frontier: Use and Abuse of the Public Land Laws in Owens Valley, California." Manuscript. University of New Orleans, Department of Geography. Subsequently published in *Annals of the Association of American Geographers* 79(4): 544–69.

Saxton, Alexander. 1971. *The Indispensable Enemy: Labor and the Anti-Chinese Movement in California.* Berkeley: University of California Press.

Schnaiberg, Allan. 1980. *The Environment: From Surplus to Scarcity.* New York: Oxford University Press.

Schumacher, Genny. 1962. *Deepest Valley: Guide to Owens Valley and Its Mountain Lakes, Roadsides, and Trails.* San Francisco: Sierra Club.

Schwartz, Michael. 1976. *Radical Protest and Social Structure: The Southern Farmers' Alliance and Cotton Tenancy, 1880–1890.* New York: Academic Press.

Scott, James C. 1985. *Weapons of the Weak: Everyday Forms of Peasant Resistance.* New Haven: Yale University Press.

Sewell, William H., Jr. 1980. *Work and Revolution in France: The Language of Labor from the Old Regime to 1848.* Cambridge: Cambridge University Press.

———. 1985. "Ideologies and Social Revolutions: Reflections on the French Case." *Journal of Modern History* 57 (March): 57–85.

———. 1986. "Theory of Action, Dialectics, and History: Comment on Coleman." *American Journal of Sociology* 93 (July): 166–72.

Sharp, Buchanan. 1980. *In Contempt of All Authority: Rural Artisans and Riot in the West of England, 1586–1660.* Berkeley: University of California Press.

Skocpol, Theda. 1980. "Political Response to Capitalist Crisis: Neo-Marxist Theories of the State and the Case of the New Deal." *Politics and Society* 10(2): 155–201.

———. 1985. "Bringing the State Back In: Strategies of Analysis in Current Research." In *Bringing the State Back In,* edited by Peter B. Evans, Dietrich Rueschemeyer, and Theda Skocpol, pp. 3–37. Cambridge: Cambridge University Press.

Skocpol, Theda, and Kenneth Finegold. 1982. "State Capacity and Economic Intervention in the Early New Deal." *Political Science Quarterly* 97 (Summer): 255–78.

Skowronek, Stephen. 1982. *Building a New American State: The Expansion of National Administrative Capacities, 1877–1920.* Cambridge: Cambridge University Press.

Smith, Henry Nash. 1950. *Virgin Land: The American West as Symbol and Myth.* Cambridge: Harvard University Press.

Snow, David A., E. Burke Rochford, Jr., Steven K. Worden, and Robert D. Benford. 1986. "Frame Alignment Processes, Micromobilization, and Movement Participation." *American Sociological Review* 51 (August): 464–81.

Snyder, David, and Charles Tilly. 1972. "Hardship and Collective Violence in France: 1830 to 1960." *American Sociological Review* 37 (October): 520–32.

Starr, Kevin. 1973. *Americans and the California Dream, 1850–1915.* New York: Oxford University Press.

———. 1985. *Inventing the Dream: California through the Progressive Era.* New York: Oxford University Press.

———. 1990. *Material Dreams: Southern California through the 1920s.* New York: Oxford University Press.

Stedman-Jones, Gareth. 1983. *Languages of Class: Studies in English Working Class History, 1832–1982.* Cambridge: Cambridge University Press.

Stegner, Page. 1981. "Water and Power." *Harper's* (March): 61–70. Reprinted as "There It Is: Take It." in *American Places,* edited by Wallace Stegner and Page Stegner, pp. 185–206. Moscow: University of Idaho Press.

Stegner, Wallace. 1982. *Beyond the Hundredth Meridian: John Wesley Powell and the Second Opening of the West.* Lincoln, Nebr.: Bison Books. (Originally published in 1953.)

Stein, Maurice R. 1960. *The Eclipse of Community: An Interpretation of American Studies.* Princeton: Princeton University Press.

Steinbeck, John. 1979. *East of Eden.* New York: Penguin. (First published 1952.)

Steinhart, Peter. 1980. "The City and the Inland Sea." *Audubon* 82 (September 5): 98–125.

Stern, Steve J. 1988. "Feudalism, Capitalism, and the World-System in the Perspective of Latin America and the Caribbean." *American Historical Review* 93 (October): 829–72.

Steward, Julian. 1930. "Irrigation Without Agriculture." *Papers of the Michigan Academy of Sciences, Arts, and Letters* 12: 269–76.

———. 1934a: see under Reports and Published Primary Sources.

———. 1934b. "Ethnography of the Owens Valley Paiute." *American Archaeology and Ethnology* 33: 233–324.

———. 1938. *Basin-Plateau Aboriginal Sociopolitical Groups.* Smithsonian Institution, Bureau of American Ethnology, bulletin 120. Washington, D.C.: U. S. Government Printing Office.

Stinchcombe, Arthur L. 1978. *Theoretical Methods in Social History.* New York: Academic Press.

Swidler, Ann. 1986. "Culture in Action: Symbols and Strategies." *American Sociological Review* 51 (April): 272–86.

Taylor, Michael. 1988. *Rationality and Revolution.* Cambridge: Cambridge University Press.

Thelen, David. 1986. *Paths of Resistance: Tradition and Dignity in Industrializing Missouri.* New York: Oxford University Press.

Thompson, E. P. 1966. *The Making of the English Working Class.* New York: Vintage Books. (Originally published in 1963.)

———. 1971. "The Moral Economy of the English Crowd in the Eighteenth Century." *Past and Present* 50 (February): 76–136.

————. 1975. *Whigs and Hunters: The Origin of the Black Act.* New York: Pantheon.

Tilly, Charles. 1975. "Food Supply and Public Order in Modern Europe." In *The Formation of Nation States in Western Europe,* edited by Charles Tilly, pp. 380–455. Princeton: Princeton University Press.

————. 1978. *From Mobilization to Revolution.* Reading, Mass.: Addison-Wesley.

————. 1981. "Britain Creates the Social Movement." Working paper. University of Michigan, Center for Research on Social Organization.

————. 1986. *The Contentious French.* Cambridge: Harvard University Press.

Tocqueville, Alexis de. 1958. *Democracy in America.* 2 vols. New York: Vintage Books. (First published 1835–1840.)

Trachtenberg, Alan. 1982. *The Incorporation of America: Culture and Society in the Gilded Age.* New York: Hill and Wang.

Turner, Frederick Jackson. 1921. *The Frontier in American History.* New York: Henry Holt.

Udall, Stewart L. 1963. *The Quiet Crisis.* New York: Holt, Rinehart, and Winston.

Useem, Michael. 1975. *Protest Movements in America.* Indianapolis: Bobbs-Merrill.

Van Valen, Nelson. 1977. "A Neglected Aspect of the Owens River Aqueduct Story: The Inception of the Los Angeles Municipal Electric System." *Southern California Quarterly* 59 (Spring): 85–109.

Vidich, Arthur J., and Joseph Bensman. N.d. *Small Town in Mass Society: Class, Power, and Religion in a Rural Community.* Garden City, N.Y.: Anchor Books. (Originally published by Princeton University Press, 1958.)

Wallerstein, Immanuel. 1989. *The Modern World-System III: The Second Era of Great Expansion of the Capitalist World-Economy, 1730–1840s.* New York: Academic Press.

Walter, Nancy Peterson. 1986. "The Land Exchange Act of 1937: Creation of the Indian Reservations at Bishop, Big Pine, and Lone Pine through a Land Trade between the United States of America and the City of Los Angeles." Ph.D. dissertation, Union Graduate School.

Wandesford-Smith, Geoffrey. 1970. "National Policy for the Environment: Politics and the Concept of Stewardship." In *Congress and the Environment,* edited by Richard A. Cooley and Geoffrey Wandesford-Smith, pp. 205–26. Seattle: University of Washington Press.

Warren, Roland I. 1972. *The Community in America.* 2d ed. Chicago: Rand McNally.

Weber, Max. 1958. *From Max Weber: Essays in Sociology.* Translated by Hans Gerth and C. Wright Mills. New York: Oxford University Press.

————. 1978. *Economy and Society: An Outline of Interpretive Sociology.* Edited by Guenther Roth and Claus Wittich. Vol. 1. Berkeley: University of California Press.

Whitman, Walt. 1955. *Leaves of Grass.* New York: Signet. (First published 1881.)

Wiebe, Robert H. 1967. *The Search for Order, 1877–1920.* New York: Hill and Wang.

Williams, Raymond. 1958. *The Country and the City.* London: Hogarth Press.

Wittfogel, Karl A. 1957. *Oriental Despotism: A Comparative Study of Total Power.* New Haven: Yale University Press.

Wolf, Eric. 1959. *Sons of the Shaking Earth.* Chicago: University of Chicago Press.

———. 1982. *Europe and the People without History.* Berkeley: University of California Press.

Wolfe, Allan. 1974. "New Directions in the Marxist Theory of Politics." *Politics and Society* 4: 131–59.

Worster, Donald. 1985. *Rivers of Empire: Water, Aridity, and the Growth of the American West.* New York: Pantheon.

Yengoyan, Aram A. 1989. "Culture and Ideology in Contemporary Southeast Asian Societies: The Development of Traditions." University of Hawaii, Environment and Policy Institute, East-West Center.

Yonay, Eliud. 1977. "How Green Was My Valley." *New West* (March 28).

Index

Compositor: Braun-Brumfield, Inc.
Text: 10/13 Sabon
Display: Sabon
Printer: Braun-Brumfield, Inc.
Binder: Braun-Brumfield, Inc.